THE MILLERS

Figure 1 (Frontispiece). A Cotswold farmer considering the ripeness of his wheat. (Author, 2000)

The Millers

*A story of technological endeavour
and industrial success, 1870–2001*

GLYN JONES

Carnegie Publishing Ltd

Published by Carnegie Publishing Ltd
Carnegie House, Chatsworth Road
Lancaster LA1 4SL
book publishing: www.carnegiepub.co.uk
book production: www.wooof.net

British Library Cataloguing-in-Publication data
A CIP record for this book is available from the British Library

ISBN 1–85936–085-8

Typeset in Goudy and Helvetica Condensed by Carnegie Publishing
Printed and bound in the UK by
The Cromwell Press, Trowbridge, Wilts

Contents

Introduction   I

Part I Background

1 *A revolutionary change*   11
   The extent and speed of change; The traditional industry;
   The milling press

2 *New processing ideas*   22
   The stages of the milling process; Hungarian refinement;
   American New Process milling; The introduction of roller
   milling at Minneapolis

3 *New ideas in Britain*   37
   Information for British millers; Gustav Buchholz, an isolated
   inventor; Attempts to import pseudo-Hungarian milling;
   Friedrich Wegmann and extensive experiments

4 *Challenges to British millers*   50
   Demand for whiter flour; Sources of wheat for milling;
   Competition from flour imports; Grist for the mill

5 *British millers search for answers*   62
   A variety of devices; J. A. A. Buchholz; Nagel & Kaemp;
   John Whittier Throop; Other alternatives

Part II The major factors: Henry Simon and the National Association

6 *Success*   83
   Henry Simon; Establishment of the Simon system; Harrison
   Carter with E. R. & F. Turner; Thomas Robinson & Son Ltd;
   Introspection and renewed confidence

7 *Resistance to change*   119
   The Bread Reform League; The 'Rollers versus Stones'
   controversy; The Germ Milling case

8 *The National Association*   137
   The founding of the National Association of British and Irish
   Millers; Continuing discussion of objectives; Appraisal of new
   machinery; Milling education

9 *Design and development*   157
    Convergence; Intractable problems; No finality

10 *Henry Simon in business*   182
    Management and money matters; Capital ideas

Part III   Scaling up

11 *Combination and enterprise: 1888–1900*   201
    Combination; Individual enterprise; District perspectives;
    The bitter cry of the country miller; Towards twentieth-century
    perspectives

12 *Scaling up and relocation: 1900–1915*   222
    Dialectic; Millennium; Hoping for harmony; No turning back

13 *Feasibility studies: 1900–1915*   246
    The involvement of chemistry; 'No finality' in machine design;
    A cure for over-production?

14 *Sea of troubles: 1915–1924*   267
    Wartime control and a new overview; Reconstruction; Trade
    organisation: Not plain sailing; Research: a glimpsed horizon

15 *Rationalisation and a new era: 1925–1939*   290
    Backwards or forwards? A waiting game; A rational solution;
    Political difficulties; New confidence

Epilogue

16 *The later twentieth century*   319
    Destruction and rebuilding; Supply – or demand for white sliced
    bread? Three big groups; Interactions

Notes   341

Bibliography   362

Index   367

Acknowledgements

For assisting the study of milling processes, for giving access to information, and for helpful conversations, the people and organizations listed here are warmly thanked; they made the project possible: H. W. Andrews; Allan Ayling; N. F. Bennett (NABIM); J. Bird; D. T. N. Booth; R. J. Catt; C. W. Chitty; H. W. Collier; Prof E. J. T. Collins; the Copyright Directorate of the Patent Office; P. Cotton; John S. Creasey; Dr M. C. S. Dixson (Simon Group); Prof R. J. W. Evans; Tony Evers; Mrs C. E. B. French (FMBRA); Dr J. Frommhold (Bühler Ltd); Robert Garnham; J. Hammond (FMBRA); P. Hancock; A. R. Heygate; M. J. W. Healing; R. R. Hiles; H. Hooker; J. Hunter; E. T. J. Hurle (NABIM); Gábor János (Ganz Machinery Holding Ltd); Dr N. L. Kent (FMBRA); Dr D. W. Kent-Jones; C. R. B. King; John Mannering; Bryan C. McGee (Satake Corporation, UK Division, successor to Henry Simon Ltd and the Thomas Robinson Group); J. Nattrass; P. H. Neil (NABIM); H. J. Norris; Gavin Owens; Patents librarians, Birmingham Central Library; C. P. Rishworth; Alan Royle; the Science Reference Library of the British Library; Mrs B. Stapleton (FMBRA); D. Seagrave; Prof Brian Simon; A. Smith; R. M. Stott (Henry Simon Ltd); Denis Swan; Conrad Syers; Prof J. Tann; I. D. Thomas (Henry Simon Ltd); J. E. Tudor; D. Wakefield; Neil Walker; R. Weibel (Bühler Ltd); R. I. Willis (Henry Simon Ltd); M. J. Wise (NABIM); Ms Ann Wood (Campden & Chorleywood Food Research Association); C. R. Wright.

The following are thanked for permission to use text or illustration: Abacus Studios for a portrait of Henry Simon; Mr R. J. R. Armstrong for a photograph of Allied Mills' Coronet Mill at Manchester; Miller Freeman for content of the journal *The Miller*; Satake Corporation, UK Division, for records of Henry Simon and Henry Simon Ltd; Simon Group for records of Henry Simon and Henry Simon Ltd; Turret RAI for content of the journal *Milling*; Mr Miles Warnick for a photograph of the Rank Hovis mill at Trafford Park, Manchester.

The late Connie French provided invaluable and kindly professional support over many years, and Bryan McGee has been a major encourager and facilitator throughout. The miller Christopher King, and Henry Simon's grandson, Professor Brian Simon, showed where exploration could continue; each contributed sound guidance and a spirit of comradeship. The finished product is dedicated to Dr Anthea Jones, who in 1975 noticed the scope, then travelled cheerfully, and also dealt with the word-processing.

Introduction

There is a well-known literature of the traditional flour milling industry, much of it concerned with the charms of rural settings and ancient crafts. The history of the dramatic changes in milling method from the 1870s onwards has been relatively neglected. It is hidden from general knowledge and appreciation in various publications for millers, chiefly the milling journals, starting in 1875 with William Dunham's *The Miller*. Dunham assisted the formation of the National Association of British and Irish Millers in 1878 and for a further fifteen years he prompted, challenged and encouraged. As much as any individual he conjured a spirit of enquiry and the chance of progress. The journal *Milling*, started in 1891 by G. J. S. Broomhall, was prominent from the turn of the century. Only a few copies of the complete series of these large volumes still exist, but their record of technological and organisational change is extensive, and includes a lively, continuing flow of description, exposition and argument. From the beginning, there was an accompaniment of correspondence which gave personal expression to competing ideas, to the energetic search for information, and sometimes to wry humour. Millers depended on the journals for up-to-date information, guidance and reappraisal; the relationship was interactive, devoted to the industry, not to a wider public. The chronicle and growing source of reference became vast in size and comprehensive in range of content, and was highly reliable.[1]

Millers met together, often locally, but crucially within the National Association, which provided a forum for debate, for the exchange of information, and for the gathering together of views and suggestions. The Association quickly became established, and its history is a chronicle of continuing useful endeavour, essential for the long-term viability of the industry. The members knew each other well, and substantial records exist of their serious discussions, and short reports of convivial occasions (one of the best-known Presidents was a star performer). Five retired millers helped to start this project; they included the very lucid centenarian Charles Chitty (1874–1979) whose grandfather was known as 'the father of the Vienna party', the eldest of a group of millers who had visited Austria-Hungary in 1877 to study changing processing methods.[2]

Radical innovation in milling was contemporary with fundamental advances in engineering and materials processing. Towards the end of the nineteenth century there were vast improvements in the design and development of many kinds of machinery. In the context of general technical progress, the changes in flour milling were notable in terms of the nature, speed, and after-effects. Within the industry itself, the innovations were revolutionary. Roller mills, purifiers and a variety of sifting and sorting machines replaced millstones and crude sieving equipment; milling capacity was concentrated at port sites,

Figures 2 and 3.
Whixall windmill and
Wrickton watermill,
Shropshire. George
Shingler (the writer's
great grandfather)
worked both these
rural mills in the
1880s. (Author)

especially at Liverpool, London, Hull and Cardiff. Change was propelled by an increasing demand for white bread; whiter flour could be produced by roller milling methods applied to hard foreign wheats, whereas traditional millstone methods were not suitable for the production of large quantities of branless flour. Expanding urban markets and public debate helped to further the popularity of white bread, to the disadvantage of owners of rural windmills and watermills, and local millwrights who had contributed significantly to parochial perspectives and were rooted in them.

It was not easy for either millers or bakers to judge the rate or extent of expansion of demand for improved quality products. The availability of processing machinery was soon assured, though there had to be a preliminary stage of trial and error, and familiarisation with new techniques. Henry Simon, who became the pioneering leader of a new field of milling engineering, installed his first roller plant in Manchester in 1878. From then on, the key phrase was 'milling system', denoting a combination of devices which contributed to the process of opening the grain and refining the flour. By the mid 1880s it became clear which engineering firms were advertising milling systems in which the term 'system' was meaningful, and by 1887 mills on the Simon system could produce enough flour to supply the requirements of 11 million people; by the early 1890s the aggregate capacity of complete Simon plants had been doubled.[3] Simon's finest project was for William Vernon & Sons at Birkenhead, completed in 1899, and marking the end of twenty years of inventive activity. From 1904 the most forceful innovator amongst millers was Joseph Rank, who commissioned Henry Simon Ltd to supply new plants at the four main port areas, impressively setting the stage for twentieth-century development on an assured technical basis.

When the National Association was formed in 1878, there were at least 9,000 addresses of flour and provender mills, the majority concerned more with horse and cart transport than with canal and railway routes. In 1887 the National Association estimated that there were 461 roller process mills in the United Kingdom, and *Milling* suggested in 1901 that there were 'over 1,000 complete roller system flour mills in the British Isles'.[4] The first national Census of Production of 1907 recorded a total of 1,254 returns from milling 'establishments', many from 'the class of country millers whose mills are of comparatively small capacity';[5] unfortunately the statistics were ill-defined, but they confirmed the general position. A generation had passed, and very many millers had been displaced, or had simply not afforded repairs and refurbishment. Where innovative activity had not been seen as vital, trade dwindled. Where aspiration was strong, mills were enlarged and more customers sought. The crucial challenge for each miller was to maintain an attitude of continual endeavour through successive phases of uncertainty. But all could be optimistic about their machinery. The mill manager W. R. Voller reported in the journal *Milling*, in 1909, that 'Engineers in this country have now reduced their work to a position of assured success. There has been a gradual elimination of factors of uncertainty ... milling engineers can now state precisely what will be done on a given plant, and in approximately accurate terms the commercial outcome'.[6]

The modern milling industry and the milling engineers have not enjoyed
the credit they deserve. Some writers have missed a British success story, by
following a fashion of expecting the opposite. British milling has been described
as lagging behind European and American practice; it has also been said that
new methods in Britain were simply copies. Budapest and Minneapolis were
regarded as centres of influence and challenge, distant, different, but sufficiently
dramatic to encourage a British response. However, dramatic technological
change through the 1880s and afterwards depended on ideas worked out in
Britain to suit British conditions, which were not relevant elsewhere. British
millers and engineers replaced the traditional form of a basic industry rapidly
and effectively. Hundreds of milling innovators and a thrusting sector of
milling engineers solved problems that would have been unfamiliar in other
countries. By the very early 1890s widespread technical change had been
fully accepted. The new position was created by enthusiastic design effort,
collaborative testing and appraisal of machinery, leading to shared experience,
and the energetic development of ideas, which were revised, improved and
extended.

Millers and milling engineers interacted. Millers had to become masters not
only of strong men and strenuous crafts but of new operations and skilful
machine adjustments. They had to be knowledgeable in buying a widening
range of raw material with differing characteristics and implications for product
quality and profitability. They had to extend their perspectives and their
command of detail, as processes were altered and increased in scale. Milling
engineers were engaged in the creative activity of their continually changing
designs of machines and processes, linking insights at the drawing board and
in the workshops, with a great deal of trying things out, arguing about
alternatives, further puzzling, and with attempts to visualise movements of
materials within the processes. It was often a fascinating occupation for those
fortunate to be employed to use imagination and take initiatives. At a time
when working drawings were issued as blueprints, good design had artistic merit;
those who were not too dour could admire the work and then begin again to
challenge the assumptions and decisions.

The nature of the basic raw material posed a long-lasting problem. English
wheat harvests varied in both quantity and quality and, although country millers
depended on the results, many farmers were more interested in yield than in
the milling quality of the grain. As the availability of machinery increased and
design improved, the already increasing supplies of foreign wheat could be seen
as essential because much of the imported grain provided 'strength'. The term
was applied to both wheat and flour, but it was easier to refer to 'strong' wheats,
while mystery surrounded the protein substance gluten yielded by a flour, upon
which depended the character of the dough and the likelihood of a well-piled
loaf. In 1904 *The Miller* commented that 'we are entirely without a theory of
any description'.[7] To try to escape from the dilemma, the National Association
initiated an investigative programme to improve British wheat, considering the
effects of soil and climate on 'strength', a puzzling term with respect to both
cause and effect; it was not possible to obtain simple answers from chemical

analysis. Kent-Jones (1950) stated that 'the history of cereal chemistry is largely a record of attempts to find out what determines strength'.[8]

Commercial issues remained crucial, largely because they represented the public life of the industry, relating individual purposes and difficulties to a community of interests amongst millers. From the 1890s, concern about increasingly overlapping trading areas in Britain was a noticeable preoccupation of journal columns and the agendas of millers' meetings. Internal competition became inevitable as regions of the country became less separate, economically and psychologically. A seemingly new period of change, characterised by consolidation, scaling up, and conflicting commercial interests, was really a further evolution. The large port millers diverged further from the country and small town millers, though there were also common problems: all millers had to withstand the pressure of foreign flour supplies, and potentially adverse factors in the free trade situation. Eventually, American millers scaled up excessively, and by the decade before the 1914–18 war technical and commercial competence in the United Kingdom milling industry had proved effectively durable against the pressure of imported flour.

Though some British millers were sceptical about expansion by colleagues within the United Kingdom, the leading port millers held market position against foreign imports. Other industries faced similar challenges during searches for optimum or viable sizes of firm, and routes towards rationalisation. As in textiles and in various branches of engineering, large firms and large productive units became common in the milling industry. The big names in milling included Joseph Rank Ltd, Spillers & Bakers Ltd, William Vernon & Sons, Henry Leetham & Sons, and Seth Taylor. The CWS soon joined the leaders. They were all still prominent in the 1920s, Ranks and Spillers continuing to the end of the twentieth century, along with the powerful group of Allied Mills Ltd.

The subject of possible over-capacity and alleged over-production in the milling industry received close attention during 1914, with discussion of a scheme to match flour production to demand. It required a majority of millers to accept a method of apportioning output quotas. There was then the intervention of the war, and Government control from 1917 to 1921, before millers could deal with renewal and reorganisation. The processing operations had still to be regarded as empirical, but there was growing recognition that cereal chemistry might be studied within a formal organisation, possibly alongside other scientific work. Larger firms set up their own laboratories, not entirely confined to routine quality control. In 1923 the Research Association of British Flour Millers was established, and had new purpose-built laboratories from 1926.

Through the 1920s there were further groupings, acquisitions and amalgamations, which were typical features of corporate industrial modernisation, based on objectives of integration and supposed economies of scale. There had been excess capacity before the war, but it was more worrying afterwards, as it became clear that there was an increasing variety of alternative foods. Calculations of the actual levels of flour and bread consumption were obscured by statistical assumptions, and were disputed. Excessive over-capacity was a hindrance to advances within the industry, to technical regeneration, and to balance between sectors of the industry. Intensive competition led in 1929 to the institution of a formal scheme of rationalisation, and productive capacity was further concentrated. The formal scheme, organised through the Millers' Mutual Association, provided for some regulation of output, and compensation for redundant businesses. There were still factors which ensured competition: price, product quality and reliability, and the market share held by imports.

After the worst of the depression years, the industry was still involved with difficult commercial and social issues, often complicated by government and forces at a distance. The National Association acted as a unifier, a mediator, and a source of expert and diplomatic representation. By 1933–34 there was a fresh phase of modernisation: *The Miller* referred to remodellings and extensions of mills throughout the kingdom. In 1935 *Milling* and *The Miller* saluted the royal silver jubilee with wide-ranging and hopeful reviews.[9] Structural change in the industry has continued, related to recent technological progress. After the 1939–45 war there was again a difficult period of recovery. From the 1960s mills owned by Associated British Foods Ltd constituted an increasingly prominent part of the industry. There have been technical surprises and some reappearances of ideas from long ago. Scientific knowledge of cereals and manufacturing methods have steadily evolved. English wheat is again important. Modern mills are impressive in outside appearance and striking inside, with machinery that looks smart and is automatically controlled, processing wheat for a range of attractive foods and for the still essential daily bread.

Some significant dates and names of innovators

1875	The journal, *The Miller*, founded by William Dunham
1877	A party of British millers, led by J. Harrison Carter, visited Vienna and Budapest to study roller milling
1878	The National Association of British and Irish Millers formed to facilitate communication within the industry
	Henry Simon supplied a roller mill plant to McDougalls at Manchester
1878–1881	Leading innovative millers tried new methods, with encouraging results for both millers and designers
1880	The Bread Reform League started a campaign against white bread
1881	A special exhibition of milling machinery at Islington provided a major focus for discussion of the prospects for technical advance
	Simon's first automatic roller mill plant installed for F. A. Frost at Chester
1882	More general use of break rolls
1883	City & Guilds examinations in milling started
1883–1885	The adoption of roller milling methods widespread
	Rollers versus Stones controversy resolved in favour of innnovation
1884	First annual convention of the National Association at Stockton on Tees

1885–1886	Improved types of purifier introduced, giving further impetus to the development of milling systems
1886	Failure of Thomas Muir's attempt to impose licences on roller millers
1887	Incorporation of Spiller & Co. (Cardiff) Ltd
	Concern about competition from United States millers
1888–1893	Early users of roller milling methods remodelled their plants to incorporate new design and increased scales of production.
	Millers in rural areas or with smaller businesses converted to roller milling
1889	William Voller published his pionering textbook, *Modern Flour Milling*
1891	The journal, *Milling*, founded by G. J. S. Broomhall
1899	Incorporation of Joseph Rank Ltd
	Vernons' new mill at Birkenhead opened
1899–1907	The British milling industry evolved towards its modern structure, with large plant development projects for the leading businesses
1901	Incorporation of the National Association of British & Irish Millers
1911	Standard bread campaign
1913	Plansifter improvements: introduced in the 1880s, rejected, revived, and later to be essential for scalping, grading, and dressing operations
1917–1921	Government Control of flour mills
1918	Flour Milling Employers' Federation set up
1919	National Joint Industrial Council for the Flour Milling Industry formed
1920	Spillers Milling & Associated Industries Ltd and Wm. Vernon & Sons amalgamated
1921	Associated London Flour Millers Ltd formed
1923	The Research Association of British Flour Millers established at St Albans
1923–1928	Rationalisation schemes discussed
1926	Henry Simon Ltd works at Cheadle Heath opened
1929	The Millers' Mutual Association formed
1933	Joseph Rank Ltd purchased Associated London Flour Millers Ltd
1935	A centenary in the history of Spillers

The terms 'plant' and 'roller mill plant' are frequently used in the following chapters. 'Complete roller plant' refers to an installation of machinery that did not include millstones. 'Combination plants' included millstones. A mill could contain one or more milling plants. A plant would be of a designed capacity: an expected rate of output, stated in sacks per hour of flour, one sack being 280 lb of flour or 2.5 cwt (127 kg).[10] Use of the terms roller mill, and rollermill, varied with author, period and custom; particular quotations have been copied exactly. The same comments apply to roll and roller. Sometimes one usage seems to sound or look better than the alternative, but *The Miller*, Voller, the translators of other classic texts, and Henry Simon all wrote 'roller mill', so this historical account is consistent with their way, as far as possible. More modern usage is 'rollermill'.

Part I

❧

Background

CHAPTER ONE

A revolutionary change

The extent and speed of change

Between 1875 and 1895 the British milling industry changed radically in method, location and organisation. Millstones were ousted, and the simple but comparatively crude traditional milling methods were replaced by processing operations that were both more elaborate and more carefully conducted. Milling was concentrated in larger production units, particularly at the ports; it was based on improvements in mechanical engineering design and on gradually increasing understanding of certain aspects of science and of the tasks of management. The old pattern of steady trade for a large number of country mills, dealing mainly with local raw materials and local product markets, in conjunction with larger steam-powered mills in the towns, was challenged and then disrupted.

Forerunners of change were rudimentary applications of roller mills in Europe, principally in Austria-Hungary, followed by importation into Britain of finer grades of flour from Hungary, and then large-scale importation of flour from the United States of America. A general preference for whiter flour developed, and many bakers soon recognised the advantage of stronger flours which gave well-piled loaves. A number of varieties of hard, foreign wheat were found to be superior to English wheat in these respects, but traditional British milling methods were not suitable for processing the harder wheats. From the early 1880s roller milling methods and machinery were rapidly improved to suit British requirements, which were modest but increasing scales of flour production, automatic working as far as was possible at that time, and means of dealing with the many different varieties of wheat that became available to British millers.

Starting in the late 1870s, the whole milling process was redesigned, and in about ten years from the early 1880s completely new methods were thoroughly established. There were many earlier experiments, but a key event occured in 1878, when Henry Simon installed his first small but complete roller mill plant for McDougall Brothers at Manchester. In April 1879, he was advertising 'Daverio's Patent Roller Mill System'.[1] Early in 1882, Simon's automatic Roller Mill System was being proclaimed, and a stream of statements in advertisements indicated a rapidly increasing range of possible machinery, with claims to achievement in sizes of plants and numbers of customers. Innovative millers experimented, saw the first effects of changes in their own mills and businesses, and became increasingly aware of alterations elsewhere. It soon became possible for them to judge their potential separation from firmly traditional neighbours. News of both inventive and innovative activity increased rapidly and the journal *The Miller* urged attention to shared investigation and practical action.

Interest was greatly increased and more clearly focused by an exhibition at Islington in May 1881. A five day show was extended to eight, during which more than twenty thousand visitors saw a comprehensive range of milling machinery presented by British firms and also from Europe and the United States, including 'machinery in motion', which was so attractive that plans for a lecture and discussion programme were set aside. There had been other well publicised exhibitions in England and abroad, but Islington in 1881 was heralded, analysed, and used as a challenge to such an extent that it continued as a stimulus for discussion and a flag for advance. It was the first big event organised under the aegis of the National Association of British and Irish Millers, a break with the tradition of meeting at Royal Agricultural Society shows, and a precursor of future official millers' annual conventions. For many millers, a general awareness of new possibilities led to closer interest and active consideration through clearer knowledge, trial, and evaluations. Those who succeeded confirmed their approval by further expenditure and increased milling capacity. When Simon addressed the Institution of Mechanical Engineers in January 1889, he could speak with confidence, as the most prominent professional engineer in his field:

> The completeness of the revolution that has taken place is exemplified by the fact that practically in less than ten years the machinery and methods of corn milling have been radically altered, at the cost of an immense amount of capital. The millstone, dating from prehistoric times, has almost wholly been discarded; and the miller has been constrained to unlearn the old method of manufacture and take up one entirely new, based upon very different principles.[2]

Economic historians have commented briefly on the changes. J. H. Clapham (1932) referred to 'the revolution in milling' of the 1880s. W. Ashworth (1969) noted 'a great transformation' in the 1880s. A. E. Musson (1978) stated that 'a revolutionary change' occurred in the later nineteenth century. Wilfred Smith (1961) referred to 'a revolution in the character of grain milling' in the last quarter of the nineteenth century: this encompassed the effects of scaling up and relocation.[3] There have been many similar judgements by prominent millers, including Voller (1923): 'That a more or less complete revolution in trade processes and methods has taken place, few will question'.[4] His retrospective assessment was concerned with much more than production methods; he recognised the altered scene in milling which had replaced traditional practice, and he was also mindful of a longer, hazardous period in commerce. These statements, from a variety

Figure 4.
Henry Simon.
(1835–1899), pioneer
in milling engineering.
(Henry Simon Ltd,
1898)

Figure 5.
Dressing a burr
millstone at Reynolds'
mill in Gloucester.
(Author, 1977)

of sources, relate to a range of perspectives. An essential aspect of an account of the technical changes is a description of the commotion, including the accelerating revision of processing ideas, the rapid spread of new machinery, the sweeping away of traditional assumptions, and the inevitable accompaniment of trade contest.

Criticism of British prestige in invention, innovation and manufacturing has often been connected to supposed time-lags in adopting new methods. The single case of the Pesther Walzmuhle in Hungary was ahead, with credit for initiative and practical development, but using unsophisticated machinery and associated laborious manual procedures that would not have been acceptable or effective in British or American mills. There was no clear route to follow, and there were limitations, in engineering terms, of even the best practice at Budapest. In 1880, Britain and America were at the same stage of gaining insight into gradual reduction systems based on roller milling. After that, there was a very long period of commercial competition in flour selling in Britain, with strong pressure from leading American millers, who scaled up so rapidly that they appeared to outpace British millers, but only in terms of their forceful exporting to a free trade country, not in the application of engineering expertise.

In the early 1880s machinery was acquired from Austria-Hungary and America, but it was not a sustained long-term market. As the journal *The Engineer* reported, imports of foreign equipment rapidly decreased.[5] British,

Hungarian and American requirements were distinctly different. What became important for the future of the UK milling industry was the application of new methods within this country, to suit British conditions with respect to variation of raw material, range of scale of production, product qualities, styles of management and capabilities of operatives. These factors required British appraisals and British solutions, which became increasingly available in the early 1880s, and widely applied from 1883.

The unusual activist was Henry Simon, who drew widely on ideas and skills of collaborators, from Daverio and Bühlers in Switzerland, from Seck in Germany, and essentially from his own staff who improved and extended his firm's design capabilities. His work shows how technical change depends on many variables: knowledge, ideas, personalities, practices, resources and opportunities, which interact. The entrepreneur not only grasps the ideas, he arranges his situation to suit many factors.

The traditional industry

THOUSANDS OF MILLERS
It is not easy to define the structure of the milling industry of the nineteenth century in relation to modernisation. The first Census of Production was not taken until 1907–8 and the hazy results did not appear until 1912. Censuses of Population of England and Wales provide some general statistics, including total numbers of millers.[6] From this vague start, the quest is exactly as it was for the first secretary of NABIM in 1878: where were the millers who might be innovators? As a first guess, might 10 per cent of millers start to form new interests?

Census	Description	Total number	Population of England and Wales
1871	Miller	30,060	22,712,266
1881	Corn miller	23,462	25,974,439
1891	Corn miller	22,759	29,002,525
1901	Millers: cereal food manufacture	23,605	32,526,075

For 1871, the thirty thousand millers included both masters and the workmen, and 340 were females. Separate statistics were provided for various ages, and for each county. *The Miller* commented on the 1881 data: 'As we anticipated they would do, these figures demonstrate the fact that the smaller millers have in many cases yielded, in the keen competitive struggle waged during the decade and now, to the larger millers, and the same remark no doubt holds good for millwrights'. For 1891, there was an attempt to show the numbers of masters and employees separately and for 1901 there was a division into urban and rural districts.

Typically for national censuses, comparisons are hindered by change of category or label between successive enumerations. Generally the Population Census data was of crude aggregate numbers of people who called themselves millers; some were juveniles. In the traditional industry, there may have been

Figure 6.
Reynolds' site at
Gloucester docks.
(Author, 1986)

a grand total of 10,000 mill addresses and at very many there was a miller and one or two assistants; many would not have been solely flour millers. There were large numbers of traditionalists who were mainly provender millers, even before innovation passed them by. Occupation statistics are also complicated by the growing numbers of mill, yard, and office workers, employed in increasing numbers by the large, modernising businesses. Also, amongst the principal members of partnerships and companies, there were not only master millers, but others who were increasingly specialising in commercial and financial aspects, and the other forerunners of mill management, the foremen.

Trade directories, especially Kelly's, gave listings of names and addresses of milling businesses for each county, and for some major conurbations. For the 1880s onwards, there was classification into users of steam, wind, or water power. For Kent, nearly 300 millers were listed in 1878. Even in 1887–88, there were 700 in Kent, Sussex, and Essex combined. From the 1880s their numbers dwindled, not dramatically at first, but steadily through the 1890s and the next decade. Eventually, thousands of small rural windmills and watermills found their methods, their sites, their products and their trading areas were no longer viable. How many of the apparent losses were mainly failures of wood and old iron in new conditions? The millstone itself had seemed immutable, though peripheral improvements were made during the two decades before roller milling was found to be the pervasive influence. Before the spread of roller milling, rural traditionalists might have seemed to fill most of the picture, but large steam-powered mills in the main centres of population were building an industrial base for change, just as other industries were gradually increasing their machinery.

SOME OF THE BIGGEST MILLS

Millers often met at corn markets and agricultural shows, but before 1875 they had no technical literature to provide knowledge of the whole country. Those who had small rural businesses would know where there were bigger mills, with five or six pairs of stones. Town millers would be aware of others of comparable size to themselves, but there might not have been much attention to distant sites. A few very large mills were known to exist, but when engineering and milling journals started to report on them, illustrations were rudimentary and descriptions were sketchy; this applied even to the large steam-powered mills in the major towns, London, Liverpool and Glasgow. The Miller set out specifically to remedy the shortage of information, but initially lacked expertise for the task.

In the first issue of The Miller on March 1, 1875, a description was extracted from The Engineer of the Royal Flour Mills at Vauxhall, on London's Albert Embankment, where Peter Mumford worked 24 pairs of stones in 1875. The machinery was supplied by Whitmore & Binyon, who also fitted up Seth Taylor's mill at Waterloo Bridge with 20 pairs of stones in 1872 and 10 more in 1874.[7] In 1878 the journal described The City Flour Mills, near Blackfriars Bridge in London, as 'not only the largest, but the most substantially built in the metropolis'. There were 32 pairs of stones, and the manufacturing capacity was about 5,000 sacks of flour per week.[8] The site was leased by Hadley Brothers, S. C. Hadley being the first President of the National Association of British and Irish Millers (NABIM). At Deptford Bridge Mills, London, built in 1870, the owners were J. & H. Robinson. In 1878 The Miller found 'in its internal organisation evidences of that departure from English traditional methods of milling which have begun to make themselves manifest in this country ... The new departure is tentatively cautious, but still it is sufficiently pronounced to separate it by a wide interval from the old system'. They had middlings purifiers and Wegmann rolls, but still had 16 pairs of millstones.[9]

The most impressively large mill at Liverpool in the late 1870s was at Boundary Street, owned by the North Shore Flour and Rice Mill Co. Ltd. In 1878 they held their twenty first annual meeting; there was no technical information in the journal report, nor in several later reports. James Wood, who had been at London's City Mills before Hadley's were the owners, and had managed a mill in Ireland, tried to introduce Hungarian methods in 1868. Previously, flour production had been confined to sizing flour for the cotton industry. Wood started a trade in baking flour.[10] There must have been a substantial number of millstones, to provide a production base that allowed the rapid scaling up when roller milling was adopted from 1883. In Glasgow, Thomas Muir owned the Tradeston Mills, which were burned down in 1872, and rebuilt and restarted in 1874 to use a half-high grinding system, with 17 pairs of stones. Previously, there had been 30 pairs. Also in Glasgow, John Ure had 20 pairs of stones at the Crown Mills in 1878.[11] Of these large mills, Hadley's ceased trading after failure to renew a lease, and a bankruptcy. Muir and Robinsons engaged in a strenuous legal action over a Muir patent. Robinsons survived and with Mumford, and especially Taylor, remained prominent in trade and in the National Association; they were still amongst the industry's leaders in the 1920s. The North Shore Co. was frequently known as one of Henry Simon's largest customers, vying with Taylor in the 1880s. Below the top of the range of productive capacity, there were by then perhaps two dozen mills of next rank. At the upper end of the scale of production, a powerful movement towards concentration was apparent by the early 1890s.

The main questions for the future of the industry were not to do with how many mills there were, in their thousands, but how many were modernising and, later, how many would survive and prosper. Innovation was possible for all sizes of productive capacity, except perhaps the very smallest, like the country windmill or watermill with one or two or several pairs of stones. However, mill buildings usually had to be replaced when a business expanded very quickly or to a new order of size, which added to the requirements for capital. Continuing innovative activity then increased the separation of the large and medium businesses from the others. When the innovative sector began to reveal itself by action, there were still many niches available for small businesses, but by the time the large firms had all joined the advance, their size gave them chances for leadership in the inevitable next stages of reshaping the industry.

A NEED FOR A CLEARER PICTURE

The report of the Council of the National Association in 1879 stated that 9,000 copies of a circular had been posted to millers, a major effort to try to contact the whole industry. The aggregate number of 9,000 was repeated at meetings, and in 1881 Joseph Westley, a prominent Association member, suggested that 'they ought not to have less than 1,000 of the 10,000 millers of the country' as members. In 1882, there were 380 members.[12] That might be taken as a provisional estimate of the potentially innovative sector, probably an underestimate, as some successful firms had not yet joined. S. M. Soundy, President in 1885, presented a report which included estimates of the extent of new machinery provision. He had approached 'many firms' of suppliers, but considered it necessary to scale up his data by a factor of three to obtain his totals. A main objective was to investigate insurance costs and he tried to value the whole industry in terms of buildings plus machinery plus stock. The most interesting feature was his estimation of numbers of relatively large mills, twenty in his top category valued at £80,000 or more, thirty in the next group between £60,000 and £80,000, and a total of 200 in the top four categories of £40,000 and above.[13] It was a new idea to publish an estimate of variation of mill size. The exercise was a rough first approximation; Soundy did not pretend otherwise. A clear picture of the industry, and of the innovative sector within it, required names and locations, and productive capacities. The big names were discerned against a less clear background of those who were mentioned less often, but who nevertheless had joined associations and had acquired machinery.

The National Association became a means of identifying most of the leading millers, though especially during the early years of roller milling the only substantial listings of millers' names were in the journal columns. Advertisements of Wegmann's porcelain rolls by his agent provided the earliest extensive lists of innovators, quoting names and locations,[14] but they soon discontinued an experiment stating numbers of machines at particular places. Wegmann's lists must have reinforced the idea that the spread of new methods was increasing rapidly. Just before and soon after A. B. Childs published names and locations of Wegmann's customers, *The Miller* gave the lists of members of group visits to Vienna and Budapest, and to Cincinnati,[15] but they were not strong indicators of a future leadership of innovation. Others visited independently. In August 1881 and September 1882, *The Miller* published lists of members of the National Association, showing also memberships of affiliated local associations. After 1882 such information was published only to members, though the number of members was often a subject of discussion at Association meetings which were reported.

Prominence and progressiveness could be seen more clearly from about 1882 or 1883, as *The Miller* increased reportage of many new installations. The whole range of suppliers, from the leading milling engineers to the smaller mill-furnishers, participated in a growing enthusiasm to provide news of activity. Lists of customers formed part of their attempts to impress others of the extent of business, implying successful methods. Both millers and engineers must have scanned the columns for current evidence of opportunity and competition. Simon's advertisements, lectures and other technical descriptions provided the most wide-ranging source of information on progress. The noticed names were not necessarily all of confirmed innovators, but a start could be made towards the identification of a leading sector of the industry, standing apart from the uncertain status of mere entries in Kelly's directories.

The milling press

Before William Dunham started *The Miller*, in March 1875, there was no regular and widespread method of communicating technical matters in the British milling industry. Previously, all that existed were publications concerned with grain trade information, including Dornbusch's *Floating Cargoes List*, which had been started in 1854, and Beerbohm's *Evening Corn Trade List*, which was first published in 1869. George Dornbusch was the proprietor and editor of a newspaper, which he published twice a day, but privately; subscribers had to sign an agreement that the information would not be passed on to others. His agents at many ports telegraphed details of cargoes in transit. Dornbusch died in 1873, but his list was continued until 1914, when

Figure 7.
William Dunham,
founder of the journal
The Miller. (*The Miller*, March 1925)

it was amalgamated with Beerbohm's *Evening Corn Trade List*, and then published as the *London Grain, Seed and Oil Reporter*. Julius Edwald Beerbohm, of Lithuanian descent, father of the writer Max Beerbohm, had come to England about 1830, and began as a corn merchant.[16] He started the *Corn Trade Journal and Millers' Gazette* in 1876. Soon afterwards, the second part of the title acquired more prominence, reflecting the gradually increasing attention to new milling ideas. In the 1880s it was advertised as a supplement to the Monday edition of Beerbohm's *Evening Corn Trade List*, which was published six days a week, with variations in content, but an accent on cargo movements. *The Millers' Gazette* had a modest coverage of milling subjects, but had several notable contributors. J. A. A. Buchholz was technical editor of the *Gazette* in 1877–78. The prominent cereal chemist William Jago contributed a series of articles in the mid-1880s, and William Voller started to contribute in 1888, with a series of short articles called 'Notes for the Milling examinations'.

In the first issue of *The Miller*, William Dunham wrote about 'the absence in this country of a 'class' journal, exclusively devoted to millers'. He had a business as a mill-furnisher, in Mark Lane in the City of London. After an adventurous early career in South Africa, as the superintendent of a sugar plantation in Mauritius, and in the Australian goldfields, he had joined an uncle, Henry Clarke, who had a mill-furnishing business in London. Clarke had acquired an interest in a method of balancing millstones.[17] Dunham took considerable interest in patents and inventions and travelled very widely in England, introducing Clarke and Dunham's patent millstone balance to many millers; the device was described in William Fairbairn's *Treatise on Mills and Millwork* of 1863. The firm also sold a range of early machines for cleaning wheat, and two kinds of decorticator, and so were well-known mill-furnishers.

William Dunham referred to the difficulty of starting his journal: 'For a considerable time we have had in contemplation the establishment of a "Millers' newspaper", which should record the state and progress of the trade. The majority of our friends, whilst admitting that a journal of the kind was much wanted, doubted if such a speculation would pay commercially'. His objective was to show the importance of information and lack of it: 'We have passed much time at the British Museum in searching for information on this subject, but beyond a few pamphlets, handbooks, and articles copied and recopied in encyclopaedias, we can recollect nothing that merited the reputation of a "Work on Milling" written by any of our countrymen, or published here'. He sent out a circular to invite support, and received 600 subscriptions. After three months he had 1,000 subscribers and nearly 2,000 before the end of 1875. The initial plan was for a journal of twelve pages, but even the first issue became sixteen pages, with eight more as a supplement. In addition to the main aspects of editorial, technical, commercial and correspondence content, extra pages were added to provide for a growing amount of advertising by mill-furnishers. The size of the journal increased rapidly: the first volume contained 348 pages, the fifth 1,000 pages. From January 1878, there was a market issue every Monday evening, mainly concerned with grain and flour trade details, and in the first issue of each month the market news was added to a much larger technical issue. In 1882 Dunham moved his offices to the Commercial Sale Rooms, at 24 Mark Lane, where he continued until 1891, Mark Lane being the hub of milling commerce.

After ten years of publication, Dunham produced a commentary on the changed condition of the industry in 1885. He stated that 'When *The Miller* first appeared the initial implement in the manufacture of flour in most parts of the world was the millstone ... Every effort to promote progress by millstone milling had our most consistent advocacy'. This was appropriate to his own traditional background, but he encouraged the investigation of new methods. He recognised the altered situation in the statement:

> The contention between Theory and practice, whether the new methods worked by the new machinery are better than the old, has so far been answered in favour of Theory, that a very large number of millers of the United Kingdom have adopted the new and since this has been clearly demonstrated, we have pursued the same policy with regard to the new as we did with reference to the old. The flour manufactured by the new methods has been hailed by many bread eaters as a superior article, which is a sign of progress; and as we welcomed every phase of that result made by the old, we think that we do our duty as a trade journal by pursuing the same policy still.[18]

From 1875 to 1891 Dunham exercised considerable personal influence on the processes of gathering and disseminating information, and in promoting interest in the new milling methods. It was said that he read every line of the journal and checked every correction. The editorials were lively and invariably constructive, directing attention to all the major features of potential change, and to matters that required the careful definition of policy within the industry. In general, though much of the content was currently topical, appropriately so in that period of rapid technical change, there was a continual accumulation of many kinds of technological reference material. Space was well-used: many pages carried two columns, each of about 90 lines, typically giving four times the number of words on a standard page of a text book on milling of the 1890s. Through this continual effort, *The Miller* created an increasingly comprehensive resource for individuals, and also provided much of the basis of news, ideas, and discussion for both formal and informal networks of communication throughout the industry. The growing record was enhanced by efficient indexing.

In December 1888 G. J. S. Broomhall started the *Liverpool Corn Trade News*. About 1873 he had begun as an invoice clerk in London with Alexander & Co., grain merchants; he was moved to Liverpool, where he continued as a grain broker and dealer until 1889. There was an initial period of unprofitability with his trade paper, but it soon became accepted, with the shortened title of *The Corn Trade News* from January 1890. From 1895, it was called *George Broomhall's Corn Trade News*. In November 1891, Broomhall started the journal *Milling*, publishing fortnightly, later weekly. He diversified into jobbing printing, and in 1894 he formed the Northern Publishing Co. Ltd., specialising in milling literature. For the first few years, *Milling* was modest in size and scope, but expanded about 1900, to include highly detailed accounts of leading mills and millers, with clear photographic illustrations. The first page of each issue of the journal still proclaimed in 1936: 'Managing Director Geo. J. S. Broomhall', and he was regarded as an authority on the statistics of the grain trade, and on milling industry productive capacity.[19] When he gave evidence to the Royal Commission on Food Prices in 1925, it was stated that for the last 36 years he had 'devoted his attention exclusively to the sphere of trade information'.

Although *Milling* became the leading journal, *The Miller* was pre-eminent from its start in 1875 until about 1900, and remains the main source of historical information for the periods of the introduction and establishment of roller milling, and also for the early years of the National Association, whose official records begin at 1886, eight years after the founding of the Association. In 1889, it was stated in the Association's transactions that 'The Council is indebted to Mr. Dunham, the proprietor of *The Miller*, for the kind permission to make use of the illustrations and reports that have appeared in that journal'. This type of acknowledgement was frequently made. Dunham provided a journal of a style that suited the individualism of most millers, and at the same time he furthered the aims of the National Association. He continually presented new perspectives to the whole industry and he fostered both investigation and argument. His full involvement in supervision continued until 1891, when illness forced him to withdraw. In 1894 he transferred the copyright to the proprietors of *The British Trade Journal*. He died in December 1894.[20] Dunham had valued assistants, including William Hepburn, described as 'the chief of the literary staff', who worked on the journal from 1877 until 1887. Hepburn was a journalist of wide experience, including several editorships. There was also Edward Martin, who started as a correspondence clerk at *The Miller* in 1881, and eventually succeeded Dunham as editor. Martin continued in charge until 1929.[21]

CHAPTER TWO

New processing ideas

The stages of the milling process

Lockwood (1945) stated that wheat grain is normally made up of about 85% starchy endosperm, 2.5% embryo or germ and 12.5% husk; Voller (1889) thought there was 90% endosperm;[1] NABIM (1991) stated 82–86%.[2] A way of describing the miller's task is to say that firstly he has to break open the wheat grain and release the endosperm, made up of coarse particles termed semolina, intermediate size particles called middlings, and finer particles including flour. Unless the product is to be wholemeal or not very white flour, the husk of bran (and the germ) must be separated. Smaller pieces of bran which are still mixed with the endosperm, or adhering to it, must also be removed if white flour is required. Highly refined flour can be produced by grinding the semolina and middlings, but the bran fragments dispersed through the material must be extracted first. The production of flour without bran is made difficult by the indentation or crease in each individual grain and by the friability of the bran, particularly of harder varieties of wheat. The soft or mellow wheats grown in Britain yielded flour with desirable flavour and colour characteristics, but they were not strong wheats and did not give strong flours. Strong wheats, which were also harder, were grown in central Europe and parts of North America but rough millstone surfaces produced severe bran fragmentation when they were used for grinding hard wheats.

In the simplest traditional practice in Britain and elsewhere the grain was broken open and a large proportion of the resulting meal was reduced in size to its finished state through a pair of millstones. This has often been referred to as the sudden death method of milling, less dramatically as low-grinding. The saleable material was sieved through a mesh (bolted), in earlier times made of cloth but latterly of wire or silk. The break and reduction processes were one, and the removal of the bran from amongst the middlings was unknown; the process lacked careful treatment. The output from the millstones was simply flour, bran and surviving middlings that had not been reduced, due to the gritty nature of that constituent. The production of middlings was considered then to be unfortunate or inexpert: the middlings were not saleable as ordinary flour. Also, the flour contained bran particles, and flour was lost with the bran. The objectives during the traditional period were to produce flour immediately and minimise the production of middlings. In the new approach, the objectives were reversed: to maximise the production of middlings, which were found to give high quality flour if carefully treated, and to minimise the production of flour at the start of the milling process, as this was of poor quality, partly because it contained dust.

Rudimentary early forms of careful processing included the French *la mouture économique* about the middle of the eighteenth century; but relatively large scale production using methods of gradual granulation and size reduction to flour fineness, was pioneered in Austria-Hungary, using millstones, to break the grain and to grind the endosperm in stages. Between the stages, the materials produced were sifted and bran was removed using sieves and early forms of purifier. Hungarian wheat supplies were fairly uniform in character, but Hungarian milling processes were laborious. These processes were used and improved for many years. Through the nineteenth century there were trials with roller mills, though when roller milling methods were much more generally used in Hungary in the 1870s many manual operations were still involved.

This more gradual procedure was called high-grinding because the runner stones were raised above the stationary bed stones far enough to avoid a severe grinding of the grain; the aim was to make only a partial splitting and breaking of the wheat at a first stage; the number of break stages varied in different mills. The basic reason for the development of high-grinding was that there were potential markets for superior Hungarian flours. It became possible to extract much of the bran from mixtures with larger particles of endosperm (semolina) or intermediate size particles (middlings), but it remained impossible to produce thoroughly white flour from mixtures in which bran powder had been dispersed through the mass. Fortunately for Budapest millers, they also had markets for very inferior grades.

Imports of more refined and stronger flours into Britain in the 1870s challenged British millers to learn how to mill hard wheats. A few attempted to adopt what became known as the Hungarian system, though the methods and their effects varied with the consultant chosen; these attempts were soon abandoned. Though Hungarian millers used both millstones and roller mills, British millers could not copy their methods. They would have had to learn meticulous procedures, employ more labour, obtain uniform raw materials and find markets for dark flour. To mill hard wheats, new techniques were required and, in Britain, gradual reduction milling was to be associated explicitly with roller milling, using continuous processing in contrast to the batch methods used in Hungary. British and American engineers quickly devised fully mechanized processes, quite different from Hungarian practice. One essential for success in Britain was the production of high yields of good quality flour from mixtures of different wheats, with the added difficulty that the resources varied through the cereal year. The British situation was unique in the requirement to deal with varying characteristics of the material to be processed; Hungarian and American millers had comparatively uniform raw materials.

In Britain and the United States gradual reduction methods using roller mills were rapidly developed to include the systematically related use of large numbers of machines. Three basic operations were involved: grinding, sieving and purifying, although additional processes have since been developed. There is analogy with the unit operations of chemical engineering. The 'break' and 'reduction' operations are both forms of grinding, but quite different processes. Scalping, grading and dressing are forms of sieving (in general terms, sifting and sorting); there is also a sieving action within the modern purification operation. The whole of the milling process when making white flour could be regarded as purification, but the purifying operation refers specifically to removal of the smallest particles of bran. The general aims were to make branless flour, and to maintain yield by rejecting only flourless bran. It was necessary for the first grinding operation to be limited to the breaking open of the grain in the course of several stages, gradually releasing the kernel and separating it fom the husk. Rolls of chilled cast iron, with grooved or fluted surfaces, were found to give the best results, the successive stages of the break operation being carried out with rolls of progressively finer fluting. The number of stages tried varied between three and seven, but four break stages soon became the general practice.

Each break stage yielded a mixture of material of large, medium and fine particle sizes, including pieces of bran, some flour, and material of intermediate size and composition, much of the material adhering together. After each break

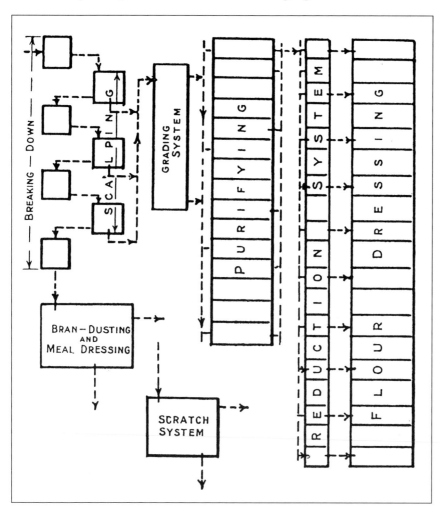

Figure 8. Block flow diagram of gradual reduction process. (Amos, 1912)

24

stage, this had to be sieved (scalped) to separate a predominantly endosperm component from a coarser bulk which formed the feed to the next break stage. Material that was sieved out, by scalping, had to be divided into fractions, according to particle size (graded), preparatory to the purifying operation. In general, it is easier to differentiate and target constituents for retention or rejection, after preliminary simple sorting. In particular, purifiers required feeds of approximately equal size particles. In gravity purifiers, air currents were directed through elaborate arrangments of channels, to flow through falling streams of semolina and middlings, projecting the different constituents into separate compartments; less compact particles, which were the more bran-laden, were deflected further by the air. Different ideas, using carefully directed and controlled airflows rising through slightly sloping sieves, led to a continuing development of purifier design in America and Britain; this became an important and interactive aspect of the evolution of modern milling systems. In these new sieve purifiers, there was a combination of separation by particle size with separation by variation of resistance to the lifting power of air currents. The differential effects within these more sophisticated devices could be used to make significant progress with mechanised refinement.

In gradual reduction roller milling, the purified semolina and middlings were reduced to flour fineness by further grinding using smooth rolls of chilled cast iron. This reduction operation was also carried out in stages. At all points where flour was produced it was separated from larger particles (dressed). In Britain, up to about 72 per cent of the wheat, or possibly more, was usually obtained as white flour. Before the roller milling era in Britain, and during wartime, extraction rates would often have been 80 per cent and higher, with significant inclusion of bran amongst the flour. Efficient late twentieth-century milling produces very white flour at extraction rates approaching 80 per cent.

Hungarian refinement

Friedrich Kick stated that gradual reduction milling, or high grinding as it was first called, started near Vienna, and that there were versions elsewhere, in and around Austria-Hungary. His entire book was not available in English until 1888, but extracts appeared in *The Miller* from the later 1870s. He attributed the start to the work of Ignaz Paur, a mill owner at Leobersdorf, near Vienna, and to his invention of a middlings purifier about 1810.[3] In an article translated from Gustav Pappenheim's *Müller-Zeitung* and printed in 1885 in *The Miller*, George Rieger was quoted as saying that the Vienna mills had 'held the front rank in the art of milling. But it was in Hungary, which till then had been very backward in milling, that high grinding reached its highest development'.[4] There were limits to the extent of improvement that could be made until they elaborated high grinding methods. Only when the operations of grading, purifying and dressing were all well developed could they grind the hard wheats effectively to produce superior flours. They concentrated on obtaining a proportion of very high quality flour; when British and American millers adopted the new methods their aim was to produce more generally improved quality.

GANZ & CO.,

LIMITED,

Millwrights and Engineers,

Works: BUDAPEST, in Hungary; RATIBOR, in Germany. Head Office: BUDAPEST.

Branch Offices: MILAN, BELGRAD, BOMBAY & MELBOURNE. Agencies throughout the world.

ROLLER MILLS MADE IN 32 SIZES.

Electrical Installations, Transmission of Power for Large Distances, Rolling Stock for Railways.

Over **14,500** Roller Mills sold up to date in different parts of the world.

Over **14,500** of these Mills are now working throughout the world.

The FINEST and MOST SUCCESSFUL MILLS IN THE WORLD are working with

GANZ'S ROLLER MILLS, awarded in 33

Exhibitions with sundry Gold and Silver Medals, First Prizes and Diplomas of Honor.

These Mills gained the Victory over Nine other principal methods in the Competition Grinding carried out under superintendence of the French Government.

Messrs. GANZ & CO., the first introducers of Roller Mills in Milling, are prepared to enter into Contracts with responsible parties for the ERECTION and STARTING of COMPLETE FLOUR MILLS on their own System.

Figure 10. The Walzmühle at Budapest, late nineteenth century. (*The Miller*, May 1890)

The rise of Budapest as the centre of new ideas in milling was directly associated with the building of the Pesther Walzmühle from 1839 to 1842.[5] During a fire in 1850, both the mill and workshops were destroyed. The rebuilt mill was started in 1851, and extended in 1868–69. The earliest stages of development at the Walzmühle were based on attempts to use rollers elsewhere: about 1830, Jacob Sulzberger had reconstructed a mill at Frauenfeld in Switzerland, and Sulzberger plants were installed at Milan, Venice, Mayence, Stettin, Leipzig, and Manheim;[6] the Budapest mill was the only one that continued to work roller milling methods successfully. All other plants were discarded. Jenkins (1887) listed the difficulties with the Sulzberger rolls:

> the high price of the rolls and machines, the frequent repairs, the great skill required to manipulate them, the extensive alterations required in the old water mills to receive them, the conservatism of the millers, their indiscriminate application to all classes of wheat, and finally the introduction of French burrs [millstones].[7]

Mill-wrighting shops and a foundry were set up at the Walzmühle, putting the company in a stronger position to support machinery maintenance and technical development. Sulzberger machines contained three pairs of rolls, placed above each other. The rolls in early machines were very small, 6 inches in diameter, and 6 inches long, grooved parallel to the axis. At first, they were used only for the break operation, smooth reduction rolls being introduced later. Oscar Oexle, who supervised the installation of the new plant at the Pesther Walzmühle in 1868–69, gave details of the mill and of the intoduction of roller mills generally in Budapest, stating that in 1867 the Walzmühle plant was arranged in five sections, two for the production of semolina and middlings,

Figure 9. Ganz roller mills advertised in 1887. (*The Miller*, April 1887)

27

Figure 11. The Concordia Mill at Budapest, now a milling museum. (R. J. W. Evans 1999)

three for the reduction operation, in what he called the Frauenfeld system. A few millstones were used. In the new plant, started in 1869, there were 40 sets of Escher Wyss rolls, their arrangement being similar to the Sulzberger machines, but with design improvements. Oexle stated that it was at the Pesther Walzmühle that the reduction operation 'was first effected with smooth rollers'. Also, he reported that until 1864 only three other mills had adopted the same method, and that on a smaller scale: 'the steam-mill at Venice and two small mills, one in Switzerland and the other in Germany'.[8]

The leading American roller mill designer, W. D. Gray, visited the Pesther Walzmühle in 1879 and stated that Sulzberger roller sets were still in use in the older part of the mill, grinding middlings.[9] It is not clear when the Walzmühle changed completely to roller milling; it may have been at the time of the remodelling of the plant and enlargement of 1868–69. During the later 1860s the number of mills in Budapest increased from three to nine. Two more were built later, and from the early 1880s there were references to the eleven mills of Budapest,[10] though roller milling does not seem to have been adopted generally there until the later 1870s.[11] Kick, in 1878, referred to 'the astonishing alterations which the Buda Pesth mills have undergone during the last few years, the most important of which is the introduction of roller mills'. He stated then that stones had been 'replaced by rollers of various constructions in all the larger mills, except for ending wheat and grinding bran'.[12]

American New Process milling

The modern history of flour milling in the United States of America begins with the use of 'New Process' milling in the later 1860s and the 1870s, methods by which American millers adopted more gradual techniques of grinding, using millstones and introducing purifiers. Kuhlmann (1929) summarised the changes: 'We may think of the decade 1870–80 as the period of New Process milling and that of 1880–90 as the first decade of roller milling'.[13] At Minneapolis advances were made in purifier design about 1870, and in the use of roller mills around 1880, leading to large scales of production in the 1880s. George T. Smith was a key figure in purifier development, his breakthrough achieved at Governor C. C. Washburn's Minneapolis mills in 1871.[14] Comprehensively mechanised gradual reduction roller milling was convincingly instituted at the mills of C. A. Pillsbury & Co. at Minneapolis by 1881.[15] The commercial success of Budapest as a milling centre had been due to progress in dealing with hard wheats, and this was true of Minneapolis. From Budapest, millers were able to sell both their fine grades of flour and their much lower grades, at least until American competition in European markets became keen. In America, problems of processing hard wheat were partially solved by New Process methods, sufficiently for a market for higher quality to start to form. With the associated higher prices for superior quality, the prestige of hard wheat and New Process flour advanced together.

The first aim was the reduction of the severity of the cutting and grinding by the millstones. To achieve this, the stones were set further apart, and the upper stones were run more slowly. More furrows were cut into the stones, leaving a smaller proportion of land, or raised area. These alterations resulted in less immediate breaking and crushing of the grain, and less attrition of the bran layers. There was a requirement for more careful attention to the milling process, and closer control of it. Two millstone operations were involved, and the stages of either could be extended, though at the start there was probably reliance on one cracking operation and one middlings reduction. These changes were tried before the general adoption of purifying, although the bolting operation was seen as worthy of attention, and was more carefully done.

Storck & Teague (1952) gave special credit to two Frenchmen, Nicholas and Edmund La Croix, who were persuaded by a mill owner to move from Montreal to Minnesota. There were others working on the same processing problems, some also in Minnesota but in a wider design context the comment was made that 'the La Croixs were the first to introduce machines which made continuous improvement possible by arangements for grading the middlings as well as sub-jecting them to an air current'.[16] Making 'continuous improvement possible' represented a breakthrough, in contrast to many routine or minor improvements. Edmund La Croix moved to Minneapolis in 1870 and worked for George H. Chris-tian, who was managing the Washburn mills. La Croix probably had knowledge of gravity purifiers from his training and experience in France, where the line of development of sieve machines included the French Joseph Perrigault's design. In his detailed account of the evolution of purifier design, Scott (1972) concluded that 'the development and general adoption of the proto-sieve type purifier was mainly due to the effort and ingenuity of three men, namely Perrigault, Edmund La Croix and George T. Smith'.[17]

The inventive thread began before Perrigault's patent of 1860 with work by the French designer Cabane. Perrigault's decision to draw the airflow through the sieve, not blow it through, was an advance. Cabane's contribution may have been the combined action of aspiration of the material on the sieve with agitation of the sieve, to move the material forward. These were essential features for progress but there does not seem to have been an effective machine for general use. In 1878, Kick made a faulty judgement: 'Cabane's principle of purifying middlings [using a sieve], if indeed right in the abstract, is not so good as that of purifying by passing a current of air through falling middlings'.[18] Development in mainland Europe seems to have left on one side the sieve idea that led eventually to modern practice. At the Washburn mills, La Croix tried to improve Perrigault's design, but an operative had to keep the sieve meshes clear by brushing, so the version was abandoned about 1870. Early in 1871, G. T. Christian, who had wide experience in the flour trade and some knowledge of improvements being made at other mills, engaged George T. Smith from another mill in Minnesota where there were attempts to improve the process. Smith was put in charge of a plan to raise quality at the Washburn B Mill, by improving the work on the millstones. In a notable letter to *The Miller* in February 1881 he stressed the importance of smooth, true and well-balanced stones.[19]

General accounts of Smith's contribution to the advance of the New Process milling made at the Washburn mill do not describe his careful attention to the stones, merely his improvement of the La Croix purifier. There had been problems with several designs: with the effect of the airflow on the lighter particles, and with the selection of appropriately graded sieve mesh. The improvements to the stones produced a good yield of middlings, and Smith turned his attention to the La Croix purifier. He improved the control of the airflow, and fitted graded sieve covers. The problem of blocked mesh was overcome by fitting a travelling brush, driven by the feed roll shaft, to clear the sieve. The results were satisfactory and, according to Kuhlmann, Christian advertised that the New Process flour was made by a patented process, encouraging widespread use of the name 'patent flour' to describe the highest quality.[20] By the autumn of 1871 Smith had left the Washburn mill, entering into a contract with C. A. Pillsbury to improve the working of two mills; in Smith's words in his letter to *The Miller*: 'to put both those mills into condition to make the same grade of flour as Mr Christian was making'. He set up the George T. Smith Purifier Co. at Jackson in Illinois,[21] but the growth of his business was hindered by a series of legal actions to establish the validity of his patents against alleged infringers. Smith was successful in a prolonged contest, one case being against La Croix, but the actions were costly in money and time.[22]

A. R. Tattersall (1921) described Smith's achievements together with a notable legal test of 1883 which dealt with the question of why a design might be classed as an invention.[23] In the Canadian Supreme Court, a judgement given in Smith's favour concentrated on the idea of the combination of machine

Figure 12. George Smith, a driving force in American New Process milling. (*The Miller*, November 1883)

features: 'By the cooperation of the constituents a new machine of a distinctive character and function was formed and a beneficial result produced by the cooperating actions of the constituents and not the mere adding together of separate contributions'. This was then held to come within the meaning of invention as applied to patents. G. T. Smith has been recognised as a leader in the design of sieve purifiers, but the importance of his work has often been described merely in terms of the single feature of the brushing action in his purifier, not doing justice to the generally improved combination of features. Various parts of the machine, including the much-noticed brushing device, allowed the principal mechanism of the aspirated, agitated sieve to become fully effective. After Smith, there were many others, continuing to improve on predecessors or vie with competitors; G. T. Smith was possibly the best-known name until well into the 1880s, but the evolution of the purifier is a complicated story of interaction.

The introduction of roller milling at Minneapolis

Success with the new purifiers led to the widespread adoption of larger-scale production, and ensured the supremacy at that time of hard spring wheat flour and the spring wheat area of the north-west. The location of Minneapolis, on the upper Mississippi, had been found to be highly suitable for the development of water-powered industrial plant. In the 1870s, rail links were created, an improvement on the steam-boat facilities on the main rivers; they allowed the growing milling centre to increase the area from which wheat supplies could be drawn, and gave better access to product markets in eastern America, and in Europe. Kuhlmann (1929) stated that there were thirteen mills in production at Minneapolis in 1870. Four were destroyed during the next two years, but by 1876 there were twenty mills with a total of 194 pairs of stones. There was an aggregate capacity of 4,840 barrels of flour per day (about 3,400 sacks). By 1880, capacity had been trebled, with a very large increase from 1879 to 1880, and another from 1880 to 1881.[24] This rapid increase was the result of continuing technical improvement from the early stages of New Process milling, leading to more confident processing methods, and a large marketing expansion.

Experiments had been made with marble rolls at a mill in Winona in Minnesota in 1873 and with cast iron rolls at the Washburn B mill at Minneapolis, but according to Kuhlmann both trials were unsatisfactory, due to excessive roll wear. Storck & Teague (1952) stated that in 1874 Christian ordered 36 pairs of smooth chilled cast iron rolls for the Washburn A mill from a Connecticut foundry, but roller milling did not become accepted practice at that time. In 1875, *American Miller* reported that experiments were being made in Chicago, at a mill in Minnesota, and at St. Louis where R. L. Downton was using rolls to reduce middlings and flatten germ, which was then dressed out in a bolter.[25] *American Miller* reported the meeting of the American Millers' National Association of 1876, but did not include any discussion of roller milling, although there were articles on Hungarian milling, reprinted from *The Miller* of London, including translations of Kick's work, and Oexle's series of articles.[26]

Storck & Teague recorded that in the same year John and William Sellers bought six Daverio roller mills, together with purifiers and reels, at an exhibition in Philadelphia. They installed the equipment in place of a millstone plant at their mill near Philadelphia; this may have been the first trial of gradual reduction, using rolls, but it seems to have been an isolated occurence.[27] William de la Barre stated that 'From my investigation I believe that the first all roller mill in the United States, where rolls were exclusively used for grinding, was that of John Sellers at Fairmount Park, near Philadelphia'.[28] A clearer preliminary to the introduction of roller milling occurred in 1877 when Oexle, who had been invited to the United States by Governor Washburn, arranged for E. P. Allis & Co. to become the sole distributors of Wegmann roller mills. By 1878, W. D. Gray of the Allis company had designed a new version.[29] He used porcelain, but altered the design of the roll bearings, method of adjustment, the method of application of pressure, and the new machine frame. Belt drives were used instead of the previous noisy gearing. Gray described his involvement in detail in *The Miller* in April 1881, hoping that his design would be successful in Britain through J. W. Throop's agency.[30]

Remodelling and extension of the Washburn mills, and general change at Minneapolis, was accelerated after a major explosion in May 1878 that destroyed the Washburn A mill and five other mills in a chain of explosions and fires, caused by ignition of mill dust. The disaster and subsequent deliberations were recorded at length in *The Miller*.[31] Storck & Teague described consequent decisions. At that time, extensions to the Washburn B mill were being prepared, with the possibility that Adolf Fischer of Budapest would provide plans for an installation based on Hungarian practice, but urgency resulted in E. P. Allis & Co. supplying a combination plant, with 30 pairs of stones and 22 pairs of Ganz chilled iron rolls. There was a fortuitous accompaniment: W. D. Gray persuaded Washburn to use space at the end of the B mill for a small experimental roller mill.[32]

Storck & Teague stated that in America 'modern milling was initiated in the Washburn experimental mill of 1878–79, as planned by Oscar Oexle and executed by W. D. Gray for E. P. Allis & Co. under the driving aegis of C. C. Washburn, and as soon thereafter revised at the suggestion of William de la Barre to include chilled iron rollers'.[33] They added that 'no single person could rightfully claim more than a small share of the credit for this achievement'. However, the Vienna-born engineer, William de la Barre, had been engaged to take charge of construction at the Washburn mills and as *Northwestern Miller* stated 'played a major role in building up the milling industry at Minneapolis'.[34] The foremost American writer on milling practice towards the end of the nineteenth century, Louis Gibson (1885) stated that 'The success of this mill led to the general introduction of rolls into this country'.[35] A replacement for the A mill was ready for the installation of the machinery by 1880. Fischer had prepared plans for the milling plant, but they were considered too demanding in manual labour, and from about that time, there was much less interest in Hungarian methods.[36] The first part of the A mill became essentially a roller mill with some stones. Before the second part of the mill was equipped,

Figure 13.
Smith's sieve type
purifier, clearly
described. (*The Miller*,
July 1880)

The Geo. T. Smith
MIDDLINGS PURIFIER.

SIMPLE, DURABLE, ECONOMICAL.

Equally well adapted to Middlings from Hard and Soft Wheat.

Manufactured in Eleven Sizes.

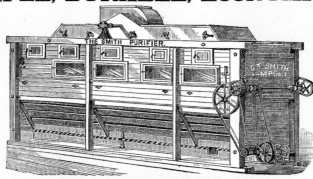

A Full Stock of Machines in Store from which Millers can be supplied at once.

CONSTRUCTION.

The Smith Purifier is constructed with from three to five grades of silk to each Machine. Over each grade of silk there is an air chamber, so that draughts of air of different forces or strength can be applied to each grade of silk. Each grade of Middlings can thus be treated with a draught of air according to its particular gravity, and in connection with each air chamber, <u>over the silk,</u> is a settling chamber, with openings from the outside (see illustration) of Machine, so that the refuse or fluff taken from the Middlings by each number of silk can at all times be examined by the operator, giving him a perfect knowledge or guide as to how the draught may be regulated.

In order to use high numbers of silk, a travelling brush is required to clean the cloth. This brush extends across the width of the sieve underneath, and travels its entire length from head to tail. It is mounted on an endless chain, and travels in one direction on ways and round pulleys. Fine silk is necessary for this reason—that it is by the delicate combination of the air draught and the silk that successful work is accomplished. With a coarse cloth the purification depends too much on the air draughts, and you lose in a measure the assistance of the cloth.

The SMITH CIRCULAR PROVER & PROOF STAFF, for Trueing Millstones.

Advice on New Process Milling.

MILLERS VISITING AMERICA are hereby cordially invited to visit the Mill of the "GEO. T. SMITH MIDDLINGS PURIFIER COMPANY," at Albion, Michigan, where every facility will be afforded them to inspect every detail of A MODEL AMERICAN NEW PROCESS MILL, which is fitted under the Smith system with Smith Purifiers, Stone Dress, and other improvements which will be fully explained. The Mill is working on the softest Wheat grown in America, and those wishing it can examine any and every part of the Mill and system at their leisure.

Write for Illustrated Catalogue. Address,

GEO. T. SMITH COMPANY,
26, MARK LANE, LONDON, E.C.

Washburn visited Europe to study developments, and sent de la Barre on a similar investigation, but with closer attention to technicalities. It was then decided to simplify plant designs, and produce six grades of flour, but this was soon reduced to three grades: patents, bakers and low grade, as the market would not accept more.

THE CINCINNATI EXHIBITION

The exhibition held in 1880 at Cincinnati in Ohio was to coincide with the seventh annual convention of the United States Millers' National Association. About forty-eight British and Irish millers attended, the party being organised by J. W. Throop; the leading spokesmen for the group were Samuel Smith of Sheffield and T. W. Hibbard of Gloucester, both of whom took the opportunity to complain that much of the American wheat that was shipped to Britain was of poor quality. Smith's assessment of the exhibition was that 'the speciality was purifiers'. According to Storck & Teague, twenty-two makes of purifier were shown. Only two manufacturers of roller mills exhibited, E. P. Allis & Co. and the Downton Manufacturing Co. The Throop Grain Cleaning Co. displayed roller mills by J. Buchholz and Ganz. Hibbard described it as the first milling exhibition at which there were complete plants working: there were six, but only one was a development beyond New Process milling, using Jonathan Mills disc mills. Hibbard then visited Minneapolis, recording his impressions for *The Miller*.[37] He reported favourably on the use of chilled iron rolls, having seen the new Washburn mill, Pillsbury's Excelsior Mill, and several other combined roller mill and millstone plants. Storck & Teague described 1880 as a 'watershed' in the development of milling in America, although neither the Cincinnati show nor the American millers' meeting demonstrated it. The purification operation was still regarded as the key part of the process. As millstones were still widely used in America after 1880, Storck & Teague's use of the word 'watershed' must refer simply to the very vigorous development of rolls by the leading American millers from 1880. It may well be a neat and satisfactory marker but does not establish a single date for international comparisons.

American milling practice then continued on its own lines, with a rapid scaling up of plants, the leading mills using automatic roller milling methods and American machinery. Bigger businesses were encouraged by expectations of large markets, their confidence generated in a simpler technical situation than in Britain, as they were asssured a steady supply of large quantities of raw material of comparatively uniform quality and characteristics. Their other main advantage was that many millers had already passed a stage of early experimental work with the purifying operation. For the next phase of technical development the lead passed to the family partnership of C. A Pillsbury & Co. of Minneapolis. In 1880 they started to build a first part of the Pillsbury A,[38] and began a period of rapid growth, punctuated by setbacks, which they quickly overcame in a strenuous programme of building and equipping. Their Excelsior Mill was remodelled by W. D. Gray in 1881, becoming the first full-sized merchant mill there to incorporate the three principal features of modern milling: it was an automatic, all-roller, gradual reduction system of 800 barrels per day capacity, equivalent to 23 sacks of flour per hour, if 24 hour working is assumed. Later in 1881, fire destroyed the Excelsior, the Empire and the Pillsbury B mills. Despite misfortunes, Pillsburys advanced rapidly. The Pillsbury A mill was completed by 1883, giving a capacity of 5,000 barrels a day, the world's largest flour mill; Pillsbury B was rebuilt by 1884.[39]

The general position reached by 1884 was described in *The Miller* in an article on Minneapolis and Budapest, called 'The two milling capitals'. Estimated daily capacity of the twenty-three mills at Minneapolis was 30,775 barrels of flour (a barrel = 0.7 sack), equivalent to nearly 900 sacks per hour if on 24 hour working. On the same basis the Pillsbury A mill would have had a capacitiy of about 180 sacks per hour and Washburn, Crosby & Co.'s Washburn A mill about 100 sacks per hour. Although flour quantities were stated as capacities, the quantities given seem to represent amounts produced. The quantity of wheat ground in 1884 by the eleven Budapest mills was said to be 5,461,015 metercentners (a metercentner = 220.46 lb).[40] If the extraction rate is assumed to have been 75%, and there was 24 hour working for six days per week and for 50 weeks per year, then that was equivalent to nearly 450 sacks per hour, or half of the Minneapolis capability.

The milling strength of Minneapolis continued to increase rapidly, but by the later 1880s, ideas of unlimited expansion and continued command of large markets had to be reassessed. From 1884 there were attempts to restrain competition, with hopes to limit output to two thirds of capacity; afterwards, alternative routes to economy of scale were sought. Between 1889 and 1891 many of the mills entered amalgamations, as outlined by Kuhlmann (1929), and by 1891 most of the capacity was concentrated in four corporations. Kuhlmann stated that 'more and more in the two decades 1880–1900, the Minneapolis mills concentrated on the export trade though they never reached the point where they were independent of the home market. The highest point they attained was in 1886–87, when about forty per cent of their output was exported'.[41] That was exactly the time of special concern and joint discussion within the National Association of British and Irish Millers.[42] There were of course other 'milling centers', though not as prominent in the crucial period for UK millers of the 1880s; Kuhlmann referred to them in relation to wheat growing areas and commecial aspects of transport. Kuhlmann and Storck & Teague dealt most extensively with developments at Minneapolis and, apart from reports of American millers' meetings, *The Miller* also concentrated almost exclusively on news of activity at Minneapolis.

GROUP OF BRITISH MILLERS AT THE VIENNA EXHIBITION IN AUGUST, 1897.

(Reproduced and corrected from July 3rd issue).

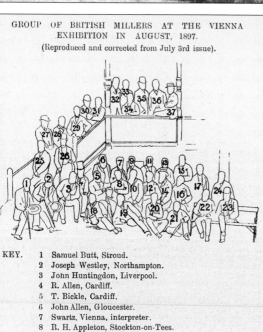

KEY.	
1	Samuel Butt, Stroud.
2	Joseph Westley, Northampton.
3	John Huntingdon, Liverpool.
4	R. Allen, Cardiff.
5	T. Bickle, Cardiff.
6	John Allen, Gloucester.
7	Swartz, Vienna, interpreter.
8	R. H. Appleton, Stockton-on-Tees.
9	G. F. Penrose, Dublin.
10	Frederick Richardson, Sunderland.
11	Henry Ibbotson, Sheffield.
12	Collins Barlow, Bilston.
13	John Thomas, Oswestry.
14	William Evans, Leicester.
15	Thos. Willacy, St. Helens.
16	John Power, Coventry.
17	Fred Stansfield, Bradford.
18	J. A. A. Buchholz, London.
19	J. W. Throop, London.
20	J. Harrison Carter, London.
21	J. R. Furlong, Fermoy.
22	G. W. Chitty, Dover and Deal.
23	J. R. Willacy, St. Helens.
24	James Greenwood, Blackburn and Burnley.
25	Joseph Huntingdon, Liverpool.
26	J. W. Mullen, Portadown.
27	J. A. Ingleby, Tadcaster.
28	Wilson Marriage, Colchester.
29	F. W. Davis, Enniscorthy.
30	W. R. Neave, Fordingbridge.
31	L. W. Roberts, Oswestry.
32	R. Shackleton, Dublin.
33	Jas. Hodden, Cork.
34	Frank Ashby, Croydon.
35	D. Carmichael, Donaghadee.
36	James Marshall, Glasgow.
37	F. Davies jun., Enniscorthy.

AUTOMOBILES AT THE B.A. MEETING.—A show of automobiles is to be held at Dover between September 18th and 21st next, simultaneously with a meeting of the British Association then taking place there. The meeting at Dover will be especially noteworthy, as it is held in conjunction with that of the French Society taking place at Boulogne, and an interchange of visits is already arranged for. The object of the show is primarily to provide an interesting display and to benefit the motor car industry. A small charge for space will be made, and prizes will be awarded to successful exhibitors. Full particulars may be obtained from the secretary, F. E. Beeton, Esq., Park Street, Dover.

CHAPTER THREE

New ideas in Britain

Information for British millers

In May 1875 *The Miller* began a series of articles on 'The Hungarian system of high grinding', with a first mention of the 'Roller or Cylinder Mill' at Pesth, afterwards referred to in the journal by its actual name of the Walzmühle. It was explained that changes in the Hungarian milling industry and extensions of wheat growing were recent developments, becoming possible only with general industrial development and modern transport facilities. In 1875, this topic must have seemed remote to most British millers, but in the following year there was much more information. In January 1876, there was a translation from Friedrich Kick's text *Die Mehlfabrication*, dealing with 'the application of Hungarian roller mills for the purpose of breaking wheat'. In March 1876, Oscar Oexle began a series of articles 'On roller mills', including many references to the Walzmühle. Details were given of the fourteen grades of flour being produced there, and dressing and purifying operations were dealt with briefly. The large number of grades must have astonished British readers, possibly seeming so strange that it merited little further attention. Roller mills by Escher Wyss & Co. of Leesdorf near Vienna were described in *The Miller*, and Harrison Carter briefly used Escher Wyss machines.[1] More obvious relevance to British millers was created when Oexle's advocacy of Friedrich Wegmann's middlings roller mill was followed by bold advertising by A. B. Childs.[2] A stage of general awareness was formed by the spread of Wegmann customers which could not have happened for Gustav Buchholz, who tried to deal with bigger initial problems during a period that lacked a medium for advertising and debate.[3]

From the first year, there was information in *The Miller* about the purification operation, described in a series of articles on 'the history of the separation of middlings and semolina' showing the relevance of purification to the production of high quality flours in Austria-Hungary and France. The notion that separations had been made over a sufficiently long period of time to have a history may have been irrelevant to some readers, but tantalising to others. There was prompting towards personal deliberation, and the spread of information. Solid facts were needed: actual machines! In the first issue of the journal, there were advertisements for middlings purifiers. A machine marketed by Bryan Corcoran was the Frenchman Cabane's design, and its prestige was indicated by medals awarded in France and Germany, and sales in France, Austria and Italy.[4] Clarke & Dunham of Mark Lane offered a Gem middlings and semolina separator, so the editor of *The Miller* was not merely an observer.[5] A. B. Childs advertised an American machine, the Excelsior middlings purifier.

Information about developments abroad was also contained in reports of the

Figure 14.
British millers' visit to Vienna and Budapest in 1877. (*The Miller*, July 1899)

Figure 15.
Members of the 1877 party, reproduced in 1899. (*The Miller*, August 1899)

37

exhibitions of milling machinery at Vienna in 1875 and 1877, and at Nuremberg in 1876. The millwrighting firm of Hoerde & Co. of Vienna showed Escher Wyss roller mills, Ganz & Co. of Budapest showed Wegmann machines. The first of these exhibitions was reported in *The Engineer*, repeated in *The Miller* with illustrations.[6] Oexle reported for *The Miller* from Nuremberg. The Vienna International Corn, Seed and Machinery Exhibition of 1877 had extra significance, as a stimulus to a more active gathering of information. A party of about forty British and Irish millers and three milling experts visited the exhibition, attended the annual general meeting of the Austrian Millers' Association, and visited mills in Austria and Budapest. The scheme for a group visit was suggested by Harrison Carter and J. W. Throop, a meeting being held to discuss it at the offices of the Millers' Insurance and Millers' Mutual Insurance Companies at 69 Mark Lane, under the presidency of Wilson Marriage of East Mills, Colchester. Carter and Throop organised the tour, and J. A. A. Buchholz assisted the group as an interpreter.[7]

At Vienna there were at least eight exhibitors of roller mills.[8] Wegmann addressed the meeting of the Austrian millers. The British millers visited mills around Vienna, before travelling by Danube steamer to Budapest, where they saw four mills: the Elizabeth, the Ofen Pesther, the Concordia, and Heinrich Haggenmacher's, but there were no descriptions in *The Miller*. In 1874, when the Walzmühle was still the only one with a large number of rolls, the Concordia had none, the Elizabeth Mill seems to have been a combination plant, and the Haggenmacher and Ofen Pesther mills were using rolls on only a small scale.[9] The visit was important for three reasons. It provided innovative millers with direct insights. On a more general level, it was the first well-publicised attempt by British millers to seek information about the new processes, and because of the cooperative effort, the 1877 party helped to encourage the formation of a National Association in Britain. Of the forty millers, about half had tried an aspect of roller milling in their own mills by 1879. In many cases the first trials were with Wegmann rolls. Amongst the more adventurous were Collins Barlow of Bilston and John Fairclough of Warrington with the J. A. A. Buchholz system, and the millers who aquired the second and fourth of Henry Simon's plants: F. Ashby of Croydon and J. A. Ingleby of Tadcaster. At least twenty-four of the group became members of the National Association of British and Irish Millers, formed in 1878, five of them serving as president: Appleton from Stockton-on-Tees, Shackleton from Dublin, Westley from Northampton, Marriage from Colchester and Ibbotson from Sheffield.

For several years the Budapest mills were open to visits by British and American millers, but from about 1880 it became less easy to gain access. From 1869, the Budapest firm of Kalnoky & Simon had published a yearly report on the Hungarian flour trade and from 1878 to 1881 extracts were translated and published in *The Miller*, but by then they also found it difficult to obtain information. In their review of 1880, they stated that their position as a private firm made it difficult to obtain comprehensive data; there was an 'absence of any systematic milling statistics'. A hope that official statistics would become available was unfulfilled, information being reserved for the private use of the

Budapest mills. After 1881, Kalnoky & Simon stopped their series of reports, but the four which appeared dealt with the significant period of increased exports of Hungarian flour.[10] In 1880, Kalnoky & Simon expressed increased concern about American competition, particularly in Britain, Hungary's largest customer abroad. Although the best flour grades, numbers 0 down to 6, had previously found a ready sale, American competition on price had reduced the Hungarian ascendancy to grades 0 to 3 and sometimes totally blocked the trade to Glasgow. The Budapest mills had worked below capacity, and had also been working for stock. Concern was also expressed by the Hungarian Government, who sent Emrich Pekar, a former director of the Istvan Steam Mills at Debreczin, to study the American milling and flour trade, and to visit Cincinnati for the 1880 exhibition there. Extracts from his report appeared in *The Miller,*[11] but after 1881 information about Hungarian mills became a matter only of general interest. Information about shipments of American wheat and flour had more direct relevance for increasing numbers of British millers.

Detailed information on particular Hungarian mills never became a subject of reporting in *The Miller,* but the machinery produced at Budapest was considered important. Grooved chilled iron rolls were in general use by 1879, and the number of different roller systems had been reduced, Ganz & Co.'s roller mills maintaining the lead. Abraham Ganz, from Embach near Zurich, had worked as a foreman in the Walzmühle foundry, and set up on his own account in the mid 1840s. Early work in casting cannon and bridge members was followed by a specialisation in casting steel railway tyres. Expertise in chill-casting had been widely recognised by the time of his death in 1867 and his successor, Andreas Mechwart, started to manufacture chilled iron rolls about 1870. Ganz & Co. were pioneers in the introduction and development of chilled iron rolls for milling.[12] Their best-known design was the Mechwart ring roller mill, marketed in Britain by J. A. A. Buchholz, and subsequently by the milling engineering firm of G. Luther, who later had works at Brunswick and Darmstadt. Despite the strength of these connections, Ganz machines, like most foreign makes, were soon superseded in Britain. Hungary was not a lone influence though very high quality flour was mainly associated with Continental products. Quite soon the situation would change as attention was switched from the Continent to the challenge of American flour entering the British market.

Gustav Buchholz, an isolated inventor

Before gradual reduction roller milling systems were introduced in Britain, from 1878 onwards, there were three major attempts to make technical progress, the first and longest-lasting being made by Gustav Adolf Buchholz, a Prussian engineer. The second was a 'movement' to import Hungarian milling as an entity, in which Oscar Oexle was the guide; it was a mirage. The third was more constructive, more public and more controversial: the attempt to make Friedrich Wegmann's porcelain rolls the governing feature of improved milling methods. Buchholz's efforts and frustrations show that it was not obvious how the wheat grain could be debranned, nor what form of roll surface should be used to break it open. Wegmann's invention was, in contrast, focused too narrowly. If they had put their existing ideas together they would still have been in difficulty. Separately they acted as *provocateurs*.

Buchholz came to England in 1847, and produced a series of designs for flour milling machinery, mainly in the 1860s, with industrial scale trials in the late 1860s and early 1870s, although relevant work continued to 1878. Gustav Buchholz was notable for inventive activity, but his designs, like much experimental work, were abandoned. His efforts were within the United Kingdom, suggesting possible advantages over consultants based abroad, who tried to arrange for the importation of 'Hungarian milling' or 'New Process milling'. Early in his career, Buchholz had been engaged in flour mill engineering, but in England he had a varied mechanical engineering experience. In 1851, he patented a printing machine; he worked on the insulation of telegraph wires and submarine cables, and he designed ship steering gear. A patent agent called Carpmael advised him to revert to milling.[13] His endeavours demonstrate how difficult it was for a versatile design engineer to make progress in this field of materials processing problems. He paid particular attention to the problem of removing the wheat husk, at first by using hulling machines, later by grooved rolls, and he tried to extend his designs to provide a complete process. The main period of trials with Buchholz's more ambitious machinery was from 1869 to 1872, at Liverpool and Bristol, in East Anglia and in Ireland. He may have worked too much in isolation, or perhaps there was mainly a shortage of competing ideas from which to learn, either in Hungary or America.

Gustav Buchholz applied for at least sixteen patents for milling machinery design, the main series being from 1862 to 1870. His work was described briefly in *The Miller* in 1875,[14] but the mid 1870s represent a short period of attempts and failures to make a breakthrough by Buchhholz and others. His first important patent was number 3113 of 1862. A hulling machine was intended to strip off much of the bran. Brushes were to be used to separate the husk, the released material of the interior of the grain being 'submitted to the action of a novel construction of crushing roller mill, whereby a large portion will be reduced to semolina fit for the market'. This basic process incorporated hopeful operations, but it was to be found by other designers that the two most basic operations, of first breaking and then reducing, should be done gradually, over a number of stages, allied to careful grading of particle sizes, the screening out of coarse material, the extraction of flour by dressing machines, and the removal of fine contaminant using air currents in purifiers. In Buchholz's hulling machine, cast iron discs fixed on a vertical spindle and fitted with steel blades revolved within a cylinder, with a clearance from another set of blades fixed to the casing. For several years in the early 1870s, a number of designers tried to solve these problems of hulling or decorticating. Other forms of disc machine were tried but these devices, like Buchholz's hullers, were too severe.

When he began his main series of designs, Buchholz had intended to use only one pair of rolls, grooved both left and right hand, to form a grid of points round the circumference. Many variations were considered.[15] He tried rolls 'with grooves in helical form, which may cross each other'. That was in 1867, and was potentially an important advance. Each new specification referred to improvements of previous designs. But the general arrangement drawing for patent 2508 of 1867 showed new ideas: a composite machine contained 'a number of pairs of rolls' in a frame, with sorting troughs below the rolls. The first pair of rolls were to be cross-cut, and other rolls 'grooved longitudinally'. The last version of this series, in 1870, stated that 'when the mill has to produce flour instead of semolina, steel cylindrical rollers, with square ribs arranged either parallel to their axes or helically, are substituted'. Differential roller speed was included. His patent 229 of 1870 described a composite machine, with six pairs of rolls in a framework. Below each pair was a sieve, 'to sift out the finer particles from the coarser, and deliver the coarser into the bite of the roller next below the sieve', so this was a gradual breaking process, an advance in general principle but still with much to consider. These designs appear to be hopeful uses of mechanisms without adequate appreciation of the characteristics of materials being processed.[16]

The first industrial installation of Buchholz's machinery was in 1862 for Fison & Co. at Ipswich. A hulling machine was included, a pair of rolls for a first break, and a series of millstones only two feet in diameter to produce semolina which was then ground on ordinary millstones of four feet diameter. The first machinery was made at Ipswich by E. R. & F. Turner, who in the 1880s were to form a successful working partnership with the milling expert, Harrison Carter. A Buchholz partial system was installed at the Albert Mills of W. J. Radford & Sons at Liverpool in 1869; in 1870, the stones were replaced by slightly grooved rolls. The plant was claimed to have been the first complete roller plant without stones in Britain. Early results led to an arrangement for Radfords to hold exclusive rights of working the Buchholz methods in Liverpool and within a radius of seven miles around.[17] It was alleged that the cost of that arrangement was never recouped; W. J. Radford's assessment in 1895 was that 'The commercial result of these installations, owing to heavy royalties, crude arrangements and other causes, was not encouraging'.

Buchholz's ideas were tried at the Bristol mill of W. Baker & Sons in 1869, by J. Stannard at Nayland near Colchester in 1871, and in the following year by S. S. Allen at Middleton in Ireland. In 1872, Proctor Baker, who was later to become the first milling examiner under the City & Guilds scheme, gave a lecture on 'the Buchholz process' to the Institution of Mechanical Engineers, at Liverpool; members inspected the machinery at Radford's mills.[18] Though there were further installations elsewhere, Buchholz's methods were not widely used. In correspondence in 1886, Stannard explained why he discarded his Buchholz equipment: 'I replaced nearly all the machinery in my mill at a heavy outlay of money and time, but owing to various causes I substantially returned to the old system … there were no purifiers and the other machines that now render the gradual reduction system a success'.[19]

Buchholz had impressed some of his miller customers. Proctor Baker suggested that he had been near 'to hitting a big thing', a view supported by Harrison Carter's manager, Gilbert Little. This judgement was modified by others, including Carter, who thought that users of Buchholz equipment had been 'ahead of their time', both with regard to the imperfections of the machinery, and limited demand at that time for higher class flour. How near was Buchholz to getting it right, in terms of mechanical engineering? He considered various roll flute profiles, included differential roll speeds, but he did not fix on a thoroughly sound specification for a pair of granulating rolls. Although Little also commended Buchholz's ideas of placing six pairs of rolls in a frame, to form what was called a concentrated break roller mill, such a scheme did not allow the elbow room required for design changes. Neither the American Cosgrove concentrated mill, which was marketed in England by Wm R. Dell, nor the American Odell concentrated mill, supplied through William Gardner & Sons,[20] seems to have become prominent in Britain. Like these American devices, the self-contained granulator that was supplied by Simon & Seck about the end of the 1870s, was developed for use in restricted space, removing a need for elevators between stages; in Simon's version there were six pairs of rolls and three centrifugal scalpers within the composite machine.[21] But when Simon & Seck's combined granulator was offered in England, work had been done on the basic operations on separate machines.

In Buchholz's case, as in the work of the systems designers in the early 1880s, there was a need to experiment with the granulation, dressing, grading, purifying and reduction processes as distinct operations. An approach that focused on separate factors would have allowed more flexible approaches to experiments, and better scope for alterations. Gustav Buchholz's work constituted energetic investigation, not successful engineering development. The American writers Storck & Teague suggested that Buchholz had 'invented the 'break' section of the modern roller mill and had placed it complete inside a single case', but also that 'it attempted too many things at once'.[22] It is possible that Seth Taylor, the most prominent of London millers during the 1880s, gave the simplest possible summary in 1889: 'Some few experiments had been made in roller milling in a crude way, but none had been successful. The system of Mr. Buchholz, introduced nearly twenty years ago, was so elaborate, complex, and difficult in working that it had been a failure; still it had been the germ of the present roller milling'.[23]

Attempts to import pseudo-Hungarian milling

Contemporary with Buchholz's main industrial scale trials there was a series of projects involving Oscar Oexle, from Augsburg in Germany. Originally from Venice, Oexle studied at the Zurich Polytechnic, served a milling apprenticeship, and became a milling engineer at Vienna.[24] His work on major extensions at the Pesther Walzmühle was in or around 1868, when the milling machinery was supplied by Escher Wyss & Co. of Leesdorf near Vienna. Oexle's earliest activities in Britain, which constituted the second of the three early and ultimately unsuccessful attempts at innovation, were from 1868 or 1869 to 1873 or 1874. At that time, Oexle was the consultant in probably the first phase of importing so-called Hungarian systems, including installations at Liverpool, Newcastle-on-Tyne and Glasgow. In 1868 Oexle was invited by the manager,

James Wood, to visit the North Shore Flour & Rice Mill Co. Ltd at Liverpool, and supply a supposedly Hungarian millstone plant.[25] In Oexle's obituary, in 1887, it was stated that Oexle fitted 'an elaborate system of middlings separators and other machines; and this, if we mistake not, was the first Hungarian stone milling plant erected in this country'. In 1870, John Davidson & Son of Newcastle-on-Tyne engaged Oexle to introduce 'his mode of treating middlings by roller mills'. It appears that steel rolls were used. There was no suggestion that break rolls were used.

Oexle was also employed by Matthew Muir & Sons at the Tradeston Mills at Glasgow. New work was planned there in 1871 and 1872, but there was then an explosion and a major fire. *The Miller* reported in 1877 on the reconstruction.[26] Oexle assisted with the remodelling, which was to be a half-high grinding system, including four break stages, using millstones. Rolls were used to reduce semolina to flour. The new plant was said to have been started in 1874. In 1875, Thomas Muir took out a patent for the extraction of germ, by flattening it between smooth rolls, and extracting it by sieving.[27] From 1882 to 1886 the patent was used in a campaign to licence all users of roller mills, which fortunately failed. In none of these projects, involving Oexle, was there a very close approach to Hungarian gradual reduction methods, nor was there a line of engineering development. It is possible that the new equipment and the new methods lasted a few years, but there was no wider diffusion, and no subsequent chronicle of satisfaction. Henry Simon provided a commentary in his 1886 catalogue:

> The continually increasing importation of this Hungarian flour induced many of the most enterprising of the British millers to make an attempt to manufacture it in this country, and several complete Hungarian plants were erected in England. Amongst others may be mentioned those by Messrs. Fison and Stannard in Suffok and Essex; Messrs. Baker Bros. in Bristol; Messrs. Davidson in Newcastle; Mr Thompson in Wakefield; Mesrs. Hay at the Craighall Mills, Glasgow; and Messrs. the North Shore Flour and Rice Mill Co. Ltd., Liverpool.
>
> All these mills were disappointing in their results, and proved commercial failures; they were able to make a small percentage of high-class flour, but the amount of low grade which they also made, the complication of the machinery, and its unsuitability for any but a particular wheat led to their being thrown out one after another, so that in the year 1878 there was not a single complete gradual reduction mill in England, Scotland, or Ireland.[28]

Simon grouped Buchholz and Oexle schemes together; what they mainly had in common was that neither led directly to a satisfactory foundation for innovation in the United Kingdom milling industry. They were certainly not gradual reduction plants in the best Budapest tradition. Oexle may have caused some of the error. For instance, in *The Miller*, in April 1876, he stated that 'the so-called 'Buchholz system' was similar to the old 'Sulzenberg system', only perhaps a little more complicated in design'. This was a reference to Jacob Sulzberger, of Frauenfeld in Switzerland, who designed a machine with three

pairs of rolls which was tried and discarded at various mills in Europe; an
improved design became the basis of roller milling at the Pesther Walzmühle.
The prestigious term 'Hungarian' was widely misapplied. Even in the mid 1880s
several leading millers used the hopefully impressive label. R. H. Appleton's
Cleveland Steam Flour Mills, at Stockton-on-Tees, were also called the
Cleveland Anglo-Hungarian Steam Flour Mills. Appleton used Seck's system
and also Nagel & Kaemp's system of gradual reduction but both suppliers were
based in Germany. Two of Henry Simon's main customers used the Hungarian
label: Henry Leetham & Sons at York called their premises the Anglo-Hungarian
Flour Mills, and at Belfast, Bernard Hughes had the Model Hungarian Flour
Mills. Widespread use of the vogue word 'Hungarian' led to trans-Atlantic
controversy. J. A. A. Buchholz wrote to *The Miller* in January 1882 to refute
misinformation by a critic in the American *Northwestern Miller*.

> 'Our millers', he says, 'representing the advanced ideas of milling in England',
> patronise Mr Simon, who 'has copied the Budapest idea so obviously that
> he cannot carry out his ideas automatically'. How ideas are to be carried out
> automatically will probably puzzle many an English reader ... If the sentence,
> however, is meant to convey the impression that Mr Simon has never put
> any of the gradual reduction mills built by him in a form which will work
> automatically continuous, our American critic is not correctly informed.[29]

In February, Simon joined in with a copy of his own letter to the *Northwestern
Miller*.

> I have achieved success because I have *not* copied any system, either Austrian
> or American Low-grinding or Gradual-reduction. In the mills which I erect
> there are no hoppers used but the small ones set immediately over the rolls.
> Neither are there any sacks employed but those which receive the finished
> flour from the packers, and those which catch the bran and offals from the
> last machines ready for the market. This is my idea of automaticity, and this
> is what falls in with 'advanced ideas of milling in England'.
>   The copying of the Buda-Pesth system in this country had never been even
> contemplated by me. Anyone who has visited those mills on the Continent
> must be aware that the great number of separate grindings, gradings, and
> re-purifications which this system renders necessary would be utterly unsuit-
> able to the requirements of the British miller.

Hungarian milling methods were not imported wholesale, nor was equipment
from Austria-Hungary specially favoured. Individual machines were acquired
from near Vienna and from Budapest, but without formation of a large or
continuing market. Many UK millers were more indebted to foreign sources as
stimulus and for a variety of individual items, a natural part of international
trade, with inward flow of machinery accepted in free-trade Britain, but not
necessarily welcome in competitor nations.

Friedrich Wegmann and the first extensive experiments

A clearer input from abroad was due to Friedrich Wegmann, who tried to make and command a market for porcelain rolls. Originally from near Zurich, he worked in France, and managed a spinning factory in Italy. With previous experience in milling, he became a partner in Wegmann Bodner & Co., near Naples.[30] This allowed him to exercise his inventive ability, at first with improvements of traditional methods, and then on the design of roller mills with porcelain rolls. In the mid 1870s, Wegmann machines became widely known in Europe, and were first tried in London at the end of 1876, for 'the softening of middlings'.[31] Wegmann's choice of porcelain for roller shells was adventurous; so also was his attempt to control the market for roller mills, by the bold, but scientifically flawed advertising statements placed in *The Miller* by Childs, and strenous legal action against competitors. Wegmann's important contribution to British milling was in raising awareness, increasing positive interest, generally provoking response. His agent, Augustus Bryant Childs, an American, settled in London in 1859, and established a mill furnishing business, starting with grain cleaning equipment and traditional machinery, then millstone dressing machines and purifiers.[32]

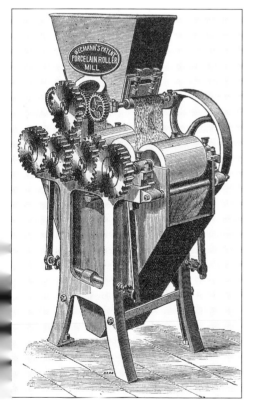

Wegmann tried rolls made of iron, steel, marble, glass and porcelain, and concentrated on the design of a roller mill to reduce middlings to flour, assuming that the stage or stages of opening the grain and granulation could be satisfactorily achieved by ordinary millstones.[33] Initially he was intent on obtaining a roll arrangement that could be used to apply pressure with a squeezing action, and a restriction of shearing effect. That implied use of equal roll speeds, which had worked in cracking large semolina particles, but not for reducing finer semolina and middlings to flour. He rejected other roll materials in favour of porcelain, but he had difficulty in obtaining adequate supplies of porcelain rolls in the form of cylindrical shells, and in solving problems of strength, wear, and methods of fixing the shells to iron spindles. In 1874, Wegmann rolls were introduced into some of the millstone mills in Budapest; he obtained a patent in Britain in 1874 for a roller mill with pairs of rolls arranged in a horizontal plane, and a second patent in 1876 for a modification, to include differential speed.[34] Possibly the earliest illustration and report in the British press is an account in *The Engineer* of the 1874 exhibition of milling machinery at Vienna. There was reference to this description in the first series of articles in *The Miller* in 1876 by Oscar Oexle, in which he very strongly advocated the merits of porcelain rolls, and also of Wegmann, for 'having brought again, and successfully, the question of rollers

Figure 16.
Wegmann's porcelain roller mill. (*The Miller*, February 1877)

before the milling public'. Oexle's second series of articles started in 1878, emphasising again the merits of Wegmann's contribution.

Oexle's advocacy, and a growing interest within the milling trade, led to a trial of a Wegmann machine in London in December 1876, after which about thirty machines were ordered. With A. B. Childs as his agent, sales of Wegmann's machines increased rapidly; 100 firms were named as users in January 1878 and 185 mills in February 1879. In December 1878 it was claimed that there were about 580 machines in use in Britain. This claim was made during the unsuccessful legal action, Wegmann v. Corcoran Witt & Co., who were selling another imported porcelain roller mill: 'Weber's improved patent self-acting, noiseless, porcelain roller mill, entirely superseding all other roller mills, with or without differential speed.' Wegmann alleged infringement of his patents and, although defeated, he gained publicity from the dispute, partly by prominent display of threats to infringers. The legal action began in the High Court in December 1878 but, due to an appeal, the case was not concluded until November 1879.[35] Battle by journal claim and counter had been energetically pursued early in 1878. Harrison Carter complained to The Miller that Oexle's articles gave unfair advantage to Wegmann, and he made particular reference to an allegation by Friedrich Kick, of a 'very cleverly conducted mode of advertising by Wegmann'.[36] Carter's protest was on behalf of chilled cast iron rolls, but there was general applicability to Wegmann's hostility to competitors, including J. A. A. Buchholz and Henry Simon, who were using chilled cast iron rolls.

The fixing of porcelain shells to iron cores had been unsatisfactory, expansion of the iron causing shell fractures. Sulphur was tried to bond the porcelain to the iron, but it sometimes melted. Lead was also tried. One roll was used to drive the other of its pair by contact, resulting in excessive wear and discolouration of the flour. It was necessary to turn worn rolls down to new, even surfaces. While Wegmann tried to reduce middlings by pressure, avoiding a shearing action, the pressure tended to be excessive, with consequent high power consumption. Due to the design and manufacturing difficulties early machines had very small rolls, some only twelve inches long which not only restricted the capacity but also accentuated the problem of providing an even feed to the nip of the rolls. With horizontal, side-by-side rolls, the feed was simply dropped into the nip; this might be done unevenly or not thinly enough. There were other difficulties. Pressure was applied by adjustable weights on compound levers, but the inertia of that mechanism prevented a quick separation of the rolls when necessary. Also, the gearing of the power transmission to the rolls was inefficient and noisy.[37]

Many of the early problems were tackled. A better way to fix the shells by clamping them to the cores with bolted flanges allowed the roll sizes to be increased. Presumably, porcelain quality was improved, and by the time of the High Court hearing of the action of Wegmann v. Corcoran Witt & Co., it was claimed that faults in the design had been overcome. Wegmann had sought guidance on the composition required to ensure a hard material, and had been advised to use a minimum of 70 per cent silica. In his legal action against supposed infringers of his patents, his case failed because his specification did

Figure 17.
Wegmann's
advertising campaign.
(The Miller, April
1881)

WEGMANN'S NEW IMPROVED PATENT
"VICTORIA"
PORCELAIN ROLLER MILL

With One Pair of Rolls, DRIVEN BY TWO WHEELS ONLY, an entirely new device.

The advantages of this Machine over all other Roller Mills are as follows :—

1. The large dimensions of these Rollers in conjunction with the new patent gear—which allows the Rolls to run at an increased speed—more than doubles the capacity.
2. Owing to the increase in the diameter of the Porcelain Cylinders, and therefore the greater angle at which the feed is drawn in between them, a much better result is produced as to the quality of the products.
3. The Machine runs equally as quiet as any belt-driven Roller Mill.
4. The pressure is applied to the Rollers by means of spiral springs only, thereby greatly simplifying the working.
5. Liability to get out of order reduced to a minimum.
6. Three scrapers to each roller acting independently one from the other and each having two adjustable weights effectually keep the rollers clean.
7. A new Friction Pulley acted upon by a lever, to be moved sideways for the purpose of putting the machine to work or stopping the same, entirely superseding fast and loose pulleys.
8. Simplicity in all the working parts.
9. Differential speed always ensured.
10. Automatic lubrication of principal bearings.

The superiority of Porcelain over Chilled Iron for reducing Middlings, Semolina, or Tailings is as under :—

CHILLED IRON ROLLS, whether polished at first or not, soon become, through wear, smooth and glassy, and will only squeeze instead of grinding.

PORCELAIN presents a continual inherent sharpness, which no art can give to any other material in equal fineness and regularity, which enables it to act upon the smallest particles of flour and to separate them.

CHILLED IRON discolours the flour, by reason of the carbon that exudes from it, and also by its liability to rust.

PORCELAIN does NOT discolour the flour and is entirely indifferent to any and all chemical influences.

CHILLED IRON ROLLS are smooth and "cake" the meal; more especially is this the case on soft material.

PORCELAIN ROLLS possess a certain porosity, and no matter how finely ground, or how long they have been used, still retain this granular or porous texture, and will reduce the middlings without "caking."

CHILLED IRON can be cut with steel.

PORCELAIN can ONLY be cut by the best black diamonds.

CHILLED IRON ROLLS require great power to reduce Middlings to the proper fineness on account of their smooth surface.

PORCELAIN ROLLS will do the same amount of work, on account of the slight pressure required, and the gritty nature of the Porcelain, with one-half the power. The flour produced by Porcelain Rolls is sharper, whiter, stronger, and more even than that produced by Iron Rolls.

No remarks need be made as to the superiority of Porcelain Rollers over Millstones, as it is a recognised fact by all. Porcelain Rollers are the only Rollers that will entirely supersede Millstones and Metal Rollers. We venture to say that this Two-Rolls Mill is by far the best Machine in the market, on account of its simplicity, cheapness, and great working capacity, and is sure to be preferred to all the Roller Mills known up to the present.

These Machines received the FIRST PREMIUM at the Late Millers' International Exhibition, Cincinnati.

Gold Medals at Nuremburg, 1876; Paris International Exhibition, 1878. Lille International Concours, 1879; First Gold Medal of the State, Berlin International Exhibition of the German Millers' Association, July, 1879, and Gold Medal Le Mans, 1880.

Over 6,000 of Wegmann's Porcelain Rollers are now in operation.

For full particulars address the Sole Licensees for the United Kingdom and the Colonies,

A. B. CHILDS & SON, 70, Fenchurch Street, London, E.C.

not have 'sufficient exactitude to describe the invention'. The main omissions were a precise description of the composition of the porcelain and a clear method of fixing the shells, the restricted description caused by ignorance or inattention to detail or an attempt to preserve a secret.

Soon after this set-back, Child's promotion of the Wegmann cause relied strongly on a vigorously conducted porcelain versus chilled cast iron controversy, maintained from 1879 to 1882. Superiority of porcelain over chilled cast iron was boldly asserted. Porcelain was said to be much harder, had a porous texture which reduced the middlings without caking, and a surface sharpness which resulted in the separation of the smallest flour particles. The most ill-judged contention was made repeatedly: that porcelain did not discolour the flour, but that 'chilled iron discolours the flour, by reason of the carbon that exudes from it, and also by its liability to rust'. Henry Simon used the oppportunity of his paper to NABIM in 1879 to counter Wegmann's allegations.[38] He described the chilling process, in which liquid iron was poured into cold metallic moulds, causing sudden cooling and the formation of a very hard outer section of each roll, containing the carbon wholly in a combined state, and making the dismissive retort that: 'Some extraordinary ideas are propagated by intense admirers of porcelain rollers, such as, for instance, that chilled iron rollers continually sweat out carbon and discolour the flour. I would recommend the believers in this theory to get their coal supplies from this seemingly inexhaustible source'.

Figure 18.
Friedrich Wegmann
(1832–1905). (The
Miller, June 1905)

Shortly afterwards, a paper was given by Dr H. Sellnick, Wegmann's scientific adviser, to the National Association of German Millers, on 'Semolina milling or high grinding'; he tried to promote a 'competitive grinding' between chilled iron and porcelain rolls. Wegmann machines were a particular feature of the accompanying exhibition at Berlin. The battle was continued in 1880, with Sellnick trying to introduce the idea of a competitive grinding to British millers by writing a long letter to The Miller. There was a strong protest from J. A. A. Buchholz, who complained that Sellnick had been trying to discredit Ganz machines from Budapest, thus impeding Buchholz's work in Britain as the Ganz agent.[39] Wegmann had been in conflict with Ganz & Co. who had built his roller mills until about the middle of 1878, after which they concentrated on their own designs and the use of chilled iron rolls. Wegmann's work was transferred to Escher, Wyss & Co. near Vienna. A restyled version of the basic machine was marketed as 'Wegmann's new improved patent Victoria porcelain roller mill'; the general form remained the same from 1881 to 1886.[40] Wegmann tried to extend his ideas back to the granulating stage of processing, by including corrugated porcelain rolls but porcelain could not be machined with a satisfactory break roll profile. Childs put the bigger scheme forward as a milling system: 'Wegmann's system of granulating, crushing and treating wheat and bran'. This was not successful and the advertising emphasis returned to the basic operation of the reduction of middlings.[41] By 1881, Wegmann claimed he had sold 6000 machines in Europe and elsewhere, but his sales in Britain were presumably a dwindling proportion, as he was losing the contest between porcelain and chilled cast iron, at least in Britain.

In his paper to the Institution of Civil Engineers, in 1882, Simon developed the case for chilled iron in more detail. He criticised the wearing properties of porcelain and its surface roughness which abraded the bran, producing darker flour, considering the surface characteristics of porcelain to be between the roughness of millstones and the smoothness of chilled iron. Wegmann's argument changed from a firm principle of applying pressure to the middlings without shearing, to a new assertion that chilled iron reduction rolls, being smooth, would only squeeze instead of grinding.[42] Henry Simon's judgement that chilled iron rolls were preferable was upheld in practice. British milling engineers transferred competitive testing to the industrial scale of trial, regularly reporting in their advertisements the satisfactory performance of their rolls. Although the Wegmann success was brief in Britain, Henry Simon conceded that 'It is undoubtedly Mr Wegmann's merit to have given an immense impetus to the application of roller mills generally by the construction of a more serviceable tool than existed before'. Machine design had been moving against Wegmann's prospects of long-term success since 1879, with the successful use of chilled iron break rolls and spirally cut fluting.

A gentler controversy was continued for many years by supporters of rounded corrugations for iron break rolls, but the general adoption of chilled cast iron rolls, fluted rolls for the break operation, and smooth rolls for reduction was simultaneous in Britain with the development of the main milling systems. Wegmann's chance must have appeared lost by 1884, when A. B. Childs was known to be marketing a new corrugated roller mill, obviously from the illustration a Wegmann-like machine but with chilled iron rolls. In 1886, there was an 'Improved Victoria' porcelain roller mill, and by 1892 roll lengths reached 40 inches in the 'Hercules' roller mill.[43] As late as 1900, Voller referred to there being, from time to time, partial revival of interest in porcelain rolls, due to sales to millers in Germany and Austria-Hungary. Wegmann was a miller with inventive ideas who does not seem to have formed sufficiently close relationships with manfacturers. His machines were useful experimental tools for millers who were investigating ways of processing middlings and often they were likely to be in the early stages of experiments with purifiers. Innovative millers were soon likely to see beyond Wegmann's context and towards integrated systems.

CHAPTER FOUR

Challenges to British millers

Demand for whiter flour

In *The Miller*, Dunham supplied three vital strands for innovative thought: a continuous chronicle of technical change, a varied discussion of the general idea of improvement, and up-to-date news and analysis of the wheat and flour markets; the chief merits of the journal may have been the discussion of these three topics. The challenge to millers was to see them interactively and respond positively. Millers and milling engineers had a shared set of queries. Would there be a substantial demand for whiter flour? Could British millers produce it? What machinery was required? Where would that machinery come from?

In the late 1870s, there was some demand for whiter and finer flour. In September 1878, an article in *The Miller* on 'The British baker' complained that

> London flour ... was not all that it ought to be and should be, and as it is quite as impossible to make good bread from inferior flour, as it is to gather grapes from thorns, or figs from thistles, the millers, who are the producers of our flour, no doubt shared the responsibility with the baker as regards the quality of our bread. A great change, however, has taken place in the British milling mind, at least in that portion of it related to the supply of flour for panification in large communities.

W. C. Hepburn, 'chief of the literary staff of *The Miller*', who had joined Dunham in January 1877 after extensive editorial experience, may have been the source of the earnestness.[1] Frequent use of the concepts and the words 'quality', 'demand', 'improvement', must have been designed to persuade. The central message was that better flour was wanted.[2]

Bakers were held partly responsible for not encouraging more progressive milling.

> If milling be a scientific process baking is not less so, but with few exceptions the British baker does not seem to have awakened to that fact. Prices and profit, trade customs and trade tricks, appear to be the subjects which are chiefly discussed in the [baking] trade associations ... The British baker is still to a large extent the venerator of tradition. He clings affectionately to the old lines and the prescriptions of his art, leaving the result to chance..[3]

Like many of the English wheat farmers supplying the milling industry, the bakers failed to collaborate in long-term mutual interests. Farmers had excuses of climate and international trade forces. Bakers had even shorter-term perspectives than the wheat growers, and were affected by local tastes and competition, and habits of tactical buying. Millers, in contrast, had to buy well in advance and risk their product against possible falling flour market prices. Fortunately for the prospects of the millers, there were dynamic milling engineers and progressive mill-furnishers who could rapidly strengthen the millers' positions, at first gradually, from 1878, and then quickly, from 1882.

In a paper to the Institution of Civil Engineers in 1882 Henry Simon remarked:

> Nothing was more common some little time ago than to be told by the miller that he could not get one farthing more for flour however beautiful he were to make it. The taste for white flour, however, has now developed, and even if this were not so, it would still be certain that that miller who gives the best value for the money would at least do the largest trade in his district.[4]

At the same meeting the views of a well-known miller were presented by W. Proctor Baker of W. Baker & Sons of Bristol, who warned that

> It is not difficult to overdo the market with fine flours, that is, to produce more than the demand will take off at sufficiently high prices ... English millers should be cautious only to adopt such systems as will enable them to make profitably those particular qualities of flour for which a demand exists in the district supplied by each mill'.[5]

He concluded that 'Popular taste fluctuates, but should it continue to move in the same direction a steady spread of the use of high-grinding systems may be looked for'. Simon's approach was more progressive, recognising that imports of superior quality Hungarian flours had been overtaken by a 'great impetus' to United States flour production and exports to the UK, so that 'an increasing demand for superior well-cleaned and white flour has thus gradually been established, which is as yet difficult for most English millers to respond to'.

Which came first, a demand for white flour or the possibility of supplying it? Hungarians, and others before them, could produce white flour, but could not supply a large market, nor at mass-market affordable prices. American millers, with their New Process methods, appeared to be capable of moving towards better quality and more of it, without matching Hungarian super fineness grades, and American supplies were competitive on price with English grades. In October 1880, *The Miller* presented an editorial article 'Pure Flour', a caption and an aim which became familiar with growing acceptance of white flour. The article hinted at the 'Which comes first?' dilemma:

> It will not be denied that at the breakfast table or the dinner-table bread that is pure in colour is a more attractive phenomenon than bread which presents the appearance of a brickbat ... might not the development of an improved popular taste in this country for pure flour prove to be the most efficient means that could be supplied to our flour makers for the production of the article in question? ... Neither Edinburgh, Glasgow, Dublin, or Belfast

would be satisfied with the bread that is consumed by the bread eaters of the metropolis.

In many editorials throughout the period 1878 to 1883, Dunham was trying to persuade all potential innovative millers that they needed to engage in processes of learning. In the simplest terms, whiter flour was to depend on new machinery. That gradual reduction roller milling in Britain produced white flour became accepted in the early 1880s and white bread was widely available from then onwards. If traditionalists in Britain remained sceptical about demand for whiter flour, they could continue to be so only if they supplied relatively isolated districts and bakers who worked for poorer communities or, for whatever other reason, aimed to produce the cheapest bread. The rapid application of roller milling across the country during the years 1883 to 1885 confirmed that caution about the demand for white flour had been replaced by determination to supply it.

Sources of wheat for milling

Addressing the National Association in December 1879, Harrison Carter observed that 'The manufacture of flour from our native wheats, and partly from the many varieties of foreign wheats, is a question for the British miller to solve which exceeds in difficulty that presented to the millers of any other nation in the world'.[6] *The Miller*, in the annual review of the year 1879, reported that

> it is quite clear that under present circumstances the sources of food supply of the country are not equal to the demand the alimentary wants of the population make upon them. Our crop failure last year was a calamity of serious magnitude, but it would have been still more calamitous had the fertile fields of America not been adequate to the supply of our deficiencies.[7]

Wheat and flour supplies from abroad became an increasingly serious preoccupation for all British millers; acreage under wheat in Britain was decreasing and population was rising. The steady fall of wheat prices seemed to be a relentless determining factor. A large increase of imports of American wheat in 1879 was followed by a large jump in imports of American flour in 1883; until 1902 the United States sent enormous quantities of wheat to the United Kingdom.[8] The dramatically poor harvest of 1879 was not just a remarkable incident, but also a confirmation of the need for new ideas, and it served as a challenge to wavering modernisers. Its impact could not have been better timed to demonstrate that innovation was essential.

The highly regarded experts on wheat requirements and home supplies, Lawes and Gilbert, contributed a paper to the journal of the Royal Agricultural Society of England, discussing the variation of crops, and the effects of climate and *The Miller* presented the main points in July 1880. From then on, *The Miller* gave detailed appraisals of the frequent reports made by Lawes and Gilbert, culminating in their major paper in the RASE journal in 1893: 'Home produce, imports, consumption, and price of wheat, over forty harvest years, 1852–53 to 1881–92'.[9] The Board of Agriculture began to collect returns of the acreage of wheat in the United Kingdom in 1866, but was not responsible for estimates of production before 1884. The Board (as stated in 1905) regarded Lawes & Gilbert as authoritative up to 1883–4.[10] According to Lawes & Gilbert (1893) net imports of wheat into the United Kingdom first exceeded home produce in 1872–73 and from the mid 1870s the major supply was constantly from foreign sources. In addition to statistics for harvest years starting in 1852–53 which were necessarily estimates, there was a summary table of 'Average annual total wheat available for consumption'; imports of flour were converted to equivalent quantities of wheat, 'reckoning 72 of imported flour to represent 100 of wheat'. The movement to strong dependence on overseas resources was emphasised in their data for the period 1884–85 to 1891–92, showing that nearly 70 per cent of wheat and flour supply for the UK was then derived from imports.

From the mid 1880s *The Miller* each year printed dauntingly copious statistics of imports from the many supplying countries, showing quantities in cwts. for fourteen previous years. The information was derived from official trade statistics, later collected together in the 1905 *Report of the Royal Commission on supply of food and raw material in time of war*, which covered the period 1870 to 1902 and gave quantities of wheat in grain, wheat meal and flour, and wheat meal and flour in equivalent weight of grain. Tables 4.1 and 4.2 use official data, presenting a simple picture of variations and interactions. The most voluminous reports were in the 'Monthly review of the state and prospects of the corn and flour trades', and in the annual summaries. There, quantities were in quarters, commonplace units for the farmers, corn merchants and millers of the time, but superseded in official statistics of the 1880s. There was frequently adverse criticism of government returns for English wheat,[11] and the wheat trade was a morass of various weights and measures and local practices. In addition, there were inconsistencies, misunderstandings and examples of non-compliance in the record-keeping at corn markets and in the returns made. *The Miller* made a specialism of the study of American wheat and flour shipments. The mass of detail in the longer reviews would have shown individual millers whether their general knowledge of the wheat market was comprehensive or limited. Yet it is not possible to study the interplay of quality and price competition in the flour market as the reviews were mainly about wheat. The journal columns provide fuller evidence of the trends and conjunctions recorded in the official statistics of wheat and flour supply. There was also a large mass of data in at least two other trade lists.

Journal articles gave descriptions of foreign wheat fields and their commercial potential, but millers required particular up-to-date information on crop prospects, actual production, quantities of wheat coming forward compared with possible stockholding, and amounts that would soon be available in the United Kingdom. They also needed to react to forecasts of interactions betwen sources, and to apparent delays. *The Miller* tried to cater for these interests in articles dealing with comparative performance and prospects of the leading supply

Table 4.1. Wheat imports into the United Kingdom, based on the *Report of the Royal Commission on supply of food and raw material in time of war* (1905), vol. 3, table A1(1)

Year	Total imports million cwt.	USA %	Russia %	India %	Canada %
1875	51.9	45	19	3	7
1876	44.5	43	20	7	6
1877	54.3	39	20	11	5
1878	49.9	58	18	4	5
1879	59.6	60	13	1	8
1880	55.3	65	5	6	7
1881	57.1	63	7	13	5
1882	64.2	55	15	13	4
1883	64.1	41	21	18	3
1884	47.3	48	11	17	4
1885	61.5	39	19	20	3
1886	47.4	52	8	23	7
1887	55.8	55	10	15	7
1888	57.3	26	37	14	2
1889	58.6	29	36	16	2
1890	60.5	28	32	15	2
1891	66.3	36	22	20	5
1892	64.9	52	7	19	6
1893	65.5	49	15	9	5
1894	70.1	35	24	8	4

countries. The year-by-year quantities display apparently erratic variations. There were several basic causes, to do with crop yields and the transfer of varying fractions of crops from grower to merchant to miller, via lengthy transport routes. J. W. Rush, editor of the *Millers' Gazette*,[12] put it economically in his paper to NABIM in 1890, 'The world's wheat crop and wheat values': 'the big wheat growing countries, such as America and Russia, are liable to sudden changes in wheat production'. There were opportunities for defensive scepticism. When Rush addressed the National Association, he said that 'No subject can be found of greater interest to the miller or corn merchant, I consider, than the world's wheat production, and there is probably no subject about which less information has, until recently, been available than about this'. That statement did scant justice to Dunham's considerable efforts. The President of NABIM, J. F. White of Dundee, thanked Rush 'for his invaluable paper', but then said that he was

> often struck with wonder in considering the amount of energy and care that was brought to bear both by Mr Rush in *The Millers' Gazette*, and Mr Dunham in *The Miller*. The mass of statistics they brought together was very interesting, but they all knew that statistics on such a scale were somewhat treacherous,

Table 4.2. United States wheat and flour supplies to the UK, based on the
Report of the Royal Commission on supply of food and raw material in time of
war (1905), vol. 3, table A1(1)

Year	Wheat	Flour	Wheat and flour reckoned as grain		US flour as % of total UK flour imports
	million cwt	*million cwt*	*% sent at wheat*	*% sent as flour*	
1875	23.5	2.3	89	11	37
1876	19.3	2.3	87	13	39
1877	21.4	1.8	91	9	23
1878	29.1	3.6	87	13	46
1879	36.0	6.9	81	19	64
1880	36.2	6.9	81	19	65
1881	36.1	7.7	79	21	68
1882	35.1	7.8	78	22	60
1883	26.1	11.3	64	36	69
1884	22.6	10.3	63	37	69
1885	24.3	11.7	61	39	74
1886	24.6	11.4	62	38	78
1887	30.5	14.9	60	40	82
1888	14.6	12.6	46	54	74
1889	17.0	10.0	55	45	69
1890	17.2	12.0	51	49	76
1891	24.2	13.7	56	44	82
1892	33.9	19.5	56	44	88
1893	32.3	18.0	56	44	88
1894	24.7	15.9	53	47	83

and many men in the last ten years could say that statistics had led them more astray than their native judgement, left to its own resources.[13]

There were two major commercial problems in the UK market: how to assure adequate supplies, and how to avoid monopolist strategies. It was desirable that there should be a balance of forces and also a place in the market for English wheat. The total annual supply from the countries not shown in Table 4.1 varied between 10 per cent and 29 per cent of the UK imports, some contributions being very small. The interplay between three countries, USA, Russia and India largely influenced the market, though there was some scope for manoeuvre. Journal comments during the short period of Russian leadership over America from 1888 to 1890 illustrated the attention directed to the tantalisingly erratic nature of Russian sources. *The Miller*'s annual review of 1888 entertained hopes for English agriculture, which were not to last long. The prospects for British wheat farmers, and those millers who made good use of home grown varieties, remained problematical and then worsened. The interactions of acreage, yields, prices and milling quality were discussed at length in journal reviews.

Competition from flour imports

Wheat and flour imports had to be studied together. *The Miller* made the point explicitly as early as January 1880, while looking back over the two years that were the start of a different era: 'Direct shipments [of flour] have been made to a larger extent than formerly, and the greatest efforts have been made to realise the desire of the transatlantic flour manufacturers for the displacement of the wheat import to this country by substitution of the manufactured article'. The threat that a greater flow of American flour might accompany a decrease in the availability of the raw material to British millers represented an intensification of a struggle. American millers were scaling up to satisfy demand that was still only potential. It was as if new moves in a game were being played.

The onset of American competition can be traced in the editorial columns of *The Miller* and in the monthly and annual 'Review of the state and prospects of the corn and flour trades'. In January 1878 there was reference to allegedly surplus milling capacity in America: 'There is virtually no competition in the American markets with foreign flour, consequently the price of that commodity in the United States is regulated by the margin of surplus manufacture, and the price it commands abroad'. In April 1878 an editorial 'American flour competition' gave the warning that 'the produce of the American mills ... might, within a comparatively short time, become one of a sharply competitive character ... nearly double the quantity of American flour is entering the ports of the United Kingdom than was the case twelve months ago'. The review of 1878 noted 'The year has seen increased activity in the efforts by the millers of the United States to introduce the products of their mills to British markets, the result being a far larger import of American flour to this country than had previously been known'. The attraction of American flour was soon increased by sending it in convenient bags, instead of cumbersome barrels.

Imports could cut into previous patterns of market share, but it was not always easy to see, in matters of collective concern, occasions for immediate individual action. In such situations, pressure had to reach some personal, critical level, financial or psychological, before action would be taken. Rather than take on the challenge to produce higher grades, some became 'mixing millers', who upgraded by incorporating a foreign, most likely American, component. How widely mixing was practised would be impossible to determine; it would not be advertised, nor publicly admitted by millers. Hearsay suggested it was commonplace. In May 1879 *The Miller* carried nearly two columns on 'Foreign flour competition': 'The cry is 'Still it comes' and in greater and growing abundance, the 'it' being foreign flour, chiefly American'. The review of 1879 repeated the previous warning and continued

> The pressure of competition from America has been still more severe in the past than it was in the previous year. From St. Louis, Minneapolis, and other United States milling centres, flour has been coming in constantly increasing

floods, the result being a diminution of the profits of our millers to an extent of which they had not previous experience.

The review of 1880, after preliminaries about adversity in agriculture, argued that imported flour should no longer be regarded as an abnormal phenomenon. Regular themes of discussion were the poor quality of English bread, pressure of foreign supplies to the major urban areas, Glasgow and Liverpool particularly, and the inferiority of London bread, frequently called 'London greys', with the constant repetition of the word 'quality'. Anxiety, as imports increased together with dissatisfaction with the average bread, continually led to exhortation. The remedy, that new milling methods were essential, was steadily made more explicit.

The statistics for 1883 were alarming. American wheat supplies were down, flour supplies very much increased and the journal observed: 'The increase in the flour exports is truly portentous; it would be so under any circumstances, but when it occurs in a year that sees the wheat shipments diminished by 10,000,000 qrs., it may well give us pause'.[14] The weakening of wheat and strengthening of flour in the ratio of those imports from America was confirmed in 1884. Review comment was: 'The American flour business continued to develop, and the flour suffers so little in transport across the Atlantic that Minneapolis and Duluth are to English country buyers almost as London and Manchester'. In October 1884, W. T. Bates contributed a long letter to *The Miller*, on 'Can we beat America?' His own answer was that 'we can, and certainly shall, eventually ...' He referred to 'the statement made by Mr Appleton at the late millers' convention that the imports of flour to this country have risen in nine years from 2.5 to 6.5 million sacks – an enormous quantity'. After discussing the range of wheats available, he gave his own warning:

> The problem of the wheat supply is the mainspring of the difficulty – the key of the position. On it depends our success or failure. To an American, of course, there appears no difficulty. America produces wheat and flour of excellent quality, and almost alone England requires a large quantity of food in one of the above forms – wheat or flour – consequently if America refuses to send the one, we must take the other.

In December 1885, an editorial 'Foreign competition and the flour trade' described the severity of competition since 1879 and was rashly optimistic: 'the time of greatest pressure appears to be over. British millers have survived the strain and are now making that headway which the magnificent mechanical appliances at their disposal render possible, and even easy'. Journal confidence was maintained in the review of 1885, but not the following year. A worsening situation became more generally apparent in March 1887, when the London Flour Millers' Association met to consider the depressed condition of the milling trade in their area, which they attributed to the large imports of American flour. They resolved that 'It is the opinion of this meeting that a meeting of the London millers, and of all the millers attending the London market, should be called to consider the advisability of placing a duty upon flour'. At the

second meeting there was a move to seek imposition of a duty on foreign flour,
and a counter-suggestion that the Association should first be asked to investigate
the causes of the depression.[15] A proposition from Wilson Marriage was adopted,
that 'the National Association of British and Irish Millers should be asked to
institute an enquiry into the causes of depression in the milling trade, and to
consider whether it would be advisable to ask for a moderate duty to be imposed
on imported flour'.

The Council of NABIM agreed to appoint a committee of enquiry, but there
were differences of opinion about the extent of depression, and about possibilities
of obtaining full and accurate information. London and Glasgow millers reported
more severe trading conditions than were apparent to some Yorkshire millers,
or to T. W. Hibbard of Gloucester. Secretary Chatterton urged millers to keep
manufacturing accounts in such a way that 'without unduly disclosing their
business affairs members of the Association might freely exchange their results
with each other'. He also explained that if protection were sought, then millers
would have to prove that they were efficient, in economic and technical respects,
and that any duty imposed would be for the public good.[16]

After a trough of depression in 1887, the recovery lasted long enough for
practical mill development projects to be completed before competitive struggle
resumed. Although the pressure became even greater and more continuous, a
sufficiently large innovative sector of the United Kingdom milling industry
provided the basis for scaling up and further development.

Grist for the mill

British millers, of necessity, acquired unrivalled skill in buying and processing
different varieties of wheat. They had to learn which varieties could be used
together to produce flour that members of the baking trade would accept as
consistent and that suited their trade. Variables included prices and particular
milling requirements, variations in the properties of the flours that would be
obtained, and the texture, crust, and the general quality of bread that could
be expected. Prices were affected by the sizes of harvests and by the competitive
commercial interplay of suppliers.

Finding reliable wheats and combining them in a grist required experiment
and incurred risk. With each variety the miller had to consider whether it
would contribute to one or more aspect of quality: strength, colour, taste, or
general appearance. With a possible mixture, he had to seek a balance of those
characteristics, and try to decide if he was likely to achieve it; to the
inexperienced it must have resembled a lottery. He had to obtain a satisfactory
yield, possibly calculated over more than one grade of flour and make a profit,
possibly without detailed costing procedures. In January 1883, *The Miller*
recognised that 'the great art of wheat mixing becomes each year of
increasing importance'. At that time, wheat could be obtained from about
twenty countries. There might be up to six main sources from which to choose,
and six more of subsidiary but worthwhile standing. English wheat remained
an important raw material for many millers, though the big port-based businesses

increasingly used foreign wheat supplies, tending towards full reliance on them. If wheat varieties were described, not merely the countries of origin of raw materials, advanced millers would be seen as choosing among many more possibilities. In 'Foreign competition and the flour trade', *The Miller* in 1885 urged the industry to look beyond the obvious resources: 'Altogether, we have not less than about thirty distinct varieties of imported wheat obtainable at our markets'.[17]

The problem of product uniformity was aired by W. T. Bates in an essay for the journal in 1887; he was then Mill Manager at Baxendells' Bee Mills at Liverpool.

> There is no definite method of mixing wheat. Let this fact always be borne in mind. Wheat varies so much that great judgment is necessary to produce even results. It is, and with us must ever be, a matter of judgement and not rule. The difficulty, too, which always presents itself to us, is that when we have obtained a suitable mixture, and made a standard flour which we are desirous of maintaining, the supply of one of our principal ingredients fails; in other words, the wheat upon which we most depended is no longer obtainable and we must find a substitute ... This matter of equivalents is, to me, of far more importance than merely mixing a few well-known and choice kinds to produce a certain flour; but this matter of equivalents is a very delicate one, and to give satisfactory advice on it is not easy.[18]

By 1890, when Voller's textbook *Modern Flour Milling* became widely used, wheat blending was an accepted practice. In Voller's first edition, there were substantial sections on wheat properties, wheat cleaning and conditioning, and wheat mixing, much expanded in his third edition of 1897. Voller's expositions were very detailed, but the technicalities had accompaniments of a common sense attitude and practical enthusiasms, as shown in his chapter of 1889 on 'Wheat mixtures and mixing', in which he stated

> There are few branches of practical milling which possess greater interest than that of blending the various kinds of wheat so as to combine those qualitites which it is the aim of the miller to concentrate in the resulting flour ... it will be well for mixing purposes to consider wheat as coming under one of three heads – strong, coloury or neutral ... As the writer understands it, strength is possessed by flour which is capable of producing bread of great size, having a porous, well expanded crumb, with plenty of spring or life in it ... for practical purposes we have but two sources of superior strength – Russia and America.

Voller pointed out that wheat buying was governed by experience and general principles and also by 'consideration of what varieties of wheat happen at the time to be in supply'.[19] The rudimentary grasp of the term strength was evident. It depended on the protein substance gluten working satisfactorily in the baker's dough and gluten was, for many years, a mysterious substance. Gluten and strength were connected uncertainly to varying grist components. Each miller had to settle on what he hoped were satisfactory combinations and proportions.

For the scientifically thoughtful, it entailed empirical practice and scrutiny, not merely more rules of thumb.

As early as 1877 *The Miller* had begun to comment on flour testing and to report on available measuring instruments . These included Pekar's method of assessing whiteness, Boland's aleurometer to test the strength of gluten, and Robine's method for estimating quantity of gluten and likely bread output. Although much research had to be done before the action of the relevant proteins could be understood, gluten became more frequently mentioned. It was commonplace by 1881 for an article in the journal, in a series on flour testing, to state that 'The strength of flour depends on the quantity and character of the gluten contained in it ... Without gluten, bread-making would be imposssible, as the dough would not rise. For instance, bread cannot be made from potato or other starches, for the reason that gluten is absent'.[20] The scientifically-inclined learned later that there was more than one protein involved, with the possibility of further complications.

From 1880 onwards Profesor Graham and William Jago offered advice; Graham was Professor of Chemical Technology at University College, London;[21] Jago was an analyst and consultant, and a pioneer in technical education. Starting in December 1884, Jago gave a series of lectures and practical demonstrations on the chemistry and testing of flour at Westminster Town Hall; the journal reported that they were

> delivered in that terse and concise yet interesting style for which Professor Jago has made himself so well known, and were thoroughly practical expositions of the subject such as millers and bakers could only take profit from hearing. Among the audience was the entire staff of Mr J. H. Carter (the milling engineer) of 82, Mark Lane.[22]

In the first edition of his text on *The chemistry of wheat, flour and bread* in 1886, Jago defined strength as a measure of water-absorbing and retaining power, adding that 'strength is also sometimes used as a measure of the capacity of a flour for producing a well-risen loaf' and that criterion has often been stated since, but increasingly with qualification and amplification. The eminent cereal chemist D. W. Kent-Jones (Kent-Jones and Amos, 1950) gave a fuller account of a later Jago version showing the limitations of simplified definitions:

> Jago (1911) defined strength as the measure of a flour to produce a bold, large-volumed and well-risen loaf. The definition broadly adopted by British millers is similar ... The difficulty of defining strength via size of loaf lies in the fact that some authorities prefer to restrict the term strength to the dough which is mainly dependent on the quantity and quality of the gluten.[23]

Indicating other complications, Kent-Jones continued: 'the existence of these variable factors which can influence the size of the loaf renders loaf volume, per se, an unreliable index of what is generally understood by the term strength'. He wrote that 'the history of cereal chemistry is largely a record of attempts to find out what determines 'strength".

Graham, Jago and others added technical detail to the general knowledge, but results still depended on the empiricism of the practical miller, for many years without his own laboratory. In addition to future work in cereal chemistry, millers themselves had to become more analytically minded. They would have to move towards close scrutiny of their products and a start of very simple testing at the mill.

CHAPTER FIVE

British millers search for answers

A variety of devices

In their history of the American milling industry, Storck & Teague (1952) made the interesting observation about the British milling industry, that 'In the early 1880s there was a greater diversity of roller milling ideas in England than at any place in the United States, although there was less decisive action throughout the entire United Kingdom than in our Northwest alone'.[1] The diversity of available machine designs in Britain, and the associated variations of method and effect, were both help and hindrance. Some millers must have been disappointed with their purchases. In America, convergence, tending towards uniformity, may have been fostered by large scales of production, together with vigorous competition. That would have been so at Minneapolis, the Northwest to which Storck & Teague referred. Simon (1882) summarised the situation. He referred to awareness of 'the absolute necessity of improvement', adding that

> The demand thus created for improved machinery has as usual been met by an ever-increasing supply. So great indeed, is the variety of machines of every kind now offered, that many a miller is bewildered by their number; all the more so as they are constructed on principles heretofore entirely unknown to the immense majority of millers.[2]

Certainly, there was a considerable variety of methods in Britain around 1882 and 1883. There were efforts by G. T. Smith from America to persuade British millers to continue using millstones. Nagel & Kaemp from Germany and Jonathan Mills in America appointed agents to sell disc mills in Britain, two quite different devices, but both in opposition to rolls. There were two overseas designers of roller mills who might have become prominent in Britain: the famous firm of Ganz of Budapest, and Gray in America, working for E. P. Allis & Co., were probably the best-known possibilities from the two continents. The trading prospects for Ganz were restricted by the many difficulties and the unorthodox ideas of their agent J. A. A. Buchholz. Gray's machines made little impact in Britain through the agent J. W. Throop; he did not have a convincing system to offer, a situation which adversely affected Buchholz and other agents for foreign machinery. Individual machines were not sufficient to provide millers with first-class mills, and did not provide agents with sound and enlarging experience; system design was not merely assembly of modules.

In the early 1880s the break operation remained the most energetically disputed part of the milling process. A multiplicity of patents for roller mill specifications had included strong representation from the Continent, but by the mid 1880s nearly all were irrelevant and leading British milling engineers turned increasingly to a concentration on purifier design. Gravity purifiers were displaced by sieve purifiers, which encompassed ideas that had migrated from France to Canada and then to the United States. G. T. Smith brought his version from America and actually met British millers.[3] His contribution was useful, but he was hampered by his speciality, which was not a system. When there was sharpened competition between purifier designs the rivals were all British firms, from the mid 1880s entirely so.

There was convergence from 1883 to 1885, when the clear leadership became fully established among British milling engineers: the main focus was then securely on gradual reduction roller milling, with increasing scales of production, and additional scope for design variations, including many to suit more modest outputs. Created by the variety of devices, an archive of discarded designs remains, accessible via descriptions in journals and available for further detailed study in patent specifications. The journal *American Miller* commented appropriately in 1889, first describing an early Jonathan Mills idea for a roller mill, in which a small diameter granite cylinder turned within a rotating granite shell; it might have been regarded as a Heath Robinson device. *American Miller* asked for contributions from readers, to illustrate the technical 'search, often in the dark, and in a zig zag course'. A Herbert Spencer saying was quoted, that 'progress does not occur in a straight line', followed by the statement:

> Scores of machines that were designed to reach higher results, many of which were successful in a measure, have been abandoned by the way, as not contributing any essential or desirable factor in modern milling. No history of modern milling will be complete without an account of these tentative machines.[4]

When major changes were introduced to millers, new ideas and equipment did not merely arrive from abroad – engineering development is not so simple – British millers acted roughly in step with the machinery system designers, several of whom might be judged to have been the leading change-agents, fired by their enthusiasm for making things work. Apparent inaction of a large number of convinced traditionalists contrasted with energetic response by several hundred British millers who took part in the first main phase of application of new methods through the industry in the mid 1880s.

J. A. A. Buchholz

An early attempt to devise a system was made by J. A. A. Buchholz, son of Gustav Buchholz, who was keen to be associated with technical improvement, but preferably using low-grinding in which the grain was crushed and the flour produced after only two passes through rolls. From 1878 to 1883 Buchholz acted as an agent in Britain for Ganz & Co.'s chilled iron roller mills, while practising as a consultant in the design and installation of milling equipment.

Buchholz was sceptical about the prospects for what he regarded as the excessive complexity of gradual reduction. His doubts concerned difficulties in dealing with varying types of wheat, the possible over-production of higher quality flour to the detriment of other grades, and the risks that would accompany hasty choices of new machinery and complicated methods. As Hungarian methods had been seen to be too laborious, Buchholz's advice was relevant. Buchholz stressed that it was necessary to devise methods suitable for British conditions, not to make imitations, but in 1887 his opinion, in a letter to *The Engineer*, was still that 'if a new grinding mechanism were to be invented, my first care would be to ascertain whether it could be adapted to low-grinding'.[5]

His earliest scheme, using Ganz 'three-high' roller mills in which the top and the bottom rolls were in a vertical plane, with a middle roll positioned slightly to one side, was to crush the grain between the top and middle rolls, sieve out the flour released, and feed the remaining meal to the nip of the middle and lowest rolls. Buchholz's specification for patent 2205 of 1879 had alternatives of using the Ganz three-roller mill, or two separate pairs of rolls, one pair having a coarsely grooved roll together with a more finely grooved roll, the other pair having a roll with fine grooves and a smooth roll. He stated that 'The object of the fluting is not to cut but to increase the grip of the roller surfaces on the bran, and to form vents for the flour severed from the bran'. So the operation was not carefully controlled breaking, but disintegrating under pressure. There was a more ambitious continuation in his provisional specification 5308 submitted to the Patent Office in December 1879: 'The object of this invention is so to treat wheat that it may be converted by one continuous operation into marketable flour, and into clean compressed marketable bran'. There were three diagrams showing the 'J. A. A. Buchholz process of milling': alternative schemes for more careful purification, and consequent production of different grades of flour. They were simple flow charts. J. H. Scott (1972) stated that 'Buchholz is credited with the invention of the milling flow sheet'.[6] However, Simon had already published a diagram of the Daverio system in *The Miller* in April 1879.

Buchholz's first installations were in 1878, for Barlow & Sons at Bilston and for Fairclough & Son at Warrington, each plant having a capacity of about 1,000 sacks of flour per week. Barlows turned over completely to the Buchholz system three years later, discarding their millstones. By 1881, Buchholz had installed new plants for Lofthouse & Hammond at Boroughbridge, F. A. Frost & Sons at Chester, and in mills at Boston, Leeds and Wakefield. John Ure engaged him to replace half his millstone plant at the Crown Mills in Glasgow, and another large business to introduce his system was at Mumford's Royal Flour Mills at Vauxhall in London, where Buchholz set up his own office. In 1882, John Ure's mills were converted wholly to roller milling, mainly on the Buchholz system. Buchholz also provided a large gradual reduction plant for W. Baker & Son at Bristol.[7]

Whereas the elder Buchholz lacked efficient purifiers, the younger Buchholz had the availability of a variety of makes and types. If he had relied on Ganz roller mills as basic machinery, and then concentrated on grading, purifying

Figure 19.
J. A. A. B. Buchholz's advertisement for Ganz roller mills. (*The Miller*, March 1879)

BUCHHOLZ & CO.,

OFFICES AT THE

ROYAL FLOUR MILLS, VAUXHALL, LONDON, S.W.

CHILLED IRON ROLLERS

Fitted with Mechwart's Patented Rotary Anti-friction Spring Pressure Ring, by

GANZ & CO., Buda Pesth, Hungary.

GOLD MEDAL AWARDED

AT THE

Paris International Exhibition, 1878.

DOUBLE SMOOTH ROLLER MILL,

With or without the ROTARY ANTI-FRICTION SPRING PRESSURE RING.

SINGLE SMOOTH ROLLER MILL,
*Fitted with MECHWART'S PATENTED ROTARY
ANTI-FRICTION SPRING PRESSURE RING.*

Three large Mills in the United Kingdom having been furnished with Messrs. GANZ & CO.'S CHILLED IRON ROLLER MILLS, entirely taking the place of Millstones, while a great number of other Mills are fitted with these Machines in various stages of the Milling process, Mr. J. A. A. BUCHHOLZ is prepared to advise Millers on the adoption of Rollers for replacing Millstones either partially or wholly.

and dressing operations, he might have vied with the leaders. Unfortunately,
he was explicitly against that next move. When he gave a paper to NABIM
in 1880, he said: 'We are spending large sums of money in dressing and
re-dressing, in purifying and re-purifying machinery, with a vista of never-ending
expenses'.[8] During 1880 and 1881, Buchholz was advertising a collaborative
arrangement with Adolf Fischer; their combined experience was offered as a
safeguard of tried, modern improvements, 'not one of those costly experiments
now being so widely practised'. Buchholz's reluctance to encourage the diffusion
of fuller gradual reduction methods continued into the mid 1880s, and the
Ganz agency in Britain was taken over by G. Luther. Buchholz's diffidence
could be attributed partly to misfortune. When Wegmann was campaigning
against supposed infringers of his patents, he tried through advertisements to
dissuade British millers from buying Ganz machines. In a High Court action,
Buchholz was successful in requiring A. B. Childs to discontinue the hindrance,[9]
but Wegmann's aura was maintained for another year by his legal attack on
Corcoran, Witt & Co.

In 1880, when technical design work was at a tricky stage, what some
development engineers wryly call 'getting it wrong to get right', Buchholz was
fixing his ideas about how to remove the bran from the wheat grains. Some
theorists thought that it might be possible to cut the individual grains along
the crease, releasing dust suppposed to be held there, with consequent significant
improvement of flour quality. Buchholz ignored this widely-held crease dirt
theory, apparently aware that it was not realistic to hope to split most grains
longitudinally, yet he devoted attention to the difficult task of peeling away
the bran.[10] He remained opposed to the idea of a cutting action, and by stating
that a 'ratchet toothed shaped fluting may be used; this will answer when
worked back to back', he rejected the alternative which soon became generally
accepted, of arranging sharp edge to sharp edge roll flutings. Kick approved of
Buchholz's fluting arrangement and the operational effect, and so possibly
reinforced Buchholz's ideas. It was the wrong choice for progress at that time.
In addition, Kick's article included Wegmann with Buchholz, as having obtained
'good low-ground flour by rollers, capable of satisfying the requirements of many
markets'.[11]

In 1881, advertisements by Buchhholz & Co. proclaimed that 'The first two
complete roller mills worked in the United Kingdom on the gradual reduction
system were constructed to the design, and under contracts of our Mr J. A. A.
Buchholz and were fitted with Ganz & Co.'s chilled iron rollers'. The claim
related to the installations at Bilston and Warrington, but these were not likely
to have been truly gradual reduction plants, even on a smaller scale. In any
case, the claim was inappropriate when he was trying to persuade millers to
adopt relatively unadventurous advances, and it might easily have been forgotten
but for occasional enquiries to the journals asking who had been first. In 1887
Carter asserted that he had been. During the controversy in the journals, there
were confused statements of technical claims and spellings; the younger Buchholz
was embroiled on ground not altogether of his own choosing, and the arguments
could not have improved his standing.[12]

The younger Buchholz remains mysterious. In June 1883, *The Miller* printed a 'Circular from Ganz & Co., Budapest': 'We hereby have the honour to inform you that in consequence of the dissolution of the firm of Buchholz & Co., of London, we have transferred our agency for the United Kingdom to G. Luther, of London, the well-known millwright and engineer, of Brunswick.' Buchholz moved to Bristol, and was a member of the firm of Buchholz, Metcalfe & Lean. In 1886 he was still regarded as a technical expert, when called as a witness in The Germ Milling Case, but his association with the Germ Milling Co. again placed him outside the group of progressive change-agents. Between 1873 and 1889 Buchholz made at least fourteen patent applications for flour milling machinery, and others that concerned associated mechanical engineering. Even the early roller mill designs had the appearance of the elaboration of mechanisms, not concentration on principal mechanisms, essential at early stages. Buchholz was an overcautious designer, lacking awareness that engineering development of a whole system would be essential; like Gustav Buchholz and Wegmann, he never had sufficiently good designs to be able to move to enthusiastic next stages. His quest was invention, and his inclination was towards detailed mechanical design. In 1890 he shot himself, leaving a regretful letter which included advice on milling technicalities and the statement that 'I have made two important discoveries. Firstly, the principle of construction for obtaining adjustment of journals (carried in bearings) in the two directions ... Secondly, the principle of construction for sifting apparatus.' J. A. A. Buchholz may be classed as a contributor to an early experimental stage of roller milling in Britain, rather than a successful guide to innovation.[13]

Nagel & Kaemp

Another attempt to introduce Continental machinery to British millers was made by Nagel & Kaemp of Hamburg through their agent H. J. Sanderson. August Nagel and Reinhold Kaemp obtained patent protection in 1878 for 'Improvements in dismembrators for flour mills, and for the comminution of various materials'. Sanderson, who had worked on flour mill installations in Germany for Nagel & Kaemp, returned to England to act as their agent. From 1880, Sanderson was at Mark Lane and in 1881 the business became Sanderson & Gillespie. Sanderson introduced Nagel & Kaemp's centrifugal flour dressing machine, an early application being at Geo. Pimm & Co.'s mill at Wandsworth. He was briefly amongst the leaders of technical development, but by 1879 there were at least nine exhibitors of centrifugals at the Royal Agricultural Society's meeting at Kilburn. Nagel & Kaemp had tried out their system on the Continent, and at the end of 1878 it was installed for Eisdell & Soundy at Reading. Other installations were in 1879 for R. H. Appleton at Stockton, and by 1881 in mills at Penrith, Cardiff and Glasgow. Soundy and Appleton were Sanderson's best known customers, the former becoming President of NABIM in 1884, the latter in 1883 and 1889.[14]

The Nagel & Kaemp system included roller mills and dismembrators, centrifugals and purifiers. Each roller mill contained one pair of smooth chilled iron rolls, driven at equal speeds. One form of dismembrator contained two metal discs, one stationary and the other rotating, each disc being armed with protruding metal studs;[15] there was also a version with a rotating disc between two fixed discs. Dismembrators were examples of a class of high-speed percussion grinders, more simply termed disintegrators. A well-known early version was designed by Thomas Carr of Bristol and a futher version became better known around 1878 as the Carr-Toufflin disintegrating flour mill. The Nagel & Kaemp machine was used to loosen grain or other material. After cleaning, the wheat was fed through a pair of rolls, and the resulting meal was then loosened. Next, the output of the dismembrator was dressed and sorted, to give flour, middlings and bran. The middlings were graded, purified and conveyed to other roller mills, the output again going to dismembrators. The process could be elaborated by increasing the number of stages.[16]

Doubts about the process became evident during 1882. When Simon addressed the Institution of Civil Engineers on 'Modern flour Milling in England', he gave a concise description of the Nagel & Kaemp scheme, concluding 'The use of smooth rollers without differential speed seems a mistake, for their action necessarily consolidates the flour into flakes, and the mechanical work spent on this has to be undone again by the mechanical work of the dismembrator'. At the same meeting in 1882, W. Proctor Baker, in his paper 'On the various systems of grinding wheat and on the machines used in corn mills', was also discouraging: 'It remains to speak of disintegrators. These, in various forms, have been tried for flour-making but not with success. The violence of the operation and the grinding or breaking of the bran which ensues, must inevitably spoil the quality of the flour made by a disintegrator from any but tough-skinned wheats'. In 1882, Sanderson & Gillespie began to advertise that 'A new two-pair roller mill with fluted or smooth rolls, has now been incorporated in the system', but Sanderson's ideas about break rolls remained sketchy; he became entangled in problems of definition, and might also have been unsure about Nagel & Kaemp's policies. In September 1883, Sanderson's advertisement merely listed 'Nagel & Kaemp's specialities. Roller mills, Dismembrators, Schrot machines, Centrifugal dressing machines, Purifiers, Turbines, Cleaning machines, Hoists'. It was hardly convincing as publicity for a system. There was absence of impressive lists of customers, unlike Wegmann's campaign, in which Childs' advertisements suggested that Wegmann machines were everywhere.

In 1883, Sanderson & Gillespie claimed that 'The first two mills in this country in which no millstones were used were on Nagel & Kaemp's system', presumably referring to Reading and Stockton-on-Tees. This reflected the fact that a series of rolls produced the final products, but their use of dismembrators separated this system from the main stream of development. In 1901 there was a retrospective appraisal of the Nagel & Kaemp system by Sanderson: the 'system of two breaks had one great defect, namely the dark colour of the break flour, due to the violent action of the dismembrators upon the only partially cleansed outer coating of the wheat ... The dark break flour, however, proved fatal to the process'.[17] It seems also that the scheme was both too complicated, and too simple. There were many steps, and numerous centrifugals but the way of opening the grain was haphazard. As with both Buchholzs, the overall scheme was misjudged, and as with Wegmann, the fluted break roll was not perceived as crucial.

John Whittier Throop

Apart from Augustus Childs, the most notable American mill furnisher living in England was J. W. Throop, whose father, G. E. Throop, had specialised in the design and production of wheat cleaning machinery. By 1876 the firm was at Aldersgate in London, with J. W. Throop in charge. He became widely known through his cooperation with Harrison Carter in arranging the millers' trip to Vienna and Budapest in 1877, and by helping the group visit to America in 1880. When he died in 1897, aged only fifty, *The Miller*'s obituary suggested that 'his best days were when … the complete roller system had not yet finally settled among us', which seemed to confirm that the so-called Gray system had little success in Britain.[18]

In May 1879, Throop was advertising 'Gray's patent noiseless roller mill for softening middlings and re-grinding bran and fine pollards … This roller mill can shortly be seen at London and Liverpool and will be exhibited in motion at the coming Royal Agricultural Show'. By the time of the Islington exhibition of 1881 there were greater hopes. In April, *The Miller* published a long description of the Gray machine, well illustrated. The text was an account by Gray himself, which he had contributed to the *United States Miller*.[19] Throop's advertisment for his display at Islington announced that 'Mr W. D. Gray, Chief Milling Engineer for E. P. Allis & Co. of Milwaukee, will be in attendance at the Exhibition and complete series of Gray's gradual reduction belt-driven roller mills will be in motion daily'. It was also reported that 'An automatic mill on the Gray system, similar to the newest Minneapolis mills', would soon be started for A. & W. Glen at their Cheapside Mills at Glasgow.

Up to November 1881, the usual Throop advertisements were headed 'Economy, simplicity & efficiency in gradual reduction roller mills' and showed two illustrations of 'Gray's patent noiseless gradual reduction machine. Two reductions and two separations in one machine'. The appearance was of box shapes, adorned with wheels and belting. The December advertisement represented progress, with a double roller mill, which had a better style. In 1882 Throop moved his offices to Seething Lane, London, very close to Mark Lane; the leading mill furnishing businesses congregated there to be near the Corn Exchange, which many millers attended regularly. From October 1882, his whole page in *The Miller* was again based on a well-illustrated Gray machine. He still referred to corrugated rather than fluted rolls, and to porcelain rolls. There was an admission of restricted progress: 'I do not urge a general cleaning out of all old machinery unless I clearly see such would be the only course to pursue to make a satisfactory and reliable mill. In nearly all instances, I can use all the old machinery, leaving it in its original position, or with as slight a change as possible'.[20] Although other machinery suppliers tried to avoid abrupt

ECONOMY, SIMPLICITY, & EFFICIENCY
In Gradual Reduction Roller Mills.

GRAY'S PATENT NOISELESS
GRADUAL REDUCTION MACHINE

Two Reductions and Two Separations in One Machine.

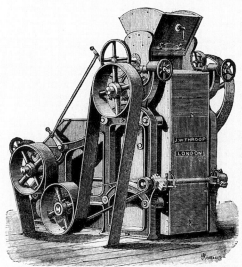 

FRONT VIEW.　　　　　　　　　　　　BACK VIEW.

No Scouring of the Chop or Meal after each Reduction by Wire Scalping Reels.

SEPARATIONS MADE ON A SIEVE
In Machine after each Reduction.

SAVING OF ELEVATORS AND SPACE UPSTAIRS by using lesser number of Reels.

This Machine is driven entirely by belt, and has all the adjustments of the renowned **GRAY NOISELESS ROLLER MILL,** and enables the adoption of a **GRADUAL REDUCTION** Roller Mill Plant at a moderate expenditure.

UNPRECEDENTED SUCCESS OF GRAY'S BRAN ROLLING MACHINE,
With Gray's Patent Belt Movement.

CHILLED IRON AND PORCELAIN ROLLER MILLS
For Middlings and Tailings.

An Automatic Mill on the GRAY SYSTEM, similar to the Newest Minneapolis Mills, Capacity 250 Sacks per Day, will be started in the U.K. about July 1.

MILLS DESIGNED by W. DICKINSON GRAY (Engineer of Allis & Co.), Designer of the celebrated Mills of

C. A. PILLSBURY & Co., Minneapolis, Minn., U.S.A.	E. T. ARCHIBALD & SON, Dundas, Minn., U.S.A.	GEO. V. HECKER & Co., New York City, U.S.A
C. C. WASHBURN, ,,	J. B. A. KERN, Milwaukee, Wis.,	A. W. OGILVIE & Co., Montreal, Canada,
E. V. WHITE & Co., ,, ,,	EDW. SANDERSON & Co., Milwaukee, Wis., ,,	A. & W. GLEN, Glasgow, Scotland.

For Further Particulars Address
J. W. THROOP, 5, Aldersgate Street, London, E.C.
P.S.—See Page IV., Cover.

Figure 21.
Gray's four-roller mill.
(*The Miller*, December 1882)

Figure 20.
J. W. Throop's agency
for Gray roller mills
from America.
(*The Miller*,
September 1881)

changes, the wording was hardly appropriate for the introduction of the 'Gray system'.

In October 1883 it was stated that Gray's automatic roller mill system was of 'English manufacture, as now built by Henry Wren & Co. of Manchester', but customers were not plentiful. By that date there were more forceful suppliers, building on tangible early results and supplying news of orders and installations completed for 'Trade Items' in *The Miller*; Throop was noticeably absent. His most important project up to 1882 was for J. & H. Robinson at Deptford Bridge, London. In 1883, Throop started the second half of Robinson's mill, making it a complete mill on the Gray system with a capacity of about 3000 sacks per

week.[21] He had also installed 'many combinations of rollers and millstones'.
The conjunction with Robinsons at Deptford may have been a misfortune,
when Robinsons became the prime target for the Germ Milling Company's
legal assault on roller millers. J. W. Throop dealt in combination plant, and so
did other and more successful mill furnishers, but the leading firms moved
quickly towards comprehensive systems, eliminating millstones. Throop used
both Gray and G. T. Smith purifiers, the latter possibly the most widely-known
American machine name in this country. Unfortunately for Throop, he was
not the sole agent for G. T. Smith.

Other alternatives

Agents for foreign machinery, including W. R. Dell and William Gardner,
illustrate the diversity to which Storck & Teague referred. They also worked
on their own schemes. They were English firms with workshops and
manufacturing skills, on which they were able to base longer-term commercial
viability than their agency business provided. In addition to these alternative
suppliers, A. B. Childs, who had become well-known with the Wegmann
campaign, tried to introduce Jonathan Mills' discs from America. But from the
end of 1884, most agents advocating machinery from overseas were running
sideshows.

DELL

W. R. Dell started his business as a mill furnisher in 1856, initially at 72 Mark
Lane. In 1871 he retired, and the business was continued by his son, W. B. Dell,
and John Fyfe Stewart. In 1873 they acquired the St James's Iron Works at
Croydon. Three years later they moved to the larger site of the Reliance Iron
Works, where they manufactured an increasing range of machinery.[22] In 1879
Dells advertised that they were 'Sole European and Colonial agents for Barnard
& Lea's Manufacturing Company's celebrated machines', mainly for wheat
cleaning, and manufactured at Moline, Illinois. At the end of the year, Dells
still headed their advertisement 'Millstone builders, manufacturers of flour mill
machinery', but since early 1878 they had been offering their Victor roller mill,
patented by John Smith, W. B. Dell and J. Fyfe Stewart in 1877, for grinding
middlings. It was a very strange design, in which the rolls had both ordinary
rotary motion and a transverse reciprocating motion.[23]

From May 1880, Dells expanded their trade, in collaboration with G. T. Smith.
Smith was a visible new technical force from America, with general though
not universal credit as the originator of New Process milling. The Smith
campaign was mainly for sales of his middlings purifier and depended partly on
improved millstone surfaces. He moved his business address in England to Dells
at Mark Lane, and advertisements included a remarkably simple description of
the action of his purifier:

> The Smith purifier is constructed with from three to five grades of silk to
> each machine. Over each grade of silk there is an air chamber, so that

draughts of air of different forces or strength can be applied to each grade of silk. Each grade of middlings can thus be treated with a draught of air according to its particular gravity, and in connection with each air chamber, over the silk, is a settling chamber … a travelling brush is required to clean the cloth … Fine silk is necessary for this reason – that it is by the delicate

THE COSGROVE CONCENTRATED ROLLER MILL.

Catalogues and Estimates on application.

WM. R. DELL & SON,
26, Mark Lane, London, E.C.

Figure 22.
Dells' agency for American machinery.
(*The Miller*, February 1885)

combination of the air draught and the silk that successful work is accomplished.[24]

By the autumnn of 1880, Smith had three 'special agents': Dells, Wm. Gardner of Gloucester and Davies & Sneade at Liverpool. Dells' suitability for collaboration with the Smith traditional processing methods was emphasised by their advertisements each January, which showed a 'record of delivery of their specialities', for instance in 1882: 460 millstones and 204 Smith purifiers.

Smith did more than anyone else to try to place millstone practice in an integrated system. Even so, the word 'process', in New Process and the Geo. T. Smith Process, was more appropriate than 'system'; many firms who used the word 'system' were soon found not to have one, or to have a less than satisfactory combination of individual machines. Smith was energetic and successful, and his sales of machinery for the various sieving and separating operations would have been impressive enough, but he felt obliged to devote time and money to patent litigation, which may have delayed further advances. In June 1882, Dells advertised that they were 'General agents for Europe for the John T. Noye Manufacturing Co. of Buffalo, U. S. A.', and they also offered Stevens rolls and the Cosgrove Concentrated Roller Mill.[25] To Smith's purifier, there was added a Smith centrifugal, and their own centrifugal.

About July 1883, Dells added another unusual and unconvincing device, Rounds Sectional Roller Mill, made by the John T. Noye Co. Dells' suggestion was that it 'Enables a miller to have a perfectly automatic mill on a small scale'. It was 'designed simply as a break mill, on which, however, the bran is cleaned. The flouring is accomplished on millstones or roller mills, as the miller may prefer'. Surprisingly it was to make 'Two to five breaks with one pair of rolls', which were divided into sections with corrugations of different fineness.[26] There was a major change in December 1885, when Dells advertised 'Investigate the new Geo. T. Smith system of roller mill separations with Geo. T. Smith scalpers, strippers, centrifugals and purifiers. A new roller mill had been patented by M. W. Clark, of the G. T. Smith Co. So G. T. Smith moved on from the millstone dependency and there was a 'new Geo. T. Smith' roller mill, described in the journal in January 1890; it was ponderous looking, compared with most contemporary British design. The link between Dells and the Stevens machines continued at least until 1887.

GARDNER

Wm Gardner of Gloucester started his business about 1860. In the late 1870s, he was advertising modestly as a 'Millstone manufacturer and general mill furnisher'. Simultaneously with Dells, in October 1880, Gardner took a full page of The Miller to announce 'American New Process Milling'. At least until the summer of 1883, Gardner included the Smith purifier as a component of his advertising, though not a major feature. By March 1883, there was a new route for possible progress, with an agency for Odell roller mills, from the Stilwell & Bierce Manufacturing Co. at Dayton, Ohio. In April, The Miller printed the makers' description of the Odell design, containing a vivid summary

Figure 23. Dells' least orthodox offer. (The Miller, June 1883)

74

IMPORTANT TO MILLERS.

AN ECONOMICAL MILL!

THE

ROUNDS Patent Sectional ROLLER MILL

Enables a Miller to have a PERFECTLY AUTOMATIC MILL on small scale which will work as economically as the largest.

SUPPLIED WITH STEVENS' CORRUGATIONS.

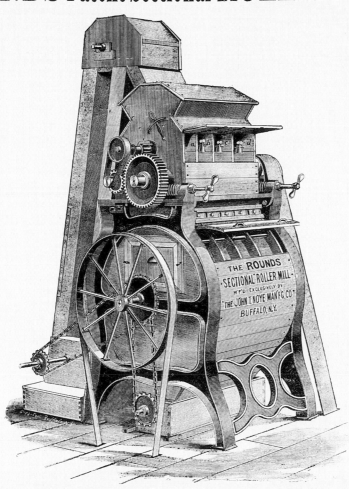

TWO TO FIVE BREAKS WITH ONE PAIR OF ROLLS.

LEADING POINTS.—A single pair of rolls divided into sections for the various breaks. Sections vary in length, and corrugations in fineness. A single sectional feed roll, with automatic feed gates, distributes the material over each section except the first (which has an adjustable feed gate), and shuts off feed when the machine stops. Two adjusting screws accurately carry the different sections into any desired position at one time, doing away with separate attachments for throwing rolls apart when stopping or starting. The short elevators transferring material from one section to another CANNOT CLOG, being driven by non-slipping chain belting.

Supplied with Reels and Scalpers complete, or with Rolls only, as may be desired, by

WM. R. DELL & SON, 26, Mark Lane, LONDON, E.C.

SOLE AGENTS for the JOHN T. NOYE MANUFACTURING COMPANY.

GARDNER'S
CHILLED IRON
NEW FOUR-ROLLER MILL. | THREE-HIGH ROLLER MILL.

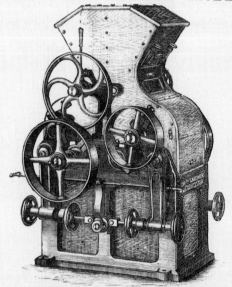

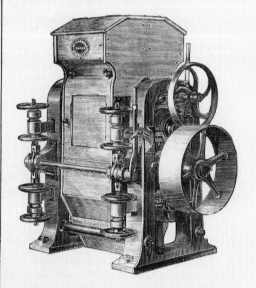

Has every important Adjustment, and the Rolls can be taken out in a few minutes without even disturbing the Hopper; and is made for Small Plants with Rolls from 7 × 12 in. to 7 × 18 in., and for larger Plants with heavier frames, from 9 × 18 in. to 9 × 30 in. Each Roll is driven by a separate belt, as shown, or can be driven by belt and gear.

I also make this class of Mill with only one pair of Rolls, same size as in the Four-Roller Mills.

These Mills can be worked on two different kinds of Feed at the same time, and should it be necessary to put more pressure on one pair of Rolls than the other, it can be done.

They are made in sizes to suit Large or Small Plants.

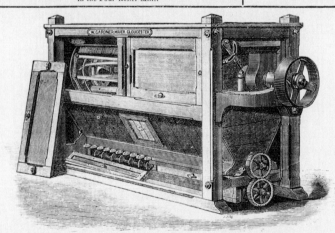

GARDNER'S
IMPROVED
CENTRIFUGAL
FLOUR-DRESSING
MACHINE.

Made with One, Two, or Four Reels in a Chest, and of Nine different Sizes.

☞ ALL THESE MACHINES are of MY OWN MAKE, and will be found to be SIMPLE IN CONSTRUCTION and WELL BUILT.

Send for Descriptive Price List of these and other Machines used in GARDNER'S COMPLETE ROLLER PLANTS to

WM. GARDNER, Millwright, &c., GLOUCESTER.

of the most difficult puzzle of break roll design: to what profile should the rolls be machined?

> A great deal is said about the relative merits of 'cutting' and 'non-cutting' corrugations ... The 'cutting' corrugation or rib, has a shearing or cutting action upon the wheat, and the 'non-cutting' or rounded rib, has a mashing or squeezing action upon the wheat. The 'cutting' or sharp rib makes the most middlings and the least amount of break flour, but if too sharp, shaped and pointed like the tooth of a circular saw, it also cuts up the bran, and makes middlings of splintered and ragged shape and uneven in size, both of which are very objectionable. On the other hand, the 'non-cutting' rounded rib mashes the wheat, makes a large amount of break flour and a proportionately small amount of middlings, which are soft instead of being sharp and granular, broad but poorly cleaned bran, and on soft or damp wheat cannot do economical work.

Odell claimed to have found a superior form of 'corrugation', but the secret was not revealed. In October there was an advertisement for the 'Odell Concentrated Roller Mill'. Its open framework made it look cruder than the Cosgrove alternative.[27] By November 1884, Gardner was offering his improved centrifugal flour dressing machines, and his own 'improved three-high roller mill'. It was reported that 'Mr Gardner, milling engineer, Gloucester, recognising the necessity of keeping pace with the times, has commenced to manufacture roller mills as well as millstones'. By April 1885, he had a new four-roller mill, and stated that 'All these machines are of my own make, and will be found to be simple in construction and well-built'. Outwardly, Gardner's machines looked strong, rather than refined. Rolls were stated to be either smooth or corrugated. In 1886, he was advertising small roller plants as 'a speciality', and frequent entries in the columns of 'Trade Items' confirmed that. In a report of 1895, there was the comment that 'With the change from stone to roller milling ... Mr Gardner's business received a considerable, and as it proved, permanent expansion'. A new works was built in 1894, easily reached by street tramway from the railway stations for a penny fare.[28]

CHILDS

A quite different device from America was publicised in 1882. A. B. Childs & Son were the agents. for 'Jonathan Mills gradual reduction mills for degerming and reducing wheat', based on a disc machine: a pair of 16 inches diameter iron discs were arranged horizontally, with the upper disc stationary and the lower one driven. It was an ornate metal resemblance of a pair of small millstones. A series of disc machines was used to split the grain; it was therefore described as a gradual reduction process, though limited to the granulation stages.[29] Mr Samuel Sidney Chisholm, of Chicago, the manufacturer, gave a paper to NABIM which was possibly stimulating, but definitely bad advice. He had two aims: to show that the action of both millstones and rolls was unsatisfactory for the operation of breaking wheat, and to claim that the disc mills which he manufactured provided a better solution. He stated that millstones

Figure 24.
Gardner's roller mills
and centrifugal
dressing machine.
(*The Miller*,
February 1885)

or rolls could be used to grind or reduce middlings, but could not grind wheat effectively. Chisholm wished to show that during the break operation the action with rolls was chaotic:

> whatever the character of the rolls' corrugation may be, it is impossible that a pair of rolls should split a grain of wheat through the crease ... All rolls

Figure 25. Whitmore & Binyon's continued interest in New Process milling. (*The Miller*, November 1885)

78

now in use break the wheat not in the manner which has been shown to be desirable, but in a haphazard manner … That the action of fluted rollers is less injurious than the millstones, and comminutes the bran in a less degree is an undeniable fact, but that they are not perfectly or even well adapted to the gradual reduction of wheat is proved by the no less undeniable fact, that the 'break flour' produced by each successive reduction grows poorer and poorer.[30]

Chisholm's case was that empirical mysteries could be replaced by a description of the supposed paths of individual grains through the disc corrugations and he implied that by his methods each grain was split accurately. Presumably a trial would have shown some supporting evidence of split grain but, despite lengthy discussion, there was no challenge about the proportion of grain that was actually neatly split. Carter, Corcoran (the strongest advocate for millstones), Hopkinson, Lund, Sanderson and Voss, all from engineering businesses, were present; they all avoided argument. None of them could have believed the speaker's theories.

In November 1883, 'A. B. Childs & Son's complete system of Gradual Reduction Milling' was advertised, but it was still a series of metal substitutes for millstones, associated with Wegmann equipment. In August 1884, Childs was advertising, much more simply, 'corrugated, smooth iron and porcelain roller mills', and offering both Wegmann machines and Wegmann designs made by special arrangement at the Oerlikon works in Switzerland, labelled A. B. Childs & Son. In November 1884 there was another forlorn prospect when Messrs Childs became sole agents for the Case Manufacturing Company of Columbus, Ohio. For several years Case machinery was given a familiar treatment of exaggerated claims; the 'Full Case System' was available, with a machine named after Queen Victoria's consort: the 'Prince Albert' roller mill.[31]

Direct competition for Chisholm and Childs was provided by James Higginbottom of Liverpool, a versatile mechanical engineer and explorer of the unorthodox; he devoted too much attention to his own disc mill.[32] From about October 1881, James Higginbottom & Co. became Higginbottom and Stuart, and it was from about that time that there were advertisements for their patent disc mill, claimed to be 'the simplest gradual reduction machine yet introduced to the milling trade'. It had 18 inches diameter chilled iron discs. The device was a basic part of their supposed system, using disc mills, roller mills and millstones. During 1883 Higginbottom was fending off Chisholm's allegations of patent infringement, but the disc machine was advertised boldly until at least the end of 1884: up to that September 165 had been sold. Higginbottom had still not accepted roller milling late in 1883, advertising:

To Millers. The millstone is the most effective flour producing machine in the world. You should add to your present mills our system of wheat breaking, bran cleaning, germ extracting, and purification of middlings, and you may then make use of your millstones for the reduction of clean middlings into flour, and thus put yourselves in the foremost position for the profitable production of high-class flour.[33]

In July 1884, his claims for the disc mill were 'the best machine for splitting wheat through the crease, the best machine for releasing the germ, the best machine for granulating wheat'. In June 1885 he announced 'The new departure in milling'. For first and second breaks he had designed a complicated 'wheat splitter', comprising six disc mills. But soon he too changed from his unorthodox break apparatus. In 1886 there was a Higginbottom & Stuart double roller mill with 'either grooved chilled iron rolls for breaking the wheat, or with smooth chilled iron rolls for reducing the middlings'.[34] Higginbottom was not an agent for imported machinery, but his oppostion to Childs, his perseverance in the wrong direction and his later work with both roller mills and sieve purifiers completes the range of beguiling excursions which the leading engineers avoided.

The period of diversity of non roller-mill methods had finished and gradual reduction methods, using chilled iron rolls had become thoroughly accepted and familiar throughout the country. The spread of ideas and equipment had depended on agents, advocates, technical advisers, and 'milling experts' acting as interpreters between millers and engineers. By the later 1880s a recognisably standard British practice had become a new orthodoxy. There were still variants, but the period of crowded variety had left only a marginal market for the many overseas sources of machinery that were not based on thorough system design for specifically British conditions. The progress of innovation was much more than the supply of machines, as the firms that were mainly agents had soon discovered.

Part II

❦

The major factors:
Henry Simon and the
National Association

CHAPTER SIX

Success

The efforts made by the Buchholzs, Wegmann, Throop (for Gray), and Sanderson (for Nagel & Kaemp), can be regarded as contributory to the introduction of roller milling, though they were mainly trial and error, and therefore only preparatory to more successful initiatives. In the early 1880s an emerging group were much more progressive; among milling engineers three names were soon in the lead: Henry Simon, J. Harrison Carter and Thomas Robinson & Sons Ltd. Simon entered milling engineering in 1878 (the firm was not incorporated until 1897). Carter entered the field slightly earlier, and Robinsons in 1882. Although Robinsons' achievements came later, they started on their new specialism during the introductory stage of full roller milling systems.

Along with these leaders, there were many other mill furnishers, with previous experience of the traditional milling industry or of other branches of engineering, who began to sell roller milling and associated machinery. But the many installations provided by the three leading firms constituted the decisive contribution to what became the full establishment of gradual reduction roller milling in Britain. Because their systems produced satisfactory results, they were enabled to move on through successive stages of development. Their systems were experimental during the period from 1878 to about 1882. After that, there were much clearer problems and targets. The successful engineers learned from predecessors and contemporaries but they were inventive and independent. There were clearly differing personalities. What they had in common was energy, membership of a new movement at a stage when it was seen to be successful, and chilled cast iron rolls.

Henry Simon

Born in Brieg in Silesia in 1835, Henry Simon studied engineering at the Swiss Federal Polytechnic in Zurich, and gained experience as a professional engineer in Germany, Russia and France.[1] Simon's life and work have been described by his grandson, Professor Brian Simon, *In search of a grandfather – Henry Simon of Manchester 1835–1899*, published in 1997.[2] An account of the Simon Engineering Group has been given by Anthony Simon (1947 & 1953) who recorded that Henry Simon 'became a naturalized British subject in 1862, and in 1867 he took a small office in Manchester, established himself as a consulting engineer, and began to look out for engineering specialities'.[3] He became a member of the Institution of Civil Engineers and the Institution of Mechanical Engineers and, beyond his professional interests, he was active in personal and financial support for numerous organisations concerned with scientific education, public welfare and the advance of Manchester's musical reputation. From 1877 to 1881 he applied for at least sixty-two patents for invention, on behalf of continental designers, only four of which directly concerned milling.[4]

In the official story of *The Simon Engineering Group* (1947), it was stated that Henry Simon urged his sons 'to search, as he himself had done, for engineering specialities and patents that could be used to improve the efficiency

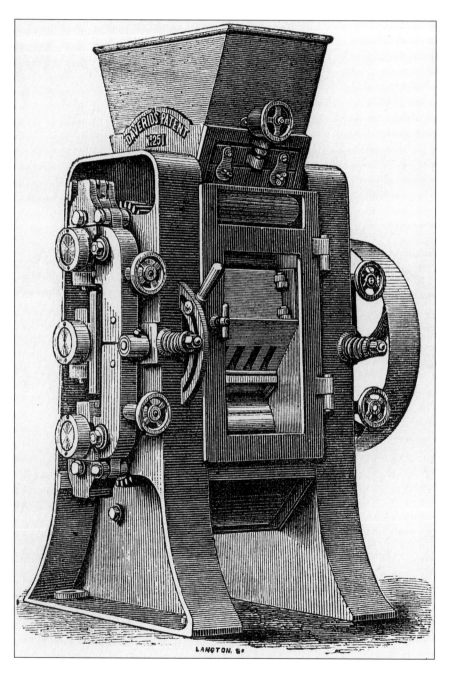

Figure 26. Daverio's three-roller mill, used by Henry Simon. (*The Miller*, September 1880)

84

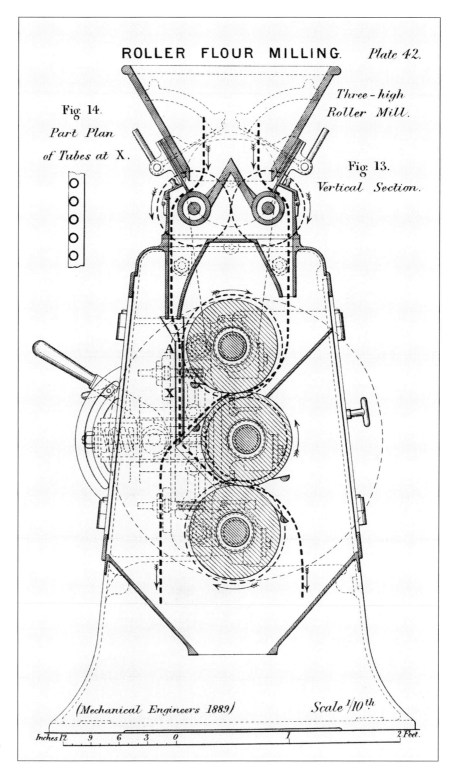

Figure 27.
End elevation of
Daverio three-roller
mill. (*Proc. I.Mech.E.*,
1889).

of large-scale industrial processes'. Simon had a strong interest in the extraction of by-products during the production of coke from coal, and formed a partnership with a patent holder, François Carves, but resistance to change was strong up to 1900. Anthony Simon (1947) recorded that 'in 1880, Henry Simon began his efforts to introduce the by-product coke oven into Britain, but from all but a few far-sighted men he met the most determined opposition. British ironmasters as a body were stubbornly prejudiced against what was known as patent coke'.

To the advantage of British millers, Simon could concentrate on their situation. When he turned his attention to flour milling, he worked in close association with Gustav Daverio of Zurich and Heinrich Seck of Frankfurt.[5] Daverio, as senior partner in a firm at Oerlikon in Switzerland, had been involved in the development of Wegmann's roller mill, but had withdrawn and set up separately, designing and manufacturing his own three-high roller mill, which Simon used extensively. Until the later 1880s Simon retained a preference for the three-high roll arrangement for the reduction operation, but soon included both two-roller mills and four-roller mills. He used four-roller mills for the break stages, with a pair of fluted chilled iron rolls, one above the

Figure 28.
Seck's centrifugal
dressing machine.
(*The Miller*,
September 1879)

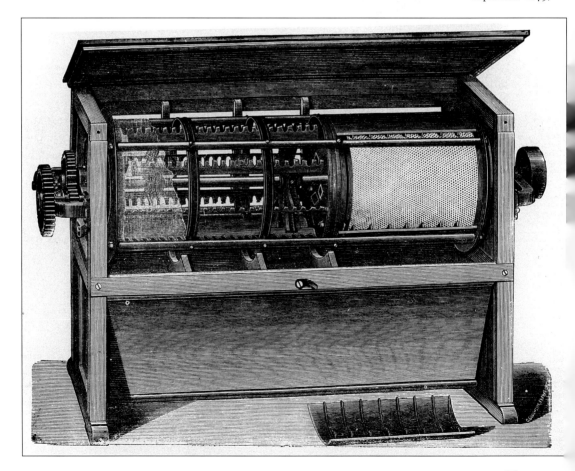

Figure 29.
Self-contained
granulator. (*The
Miller*, September
1881)

other, on each side of the centre line, the pairs working independently.[6] Other firms used two pairs, all in a horizontal plane.

Simon and his collaborators had to solve many mechanical design problems. If at least at the start the experimenters and draughtsmen were mainly in foreign firms, Simon was still responsible for successful operation in British conditions. He certainly had to be thoroughly conversant with the mechanical detail and be confident that decisions were being made efficiently. This applied to sizes of rolls and their speeds of revolution, and particularly to the design of break rolls: choice of speed differential, determination of flute profiles and sizing, and arrangement of the spirality of the fluting. He gave sufficiently detailed information in his first two publicly presented technical papers to confirm that confidence;[7] he was not in doubt about the technical integrity of the designs, nor secretive about the principles involved. Although roller mill ideas continually evolved, making the pioneering work look unsophisticated, many fundamental features retained validity.

By the mid 1880s expertise was developing rapidly and there were increasing requirements for machine-making: roller mill construction was concentrated at Uzwil in Switzerland, based on a long-lasting relationship with Adolf Bühler and his successors, who became leading European specialists in roller mill production.[8] The timing and details of the collaboration with Bühlers, and the connection with Daverio, have remained mysterious. The key year may be 1882. From then on there was a distinctly new look to machinery, and the assured treatment of the many less obvious features included improved methods of regulating the feed of material to the rolls. In the 1892 Simon catalogue maximum roll length was 40 inches; in 1898 the heavy pattern four-roller mill was available with rolls up to 60 inches long, an enormous contrast with the 12 inches long rolls of early machines. It was less easy for Simon to give a clear yet simple exposition of the equally or even more mysterious dynamics of purifying operations, but there was already some existing experience of the use of gravity purifiers amongst British millers, and there was soon some knowledge of G. T. Smith's different approach. Simon himself became closely involved in the design of purifiers in the mid 1880s, and also in the development of the roller mill, becoming increasingly involved in more highly developed systems and larger scales of operation.

INTRODUCTION OF THE SIMON SYSTEM

In August 1878, Simon supplied a plant for McDougall Brothers' mill at Poland Street in Manchester, which became known as the first complete roller mill plant, without millstones, in Britain. Little (1887) stated that there had been a previous trial, with a combined roller mill and disc machine from a German maker; he also quoted a letter from Arthur McDougall: 'In our little experimental mill, erected by Mr Simon, we obtained a straight run flour of very good quality, and a little low grade … After running this small plant for about six months we were more than convinced of the suitability of the roller system'.[9] Simon (1882) gave his account of the experimental stage at Manchester: 'Its success was so decided that this firm gradually extended their roller-plant, until in the two following years rollers had entirely replaced stones. More than seventy roller mills have been supplied to them, besides dressing and purifying machinery'.[10] The first successful plant of 1878 was said to grind 700 sacks of wheat per week. The nominal capacity was probably three sacks per hour of flour output. Roller plants were installed in 1879 for Ashby, Son & Allen at Croydon, for E. Shackleton & Sons at Carlow and Athy in Ireland, and for J. A. Ingleby & Sons at Tadcaster near Leeds.[11] The Tadcaster plant was capable of grinding 15 cwt. of wheat per hour, which was equivalent to production of about 4.5 sacks of flour per hour. The Croydon plant was stated to be the same size.

Initially, the Daverio three-high mill was a clear feature of the system, while the dressing machines and purifiers, essential to its success, were designed by Seck.[12] During the early stages of introducing and developing his system, Simon also used a self-contained granulator, a combination of up to five pairs of rolls, together with centrifugal dressing machines; it was still in use about 1880 and 1881, a plant at Croydon being an example.[13] It was also a feature of Simon's display at the 1881 Islington exhibition. Simon offered single middlings reducing mills for trial, free of charge. The copious statistical and geographical information that he published showed a substantial involvement in propelling the changeover to rolls. Also Henry Simon had to attend to the problem of countering Wegmann's campaign against iron rolls …[14] Simon sold the whole of his displayed machinery at the 1881 Islington exhibition to the Britannia Mills Flour and Bread Co. Ltd. of Birmingham. By the end of 1881, he had installed an aggregate of about 100 sacks per hour of roller mill capacity in complete plants in addition to contracts for partial introduction of new methods. There was a doubling of that total in 1882, considerably more than a doubling in 1883, and almost another by the end of 1884, making a total capacity installed in complete plants of 934 sacks per hour, which could possibly have supplied more than six million people with flour if those plants had been run for 126 hours per week.[15]

In 1881, there was another 'first'. Simon put in an automatic roller plant for F. A. Frost & Sons at Chester, the materials-in-process or intermediate products (mill stocks) being mechanically transferred from one operation to the next without the need for sacking or manual handling. It does not seem that any great claims or prominent advertisements were made at the time. Anthony Simon (1953) stated that in 1881 there was 'a major step in transforming a slow, laborious and costly batch process into an automatic continuous process'.[16] There were arguments about the claim during the 1880s, particularly after Simon's paper to the Institution of Mechanical Engineers in 1889. He had said that 'The first complete roller-mill without the use of stones was built by the writer in 1878 for Arthur McDougall of Manchester, and in Ireland for Messrs. E. Shackleton & Sons of Carlow, in 1879; the first automatic roller flour mill in England for F. A. Frost & Sons, of Chester'.[17]

Harrison Carter thought otherwise, believing he had been first but, as with so many claims of technical 'firsts', early successes were often tentative, prior to improvements. Although there were millstone plants with mechanical conveyors for transferring materials-in-process, the potential for scaling-up became relevant to a large group of innovative millers for the first time, strongly reinforcing the trend of technical change. Automatic feed mechanisms were designed in the early 1880s to control the supply of material to roller mills and purifiers. In contrast, millstone plants usually involved some sack work and some shovelling. Material had been fed to the main machines through hoppers without sophisticated methods of regulation. The practical outcome was that the introduction of automatic working in roller mills allowed progress towards much larger scales of production and, though seeming obvious, the general technical progress probably took many millers by surprise.

From 1882 onwards, there was a striking new emphasis in Henry Simon's advertisements; he could claim the leadership confidently and with evidence. He made basic technical points, his plants were 'suitable for either hard or soft wheat', and the process could be 'entirely under control as to mixture of flour into one straight grade or into (the) best number of qualities, to suit every market'. But he could also say that his system was 'working in the largest number of mills'. A clear indication of leadership was Simon's successful work at the top of the range of plant capacity. In April 1882 he could claim that 'By far the largest roller mill in [the] United Kingdom, capable of grinding 5 tons of wheat per hour, is successfully working on this system'. He guaranteed an extraction of 75 per cent of flour, which was higher than later expectations. At that rate, five tons of wheat per hour would have been equivalent to a flour output capacity of 30 sacks per hour, or ten times the capacity of his first plant for McDougalls. The 30 sack plant must have been at Falls Road in Belfast, installed at Bernard Hughes' mill. In the same journal issue Simon stated that he had successfully introduced his system 'in twenty-five large and small mills varying in capacity from 8 cwts. to 5 tons of wheat per hour, in the following towns'.[18]

Greenock	Dublin	London	Croydon	Tadcaster	Ayr	Bridgwater
Liverpool	Glasgow	Belfast	York	Chester	Athy	Birmingham
Loughboro	Leeds	Paisley	Carlow	Doncaster	Cahir	Manchester

Establishment of the Simon system

Three years, 1883 to 1885, provided evidence that there was a movement through stages of progress. News of activity was firstly to do with individual businesses, but there was also an overall impression of speed and decisiveness. This was encouraged by the milling engineers. *The Miller* could hardly have avoided being caught up in the movement, so that journalists and millers found that it became easy to use the word 'revolution'.[19] Simon soon sensed the first upturn of 1883 and in April and October 1883 he published maps showing the geographical spread of his work. These first two were simple experiments, but he must have realised the challenge to himself, as well as to his competitors. From January 1885, he gave a series of annual reports, using maps and often supported by lists of milling businesses where his system was in use, or was being installed.[20] The density of the symbols on the maps rapidly increased, showing plants started into operation, plants erected or in course of erection, and combination plants. The lists confirmed the care in the mapping, and the series was continued until at least 1898. No other form of report showed the spread of roller milling systems so clearly.

In numerous statements, including his advertisements, Simon publicised the advance. By March 1884, he claimed that his automatic roller mill system was 'now adopted in over sixty mills in Great Britain and Ireland alone, with a weekly power of production of 100,000 sacks of flour'. He also made clear that 'This does not include the very large number of single machines of all kinds working in other mills'. In May 1884, Simon was advertising that he had 'built the largest complete roller mills in the United Kingdom'. He was referring to the work at Hughes' mill at Belfast, and the North Shore Co. at Liverpool, each for a total capacity of 10,000 sacks per week.[21] Both firms had reached a capacity of 60 sacks per hour by 1884. By July, he could state that he had twenty-five repeat orders for complete plants, and by October that he had '102 orders now booked for complete plants in the United Kingdom alone, not

Figure 30.
Flow chart for early Simon small capacity plants. (*Proc. I.C.E.*, 1882)

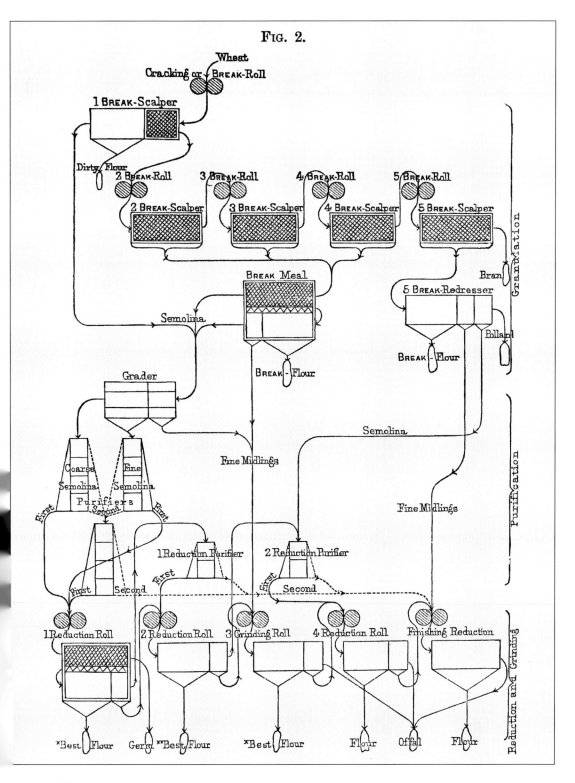

Fig. 2.

including a large number of mills partially remodelled'. There was an invitation: 'H. Simon's Roller Mill Facts for 1884, along with a map of the United Kingdom, showing where these plants are at work, sent gratis to Millers on application'.

Data describing the diffusion of the Simon system appeared in journal supplements. Unfortunately, when journal issues were bound, supplements were often discarded; otherwise, the extent of Simon's activity might have been better known in later appraisals. In particular, clustering of new installations at the ports can be clearly seen in relationship to time scale. The involvement with port mill development around Liverpool is striking. By the mid 1880s there was strength of innovation in a region from Liverpool and nearby Cheshire, across the country to York and beyond. Hull and the Bristol Channel ports had not yet become very prominent, compared with their importance a few years later. London and Glasgow had been catching up, though Seth Taylor's mills, the biggest in London, were not converted to roller milling until 1884 and 1885.

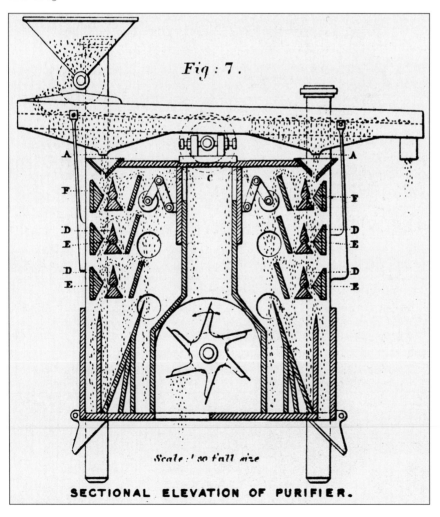

Figure 31.
Gravity purifier. (*Proc I.C.E.*, 1882)

In November 1884, Simon introduced another new advertising feature, detailing the 'Record of Application of Simon's Roller System in Liverpool alone', shown here. There was a series of similar tables, unfortunately printed on very fragile paper. The North Shore Flour and Rice Mill Co. Ltd was the one big milling business in the district, a limited liability company since 1857;

SIMON'S ROLLER MILL SYSTEM.

SIMON'S PATENT REFORM PURIFIER

PATENT REFORM PURIFIER

HENRY SIMON   MANCHESTER

AN IMPORTANT & NEW DEPARTURE IN PURIFICATION

WILL PURIFY THE VERY FINEST STUFF

That no other Machine can Touch.

ABSOLUTELY SELF-CONTAINED.

REQUIRING

NO STIVE ROOM.

NO DUST COLLECTOR.

NO CONNECTING PIPES.

All Middlings, Tails, Dust and Fluff automatically collected and delivered by the Machine.
ALREADY INTRODUCED IN SOME OF THE BEST ENGLISH MILLS.
CAN BE SEEN ON APPLICATION.

HENRY SIMON, 20, Mount St., MANCHESTER.

Figure 32.
Sieve-type Reform purifier of 1885. (*The Miller*, April 1885)

SIMON'S ROLLER MILL SYSTEM.

SIMON'S PATENT ELECTRIC LIGHTING ARRANGEMENT

CAN BE APPLIED TO ALL PURIFIERS.

SIMON'S
PATENT "REFORM" PURIFIER

Now **IN USE** in the Leading Mills in ENGLAND, FRANCE, BELGIUM and GERMANY. In AUSTRO-HUNGARY, the mother country of Purifying, SEVERAL HUNDREDS HAVE BEEN SOLD, and with one exception EVERY LARGE MILL in BUDA-PESTH has ADOPTED THIS MACHINE.

PATENT ELECTRIC LIGHT ARRANGEMENT
For MIDDLINGS PURIFIERS.
Simple, Cheap & Effective.
Can be used in all Flour Mills, without exception, even where the Electric Light is not in use for the remainder of the Mill.

For full particulars, apply to
HENRY SIMON, 20, Mount St., MANCHESTER.

Figure 33. Improved Reform purifer of 1887. (*The Miller,* December 1887)

it was uniquely constituted among the larger milling businesses at the start of roller milling. Edward Hutchinson's Mersey Mills were to be amongst the biggest mills in the United Kingdom within a few years, but in the mid 1880s he was still experimenting. Jacobi, Tongue, Ross and Radford were principals of mills which other millers acquired and developed; with previous experience, the incomers then used these part-formed opportunities to establish bases at

Liverpool, from which they expanded. In 1888 William Vernon purchased Jacobis' mill and modified it, and in 1891 purchased Tonges' mill and enlarged it. Arthur McDougall rented the Ross mill in 1889 and remodelled it. Buchanans acquired Radford's mill. The North Shore Co., Hutchinsons, and these three

SIMON'S ROLLER SYSTEM.

HENRY SIMON'S
4-ROLLER MILL

SMOOTH AND NOISELESS WORKING.

UTMOST EFFICIENCY & DURABILITY.

HENRY SIMON

With ROLLS of about 6, 7, 9 & 10 in. diam.
And about 16, 20, 24, 32 & 40 in. long.

H. SIMON has supplied these 40 by 10 in. Roller Mills to a number of WELL-KNOWN FIRMS, one of them remarking—

**"The 40 in. Roll is no trouble at all.
It works more like a clock than a Roll."**

HENRY SIMON, 20, Mount St., Manchester.

Figure 34.
Simon system
four-roller mill in
1889. (*The Miller*,
February 1889)

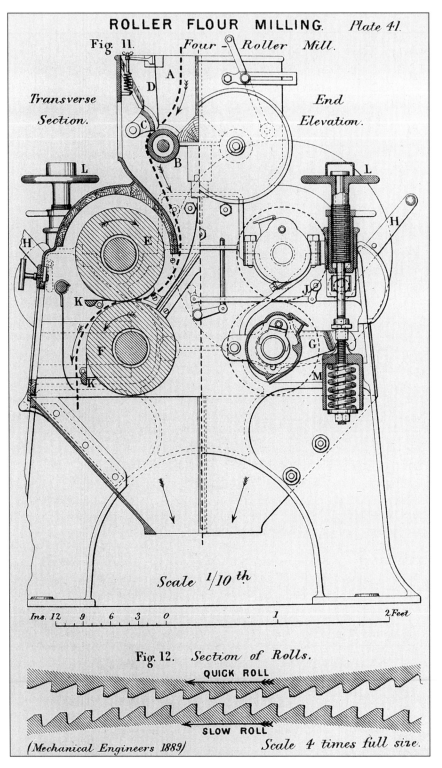

ROLLER FLOUR MILLING.   *Plate 41.*

Fig. 11.   *Four - Roller Mill.*

Transverse Section.

End Elevation.

Scale ¹/10ᵗʰ

Ins. 12 9 6 3 0   1   2 Feet

Fig. 12.   *Section of Rolls.*

QUICK ROLL

SLOW ROLL

(Mechanical Engineers 1889)   *Scale 4 times full size.*

THE MILLERS

Figure 35 (*left*).
End elevation of
Simon system
four-roller mill. (*Proc.
I.Mech.E.*, 1889)

Figure 36 (*opposite*).
Vernons' mill at
Birkenhead opened in
1899. (*The Miller,*
October 1899)

96

SIMON ROLLER SYSTEM

"The Miller" Prize.

BAKERS' EXHIBITION, AGRICULTURAL HALL, ISLINGTON, SEPT. 16th to 23rd.

ENGLISH versus HUNGARIAN FLOUR.

MESSRS. W. VERNON & SONS' NEW BIRKENHEAD MILL.

WINNERS of the PRIZE CUP,

MESSRS. W. VERNON & SONS.

LATEST NEW MILL ON THE SIMON SYSTEM.

HENRY SIMON LD.: 20, MOUNT ST., MANCHESTER.

later arrivals became, and remained for many years, the best-known names and the biggest businesses in the Liverpool area, joined later by others. Birkenhead then became a prominent district for expansion.

Complete plants on Simon system at Liverpool [22]	Capacity sacks per week	Date of order
Messrs A. Jacobi, Union Mill, Commercial Road		1881
repeat order	1150	1882
North Shore Flour & Rice Mill Co. Ltd, Boundary Street	3300	1883
Messrs J. Tonge & Son, Toxteth Mills, Mill Street	2000	1883
North Shore Flour & Rice Mill Co. Ltd, Boundary Street	6500	1884
Mr G. Lunt, Soho Flour Mills, Soho Street	1000	1884
Messrs Ross Bros, Kinross Mill, Commercial Road	1150	1884
Mr J. Radford, Stanley Mills, Westminster Road	1150	1884
Total	16250	

In 1886, 1893 and 1898 Simon published catalogues in which he included appraisals of technical progress and statements of numbers of plants installed on the Simon system. In the 1886 edition he included an essay 'On roller flour milling', in which he stated that the Simon system 'which in May 1882 had been adopted by some twenty five British millers, of whom about a dozen had proved their satisfaction and confidence by doubling, and even trebling, the plants originally erected for them, had been adopted by the New Year 1883, for 40, by the New Year 1884, for over 60, by the New Year 1885, for 100 complete Roller Plants; and now in April 1886, this number is raised to over 160'. Much of Simon's 1886 essay concerned developing machine design, but he referred particularly to modernisation at Liverpool and Glasgow, where there had been strong competition from American flour. Henry Simon obviously had a liking for statistical information. He stated that

> At the beginning of the year 1886 the total capacity of the whole of the mills now working upon Simon's Roller System in the United Kingdom alone is between ten and twelve million sacks of flour per annum; and some idea of the magnitude of this production may be gained when it is stated that to produce the wheat required for these mills over two and a half million acres, equal to about 4,000 square miles of land, are necessary, and to convey it, upwards of 225,000 railway wagons, making, without the necessary engines, a train of about 1,000 miles in length, are requisite.[23]

In Simon's total of over 160 plants, he included 'plants erected for the two largest flour milling firms in the United Kingdom, the North Shore Flour and Rice Mill Company ... amounting in aggregate to about 100 sacks per hour; and Mr Seth Taylor ... bringing his output up to fully 100 sacks of flour per hour'. So the North Shore Co.'s third order to Simon had resulted in another large expansion, and Taylor had joined in the setting of a new standard for the size of very large mills. Thirty businesses had been supplied with two or more plants, with seventy-one plants between them; the pattern of supply to this group is shown in the table. Simon's original data was in four columns

Firm or company	1878	1879	1880	1881	1882	1883	1884	1885
Andrews, Belfast						*	*	
Ashby & Allen, Croydon		*		*		*		
Bannantyne, Limerick						*	*	*
Buchanan, Glasgow					*			*
Field, Banbury							*	*
French, Darlington								**
Frost, Chester				*		*		
Gilliland, Londonderry					*	*		*
Going & Smith, Cahir				*	*			
Hallinan, Cork							*	*
Hughes, Belfast				*		*		*
Ingleby, Tadcaster		*			*			
Kirby, Hull						*	*	
Leetham, York					**	*	*	
McDougall, Manchester	*		*		*			
Mills, York					*			*
Milner, Elland						*	*	*
North Shore Co., Liverpool						*	**	
Primrose, Glasgow				*			*	
Rishworth, Leeds				*		*		
Shackleton, Athy		*		*				
Shackleton, Carlow		*		*				
Spiller, Cardiff				*	*			
Star Corn Millers, Oldham						*	*	
Taylor, London							*	**
Trevithick, Hayle					*	*		
Tucker, Abergavenny							*	
United District, Sowerby Bridge							*	*
Walmesley & Smith, Barrow						**		
White, Partick					*		*	

Dates of repeat orders for Simon complete plants [24]

showing date of first order, first repeat etc. It has been modified to show gaps between orders, the timing of action of early innovators and well-known firms, and increasing activity during 1883–1884. It shows the comparative lateness of Seth Taylor's entry. In addition to Taylor, other eventual big names in milling were Spillers, Leetham, the North Shore Co. and McDougall. J. Rank of Holderness Road, Hull, was listed (but does not appear in the table); a 6 sacks per hour Simon plant at the Alexandra Mill was started in April 1885. [25] Names and locations were supplied of 116 customers for complete plants, to whom a total of 157 plants had been supplied by 1885.

Size of plant is more difficult to study, also range of plant size and the variation of size across the range. While Simon pointed out that he was supplying large capacity plant, he also repeatedly stressed his willingness to deal with all sizes of installation. At the stage of the introduction of roller milling in Britain, there was an innovation entry barrier in terms of plant capacity. Whereas small experiments were possible with purifiers and middlings rolls, the smallest complete plants recommended by Simon in 1879 were about 3 sacks of flour per hour capacity, which could have supplied a population of 5,000 people by being run for only 30 hours per week. During the first surge of innovation up to 1885, typical plants ranged up to 20 sacks per hour, but the largest were already twice that, a considerable stride towards the large port mill plants of the 1890s.

Harrison Carter with E. R. & F. Turner

James Harrison Carter had practical milling experience. Like Simon, he was a consultant and contractor, associated with both design and inventive activity. Both were principal agents of change, through their determination to act as advocates in lectures, correspondence, general debate, and publicity for new ideas. Though they were quite different characters, with contrasting backgrounds, together they had a persuasive influence on the progress of millers through stages of decision making. Carter had started a mill furnishing business about 1873, after responsibility as a miller in England and Ireland. He had reconstructed a mill near Brighton, and another at Aberdovey.[26] He styled himself as a milling engineer, although not formally trained as an engineer, but he had served an apprenticeship to a miller in Sussex and combined extensive knowledge of traditional milling practice with inventive ability. Carter's main activity as a milling expert lasted only from 1877 to 1888. He had premises in Mark Lane near the London Corn Exchange and the offices of *The Miller*. Mill furnishers with offices and showrooms in Mark Lane included G. P. Witt, W. R. Dell, Frederick Nell, Sanderson & Gillespie, Whitmore & Binyon and Brian Corcoran.

By May 1878, Carter's advertisements included an illustration of 'Carter's English chilled iron roller mill', and the assertion: 'Chilled iron roller mills only, are used in the great majority of Austrian and Hungarian mills, in preference to porcelain'. Some of the roller mills of that time were quaint in appearance; in a mere two years they were markedly improved. This certainly applied to Carter's machines. Years later he recalled: 'I exhibited at the Royal Agricultural Show, Bristol, 1878 the first iron roller mill for flour mills ever exhibited in this country'.[27] That was in July, and he had already shown it in Paris in June. With comment on the Paris exhibition, *The Miller* printed an illustration, in usual woodcut form, giving a 'general view of Mr Carter's

Figure 37.
J. Harrison Carter.
(1840–1906). (*The Miller*, May 1906)

novelty, the idea of which was inspired during his visit to Vienna and Buda-Pesth with a party of British and Irish millers in the autumn of last year'. Initially Harrison Carter combined his three-roller mill, to deal with middlings, with fluted rolls from Escher, Wyss & Co. for the first part of his system. When he addressed the National Association in December 1879, his contribution, at that very early stage of the spreading of new ideas, was lively, though he had to contend with one member of the audience who arrived late, and intended to be a disbeliever. Carter was able to talk at length about the use of millstones; in contrast he could refer to communication with Professor Kick.[28]

From 1880 Carter had a comprehensive system and from 1882 Turners also manufactured break rolls, which he was then able to use in place of Escher Wyss machines. By 1883 four-roller mills, which were later to become a general standard, were available from Turners and from 1883 or 1884 they were able

Figure 38. Carter's first roller mill of 1878. (*The Miller*, June 1878)

CARTER & TURNER'S
PATENT ROLLER MILLS
FLUTED AND SMOOTH.

DURABILITY.

EFFICIENCY.

HURT'S PATENT AUTOMATIC FEED

CARTER & TURNER'S PATENT
ROLLER MILL.

C. CLOSHEIM. FRANKFURT A. M.

Fitted with 2, 3 or 4 Rolls per Machine
ROLLERS VARYING IN SIZE
From 15 in. long by 8 in. diameter to 30 in. long by 16 in. diameter.

J. HARRISON CARTER, 82, Mark Lane, LONDON, E.C.
See Advertisements. Pages i. and ii. Wrapper.

to build complete sets of mill machinery for use in the Carter system.[29] In association with the Ipswich engineering firm of E. R. & F. Turner, Carter also took charge of marketing and the installation and commissioning of plant. Turners were his machine makers, and mechanical engineering design was carried out both by Turners and within Carter's own firm. Although patent 2626 of 1879 for the widely used three-roller mill was registered by E. R. Turner, F. Turner and Carter, it was stated by E. R. Turner that the machine had been invented by Carter.[30]

Carter's patents extended from his design of a disintegrator for crushing beans, nuts and cattle food, a feeding device for use with millstones, and a flour mixing machine of the 1870s, to design work on centrifugal dressing machines in 1890. In 1886 there were two patent applications relating to bicycles and tricycles, including a gear case: in French, the name for a cycle gear case became a 'carter'. In 1877 he used semolina and middlings purifiers designed by Carl Haggenmacher of Budapest, but, like other leading milling engineers and milling experts, he worked continually on the development of purifiers. In 1886 he took out a patent with G. F. Zimmer, a German engineer who acquired British citizenship. The collaborative design was concerned with sorting break stock, to allow separate treatment of various particle sizes. Zimmer became Carter's chief draughtsman and designer, and later chief milling draughtsman for Turners.[31] In the *Encyclopaedia Britannica* of 1910 the section on 'Flour and Flour Manufacture' was initialled G. F. Z. and was surely composed by Zimmer, who referred to Carter and commented favourably on Wegmann, but did not mention Henry Simon.

Carter's first major plant, installed in Dublin in 1880, was provided for Patrick Boland, a baker. The mill manager, John Mooney, who was to become President of NABIM in 1894, ordered a complete roller plant to replace 41 pairs of stones, out of a total of 63 pairs. There were six break stages, using Escher Wyss grooved, chilled iron roller mills. Middlings and semolina were reduced by nine Carter three-high smooth chilled iron roller mills and four Wegmann porcelain roller mills.[32] The project for Boland continued to be a fixed point of reference; in 1885 he advertised that 'J. Harrison Carter personally designed, erected, and started the first roller mill in the world which finished off all the products in one continuous operation'.[33] This claim was based on eliminating the manual handling of mill stock. In March 1881 he patented an automatic feeding device for use with roller mills or purifiers.[34] In the Dublin plant, stock hoppers or bins had been used over the rolls, but in plants at Glasgow and Salford they were said to have been eliminated. However, material must have been passed through a small hopper leading to the automatic feed regulator.

Carter was proud of work done at Salford, where Frederick Moss had bought the West Gore Street Mills about 1876, with six pairs of millstones, purifiers, and rollers for the treatment of middlings. Members of the family firm visited Budapest and America, and decided to adopt Carter's 'controllable automatic system'. The change-over was at the beginning of 1882, prior to which Moss had been working 15 pairs of stones. Carter wrote to Moss: 'Your plant was undoubtedly the first successful automatic roller plant in England'.[35] Claims for

Figure 39.
Carter and Turners'
roller mill of 1883.
(*The Miller*, March
1883)

firsts were controversial in the absence of full general arrangement drawings and specific detail drawings. Between 1879 and 1882 roller mills were purchased from Carter by Spiller & Co. of Cardiff, followed in 1883 by an order for break roller mills capable of producing over 3,000 sacks of flour per week. Prestige could be enhanced by association: Carter reported that his system 'was, during 1884, erected for and ordered by six members of the Council of the National Association', and also 'was ordered by and erected for five members of the Vienna party'.

Carter's main achievements were during the general surge of activity of 1883 to 1885. In June 1885 he published a list of thirty-three complete roller plants that had been started or ordered since June 1884.[36] These included installations for Arthur McDougall at City Mills, Manchester, Davidsons at Phoenix Mills, Newcastle-on-Tyne, and John Greenwood at Blackburn. Of twenty-six plants in England, five were for mills in or near Liverpool. There was a range of capacity from 300 to 6,000 sacks per week. From this and information about particular mills it is clear that Carter was supplying large plants. In December 1884 he personally started the new plant for Arthur McDougall at Manchester. Immediately after the start, erection of another was begun, to increase the capacity to between 30 and 40 sacks per hour. The Davidson order was placed in December 1884 for a similar capacity, with seven break stages.[37]

The installations at Newcastle and Blackburn were considered by Carter's employees to be two of his most noteworthy projects. The firm of John

Figure 40.
Flow sheet of Carter's system: increasing complexity.
(*The Engineer*, November 1887)

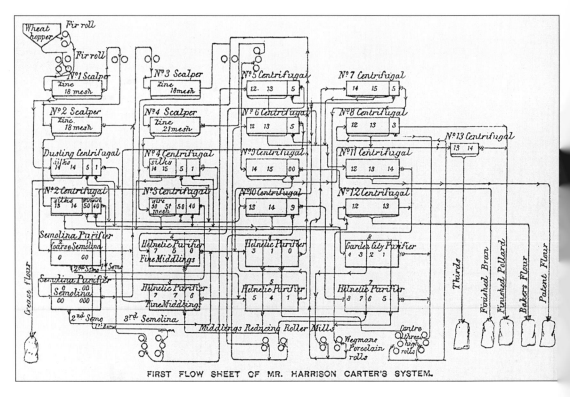

FIRST FLOW SHEET OF MR. HARRISON CARTER'S SYSTEM.

Greenwood & Sons had mills at Blackburn and Burnley and was said to have had 100 pairs of stones. Greenwoods investigated new methods for ten years before adopting Carter's system. Gilbert Little, who had been employed in a managerial position by Carter, contributed a series of articles to *The Engineer* in 1887 and 1888 on 'Roller milling – it's birth and development' in which he described Greenwood's efforts. From 1872 to 1882 they experimented with high grinding, mainly with millstones, but gradually trying rolls. They bought purifiers in 1874 from A. B. Childs and in 1876 from Walworth & Co. at Bradford. In 1878 Wegmann rolls were tried. G. T. Smith's purifiers were introduced in 1880, followed by experiments with Gray rolls and Simon fluted rolls. They then decided to install roller plant at Burnley.[38] *The Miller* recorded that during 1883 they progressed from a first trial to a 20 sack plant at Junction Mills, followed by a 14 sack plant at Pillingfield Mills. In 1884 the Carter system was installed at Blackburn, to give 30 sacks of flour. In 1889 Greenwoods were said to have about 100 sacks per hour capacity at Blackburn and Burnley combined, all on the Carter system.[39]

As an advocate for the new methods Carter was as active as Simon. Both wrote to *The Miller* on points of technical controversy. Carter gave papers to NABIM, to milling operatives and to other societies, and was on the committee

Figure 41.
Woodcut of Turners'
fitting shop. (*The
Miller*, June 1885)

Figure 42.
Carter's last project: at
Cardiff for James
Tucker. (*The Miller*,
April 1892)

that organised the exhibition at Islington in 1881. His claims point to success and to vulnerability; the status of first with an automatic plant became the subject of contention. In *The Engineer*, in 1887, it was stated that J. A. A. Buchholz had 'designed the first automatic roller plant in the world, and carried out his invention with perfect success at the mills of Messrs Barlow and Sons, of Bilston, in 1878'. Carter objected and drew the more restrained Buchholz into an argument that had previously been aired in the *Corn Trade Journal*. Buchholz replied that 'to all intents and purposes', Mr H. Simon had anticipated Carter.[40] Buchholz's Bilston installation and Carter's Dublin project were experimental steps and soon surpassed by other designs and machinery. The Carter automatic feed patent of 1881, for a device to smooth the flow of material to roller mills or other machines, was an important feature, but several alternative devices were soon available and in 1882 Carter was advertising that he had abandoned his design, in favour of Hurt & Strathern's patent automatic feed, which he frankly stated he considered simpler and superior to his own version.

All the machinery used in the new systems required constant development effort; Gilbert Little stated in 1887 that there was 'a great change in the design of milling machinery ... from the more general introduction of the granulating rolls in 1882'. That coincided with the extension of Turners' range of manufacture and with the entry of Robinsons of Rochdale. Turners' extended capability enabled Carter to claim that he had the first all-English milling system, but in 1887 Gilbert Little stated that the Carter system was not being developed. In *The Engineer*, Little asserted that

> The Carter system has been among the most successful, and taking numbers of mills equipped as the indication of popularity, it ranks next to the Simon, though it is only fair to Messrs Thomas Robinson & Sons, Rochdale to mention that while they were late in entering the field, they have secured a very large share of the more recent orders, and are now next to the first in the race.[41]

In 1888 Carter retired from his business of full-time consultant and contractor. In the same year Simon had tried to introduce the Haggenmacher plansifter, the forerunner of new forms of gyratory sieve for flour dressing, that eventually displaced other types of sieving machine and W. T. Bates (1908) suggested that these two events of 1888 were connected; it appeared that Carter believed that he could not compete with such an advance. At that time, the development of the plansifter failed, so that it could have been nothing more than a bogey, as Bates called it.[42] Carter had contributed to all the stages of introduction, establishment and diffusion of the new methods, and the expertise that could be transferred was then used within Turners' engineering firm, which acquired his stock and interest and continued as one of the leading firms of milling engineers.

Harrison Carter apparently regretted his early departure and tried to resume as a consultant; perhaps he lost confidence during the temporary depression of 1887. In 1891 he read a paper at the Society of Arts in 1891, and exhibited plans of a large mill for Messrs James Tucker Ltd of Cardiff. The audience included representatives of the three leading milling engineers, Simon, Robinsons, and Turners, and from Whitmore & Binyon who secured the contract for the 50 sacks per hour plant at Cardiff.[43] *The Miller* commented that 'It is beyond question that a distinct charm has been imparted to this dissertation on 'Modern Flour Milling' by the fact that its author has had a large share in shaping the milling history of these times'. In 1894 Carter announced that he was erecting entirely new buildings and plant for the manufacture of flour mill machinery. He advertised that 'From the first I personally made out the flow sheet for every new plant, and started nearly all of them, and shall hope to do the same in the future'.[44] He reminded readers of *The Miller* of his previous claims to fame, but his health deteriorated and although he lived until 1906 his achievements were mainly concentrated in the earlier period of the establishment of roller milling.[45] Meanwhile E. R. & F. Turner stated that there was continually increasing demand for 'The best four-roller mill in the world'. Its outward appearance during the early 1890s was still a reminder of the Turner-Carter collaboration.

Thomas Robinson & Son Ltd

Thomas Robinson started in business with a sawmill at Rochdale about 1840. His son, John, developed a particular interest in the manufacture of woodworking machinery, and in 1854 larger premises were needed; the site was near the railway station, so the address became the Railway Works. John Robinson died in 1877. His eldest son, James Salkeld, became head of the firm, the directorate including his brothers Thomas Nield, Charles and Arthur. In 1880 Thomas Robinson & Sons became a private limited liability company. J. Salkeld Robinson died in 1892, aged forty-three years. A new limited company was

ROBINSON'S ROLLER SYSTEM.

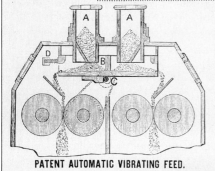

PATENT AUTOMATIC VIBRATING FEED.

The following are some of the advantages of this Feed:

I.—It is the most Automatic Feed yet introduced.—When the flow of material into the hopper increases, it presses down with greater weight on the vibrating sieve, which, in turn, gradually increases the flow on to Rolls.

II.—It Feeds equally well on both wheat and middlings.

III.—Its Simplicity.—Its whole construction is so simple that it cannot possibly get out of order.

IV.—It never requires adjusting.—When once started the miller never needs look at it again.

V.—IT CAN BE FITTED TO ALMOST ANY KIND OF ROLLER MILL OR PURIFIER.

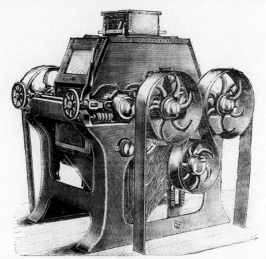

DOUBLE HORIZONTAL ROLLER MILL, WITH PATENT AUTOMATIC VIBRATING FEED.

GRINDING & RE-FLUTING ROLLS.

We have recently put down a complete Plant of most modern construction and we are, therefore, prepared to Grind and Re-flute Rolls of any dimensions.

THOMAS ROBINSON & SON,
ROCHDALE. LIMITED

Figure 43.
Robinsons' four-roller mill of 1886. (*The Miller*, October 1886)

Figure 44.
Robinsons' early purifier. (*The Miller*, February 1886)

108

ROBINSON'S ROLLER SYSTEM.

IMPORTANT TO SMALL MILLERS.

Howarth's PATENT Concentrated Roller Mill

CAN BE SEEN AT WORK ON APPLICATION.

PURIFIERS.

Having Purchased the "ŒXLE" Patent Purifier and Travelling Cloth Dust Collector Combined, No. 1,024, 10th March, 1881; also obtained Sole use of the "HOLGATE" Purifier, we have combined the leading features of both, which we call

THE "X L" PURIFIER.

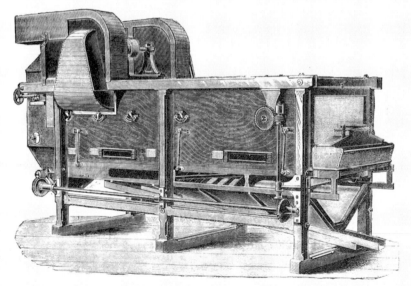

NO STIVE ROOM.

NO TRUNKING.

THE CHEAPEST AND BEST PURIFIER IN THE MARKET.

THOMAS ROBINSON & SON,
LIMITED.

WORKS: ROCHDALE. ‖ 2, Victoria Mansions, Westminster, London, S.W.

formed, with T. N. Robinson, a professional mechanical engineer, as chairman.[46]
In 1962, D. W. Povey, a director of the company, explained the move into
flour mill engineering: 'In 1882, a consignment of milling machinery arrived
in this country in a badly broken condition and Robinsons were asked to repair
this. Seeing in this new field an ideal oppportunity for further expansion, the
company took comprehensive steps to enter the market'. Povey referred to their

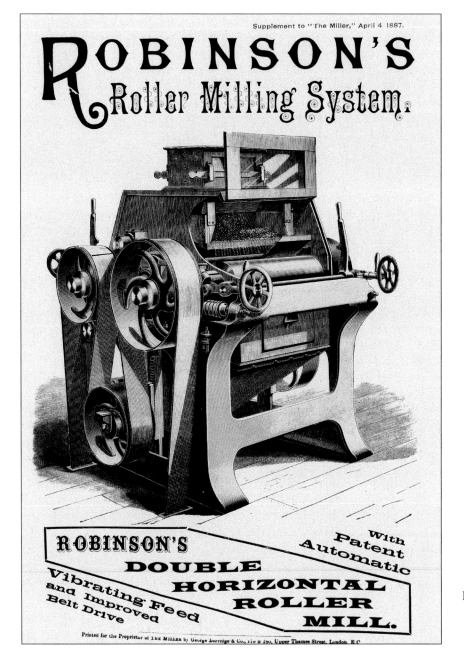

Figure 45.
Robinsons' improved
roller mill of 1887.
(*The Miller*, April
1887)

advantages: 'There were, for example, existing pattern shops and foundries, fully equipped fitting and erection shops were available and there was the further advantage that they could equip themselves with woodworking machinery of the very latest design, at a lower cost than any competitor'.[47]

In February 1883 *The Miller* had a whole page advertisement devised by Frederic Nell on behalf of a collaboration, within which Nell would supposedly be the milling expert and London agent, already used to London-based commerce. Nell was a mill furnisher, noticeable mainly as an agent for several American machines. He stated that he had concluded arrangements with Robinsons, 'a sure guarantee for first-class English manufacture, whereby this company is now preparing to enter into complete contracts for erecting, from first to last (including engines, boilers &c.), complete roller mill plants on the gradual reduction system, at most reasonable prices'. Nell referred to 'non-cutting rolls or any other design purchasers may prefer', but the non-cutting alternative was emphasised, a relic of his experience with American Stevens machinery. The rolls could be 'smooth or corrugated'. At that stage the advertisement heading was 'Nell's non-cutting roller mill system'. In August the label became merely 'Gradual reduction system', and another roller mill design was available. Whereas the previous design had two pairs of rolls in a horizontal plane, 'Nell's double height roller mill' had smooth rolls arranged as vertical pairs. The Robinson-Nell display at the York RASE show included the Excelsior middlings purifier, a Huntley, Holcomb & Heine design from America that Nell had used previously.

The journal provided a description and illustration of the Rochdale works.[48] This was perhaps an early hint of changing attitudes within the collaboration, Robinsons increasing their perceivable presence. A journal page in April 1884 was distinctly divided into two parts. Under a bold heading 'Roller milling' there was a simple illustration of a new first-break machine, but below it was another possibly Nell-type protest: 'Notice. Millers! Take warning! In this business, as in most others, there are not wanting, unfortunately, 'Jerry Builders', who pretend to do a great deal for a very little, who in order to obtain a back-door start, invariably put in too little machinery'. It appears that Robinsons, rather than Nell, were seriously studying the problems of the break process, but an early choice of design would soon have to be discarded. *The Miller* published concise descriptions of new machines as they entered the market, and in May Robinsons' first break machine was introduced:

> it is necessary that while breaking the wheat the first break rolls make in the operation the smallest minimum of flour ... [the machine has] three horizontal rolls, the middle one of which is stationary, and is provided with two smooth and two corrugated surfaces. The two outside rolls, which work against the centre roll, are grooved with half-inch corrugations, and the middle roll can be adjusted so as to allow its smooth or corrugated face to be worked against the revolving rollers.

The stationary middle roll was a curious notion from Oexle; Robinsons bought manufacturing rights and persevered for possibly two years, also temporarily

Figure 46. Robinsons' fitting shop, illustrated in 1903. (*The Miller*, February 1903)

trying other Oexle ideas. Simon had tried smooth rolls on a 'cracking process' at the start of the break operation to 'open out [the individual grains] at the crease, thus letting the dirt which lodges there and on the surface fall away'. Voller (1889) rejected the idea that wheat grain could be split accurately along the crease, and wrote that 'Concerning the crease dirt theory, it appears to have been propounded and accepted on very slender premises'. Voller commented: 'In the early days of the gradual reduction system no part thereof excited greater curiosity than the first break. Milling experts and millers alike appeared to attach much importance to every circumstance which could be connected with it'.[49]

From June 1884 advertisements showed that Robinsons were becoming prominent, and Nell's contribution was ill-defined. There was also the statement 'We can fully equip a full roller mill with our own machinery throughout'. The review of the RASE show, held at Shrewsbury in the July, dealt with Robinsons' exhibit without mentioning Nell. They showed a new patent double purifier. There was a terse reference to 'Case patent', which presumably meant the American Case Manufacturing Co. Nell was offering the Excelsior machine on his own account. Robinsons were working on their own designs, making three relevant patent applications in June 1884, all in the name of Thomas Nield

Robinson; they were part of on-going effort as they moved away from Nell's piecemeal collections of machinery.[50]

In October 1884 Nell stated that 'In order to guarantee despatch in the execution of contracts, and to insure the highest class of machinery, I have placed the building of my various machines in the hands of Messrs Robey & Co., Lincoln'. Robinsons merely reported 'Messrs Thomas Robinson & Son Ltd beg to say that Mr Frederic Nell has ceased to be connected in any way with their firm'. They were soon able to report that they had 'Complete plants now in operation from 3 to 30 sacks per hour, which can be seen by appointment'. In March 1885 they published a list of 'recently erected complete plants' for eleven firms, including the Rochdale District Cooperative Corn Mill Society and the Halifax Flour Mill Society. From December 1884 Robinsons' advertisements prominently displayed their own double horizontal roller mill, far superior in appearance to Nell's archaic-looking machine.

After Nell's departure, Robinsons made fuller use of their expertise in workshop practice and progressed under the leadership of T. N., C. J. and A. M. Robinson. It is not clear when Robinsons overtook Harrison Carter. Around 1885, at the time of Carter's most impressive projects, Robinsons were still newcomers. Although Robinsons were making progress, they were not obviously carrying out massive projects in 1886 and 1887. They were active in a market where numerous medium and smaller projects were shared amongst many firms, including Higginbottom & Stuart of Liverpool; Hind & Lund at Preston; Hopkinson at Retford; Houghton at Grimsby; Munden, Armfield of Ringwood in Hampshire; and Whitmore & Binyon at Wickham Market in Suffolk. Robinsons' first highly publicised major project was for the CWS at Dunston-on-Tyne in 1891.

Introspection and renewed confidence

In July 1887, *The Miller* gave full coverage to the report of the special committee of the National Association 'appointed to investigate the present depression in the milling trade'. It was the most detailed appraisal that was published on the innovative sector of the industry. When Wilson Marriage presented the report at the London convention, he stated that very few millers had supplied information in response to questions sent to them, but the committee acknowledged the aid of J. H. Chatterton, 'in whose office a good deal of valuable and authentic information has been recorded from time to time'. In addition to assessments of national roller mill capacity, and general statistics of the industry, the report provided data of import duties levied on wheat and flour by other countries. The Census of Population figures were quoted for 1851 to 1881, showing rising population and smaller numbers of millers, with the comment:

> They are only to be taken as indicating the ratio of decrease in the number of persons who, at the several enumerations, described themselves as "millers of corn" in the census returns, and not, by any means, as a statement of the total number of men employed in mills. Labourers, carters, engine drivers,

stokers, millwrights, fitters, clerks, travellers, &c. would be entered separately under their various occupations, although all such are employed on, and necessary to, the staff of a big corn mill.

As a statistical analysis of the industry, the big step forward in the report was a tabulated 'return of complete roller process mills in the United Kingdom, made up to 1st May, 1887'. It gave the aggregate capacity of 461 mills, of which 419 were classified by size.

			Numbers of roller process mills (Source: NABIM, 1887) [51]			
Capacity sacks per hour	Numbers of mills	Total sacks per hour	Capacity sacks per hour	Numbers of mills	Total sacks per hour
1	7	7	15	9	135
2	31	62	16	4	64
3	54	162	18	1	18
4	51	204	19	1	19
5	40	200	20	15	300
6	37	222	24	3	72
7	21	147	25	3	75
8	49	392	30	6	180
9	5	45	40	2	80
10	45	450	45	3	135
12	25	300	70	1	70
13	1	13	90	1	90
14	4	56			
Totals of the tabulated data				419	3,498
Mills of unknown individual capacity				42	312
Totals				461	3,810

The report stated that the total capacity of about 3,800 sacks per hour was

> irrespective of the amount [of money] expended by millers in partially adapting millstone mills by adding rolls and purifiers, and for the improved wheat cleaning apparatus which has been added to nearly every mill in the country, whether on the old or new system.

There was an analysis by county of the 461 mills, but not giving names or exact locations, presumably to preserve confidentiality. In the table of capacities, the largest estimates were one mill of 90 sacks per hour, and one of 70 sacks per hour, followed by five other large mills clearly exceeding 30 sacks per hour. Candidates for the largest would have been Seth Taylor of London, the North Shore Co. at Liverpool, and Hughes at Belfast. Taylor had two main mill sites. The North Shore Co. had three main buildings, but all at the Boundary Street site. Many millers would have been able to judge which mills were included in their own areas, and at least some of the largest mills could have been identified by attentive readers of the journals. Overall, the average capacity was a little more than 8 sacks per hour, but total capacity was impressive; 3,810 sacks per hour was equivalent to a possible production of 480,060 sacks per week, by working an 126-hour week (6 a.m. Monday to noon Saturday), or enough to supply 5 lb of flour per week to nearly 27 million people.[52]

Large mills often worked continuously. Simon had referred to millers having millstone plant 'at work day and night' and he regularly implied that his new roller mill installations could be expected to be run continuously. John Ure's Crown Mills at Glasgow were run 'steadily day and night' throughout the early 1880s; this included several years using roller mills, and also the previous millstone plant. Seth Taylor's Waterloo Mills in London 'had been running very satisfactorily, and almost constantly, day and night' in the mid 1880s. In 1884, Frederick Moss at Salford, with his new automatic plant of more modest capacity, installed the previous year by Harrison Carter, stated that the mill had been working on a 144 hour week. In the summer of 1887 Simmonds & Morton were running their Stevens roller plant at the Westminster Bridge Mills on a 144 hour week: 'We run most weeks from 12 p.m. Sunday night to 12 p.m. on Saturday night without stoppage of any kind, even for oiling'.

The large numbers of fifty-five mills in Lancashire and ninety-six in Yorkshire were particularly striking. There were fourteen in Cheshire and twenty in Durham. Otherwise, there was widespread geographical distribution; only Staffordshire and Gloucestershire had more than ten mills in the list. Middlesex had only four. Surprisingly, Cornwall was credited with eight mills and Cumberland with seven; presumably they were mainly small. If the tabulated entries of 419 mills in the original table are grouped into a small number of categories, it is easier to see a pattern of size variation. The forty-two mills of unknown individual capacity grouped together at the end of the original table, with an average capacity of about 7.4 sacks per hour, would presumably increase the numbers in the three lower capacity groups, but it seems likely that the simple pattern of the five groups would not be greatly disturbed. (For the data in the Census of Production of 1907 there are similar problems.) The thirty-four largest mills possessed 26 per cent of the total capacity.

Capacity sacks per hour	Numbers of mills	% of total capacity of 461 mills	cumulative % of total capacity
1–4	143	11.4	11.4
5–8	147	25.2	36.6
9–12	75	20.9	57.5
13–20	35	15.9	73.4
24–90	19	18.4	91.8
others	42	8.2	100.0

The supposed depression of 1886–87 had followed a period of unprecedented innovative activity. The committee's conclusion was that the depression arose 'not from any want of skill or enterprise, or lack of suitable machinery, but from the action of external causes, which, it is hoped, would not be permanent'.[53] Fortunately, or through the advantages of technical progress, the trough was soon succeeded by distinct improvement and the journal appraisal of 1888 confirmed that the depression had been temporary. The pressure of external competition eased. In August 1889 the National Association held their annual convention in Paris, possibly a sign that better times were possible. The eleventh annual report of the Council described the new state of the industry:

> The altering conditions of the trade were pretty fully reported on to the Convention in 1887, when it appeared there were to that date 460 complete roller process mills in the United Kingdom. This number has now [1889] been increased to about 540, and not only has there been a great change in the system of manufacture, but the milling trade of the country has quickly gravitated to the towns situated either near the sea coast or on the banks of navigable rivers, where foreign grain, which is now the main source of food supply, can be obtained without the expense of transhipment or conveyance by railways.[54]

The continuing record of Henry Simon's work demonstrated the strength of the second main phase of diffusion of roller milling, and the increasing relevance of mills at the main port areas. In ten years he had done more than anyone else in Britain to establish the new branch of mechanical engineering. His paper to the Institution in 1889 showed that he had not only identified the scope for industrial innovation, but also the professional expertise required: 'The principle of progress now recognised in milling is indeed the same as in other establishments or manufactories ... namely, increased elaboration and more scientific treatment ... This change has called forth an entirely new class of milling engineers'.[55] With his catalogue of 1892, in which Simon published his paper 'The present position of roller flour milling', he reported the increasing number of mills erected on the Simon Roller System:

Year	1886	1887	1888	1889	1890	1891
Total	160	184	231	294	344	380

By June 1892 the total was '394 Simon Roller-mill Plants in the United Kingdom, the British Colonies, India, and other countries'. There were not many installations outside the United Kingdom up to 1886. In January 1893 Simon reported that 'The Simon system is equally well adapted for the smallest [one sack per hour] and the largest [fifty sacks per hour] installations', and that 'the total number of roller plants on this system now considerably exceeds 400'.[56] He provided the eleventh edition of his map of the United Kingdom as a journal supplement, showing that installations included much more than the basic processing machinery. In addition to the representation of roller plant erected or in course of erection in 1892, work prior to 1892, and extensions, the map also showed instances of grain cleaning, washing and drying plant, and grain silo storage installations. There was also reference to work overseas: 'Over 70 Simon plants have been erected in Australia, New Zealand, India, S. Africa, S. America, Japan, New Caledonia, Portugal & Germany'. The largest overseas project was probably a large mill built and equipped at Rio de Janeiro in 1888, with a capacity of 60 sacks per hour, which was described in the paper to the Institution of Mechanical Engineers in 1889. Simon repeatedly referred to projects at the ports. The issue of his circular, coinciding with the NABIM convention at Liverpool in June 1893, included information about main centres of concentration, apart from the Bristol Channel area.

> The total capacity of roller flour mills working in Liverpool alone is estimated at 310 sacks of flour per hour, or about 44,000 sacks per week. Of these, over 33,000 sacks (more than three-quarters of the whole) are manufactured by mills working with my machinery thus leaving only 75 sacks per hour to be made by mills on other systems. It is a remarkable coincidence that the capacity of roller plants working on my system in London and Liverpool exactly corresponds, namely, 235 sacks of flour per hour in each city. Almost the whole of the flour manufactured in Glasgow, Hull, and York is made by roller plants erected by me and on my system.[57]

In comparison with the records of Simon's work, which include copious statistical data, the chronicle for other milling engineers, even for Robinsons and Turners, is fragmentary. During the 1890s there were occasional brief statements. Salkeld Robinson's obituary of 1892 gave a little indication of progress of the Rochdale firm. 'Many of the flour-producing societies of Lancashire and the northern counties have installed the Robinson system, the most noteworthy example being the great Cooperative mill at Dunston on Tyne, which was fitted with a plant of 40 sacks capacity per hour'. Robinsons reported in 1897 that 'During the last fourteen years we have erected 394 complete new roller flour mill plants and during the same period we have re-modelled to our system 127 existing roller mill plants, making a grand total of 521 plants working on the Robinson roller system. The total weekly capacity of these plants is 285,000 sacks or fifteen million sacks of flour per year'.[58] In contrast, Simon claimed his plant provision had reached that aggregate during 1887–88. He had five years start on Robinsons, but had probably extended the lead, by equipping very large mills.

In January 1895 Simon published a chart showing the growth in annual capacity of mills on his system from 1878 to 1894, when the total exceeded 32 million sacks of flour.[59]

Growth in capacity of roller flour mills erected on Henry Simon's system from 1878 to 1894			
Year	Cumulative totals		Yearly increase
	sacks per annum	sacks per hour	sacks per hour
1878	26,208	3	3
1879	174,720	20	17
1880	428,064	49	29
1881	917,280	105	56
1882	1,886,976	216	111
1883	4,114,656	471	255
1884	8,159,424	934	463
1885	11,356,800	1,300	366
1886	12,457,536	1,426	126
1887	14,230,944	1,629	203
1888	17,594,304	2,014	385

1889	21,997,248	2,518	504
1890	24,775,296	2,836	318
1891	25,876,032	2,962	126
1892	28,540,512	3,267	305
1893	30,838,080	3,530	263
1894	32,200,000	3,685	155

All the quantities, except the last, were exactly divisible by 8,736, the product of 364 (days) × 24 (hours), therefore the data represented absolutely full-time working, except for Christmas Day! Hourly capacity would have been simpler to use and obviously formed the basic data, whereas output in millions of sacks was of limited practical value even though it looked impressive. Some of the early capacity included would have been replaced by 1895, and the data probably included overseas work. There is clear evidence of the busy period from 1883 to 1885, the slacker years 1886 and 1887, and the much increased activity from 1888 to 1893, representing two surges of innovative activity in the UK. The chart may have been published only once, and then quite without comment. It seems to have been a unique statistical item, showing his remarkable effort.

CHAPTER SEVEN

Resistance to change

Resistance to change in relation to innovation in milling was evident in several much publicised episodes: the start of a wholemeal versus white flour argument, which was emphasised by the Bread Reform League; the 'Rollers versus Stones' controversy; and The Germ Milling Case. The third was not originally a form of resistance, but probably persuaded some millers to be cautious about innovatory change. The controversy that was destined to last was wholemeal versus white flour.

The Bread Reform League

From the autumn of 1880, Miss M. Yates, a member of the Ladies Sanitary Association, and Hon. Sec. of the Bread Reform League, led a campaign against white bread and for the promotion of what she called 'finely ground meal, containing all the nourishment of wheat'. *The Miller* discussed philanthropy, nutrition, digestion, demand, and the inferiority of London bread. Miss Yates recommended a Dr Campbell Morfit's process, which could produce the recommended wheat-meal only on a relatively small scale. The journal wondered what exactly was produced from which the 'reformed bread' could be made: 'So far as we are aware no really effective method of decortication is yet in existence, nor, considering the physical configuration of a grain of wheat, is such a method likely to be forthcoming'. Miss Yates used seemingly scientific language, and bold images in a letter to *The Miller*:

> We are not however taking a mere chemical analysis as all-sufficient to establish our point; for a long personal experience amongst Egyptian fellaheen and Sicilian peasants, who scarcely ever touch meat, has convinced me ... that wheat meal bread is much more sustaining than white bread, and that a much larger amount of work can be done on it than on white bread'.[1]

Much of the campaign was on behalf of the children of the poor in London. The League based their campaign on assertions by Professor Church and others that white bread was deficient in food value. But although Miss Yates paraded authorities and percentages of chemical components, there were flaws in the assumptions. Analysis of raw materials was not enough. Meetings were held in London, notably at the Mansion House, in December 1880, when the Lord Mayor presided and at least nine London millers attended. The Lord Mayor closed the meeting with a statement 'Miss Yates has no commercial aims; what she is doing is for the good of the country'. Mr S. Morley MP had contributed the only caution: 'It might be a matter of controversy how far the statements which had been made were true – if they were not true they ought to be controverted. If true, however, there would be a revolution in connection with our food supply'. Unfortunately he then became vaguer. The report said 'He had been reminded that there was the same difference between white bread and this real brown bread as there was between real and mock turtle'. Then Mr Morley fell off the fence:

> As a citizen of London, and as one who was deeply anxious to promote the adoption of plans for the well-being of the people, he was desirous of becoming a member of the League, and he advised others to do the same ... He quite believed that the bread which hitherto had been most admired for its whiteness was mischievous and full of dangers, and that they should avoid it, and get the honest article.[2]

The Rev. Professor G. Henslow read a letter from Dr Morfit, not an ideal witness for his own process. 'Of 50 samples of bread from as many different bakers, and said to be made by my process, which have recently come under my notice, no two are alike. No one realised the character of the real article, and some were beneath consideration.' Professor Henslow described the process: 'A grain of wheat was really a seed invested with a husk like a pea-pod containing but one pea and closely fitting it. In the decorticating or, as the word signifies, bark-removing process, the outermost layer, or epidermis, was removed'. He then said that wood fibre was eliminated and 'By Dr Morfit's process, the denuded grain was ground in a steel mill, something like a coffee mill, so that the grain was broken into minute fragments of a granular form'. The journal described the meeting as 'a conference at which there was no conferring'.[3]

CONFRONTING THE LOBBY
Opposition to the League's position was provided in lectures by Charles Graham of University College, London, and William Jago. Both maintained that much supposedly nutritive content of the bran layers of wheat was inaccessible to the human digestive system. Their general conclusion and advice to millers was to remove the bran and the germ, which was also detrimental to the keeping quality of flour. In the Cantor Lectures to the Society of Arts at the end of 1879, Graham had criticised average bread, presumably London bread, and suggested that its inferiority was due to lack of skill in milling and baking. From then until the mid 1880s, he continued to urge millers to eliminate the bran, and Jago was equally clear on the point.

A total refutation of the Bread Reform League's case was provided by Professor Graham, in a long and technically detailed article in *The Miller* in February 1881. He referred to 'the so-called conference at the Mansion House', to which he had not been invited, and his general conclusions included statements that:

> The speakers at the Bread Reform Conference made use of *chemical analysis* to show that the world is utterly wong in preferring white bread to brown bread, or *whole-meal* bread ... we must eat bran or be guilty of sinful waste and crass ignorance of what they are pleased to call science. But why listen

to likes and dislikes at all, and not urge upon all the necessity of eating grass, hay, oats, straw, and any other vegetable substance that chemical analysis indicates to be valuable, and that *good economy* shows to be cheap.[4]

Miss Yates and her supporters were apparently only cursory readers of the milling press which nevertheless she used for exhortations. In August 1881, there was a report of the Bread Reform League's conversazione at the Kensington Hall. Miss Yates found a new theme in her paper called 'The Bread of the Olden Days': 'An old English revival has now set in, and we are surrounded by mediaeval architecture, antique furniture, and brown and yellow coloured lace and drapery. Let us carry the movement a step further and bring into fashion good old English Brown Bread'. *The Miller* commented 'the craze for the mediaeval which has taken possession of a section of society has not yet penetrated far below the surface. We have not heard of ladies discarding their grand Erards and Broadwoods and adopting in their stead early English harpsichords and spinnets'.[5] But the League continued with its mission. They issued leaflets at their meetings, listing the names of patronesses with titles. Henry Simon protested in the journal in March 1882:

> I have, no doubt along with others, again been favoured with a set of circulars from the Bread Reform League, and I really think that it is time to draw public attention to the manner in which these enthusiasts are pushing their hobby ... I should really like to know whether the 24 duchesses, marchionesses, and ladies whose names head the prospectus of the League, along, it is true, with a number of medical and purely scientific men, have each of them, before granting the use of their names, taken any serious trouble to ascertain whether the assertions made in their name are well founded.

The aspiring reformers of the Bread Reform League lacked a sense of numeracy. There was a failure to see the contrast between scales of production of even modest milling businesses and the kitchen scale of operation of the Morfit process. Percentages of chemical components were used, often inappropriately; Dr Graham had protested that it was 'not science, but its pretentious caricature'. Miss Yates possessed only a sketchy idea of the strengths and activities of the labouring poor she reckoned to help. Although millers' delivery men and bakers' labourers could move sacks weighing two and a half hundredweights, Miss Yates imagined a man could carry between 400 and 500 pounds, despite her own claim that labourers were not able to work effectively due to inadequate nourishment. *The Miller*'s literary staff spotted the effect of fantasy, but did not give detailed rebuttals, preferring gentle mockery of the League: 'Strong asssertions have the same effect upon the popular imagination [as that] which that blessed word Mesopotamia had upon Dean Ramsey's old Scotch woman, who enjoyed her sermons in proportion as they transcended her comprehension'.[6] By 1883, the scope for the League was disappearing, with two years of post-Islington reassessment of the state of the industry and general innovative activity. In 1884 Frederick Moss, the Salford miller, gave a direct, business-like view: 'Gentlemen say that roller-mill flour is not so good as stone flour, and that it is not so nutritious. We do not care a straw about that. So long as our customers come to us and say 'Give us white flour', we are not going to give them flour which they do not want'.[7]

In 1884 and 1885 W. T. Bates provided lengthy and humorous commentaries on the subject in the correspondence columns. Bates, who had started work at the age of ten, became a successful mill manager and mayor of Nuneaton.[8] He came to prominence as a regular correspondent to *The Miller* during the Bread Reform League and the Rollers versus Stones controversies and was probably the most frequent contributor to the journals, regularly producing long articles for *The Miller* and latterly also leaders and copy for *Milling*. Bates wrote in April 1884, wondering whether the League was 'defunct or dormant', and criticising London bread:

> There are reasons why we eat this – we can get no other. A greater error was never foisted on the British public than that Londoners prefer dark or 'wholesome' bread ... As an atom in this great conglomerate, I protest against the assertion that Londoners prefer it – they have never been consulted in the matter ... I should like to see bread made in London – and I hope before long I shall see it – which can be eaten without the aid of Whitechapel or Thames mud, butter, and turnips and treacle jam – pure bread, that need not be taken with eyes shut, as medicine.

Bates compared London bread adversely with that of 'Dublin, Belfast, Liverpool, Glasgow, and nearly every other large town in the kingdom, excepting, perhaps, Birmingham'. Simon installed plants for Seth Taylor in London in 1884 and 1885, so at the time of Bates' protests a solution was available. Not only the big mills in London had been changing over completely to roller milling but also others whose owners had previously been cautious, such as Mead at Chelsea, French at Bow, and Kidd & Podger at Isleworth. Whether Bates actually thought the League was defunct, or was craftily casting a fly, is hard to tell, but the League still existed. In September 1884 it was organising an exhibition in London 'to promote the production of finely-ground cereal foods, and to provide wheat meal breakfasts and meat dinners, at cost price, for poor children at Board Schools during the winter months', and on a turquoise coloured leaflet the League advertised that they had twenty-five patronesses, who were either duchesses or had other titles. Bates signalled the end of significant controversy in April 1885, again to the editor of *The Miller*. Prompted by the fact that the League was organising a Dietetic Exhibition to be held at South Kensington during the spring, he declared that 'to return to the clumsy method of our forefathers is retrogressive. They were far in advance of their ancestors, striving by all means to reach the perfection we now attain. They did not make dark flour because they preferred it, but because they could make no better'. Bates attacked the most basic point:

> The value of any food lies not so much in its original properties as in its assimilation in the body. We know perfectly well that unless food is properly digested it does no good, and the experiments of Reubner and Mege-Mouries

have proved conclusively that the largest part of bran flour or whole meal passes through the body undigested, unassimilated. If we must eat the husk or shell or covering of our grain, why not go a little further and eat nut-shells, egg-shells, crab, and lobster-shells, or even the tiny shrimp-shell?

The posturing of the Bread Reform League could take place only when knowledge of cereal chemistry was at a restricted stage of insight. Although Professor Graham and others were making progress, the millers had not yet been provided with a helpful literature. Deeper insight and discussion depended on the slowly increasing scientific understanding of the composition and properties of wheat and flour, the chemistry of nutrition and the physiology of digestion. Even flour colour could not be assessed simply: superfine flour and Hungarian flour implied whiteness and freedom from bran specks, but 'white flour' and 'pure flour' were arbitrary descriptions. Flour that had a golden bloom was sometimes regarded as the best. In ordinary language, the only sound prescription was for 'whiter flour' and avoidance of the London 'greys'. The next energetic campaign against white bread was not until 1911.

The 'rollers versus stones' controversy

At the first annual meeting of the National Association in June 1879, Sanderson, Nagel & Kaemp's representative in Britain, suggested that millstones would be discarded. Henry Simon's view was that millstones would still be used for a considerable time, but in a subordinate position. *The Miller* was cautious about the prospect of complete replacement of millstones, suggesting that 'a large body of evidence' should be collected. The correspondence columns had been serving a wide field of enquiry about flour dressing, purifying, the operation of water wheels, weights and measures, and characteristics of different varieties of wheat, and frequently about the use of millstones: how to dress them, how to balance them, whether to use machines for millstone dressing. Bryan Corcoran, son and grandson of two other Bryan Corcorans, all mill-furnishers and millstone builders, became one of the most noticeable contributors to general discussion and from 1880 he became the leading advocate for traditional practice.[9] He maintained his position as a specialist in the construction of millstones into the twentieth century.

Resistance to technical change took several forms, which could be strict adherence to previous practice, blunt opposition to new technicalities, or simply the rejection of white flour. Also it was possible to avoid complete change by hoping that a small amount of extra machinery would be sufficient. In the early 1880s various alternative were tried, but were then discarded, leaving the milling trade gradually to divide into a group of innovative roller millers and a large group of firm traditionalists, who eventually went out of business or relied on provender milling.

When G. T. Smith addressed NABIM in 1880, he proposed technically unadventurous methods, and therefore less expensive decisions; they were not reported in full in *The Miller* and impact was limited. At the request of *The*

Figure 47.
G. T. Smith's
elaborate millstone
dress. (*The Miller*,
September 1880)

Miller, Smith supplied a description of his pattern of millstone dress, which had been shown at the Cincinnati exhibition. He claimed that the dress could be put into an ordinary pair of stones without changing the leading furrows, but his preferred arrangement had fourteen leading furrows and many small ones in each 'harp', or section between them. This left a very small proportion of land, which was to be rubbed smooth with sand and water. It was not likely to appeal to the majority of millstones dressers, being much more complicated than standard British patterns.[10] As his expositions were mainly concerned with directions on how to set up millstones and improve their condition, there was an implication that much millstone practice was inadequate for the production of high quality flour. So New Process milling in Britain was not, as some hoped, a rescue for the millstone. Smith's improvement of the purification operation inadvertently encouraged the move to complete roller milling systems. When the range of machines which Dells offered for sale was expanded around 1884 to include Geo. T. Smith centrifugals, scalpers, and graders, in addition to his purifiers, there was no reprieve for traditional millstone methods. Also anyone who read about American practice soon learned that New Process milling was a thing of the past.

For traditionalists, two main questions emerged: were millstones being used as well as possible, and were the operating principles clearly understood? Corcoran's response to the first was that millstones could be dressed and balanced more carefully, and that with careful attention they were superior to rolls. The second question was difficult to deal with, except by trial and observation of results. Carter suggested that the grain travelled in a spiral path between the stones, often with too long a period of contact; he criticised the abrasive action of low grinding, particularly during the action of breaking the grain. Corcoran believed that the wheat was cracked effectively at the eye of the stone, and processed satisfactorily during the rest of its passage, provided that a suitable dress was used.[11] Unfortunately for his case, he was not able to produce a dress of the required versatility. He tried to promote a design by R. Smith of Stone in Staffordshire, but it was far too complicated to become a practical proposition, as an illustration in *The Miller* in December 1880 showed. There had been other suggestions during the previous few years, including the Jones New Patent Millstone Dress from America.

The rollers versus millstones controversy was at its sharpest until 1883, exercised in the correspondence columns, and also at lectures to operatives. At meetings of the Amalgamated Society of London Operative Millers, the usual subjects of discussion were the very long hours of work, and low pay, but for a year from March 1882, resistance to new methods was strongly expressed. Carter first addressed the Regular Millers of Ireland Trade Society in Dublin on the 'Relative merits of millstones and rollers'.[12] The London operatives followed their lead, inviting R. R. Smith, Carter, Bryan Corcoran, Theodore Voss and George Miller. Leading master millers presided at the London meetings. Corcoran and R. R. Smith, who was about to retire from working a small mill at Bungay in Suffolk, were advocates in the cause of millstone milling. Throughout the series of meetings, Carter had to contend with the continual disapproval of his ideas. Apart from Voss, who reviewed the development of gradual reduction methods in Hungary, and tried to encourage interest in technical education, the other speakers engaged in polemic. Carter's only firm support was from W. T. Bates, then a foreman at F. D. Collen's Metropolitan Mills at Rotherhithe. At that time, Bates had no personal experience of roller milling, but he became a fluent advocate for the new ideas, investigating the situation by personal correspondence with Simon, and with millers in Glasgow, Liverpool and Dublin.[13]

Corcoran's paper published in October 1882 was 'Modern milling', an inappropriate title for retention of traditional practice and the complete rejection of Carter's expositions on roller mill systems. Corcoran stated: 'There is no doubt in my mind that the present temporary success [with rolls] is due to want of proper care in working millstones'. His ostrich-like position was that because there were nominally 10,000 millers in the United Kingdom and a relatively small number worked the roller system, he could dismiss the innovators: 'This small proportion does not justify the amount of public attention claimed'. He rejected the American G. T. Smith's requirements for smooth millstone surfaces, and said of millstone high grinding 'I have never seen, and know of no mill where it is being carried out in this country'. So he may have left many traditionalists with no path to follow. He had much to say about elaborations of millstone dress; the prescriptions had geometrical interest, but would not lead to even the crudest levels of engineering science. Rule of thumb would merely become more complicated. Carter commented in good humour: 'I make this offer to Mr Corcoran on behalf of myself and half-a-dozen other roller-mill makers, if he and half-a-dozen other millstone furnishers will undertake never to sell any roller mills, we will undertake never to sell another millstone'.[14]

Voss, a milling engineer associated with the firm of Corcoran, Witt & Co., spoke in favour of combined plant. His view was that 'the milling world was at present in a state of transition'.[15] He was constructive and conciliatory, but not able to cross a Rubicon: 'The *exclusive* adoption of roller mills, or any other gradual reduction machines, is not so advantageous as their intelligent combination with stones in such a manner as to use each machine to its greatest advantage'. George Miller's title was 'The transitory aspects of milling', a phrase which could be used to suggest that rolls would be discarded. He pretended to be impartial but was not: 'It must not be understood that I am speaking in utter condemnation of the roller mill. It is a useful auxiliary. But its actions are so slow that it can only be entertained where a slow mode of treatment is absolutely essential'. He considered rolls unsuitable for breaking damp English wheat. *The Miller* commented on George Miller's approval of combining rolls with stones:

> It will be seen that this is the view of Mr Voss, only that gentleman would use the roller mills for breaking the wheat, and the millstones for flouring the middlings, whereas Mr Miller would reverse the duties of the working agencies. A combined millstone and roller system is already in operation in London, viz., St. Saviour's Mill (Mr Seth Taylor's), on the lines Mr Miller favours, and in a very short time Messrs. J. & H. Robinson's mill at Deptford Bridge will be in operation on those approved of by Mr Voss.[16]

George Miller spread the campaign to the *Millers' Gazette*. As a result Henry Simon felt obliged to join in and wrote to *The Miller* in May 1883:

> Sir, – Not content with reading his extraordinary paper, Mr G. Miller has since that time occupied a large portion of space in correspondence, containing numerous statements attempting to prove that milling with stones not only produces better flour, but is commercially more profitable than milling with rollers ... I felt it incumbent to take steps to ascertain the correctness or otherwise of Mr Miller's facts.

Simon quoted supportive customers, one saying 'If the taste for white flour continues Mr Miller will get his eyes opened', another that George Miller's statements were 'absolutely absurd'. In reply to George Miller's suggestion that the rival methods of processing should be examined practically, Carter proposed a visit to a mill using his system.

Fulfilment of this plan was delayed, possibly because Carter was busy with large projects, including the plants for John Greenwood & Sons at Burnley and Blackburn, but in October 1884 about eighteen London operatives and more than forty others, including many master millers, visited Greenwoods' new mill at Blackburn. They saw a 30 sack plant working entirely on foreign grain, and the visit led to a marked change of attitude by many of the London Operatives' Society, which was clearly shown at a meeting of the Society at the Star Coffee House, Deptford in November 1884.[17] In March 1885, *The Miller* published a letter from the Society's secretary to Carter, including

> the progress that has been made in the minds of operative millers since you read your first paper before them some three years-and-a-half ago has been considerable, and it is to you their thanks are due in a great measure for much of the knowledge they have gained in roller milling.

COMBAT IN THE COLUMNS

The extent to which the publicised views of the London operative millers represented the views of others is unknown, but *The Miller* paid them close attention. Some were sceptical, ill-informed or indifferent to the new ideas. After 1883, polemic was continued less strongly in public, as more members of the trade became aware of the success of the new machinery. During the first half of 1885, there were attempts to continue the controversy in journal correspondence, but they were only echoes of previous dramatic presentations. Corcoran had lost his main audiences. He would continue to be prominent in the remaining millstone trade, but his peformance in print gave easier opportunities for opponents to dissect his statements at leisure, and compose more telling, sometimes humorous replies. In May 1885 George Miller, who had escaped from his transitory phase, tried to rationalise his change of mind:

> It has on several occasions been suggested through the columns of your valuable journal that many of the combatants in defence of the millstones have been put *hors de combat*, or at least they have been so cowed by the overwhelming forces of the rollers, ... I may be asked how it was that I did not realise the merits of the roller mill sooner. Was it prejudice, weakness of intellect, or a low scale of mental capacity generally? No, it was none of these things. It was simply want of experience in roller milling when reduced to a system.

In June, Wm. Fairclough from Cornwall emphasised the defeat of the rearguard.

> It was with not a little humorous satisfaction that we roller millers (who have been confined to the regions of folly and the verge of insanity by more than one stone miller) heard of the full conversion of Mr G. Miller, one of the strongest advocates of the old millstone ... I fail to see much foresight or progress in a man who is forced, as it were, to walk up the rack by the public demand for a better article than he is able to produce.

W. T. Bates referred to the Millstones *v*. Rollers dispute in 1907, in 'Twenty five years of roller milling: a retrospect'. 'My first attempt at milling journalism was made, I think, in opposition to an article by George Miller ... It was not

of dress (stone divided into quarters) the master furrows have least, and the other furrows have each more and more drift as they get shorter.

The speed of the surface at different distances from the centre is very different. In a 4 ft. stone, making 120 revolutions per minute, the

FIG. 9.—FACE OF STONE DIVIDED INTO ZONES.

number of feet per minute at a 12 in. eye is 377, at 12 inches from the centre, 754, at 18 inches, 1,131, and at the skirt, 1,508 feet. These positions are indicated by the circles in Fig. 9. The centrifugal action driving the stuff out increases with the speed. A grain of

FIG. 10.—SECTION OF RUNNER AND BED-STONE FACE.

wheat does not travel down the furrows, as shown above, but entering a furrow is caught and passed between the lands (Fig. 10) till thrown by the next furrows, and caught by next lands, gaining impetus to travel towards the skirt from the rotating runner, and thus continuing its journey till it gets out in a state of reduction according to the setting of the stones, dress, &c. There have been many ideas of the course of a grain of wheat between the faces, but it seems to me to depend upon so many circumstances, such as speed of stones, nature of burr, amount of swallow, drift, dress, quantity of feed, and nature of work being done, that it is difficult to indicate it by a clear line, especially as it is likely to be different on runner and bedstone; nor do I think a line would suffice, for the wheat is gradually reduced and occupies more surface, like the tail of a comet. When it once gets past the breast it is probably out like a flash of lightning, although near the eye it may travel round some distance.

The furrows distribute the feed and ventilate the stone; if the furrows are deep and like the first section shown (Fig. 3A), whole corns will escape, or if the drift is too great, some portion will escape unfinished. The fewer quarters there are the greater the drift of the small furrows.

FIG. 11.—DRESS.   FIG. 12.—DRESSES.

The illustrations represent 4-ft. stones with nine fours with the sun and fourteen threes against the sun respectively. The description of dress that is necessary depends upon the quality of the stone and nature of the work to be done. Each part of the face should have its proper work, and not more than its share. For ordinary work ten fours give the greatest satisfaction generally, wears evenly, and gives a broad bran; a large fly is considered to make clean bran. The number of furrows in ten fours is forty, in fourteen threes forty-two, and though very nearly the same in number, they are very differently distributed over the face. In the fourteen threes the smaller furrows have less drift and cross each other at a more acute angle; but the great objection to so many furrows in the eye is that the wheat is cut up immediately on entering the stone, making small bran, and often crowding the breast, where the stuff is murdered and the face worn in rings; this may be relieved by continuing the second furrows into the masters, as shown in half the illustration. It may be doubted whether the great drift in the small furrows is not a safeguard in helping the stuff to escape after passing the preceding lands; and may not the different angles in succession be also beneficial.

More land is required for soft than for dry hard wheats, and they should have nearly a uniform drift. The eye burrs should be smooth for treating wheat, the breast closely dressed, and the skirt finely cracked; roughness makes greys and bran dust. The face should be short for granulating, and a long face is necessary for softening and reducing to fine powder.

There are many devices for sickle shape and circular furrows. For making middlings it is generally considered that the furrows at the skirt should have nearly a uniform drift. It is sometimes done with many master furrows and one short furrow between, with the same drift and tapered lands like the half-size model kindly lent me.

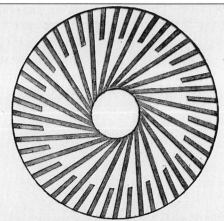

MODEL DRESS FOR A FOUR-FEET MILLSTONE.

This represents a model of a dress the maker thinks 4-feet millstones should have, which was shown at the meeting by Mr. Corcoran. The model was half-size, and the maker says:—" The wheat is supposed to be gently split open by the points of the eye-lands, each half spread out flat by the widening face of the same, which should be kept as smooth as glass, and finally, the thick bran scraped clean by the last seven inches of sharp cutting skirt. The action should be uniform, as every furrow has the same drift, and therefore they all cross each other at the same angle.

DIMENSIONS.

Stone	...	...	4 feet.	Eye ... ... 12 inches.
Eye-burrs	...	...	...	11 inch ring of hard white burr.
Bedstone skirt	...	...	7	„ close violet „
Runner skirt	...	...	7	„ free nutmeg „
Bedstone	...	...	...	To stand all over.
Runner	...	...	...	„ 7 inches in breast, and eye-burrs gradually depressed 1-16 inch.
24 leading furrows	...	All ½ inch deep throughout.
24 intermediate furrows	...	All ¼ „ to back edge.

I do not claim to make a great excess of middlings over any other dress while cleaning the bran, but that while we get rather more in quantity, they are much more even in size, with fewer large ragged semolina than the quarter dress would give. For half furrow and half land in a 4-feet stone the 48 furrows should be 1½ in. The white represents the "lands," which lead right up to the eye, and the shaded lines the leading and skirt "furrows."

I borrow a woodcut from THE MILLER (page 623, vol. v.) of a dress by J. Cast (Fig. 13), showing few furrows in the eye and a circular furrow

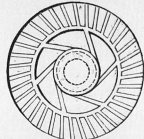

FIG. 13.—DRESS. (J. CAST.)

to feed the skirt. I also borrow from page 63, vol. ii., woodcut of very different dresses by "Amicus" (Fig. 14).

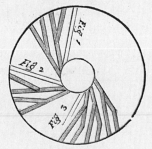

FIG. 14.—DRESSES: (AMICUS.)

I come to the conclusion that where the object is to finish everything in passing once through the stones, viz., breaking and opening the wheat, disengaging and reducing the middlings, making all the flour possible and cleaning the bran, the quarter-dress is the best, as it combines all the very long before we were in violent oppostion to one another, I for, and he against rolls … and I lived to regret some of the bitter invectives I heaped upon him in the heat of controversy'. His apology seems unnecessary, as his contributions were invariably well-mannered. During the controversy Bates and Miller were both foremen, responsible for mill production, Bates in his early thirties, Miller twenty years older. When Miller read his paper to the operatives, he was at Reynolds & Allen in Gloucester, but he became manager of Nelstrops' mills at Stockport. Bates was successively with Marriage, Neave & Co. at Battersea, Baxendell & Sons' Bee Mills at Liverpool, and John Knowles' mill at Nuneaton. Both contestants, therefore, became managers of roller mills.

DIRECT CRITICISM OF ROLLER MILLING

Opposition to the new technicalities could be expressed by supporting any of the hearsay criticisms of roller mills: that they gave insufficient yield, required too much power, or could not be used on soft wheat. The insufficient yield allegation was contested by Carter and Simon who were seen to hold the advantage when roller-made flour started to command better prices. Previously, it had been possible to sell flour grades that contained 80 per cent of the grain, but around 1880 new standards of acceptance were being set. Increasing confidence by roller millers who could obtain about 70 per cent, or a higher yield of the newly popular products, resulted in the challenge being returned to the traditionalists. It was frequently asserted by detractors that rolls required more power than millstones; this issue was complicated by the lack of comparable data, with similar feed rates, and without the inclusion of other plant. Simon (1882) stated that the Simon plants at Tadcaster, Croydon and Carlow, erected in 1879, required an average of 2.5 h.p. per cwt. of wheat ground per hour for 72 per cent extraction. This was equivalent to about 8.7 h.p. per sack of flour per hour. Possibly the first well-publicised data related to Frederick Moss's mill at Salford, but the information was not widely known until 1883. Moss stated that he could obtain a far higher output with rolls than with stones.[18] There had been no alteration to the engine or boiler plant. There was a trap which millstone advocates needed to avoid; many of them used feed rates that were too high for the effective use of their millstones unless they were content with a coarse product. Another factor that made it difficult to obtain comparable data was that roller millers were the main users of the harder wheats, which took more power to process, whereas stone millers could not even deal with such wheats effectively.

During the early 1880s, for many millers adherence to traditional practice could be based on their security of local trade, unsophisticated taste, and enough mellow wheat for their relatively small production requirements. As foreign wheat became more generally prominent, and not merely at times of poor

Figure 48 (*opposite*). Corcoran's paper on millstones: orthodox and fanciful alternatives. (*The Miller,* October 1882)

Figure 49. The miller and controversialist W. T. Bates. (*The Miller,* December 1899)

English harvests, they could avoid technical problems only if they did not buy the harder wheats. This remained possible until the innovative sectors of the industry impinged extensively, increasing their trading areas, and showing quality or price differences. One of the best known millers who seems to have expressed caution, which could have helped the traditionalist position, was Wilson Marriage, who was taken to task by Henry Simon for a speech allegedly containing 'the old truisms about the impossibility of introducing the roller system into England'.[19] Marriage's stance was less one of direct opposition to the methods than a belief in the superior taste of the flour produced in the southern part of East Anglia.

As the design of roller plant was rapidly developed, and included more machinery, comparison became even more difficult. Traditionalists were left with the complaint that millstones had not been given enough opportunity. Power requirements became a matter of general mechanical engineering with only echoes of the controversy. Details of power requirements were not made widely available until 1887, when Simon provided a paper for NABIM, based on extensive trials by William Stringer and the chief engineer of the Boiler Insurance Co. of Manchester, the tests being made at the Kirkdale Roller Mills at Liverpool. A very detailed report and analysis was published.[20] The summary contained a statement that 'when packing 8.5 sacks of flour per hour from a medium mixture of wheat, we find that the total power absorbed by the entire plant (exclusive of the friction of the engine and some shafting outside the mill) was 66.3 h.p.'. That was equivalent to 7.8 h.p. per sack of flour produced per hour. The total included the power required by the break and smooth rolls, and scalping, dressing and purifying machinery, shafting and conveyors.

There were many technical contributions to the new confidence, relating machinery designs to processing needs that the millers could reckon were basic. For instance, the question of whether roller milling methods could be applied successfully to the soft wheats had been finally settled by 1886. For leading adopters of roller milling, it had been settled in the earlier 1880s, but there had been doubters elsewhere. In 1886, T. W. Hibbard, by then a prominent member of NABIM, addressed the Association on 'Gradual reduction by roller milling, applied to soft wheats'. His theme was that hard foreign wheats were the main raw material for the larger mills, but soft British wheats were useful for many millers; British wheat was cheaper, it yielded flour that had a good flavour, and kept well. Hibbard's paper gave a technical description of adjustments needed to ensure satisfactory milling results.[21] Excuses for looking away from technical advance were being reduced to financial and market limitations of small businesses, and technical abilities in those situations.

The germ milling case

There was another issue of general concern to millers in the mid 1880s which acted indirectly to inhibit progress. Thomas Muir of Glasgow, through his Germ Milling Company, was claiming that all roller millers should pay him royalties for infringement of his patent, No. 2560 of July 1875: 'Improvements in the manufacture of meal and flour from wheat, maize, and other grain, and in obtaining a valuable product during the said manufacture'. The basic objective was to separate the part of the broken grain which contained most of the germ, to pass that through smooth rolls, flattening the germ, which could then be sieved out. The patent was for a process, not machinery. Muir regarded his process as novel, and a major solution to the problem of improving flour quality. He could not see it as merely a step on the way using machinery experimentally. Muir created a conflict, wisely controlled by some of the members of the National Association, so that it stayed in the background to more constructive technical progress. He involved the Association, partly by criticising secretary Chatterton's work of building a defensive position.[22] When the attack moved towards a legal test, Chatterton acted as secretary of the defence association, but the issue affected all innovating millers, and Muir's noisiest publicity was bound to involve the National Association.

PREPARING FOR BATTLE
A description of Muir & Sons' Tradeston Mills at Glasgow appeared in *The Miller* in July 1877, with reference to the patent, to Thomas Muir, and to a statement that Muir regarded the removal of germ as his invention. Assistance was acquired in 1879: Mr Alderman Hadley, the Association's President, apparently said that 'The germ of wheat has a most deleterious effect on the quality of flour, and if we could find some means to extract the germ from the semolina before it is manufactured into flour, we should have a superior class of flour, for which we should get a higher price'. *The Miller* reported Muir's first version of his case, presented to the first annual meeting of the Association in June 1879.

> His object in getting the patent was not the prospect of great pecuniary advantage at the time, such novelties being slow of introduction; but as he was informed by the best experts that such a thing had not been practised in this or any other country, he thought he may as well protect it.

Conflict became serious in the autumn of 1881, and was not resolved until the end of 1886, five years of manoeuvring and anxiety. Journal advertisements stated: 'The Germ Milling Company, Limited, having acquired Mr Thomas Muir's Patents for Degerming Grain, intimate that they are prepared to grant Licences to Millers, Brewers, and Distillers throughout the kingdom … Application to Mr Thomas Muir, Patentee & Manager, Tradeston Mills, Glasgow'.[23] In December 1881, secretary Chatterton published the opinion that 'the Company's offer to grant licences may be disregarded'. Muir wrote, not without humour: 'Was the idea of Hebrew origin … is it a myth, or has it simply growed?' He continued, 'I must add that my claim has been substantially acknowledged by many of the leading millers in the country, and I consider this action of the Council of the Association as an attempt to snuff me out'. In January 1882, *The Miller*'s review of the previous year included: 'A little cloud, not bigger than a man's hand, rose on the milling horizon in the later part of the year, and it remains to be seen how far it will spread during the

year which has just commenced. We refer to the degerming of wheat question'.
A year later, the journal mentioned the cloud briefly: 'It still exists, but in its
original dimensions, and if it contains any destructive matter, the prudence of
both parties supplied a conducting rod sufficiently effective to carry off such
matter without resulting in mischief'. But during 1882, the situation worsened.
In February, Muir's provisional and full specifications for letters patent appeared
in the journal, including:

> the larger portions or sizes of semolina in which the germs are found
> concentrated I pass forward to and between rotating rolls ... The semolina
> or fleshy portions of the grain is easily crushed or broken into flour, but the
> germs, which are elastic and of an oleaginous nature, pass from the rolls each
> as a flattened mass' ... I thus obtain an entirely new and novel mercantile
> product, which I name 'germ meal' the absence of which from the flour
> much improves its quality.

A letter from Henry Simon appeared in the same issue of *The Miller*:

> Sir, It may interest you to hear that already in the first edition of Professor
> Kick's well-known work on the *Manufacture of Flour*, printed in 1871, the
> following passage is to be found on page 82:- 'There are certain classes of
> middlings containing from 30 to 40 per cent. of germs. If one lets such
> middlings pass through rollers set to the proper distance these germs are
> easily flattened, whilst the middlings are crushed, and it is then easy to
> remove them by dressing machinery'. Please note that this was printed in
> 1871, so that the system was therefore necessarily known some considerable
> time before, Professor Kick's statement being not at all made as if communi-
> cating anything strikingly new or unknown in milling practice.

Simon's contribution introduced a possible counter to Muir, by use of a standard
attack on a patent when a 'prior publication' can be cited, but Kick's book of
1871 was in German. Relevant material from Kick's work was published in *The
Miller* in 1876, soon after Muir's patent, but Kick's book was apparently known
in the Patent Office in London in 1871. Many millers must have wondered
whether Muir had secured a master patent; what would be the scope and
interaction of the many other later patents for individual machines and methods?

LITIGATION

Older millers were aware that there had been a patent by Bovill for an alleged
improvement of grinding by millstones, using a flow of air to make a partial
separation of material passing between the stones, and to cool it. Bovill was a
reminder and a warning to the cautious and to some with actual unfortunate
experience; there were numerous legal actions by Bovill in the 1850s and 1860s.
Aware of this previous battle, the National Association discussed the contention
with Muir in detail during 1882; the Council considered and reported that as
'all the operations described in the specification and the combination of them
were well known and employed prior to the date of the patent', Muir's claims
could be disregarded. An attempt was made to strengthen resistance: if legal

action for infringement were taken against any member, the Association would 'be recommended to defend the same'. Israel Rishworth of Leeds objected to joint financial liability. Other speakers gingerly tested the wording of official statements, and the possibilty of a conflict between accepting the Council report and being free to discuss it further. Frederick Richardson of Sunderland, the President, stated that 'It is a recommendation of the Council; it does not bind the members to subscribe to it'. It was recorded that 'The report was then adopted unanimously and with enthusiasm'.[24]

A year later there was further advice. 'Should any action be commenced by the patentees, your Council will immediately call a special meeting for the purpose of forming a defence fund to resist the claim'. By September 1883, R. H. Appleton of Stockton on Tees, the new President, had received 'letters from all parts of the kingdom, from parties who had received letters from Mr Muir, threatening them'. Frederick Moss of Salford said that Muir had 'kept calling on him from time to time, informing him that he had settled with one and another'. Rishworth had settled. The Liverpool Association were disconcerted; according to Moss, 'when they wrote to Mr Chatterton asking what the National Association meant to do, they got a vague reply but no real information'. Several Liverpool millers had settled, but Moss refused.

In November 1883, Muir wrote to *The Miller*:

> The Germ Milling Co. had thought, and so had I, especially seeing so many settlements had since been made ... that proceedings at law might be avoided. If action at law must be taken ... not one iota of the just claims will be abandoned, and the full measure of the savings effected by the process, perfected and first worked out by me, will be enforced.

He challenged the Association:

> I might say no list of members of the Association has been issued by the Association this year. This I do know, however, that of the 31 members ... who formed the old and new Councils, I have settled with thirteen, the large number of 13 are not working my patent process, and there are thus left 5 to enter the cave of Adullam.

In 1884 and 1885, leading millers were busy with a quite new level of innovative activity, and the Association was widening its scope by holding annual conventions, while Muir was practising divide and rule tactics. The Association tried to prepare informally to resist a formal attack. Then, early in 1886, the dispute was intensified; Muir decided to act against J. & H. Robinson of Deptford, presumably partly because Henry Robinson was the Association's treasurer. Chatterton wrote to *The Miller*.[25]

> The attention of the Germ Defence Association has been called to a great number of letters, by which the Germ Milling Company – although an action is pending in which the validity of Muir's patent is openly questioned – have thought fit to endeavour to intimidate millers into paying royalties under that patent. I shall be glad if you will allow me, through the columns of

your valuable journal, to request all millers receiving such circulars to communicate at once.

The Germ Milling Company wrote:

Though Mr Chatterton invites millers to communicate at once with him as secretary of the Germ Defence Association, his letter carefully conceals the names of the millers forming that Association; nor does he venture to state how much, even by way of estimate, those whom he invites to join the so-called Germ Defence Association may become liable to pay for the proportion of Mr Robinson's costs, charges, and expenses, which he may incur in any legal defences, or otherwise, in contesting the patent.

There were further threats: higher payments would be demanded after litigation. The National Association report to the 1886 Dublin convention was in simple terms:

in consequence of many of your members having, for the sake of peace and quietness, accepted licences … a strong Defence Association, apart from your organisation, has been formed for the purpose of testing the validity of these claims, and during the year a very large portion of the time of those gentlemen who attend your affairs has been occupied in preparing the defence.[26]

The trial of the Germ Milling Co. *v.* Robinson was in the Chancery Division of the High Court, lasting from 22 to 29 June. It could have taken much longer, but there was a surprise on the seventh day. Other patents were considered at length, and repeatedly, mainly for the plaintiff's two QCs to try to show the importance of Muir's position, contrasting the objectives of other designers, including Gustav Buchholz and Wegmann. Kick's work was examined frequently, as possible evidence of anticipation. Proctor Baker of Bristol did not accept that Kick's book described Muir's process; his firm had paid £50 for a licence. Robinson Greenwood of Blackburn and Burnley regarded Muir's process as useful, and had bought a licence for £211. Edgar Appleby of Blackburn had bought a licence for seven shillings per sack for twenty four hours production. J. Buchholz was encouraged to discount any relevance of Wegmann's work, and he refused to accept Kick's descriptions as adequate. William Jago confirmed that it was desirable to remove the germ. There were long examinations of witnesses, to compare alternative processing steps. Muir was examined on the seventh day. Cross-examined by Mr Romer QC, for the defence, he stated: 'The flour which I made in June, 1875, I sold in the ordinary course of business'. He agreed that he was referring to flour 'we were making by our new process'. The case collapsed! To the lawyers on both sides it was obvious that inadvertently Muir had admitted to being a 'prior user'. After a lunch adjournment, there was a tentative attempt by Muir's side to suggest that use of the process prior to the patent was only experimental, but the judge dismissed the action.

A LAST THROW

Muir tried again with a motion in the Court of Appeal for the grant of a new trial. The journal reported that the notice of appeal was on the ground that evidence given by Muir 'that he had sold flour manufactured by the patent process in June 1875, prior to the grant of letters patent to him, was a mistake and not in accordance with the fact, and that the plaintiffs have since ascertained, and are now in a position to prove, that such flour had not, in fact, been sold until some months after the date of such letters patent'. The hearing of the application for a new trial began on November 8.[27] In an affidavit, Muir stated that 'I was entirely mistaken at the trial that in the month of June 1875, I was selling fairly freely, and in the ordinary course of business, flour made according to my invention'. Affidavits from Muir, and from two of his foremen, who supported his new statements, formed the basis of his attempt. Lord Justice Bowen questioned Mr Theodore Aston QC, acting for the plaintiffs.

> Lord Justice Bowen: 'At the trial you might have asked the witness to produce his books'.
> Mr Aston: 'I was taken by surprise'.
> Lord Justice Bowen: 'But you might have called for the books'.
> Mr Aston: 'The learned judge stopped me. He would not allow me to put the question 'What were the dates?' He would not allow me to shake the witness'.
> Lord Justice Bowen: 'You might have asked him to put in his books. That would not have been to cross-examine your own witness. During the adjournment your witness might have referred to his books' …
> Mr Aston: 'I do not think Mr Muir was in a condition to look into anything. After he had gone out of the witness-box he was very greatly confused'.
> Lord Justice Fry: 'When he was told the effect of his evidence'.
> Mr Aston: 'I don't deny that I told Mr Muir that it was impossible to keep up the case if what he had said was true. I do not know who was the more surprised – the witness or his counsel'.

Not only Muir was confused; there was confusion about germ meal and germless flour: which should be considered the relevant part at various stages of Muir's experiments, and therefore what exactly he might have been selling, or now claiming that he was not selling? There were doubts about alterations during the experiments, and when a settled process had been reached. But it gradually became clear that the plaintiffs would not be able to convince the judges that the affidavits were credible, and that 'it would be too dangerous a thing to allow fresh evidence to be given by a witness after he had considered what the result of his previous evidence was'. Muir failed to provide tangible evidence and could not remove the effect of his statement at the trial that he had actually been a prior user. The three judges agreed in rejecting the application for a new trial.

According to *The Miller* a germ meal was not useful: 'millers as a class have not the slightest intention of extracting it with a view to the obtaining of a separate product'. Extraction was to improve flour quality. The grant of a patent

was misguided, but the move that eliminated it again suggested a game of
hazards. The journal then took the focus off Muir: 'we are not sure but that
the Patent Office is largely responsible for the unfortunate position in which
the Germ Milling Company now finds itself', commenting on invention and
patents:

> The wider notions of mechanics, the more general conceptions of any trade,
> will on research be usually found to have been conceived if not embodied
> in some more or less practical form, long before the period when the adaptation
> becomes of general acceptance. Thus it is that the more particular and
> technical an invention is, the more it may be said to be the proper subject
> of a patent, while the more general it is the more unfitted it is for patenting,
> and the more likely is the patent, if granted, to be subsequently upset.[28]

Chatterton sought financial contributions. It had been suggested that demands
for royalties would have approached £200,000. The Germ Defence Association's
costs were estimated as about £7,000.[29] Their final meeting was in February
1889; the final amount was £5,891. Comment appeared in *The Miller* in March
1889, together with the list of subscriptions and donations which covered the
costs.

CHAPTER EIGHT

The National Association

The founding of the National Association of British and Irish Millers

Prior to the founding of the National Association (NABIM) in 1878 there were many contributions to the pool of ideas concerning association. An early suggestion was for a protection association, as a safeguard in dealings with the baking trade. In articles in *The Miller* on 'The present condition of the baking trade' there was a review of difficulties which millers experienced in selling flour without clear contractual agreements. One common grievance had been 'the sack question', the unsolved problem of how to charge for branded sacks, or prevent bakers using them as aprons, floor mats, cleaning materials, or overclothing in bad weather. Lack of agreement about how to charge, or how much to charge, caused ill-feeling; millers sued offending customers. Much more of a challenge, trouble arose due to variation in conditions of sale, terms of credit, and discounts. Frequently flour sales were booked without firm agreement about delivery dates or, for large orders, dates of stages of delivery; 'forward sales' became risks of future cross-purposes. In times of falling flour prices, bakers often delayed taking delivery. When prices rose, in step with rising grain prices, it was difficult to sell flour in areas where some bakers had given orders for many months' supply at lower prices. These problems were accentuated by price-cutting to obtain orders. There was also a shared interest in insurance. A widely held opinion was that rates of fire insurance for mills and machinery were excessive, and attempts were made to obtain better terms, for instance by seeking support for mutual insurance schemes. Also, *The Miller* put forward a proposal for a Millers' Benevolent Institution to 'form some efficient, permanent, and comprehensive combination, whereby every member of the trade might feel perfectly secured against the many vicissitudes of industrial and commercial life'.

At the end of 1875, *The Miller* commented on the inadequacies of the London Smithfield Show, from the points of view of millers and mill-furnishers, hoping that a 'special annual exhibition of millers' machinery will sooner or later be inaugurated'.[1] Harrison Carter took up this point, suggesting that 'Meetings of millers should be held and papers read and discussed'.[2] In contrast with the previous subjects of concern, Carter's accent on communication was the most significant for later development. There was opposition. Amongst journal correspondents, some members of the trade did not believe that association was advantageous. The visit to Vienna and Budapest, in 1877, by a group of millers led by Carter, gave *The Miller* a tangible opportunity for direct encouragement:

> We have pleasure in drawing our readers' attention to this associated journey, because we think that the time is not far distant when millers in the United

Kingdom will see it in their interest and that of the community at large to form Associations ... to seek out and apply the best means of manufacturing that article which is so important to all – the staff of life.[3]

This was not yet a clearly focused scheme. However, *The Miller* continued to publish statements in favour of association, and in editorials and correspondence columns the heading became 'Millers' organisation'.

INAUGURATION

The Miller not only pronounced on the need for organisation, but also indicated the basic stucture required: 'The organisation should be national, but, at the same time, local; in other words, the national organisation must be composed of local organisations subordinated to a central governing or administrative power, elected by the various organisations and fairly representative of each'.[4] The full achievement of this objective was to prove both elusive and a continually renewed ideal. Evidence of advantages of association was provided by the Sheffield and Rotherham Millers' Association, formed in 1877 with the aim of setting up uniformity of trading practice by fixing terms of flour sales and eliminating forward sales of flour. The chairman was Samuel Smith, who was to lead a party to Cincinnati in 1880, and to become President of NABIM in 1882. Another prominent member and a future President of NABIM was Henry Ibbotson, who had visited Vienna and Budapest in 1877. Ibbotson and Emrich Pekar, of Budapest, had addressed the group in 1877.[5]

A report of their first year of activity and a letter urging the formation of local associations in other areas, were printed in the journal in February 1878, and reference was made to these two items in one of the most important editorials *The Miller* produced. Attention was drawn to a meeting to be held at the New Market Sale Room of the Corn Exchange Hotel in Mark Lane, on 11 February, 'for the purpose of forming a National Association of British and Irish Millers'. Alderman Hadley, of the City Flour Mills, was to be the chairman, and notice was given by W. C. Hepburn of *The Miller* and D. G. Tepper of *The Corn Trade Journal*, acting as temporary secretaries. Dunham and Beerbohm paid all the expenses of the first meeting. The key resolution was put forward by John Fairclough of Warrington, a member of the Vienna party, that 'this meeting is of opinion that the time has arrived when, in the interests of the trade, it would be advisable to form a National Association of British and Irish Millers, for mutual advancement and protection'. At least ten future Presidents of NABIM attended, from London, Sheffield, Colchester, Gloucester, Northampton, Reading, Stockton-on-Tees and Sunderland.[6]

Particular attention was paid to the need to acquire expert advice on new machinery, possibly by an arrangement 'under which a new patent applicable to milling is thoroughly tested ... before it is recommended to the trade as being worthy of acceptance', but it was an oversimplification of the problem of system design and performance. J. A. A. Buchholz suggested that the Association should include mill-furnishers, milling engineers and millwrights. This was resisted by Alderman Hadley, but supported by several prominent millers: Frederick Richardson of Sunderland, leader of the Vienna party in

1877, John Fairclough, and Peter Mumford of Chelsea were in favour of Buchholz's suggestion, as a way of obtaining general technical discussion and advice and this was eventually accepted.

A provisional committee was set up to make a draft code of rules and an inaugural meeting was held on 29 April 1878. S. C. Hadley was elected President, an office he held for three years. Hepburn and Tepper contributed to the drafting of the constitution. A Council was elected to supervise Association affairs, and J. H. Chatterton, of the Millers' Mutual Fire Insurance Company, was appointed secretary of the National Association. Like William Dunham, John Henry Chatterton had sought fortune overseas, trying Australia and then working his way round the world. Returning to England, he worked for a wine merchant and learned Spanish, and then for the Western Gas Co., and for the Sunderland Water Co.[7] Chatterton remained the secretary until 1890, and continued to assist the London millers until 1904. In all the Association's early projects he was an invaluable facilitator. He was obviously energetic, and reputedly whimsical, often arriving at mills on his tricycle, his practical application of a gift from the London millers' association.

Figure 50.
J. H. Chatterton
(1835–1929), first
secretary of NABIM.
(*The Miller*, March
1928)

The draft rules provided for the membership to consist of 'Master Millers in all parts of the United Kingdom, and of Milling Engineers, Millwrights, Millfurnishers, and others directly connected with the milling trade', and this composition was adhered to through various revisions. General aims included: 'The collection of information bearing upon all departments of the trade, technical, practical, and commercial, with a view to improve the quality of its products and increase the ratio of its profits' and a statement that the Council of the Association would:

appoint technical, statistical and commercial committees, whose duty it shall be to examine and estimate the practical value of new machinery and new processes in milling, collect information with regard to the grain harvest prospects at home and abroad, and such other statistics as may be deemed useful to the Association; and to make suggestions with regard to the best methods of dealing with such subjects as sales and purchases, credits, weights and measures, sacks, insurance, patents, &c.

CONFIRMATION OF GENERAL PURPOSES

The draft rules were revised and approved in June 1879: the Council was to 'appoint technical, practical and commercial committees, whose duties shall be to estimate the value of new machinery and new processes in milling, and to collect all such information at home or abroad as shall in anywise be deemed beneficial to the Association'. The overall aims of the Association and the particular objectives remained the same in the next revision, made in 1889.[8] In the amended version, the emphasis on information collection and exchange gave way to a simple statement of association, and responsibility for the collection of information was formally passed to committees.

The first phase of development of the Association was marked at the first annual meeting, held in the hall of the Worshipful Company of Bakers, in Harp Lane, London. Henry Simon supplied a paper on the Daverio system, and a paper on the Nagel and Kaemp system was read by H. J. Sanderson.[9] A report was received from the Practical Committee, whose main recommendation was that attention should be directed to the problem of optimising flour extraction rate in relation to flour quality. The financial report stated that 146 members had paid the guinea subscription, and that subscriptions had also been received from the London, Liverpool and Sheffield Associations; it seems that by June 1879 the total membership was about 200. Efforts were made to build up interest in as many places as possible: a circular was prepared, giving the rules and reports of meetings, and sent to 9,000 millers as an invitation to join. In the draft rules the Council were required to form branch or district associations in all parts of the country and to arrange for their affiliation to the National Association. This policy was maintained, though it soon became clear that the viability of local groups depended on the strength of local initiative and leadership, and on the willingness of the millers in a particular area to meet and cooperate. According to *The Miller* in January 1880, there were by then seven affiliated associations: Sheffield and Rotherham; London; Liverpool District; Northamptonshire; Devon; Hampshire, Wiltshire and Dorset; Gloucestershire, Bristol and South Wales. There were also four other associations: Leeds; Colchester; Edinburgh and Leith Millmasters; Glasgow Merchant Millers.

Continuing discussion of objectives

There was a short period of uncertainty about the best policies to pursue, how to create a strength of leadership and, at the same time, create a wide basis of membership and organisation. A particular problem arose in 1879 and 1880, when the Council decided that detailed reports of meetings of the National Association would not be published in the journals; reports would be for members only, and could not be printed until funds became available. *The Miller* referred to the 'policy of silence and secrecy'.[10] It was an attempt to encourage millers to join and participate, instead of passively accepting the advantages of receiving information through the journals. Annual subscription to *The Miller* was five shillings for the monthly technical issues, which included trade advertisements, and the annual cost of those, together with the weekly market issues was only twelve shillings and six pence, compared with the guinea (twenty-one shillings) for an annual subscription to the Association.

With the exception of a meeting in February 1879, when J. W. Mullin read a paper on 'The manufacture of flour', and another in April 1880, *The Miller* managed to bridge the gaps. In December 1879 Harrison Carter gave his first important paper, which was printed. Within the Association, one idea was to publish quarterly, and that would have provided records, possibly private, and inevitably with the loss of immediacy of communication and discussion which the journals were able to promote. As members of the National Association, the editors of *The Miller* and *The Corn Trade Journal* were put in a difficult position. Dunham did not attend the meeting in April 1880 which was addressed by J. A. A. Buchholtz and G. T. Smith; two of Dunham's staff attended, but the brief report that was published in *The Miller* was composed by the secretary of the Association, and did not do justice to the occasion, missing an opportunity to encourage debate.

At this time, Dunham gave extensive space in the journal to reports from T. W. Hibbard about the visit by Association members to the milling exhibition at Cincinnati, and Hibbard's tour of American mills. In editorials, Dunham argued that 'policy should be inclusive in the widest sense', and that Association meetings should be 'to some extent peripatetic'.[11] Full publicity of Association meetings was resumed in August 1880 and the Association entered the crucial phase of its own establishment, notably with preparations for the milling machinery exhibition of 1881. Between 1880 and 1883 it gradually became apparent that the idea of association was attractive mainly to the principals of the larger milling firms, and that most of the small country millers were unlikely to join.

J. H. Chatterton attended many meetings of local associations, to give general encouragement, to discuss local objectives and to advise on the relationship with the main Association. The attitude of many country millers was illustrated when he visited the still independent Colchester District Millers' Association, in October 1880. In reply to Chatterton's explanation that the national body required a subscription from each member of a local association at the rate of two shillings and sixpence per pair of stones, the reply was that 'The country trade will not afford it'. During the early 1880s there was strong support from the five major industrial areas of London, Liverpool, Leeds, Sheffield and the Bristol Channel and South Wales area, also from Northamptonshire, but continuing invitation by members of the National Association, and exhortation by Dunham, did not persuade very many of the small country milling firms that they would benefit from association.

In 1880, the question posed by detractors of the work of the Association was 'What is the good of it?' *The Miller* produced a detailed answer, including 'Union had been promoted among members of the trade, to an extent that had been thought impossible' and 'There had been beneficial discussions about machinery and methods that would lead to improvements in product quality'. The Council of NABIM regarded the Islington exhibition of 1881 as the 'tangible answer' to the question 'What is the good of Association?' and hoped that it would encourage many more millers to join. R. H. Daw suggested that a full list of members should be printed; details were published in *The Miller* in August 1881 and also in September 1882, including names and addresses and dates of joining, together with the names of members of the affiliated Associations and the rules of the National Association. During 1882 and 1883,

APRIL 4, 1881.]   THE MILLER.   129

International Exhibition

—OF—

FLOUR MILL MACHINERY.

LONDON, 1881.

THE

𝕹ational 𝕬ssociation of 𝕭ritish & 𝕴rish 𝕸illers

WILL HOLD AN

INTERNATIONAL EXHIBITION,

OF

Flour Mill Machinery,

Bread Making and Biscuit Baking Machinery,

And all kinds of Machinery connecte dwith

Cereals and Farinaceous Products.

IN THE

𝕬gricultural 𝕳all, 𝕷ondon

ON

Tuesday, May 10th;   Wednesday, May 11th;
Thursday, May 12th;   Friday, May 13th;
Saturday, May 14th.

Forms of Application for Space and full particulars may be obtained from

JOHN H. RAFFETY,

Managing Director,

AGRICULTURAL HALL, LONDON;

OR FROM

J. H. CHATTERTON,

Secretary.

OFFICES—61, MARK LANE, LONDON, E.C.

Nearly the whole of this Magnificent Hall, measuring 380 feet in length by 215 feet in width, the largest covered space that has yet been made available for an **EXHIBITION** of **MILLING MACHINERY IN MOTION**, has already been allotted.

Figure 51.
Notice of the momentous Islington exhibition of 1881. (*The Miller*, April 1881)

The Miller provided regular commentary on the new situation of technical change and continuing development, the National Association being shown as a factor in the progress of the industry.

By the autumn of 1883, the journal could indicate the standing achieved by the Association, through an editorial statement that 'the question 'What is the use of it?' has ceased to be asked by all except the most indifferent to the milling progress of the United Kingdom'. *The Miller* urged the Association to make investigations and report through technical, practical and commercial committees, stating that 'data can now be obtained in abundance' for the solution of the problem of quality versus quantity in flour production, but the field for information search and analysis was developing too quickly for part-time committees to deal with adequately, and much useful information was becoming available to all millers in the growing volumes of the milling journals and in lectures at the meetings of NABIM. At a meeting at the end of 1883, there were three items that represented the next stages of more confident activity. Milling technology was discussed in the context of the newly formulated City & Guilds scheme of study. The analytical and consulting chemist William Jago presented a paper which was the start of more active interest in hearing experts, some concerned with the basic practicalities of milling, others with subjects of a scientific or technical nature, increasingly relevant to the industry. Thirdly, the decision was taken to hold annual milling conferences, this plan being supported by all the affiliated groups.[12]

THE MEMBERSHIP

Starting in 1884, three-day conferences were held at main milling centres and other towns where membership might be increased, the first four meetings being at Stockton-on-Tees, Glasgow, Dublin and London. By 1881, the number of members had reached 338, and in 1887 the total had increased to about 400. From 1888 to 1892, membership numbers were below 350, but then increased again. Around 1890 local associations that continued the formality of affiliation to NABIM were those at London; Sheffield & Rotherham; Northamptonshire; and Leeds. There were at least seven other existing local millers' associations: Colchester; Birmingham and District; Northumberland, Durham and North Yorkshire; two in Scotland and two in Ireland. The Gloucestershire, Bristol and South Wales District Branch seems not to have been active after 1889.[13] Lancashire was an area with some spirit of independence, but individual memberships were maintained in all regions.

In the early years of NABIM, the list of members contained a small number of names of firms, and a large number of names of principals of milling businesses, together with senior members of mill engineering and mill-furnishing businesses, and a few journalists. The Association was originally meant to be made up of individuals, so when the titular head of a firm was the most active member the principle of individual membership was fairly effective, but when the direction of a firm's main activities passed to other members, the definition of membership became less clear. The basis of membership was frequently discussed. When the rules of the Association were revised in 1889, it was stated that 'The objectives of the Association shall be by all available and legitimate means to protect and promote the Milling Interest in all its branches'.

The numbers of members from milling engineers' and mill-furnishers' businesses increased steadily; totals seem to have been about seventeen in 1881, rising to thirty-six in 1889. In 1889, the three leading firms of milling engineers contributed fourteen members. At Simon's offices at 20 Mount Street,

Manchester, the members of NABIM were Simon, Ingleby, Stringer, all well-known at NABIM meetings, W. W. Stephenson, J. W. Walworth, and R. Witherington who had previously been with Robinsons. At Robinsons' works at Rochdale there were J. Salkeld Robinson, C. J. Robinson, T. P. Fielden, and A. R. Tattersall who became a frequent contributor to the journals. With Harrison Carter at 82 Mark Lane were G. F. Zimmer and H. J. Davis. Peirson Turner, Carter's manufacturer, also quoted Carter's address. Of the journalists who had helped to start the Association, Dunham and Beerbohm were members. Beerbohm's assistant, D. G. Tepper, was succeeded by J. W. Rush, who became a member. Rush was regarded as an authority on grain and flour trade statistics. The 1889 list included a fifth journalist, Samuel Woods of Dornbusch's *List*. There was also one member of the Patent Office, Rhys Jenkins.

In the 1890 NABIM report it was stated that the enrolled membership was 'barely more than four per cent of the total number of master millers in the country', but most innovative millers throughout the country were members. Estimates by NABIM of the total number of mills were: 10,450 in 1879; 8,800 in 1887; about 8,500 in 1889.[14] At a meeting of the Council of NABIM in 1890, Peter Mumford, one of the three most prominent London millers, stated that 'the idea had got abroad that the National Association of British and Irish Millers was, above all, a large millers' association'. He added, 'That was not the case. It was as well calculated to be useful to small as to large millers'. Nevertheless, the thirteen members of the Council who then discussed the problem, were all prominent millers, though not necessarily all owners of very large businesses; they included Frank Ashby, Arthur Baker, Stephen Cannon, Wilson Marriage, John Mooney of Dublin, Peter Mumford, Seth Taylor, John Ure who was possibly the best-known of Glasgow millers, John White of Dundee, and William Vernon of Uttoxeter.[15] Discussion of membership numbers often led to reviews of objectives and suggestions for the improvement of facilities or services. F. Ashby of Croydon considered that 'a consulting library and reading room of trade periodicals would be of the greatest value' to members. White suggested that the Association could obtain expert advice on the chemical composition of wheat and flour, and that 'a mechanical expert might be provided for advising on the mechanical value of new inventions'.

MR. SETH TAYLOR.
(*From a photograph by Byrne & Co., Richmond.*)

Figure 52.
Seth Taylor
(1836–1917), doyen
of London millers.
(*The Miller*, July 1887)

Appraisal of new machinery

Familiarisation with the new technicalities was facilitated by demonstrations of an increasing variety of new machinery at a series of exhibitions held between 1877 and 1881. The first main kind of exhibition was at the annual show of the RASE (Royal Agricultural Society of England): in 1875, 1876 and 1877, respectively at Taunton, Birmingham and Liverpool,. At Taunton, Bryan Corcoran, W. R. Dell & Son and William Gardner exhibited traditional equipment. In 1876, middlings purifiers of English manufacture were shown: Dell's Economic Purifier and Walworth's Patent Middlings Purifier and Separator. The year 1877 marked the new departure towards roller milling: there was what *The Miller* called 'an absolute novelty', a roller mill for softening middlings, with rolls made of porcelain – Wegmann's machine exhibited by A. B. Childs. There were wheat cleaning machines, including two shown by Throop. It was estimated that between 800 and 1,000 members of the milling trade had attended the Liverpool RASE show.[16]

Another main type of exhibition was the 'International exhibition', and the visit by British millers to Vienna in 1877 was to one of a series of exhibitions there; in 1877 they saw strong evidence of technical change for the first time.

At Cincinnati in 1880 change was seen as gradual, perhaps giving a false sense of security to some British millers, but not to T. W. Hibbard, who recognised the power of increasing scale and its potential for becoming an important factor in technical development. Between the 1877 Vienna exhibition and the event at Cincinnati there was the Paris exhibition of 1878, at which Carter showed his first, strange-looking design of roller mill.

The RASE show at Bristol in 1878 was important for British millers, even though any of them who had visited Paris could have seen roller mills by Ganz, Escher Wyss, Wegmann, Daverio, Nemelka and Worner. Members of the newly-formed National Association saw machinery exhibited by Carter, Corcoran, Corcoran & Witt, Dells, Gardner, Hind & Lund, Hopkinson, Houghton and Walworth, amongst a total of fifteen exhibitors of milling equipment. Carter showed his middlings roller mill, Corcoran, Witt & Co. showed Weber's porcelain roller

Figure 53.
William Voller,
pioneer in technical
education. (*The Miller*,
April 1900)

mill. Buchholz showed the Ganz roller mill at a separate site. *The Miller* regarded the Bristol event as the most important that had been held, with an 'unprecedentedly large attendance of millers'.[17]

The trend of advance continued, with a much more impressive event at Kilburn in 1879, with thirty-one exhibitors of milling equipment.[18] Progress was partly due to the RASE's choice of the metropolis, but, according to *The Miller*, 'also due, to a great extent, to the increased interest that has been manifested by millers, during the last few years, in the adoption of improved machinery'. There was a much larger representation of roller mills, with twelve exhibitors of chilled iron rolls, and three exhibitors of porcelain rolls, providing a total of twenty-six machines for inspection. There were eighteen exhibitors of middlings purifiers, twelve exhibitors of centrifugals, and there was a large variety of wheat cleaning equipment. Chilled iron rolls were shown by the firms who were to become prominent: Simon, with the Daverio design; Carter,

with two designs; Buchholz, with Ganz designs; and Throop, as agent for the
American Gray machine. There were also Fiechter's 'Fir' cracking mill, Nell's
'Champion' middlings mill, and an over-complicated design by Smith, Dell &
Stewart, in which the rolls had a transverse reciprocating motion, in addition
to rotation.[19] The Kilburn show was a success despite heavy rain on a clay site
and a resultant quagmire. Cincinnati provided the big event of 1880, but there
was also an RASE show at Carlisle, smaller than usual, also held in poor
weather. Turners of Ipswich exhibited Carter's roller mill, and also Braun's
fluted roller mill for breaks, made by Escher Wyss. Wegmann introduced his
granulating rolls and Buchholz showed his low-grinding method.

By this time, grain cleaning equipment and a large range of purifiers had
become generally familiar, while a wide variety of roller mills had been presented
to the trade. Many machines were of Continental or American design and
manufacture, but British equipment was becoming increasingly evident. Many
millers were considering the new methods. The trend was recognised and
reinforced when the National Association discarded the cautious 'silence and
secrecy' strategy, and found a major new objective in planning and promoting
a special milling exhibition. At the RASE shows, milling machinery had not
been specially classified or concentrated and, although Hadley and others had
been keen to associate themselves with a general policy of meeting where the
Society held its main annual event, millers and milling engineers were not able
to discuss new equipment in satisfactory conditions. Machinery had been
operated, but a covered site was needed, with provision of mechanical power,
if realistic demonstrations were to be given.

A SPECIAL EXHIBITION: ISLINGTON IN 1881
The idea of an annual milling exhibition in England had been suggested in
The Miller in 1875, and supported by Harrison Carter. In April 1878, the Journal
urged the new National Association to arrange a special exhibition, in
conjunction with the RASE. Dunham presented the idea again in August 1880,
but then specifically as a project for the Association. On this occasion also,
Carter was prominent, having requested Dunham to raise the issue.[20] At the
annual meeting of NABIM in July, Frederick Richardson suggested that the
Council might organise an exhibition at the Agricultural Hall at Islington. By
October, arrangements had been made to hold an international exhibition of
mill machinery at Islington in May 1881. The organising committee included
the London millers Robinson and Mumford, Wilson Marriage, Harrison Carter,
Stewart (of Dells), Binyon, Sanderson, Hepburn of *The Miller* and Tepper of
The Corn Trade Journal. The decision to carry out the project in 1881 was
influenced by plans in Vienna; the Austrian Millers' Association had hoped to
organise an exhibition with working machinery for 1881, but considered the
date to be too early for adequate preparation. Their decision to hold back the
Vienna event until 1882 left the field clear.[21]

The Islington exhibition was planned to last from 10 to 14 May, but was so
successful that it was extended for another three days; altogether there were
nearly 21,000 visitors. Papers on 'American Milling' by Andrew Hunter of

Chicago and on 'Siemen's System of Electric Lighting' by a Mr Antill were to have been given in the Berners Hall, but remained unread, due to the maintenance of interest in the many exhibits of 'machinery in motion'. Many firms had individual machines working, but the leading milling engineers operated enough machinery to demonstrate their systems. There were at least sixteen exhibitors of roller mills, a wide range of equipment being included by leading firms: Buchholz, Carter, Childs, Sanderson & Gillespie, Simon and Throop. Other firms that showed roller mills were Fiechter, Hopkinson, Miller & Herbert, Munden Armfield and Seck, all of whom were to become well-known in the trade. Also there were Joseph Baron, Joseph Bedford, and Corcoran & Witt, and at least one roller mill was displayed on some other exhibits. *The Miller* supplied extensive illustrated descriptions of the whole range of machinery.[22] Editorials encouraged the stages of anticipation, participation and reappraisal of the event; an exuberant report in June began: 'For Islington ho!' and included the statement: 'The Show, it had been widely proclaimed, would inevitably eclipse any Exhibition of the same character which had been held at home or abroad. What they actually saw, on entering the Hall, however, greatly exceeded their expectations'.

A TURNING POINT

It is difficult to assess the effects of the Islington Exhibition in detail, as there is little personal evidence about the subsequent stages of decision making. But there is plenty of other evidence of the successful progress of innovation after 1881. In Simon's list of the thirty firms that had given him 'one or more considerable orders' by 1886, seven had given their first order and eight had given a repeat order in 1881 or 1882.[23] His advertising showed his increasingly successful activity from 1882, and from 1883 he was able to publish impressive information on the spread of his system. There seems little doubt that small-scale modernisation increased markedly in 1881, or soon afterwards, to be followed by the gradual development of much larger plants; Simon was explicit about the importance of that year,[24] stating that: 'The Exhibition at Islington in 1881 marks a very decided epoch in the matter. Millers were astonished to find Roller Milling so prominent, so successful and so promising for the future, notwithstanding that the majority of millers looked upon it with suspicion as a craze ...' In 1923 Voller gave an authoritative assessment:

> If the modern history of British milling is ever attempted on a scale com-
> mensurate with the importance of our trade, a position of singular interest
> will certainly be assigned to the year 1881, the point at which accelerated
> reform actually commenced. In the Agricultural Hall, Islington, the greatest
> International Exhibition of milling machinery was held in that year.[25]

Voller described the next ten years as a period of great difficulty, 'a time of selection and development', and stated that millers reacted in one of three ways. Some retained millstone methods and had 'a hard future'. Secondly, there were firms that were only partly persuaded that drastic change was required, tried composite mills, followed by modernisation during the later 1880s, and that experience was costly. Thirdly, many firms were quick to seize the opportunity, installed full roller plant, and were usually well repaid for their confidence. By the end of 1881, the journal had detected 'no outward visible sign of a 'boom' being in progress in mill conversion', but reported that 'All our leading engineers and mill-furnishers have orders flowing in upon them'. At the start of 1883, the journal was still referring to the courage of those who had adopted the new systems, but at the start of 1884 it was stated that 'there are few places in the United Kingdom where there are not flour mills worked on the gradual reduction method'. Although millers did not make it generally public, it was known that 'in most cases the adoption had resulted beneficially'.[26] The National Association should be credited with a major contribution.

TALKING 'SHOP'

Further progress required exposition by milling experts, the supply of well-explained trade literature and opportunities to see full-scale plant in normal operating conditions. Carter and Dunham had been assiduous in urging that papers should be given, but the two that were to have been presented at Islington were not on subjects that closely supported the main activity. In 1882, Henry Simon, Proctor Baker and W. B. Harding gave lengthy papers on roller milling at the Institution of Civil Engineers, to an audience of professional engineers and master millers.[27] In 1883 Jago related practicalities of bread making to the basic chemistry, and James Higginbottom described his attempt at gradual reduction without using break rolls.[28] Then in 1884 the Association embarked on annual three-day conventions, for formal discussions, social togetherness and learning. Starting at Stockton-on-Tees, lecture subjects included:

1884   Book-keeping for millers, by J. H. Chatterton, and by F. Stansfield.

1885   On electric lighting, by W. Hartnell of Leeds; American roller milling, by M. W. Clark of the G. T. Smith Middlings Purifier Co.

1886   Gradual reduction milling applied to soft wheats, by T. W. Hibbard.

1887   Roller milling, an historical sketch, by Rhys Jenkins of the Patent Office; Milling technology, by A. R. Tattersall; Records of tests as to the power consumed by various machines used in roller mills, by Henry Simon.[29]

1888   The Carter and Zimmer sorting system, by Harrison Carter; The Simon-Haggenmacher patent sorter and dresser, by Henry Simon.

1889   Observations on the colour of wheaten flour considered from the standpoint of the manufacturer and merchant, by F. Ashby.

1890   The world's wheat crop and wheat values, by J. W. Rush; Roller milling in small mills, by Alph Steiger.

In his lecture in 1884, Chatterton was not merely concerned with the details of office practice; his aim was to encourage millers to keep records that could be used to compare the results of different milling systems.[30] In 1888, a special feature was the presentation of papers on the same day by the principals of all three of the foremost milling engineering firms; Carter and Simon were concerned with the development of new machinery. Charles Robinson of

Rochdale discussed 'the continuous advance and improvement of commonly accepted methods'.[31] The examples from 1889 and 1890 represented three other areas of increasing importance: early ideas concerning scientific testing, problems of choosing wheat supplies in a complicated world-wide market, and the difficulties of trying to produce high quality flour on small non-automatic plant.

As the number of installations of the various systems increased, there was greater opportunity for millers to visit new plants. As early as 1880, Simon was advertising that he could organise visits, and Carter made similar arrangements though, as could be expected, some millers accepted visitors willingly, while some preferred privacy. When Carter suggested that the London operatives should make a group visit to one of his installations, he stated that millers who were using his plants 'in almost every instance, have opened their mills without stint of inspection of any person who chose to come and see them'. During this early period, *The Miller* published many very short statements about new installations, and some more extensive descriptions of mills, but detailed records were not available for most mills or their equipment. This might have been partly due to a lack of skills in technical report-writing, and to the difficulty of including illustrations. Presumably, it was also related to the priorities of millers and engineers, who had to be busy with practical matters, with acquiring confidence in their own new work, and with gaining the assurance of competitive leadership.

There was also a period of more widespread opportunity to see full-scale plant, provided through arrangements by NABIM, during the conventions at Glasgow, Dublin and London, in 1885, 1886 and 1887.[32] In 1885, visits were arranged to eleven mills in Glasgow, and others at Greenock, Leith and Edinburgh, and it was possible to inspect plants supplied by Simon, Carter, Nagel & Kaemp, Throop and Buchholz. There were more than seventy visitors to the Craighall Mills at Glasgow to see the Simon system there. In 1886, there were visits to at least ten mills in or near Dublin to see plants by Simon, Carter, Robinson, Throop and Fiechter, including Patrick Boland's Ringsend Road Mill where Carter had erected his first major roller plant in 1880. In 1887, the main London mills were open for inspection. Simon roller systems, installed during the previous three years at Seth Taylor's St Saviour's and Waterloo Bridge Mills, could be compared with American machinery at J. & H. Robinson's Deptford Bridge Mills, which had Gray roller mills and gravity purifiers and also G. T. Smith purifiers. At the Royal Flour Mills at Vauxhall Bridge, Mumford had mainly Ganz three-high roller mills, but also roller mills from Houghton of Grimsby and Herbert & Law of Edinburgh. Another Simon plant was available at Marriage, Neave & Co.'s Albert Bridge Mills at Battersea.

The Council of the National Association discussed the possibility of a second special milling exhibition, to be held in 1887. Chatterton approached more than seventy firms that were thought likely to be interested in exhibiting. Thirteen engineers were 'decidedly against this project being carried out', including Simon, Carter, Dells, Corcoran, Whitmore & Binyon, Childs, Gardner and Throop, a group that represented a wide variety of technical and comercial styles, and the innovative leaders. The project was shelved and eventually

dropped. Milling engineers continued to exhibit on a small scale at RASE
shows, and the possibility of another special exhibition was occasionally
reviewed. In 1892, there was an attempt to provide one at Islington, but it
was not a success, and when the idea was raised again in 1896, *The Miller*
commented that the 1881 exhibition 'had been invited by the conditions of
the time ... But now the country is one vast milling exhibition'.[33]

Milling education

THE START: THE CITY & GUILDS INSTITUTE

A growing theme of discussion in the milling trade in the late 1870s was the
apparent scientific basis of new methods and the consequent new knowledge
involved. Arguments about the appropriateness of describing milling as a science
or the new ways and outlooks as scientific were combined with exhortations
to millers to study chemistry and mechanics. Correspondence on this theme
started in *The Miller* as early as 1875, and there were series of articles on
'Scientific and practical milling' and 'The science of milling'. An awareness of
more sophisticated ideas led gradually to interest in the practical requirements
of retraining mill staff, but change of outlook was inevitably affected by the
variety of the equipment and unevenness of technical advance. There was
comment on the inadequacy of the apprenticeship system and increasing
frequency of reference to milling operatives as a class, in the contexts of
technical awareness, training and proficiency.

Commenting on the presentation of technical papers by Simon and Sanderson
at the first meeting of NABIM in 1879, Dunham observed that 'the want of
technical education is a serious hindrance in any industry'. Later in 1879,
Dunham noted 'a deeper interest in the scientific aspects of flour manufacture'
by both master millers and their employees, particular evidence being a large
attendance of foremen millers and millwrights at the Kilburn show.[34] So far,
milling operatives were not much involved, but it became clear to the more
innovative millers that the successful use of the new systems would depend on
the technical insights acquired by master millers and on the abilities of
supervisors and operatives. The idea of setting up special millers' training schools
was aired occasionally but funds were not available, and it was not envisaged
that facilities could be provided for all the work force.

A cautious response by the journal took account of the situation in America,
and reports of the 1880 convention of American millers at Cincinnati. *The
Miller* suggested that neither United States nor British millers were ready for
the development of millers' training colleges, but that 'the time is coming when
every industry will have its special training school'. A practical alternative
existed, that could be used to encourage all who were involved in milling to
increase their technical skills and understanding: Dunham argued that milling
would be a suitable subject for examination by the 'City and Guilds of London
Institute for the advancement of Technical Education', and he proposed that
the subject should be added to the existing list of thirty-two others dealt with
by the Institute.[35] He urged that 'the authority which could negotiate for the

recognition of milling with best prospects of success is undoubtedly the National Association of British and Irish Millers'. J. H. Chatterton sought to direct attention to the need for a training scheme and for the involvement of the Association.[36] He referred to 'the apathy, indifference and even hostility of those employed ... Foremen, as well as operative millers, who, shut up from one year's end to the other in the same mill, naturally eye with suspicion any innovations on old routine'. Writing to *The Miller* he suggested that master millers should allow their foremen and operatives to visit the Islington exhibition. He emphasised the opportunity of 'seeing in active work all the latest devices'. There was a satisfactory outcome, the journal reporting that 'Of the twenty and odd thousand visitors who entered the Agricultural Hall, Islington, from the 10th to the 18th ult. inclusive, a very large number were of the foremen or operative class'.

After the Islington Exhibition, Dunham returned to this project. He combined a criticism of backwardness in technical training and a report of the building of a Central Institution for the City and Guilds Institute with details for a milling education scheme.[37] Less than a year later, Chatterton reported that both *The Miller* and *The Corn Trade Journal* had drawn attention to the fact that the City and Guilds Institute had accepted baking as an examination subject and that subsequently a successful approach had been made on behalf of milling.[38] The syllabus included the study of the properties, varieties and treatment of wheat, grinding, flour dressing, flour testing and the operation and power requirements of mill machinery including millstones and rolls. To fulfil the Institute's requirement for the associated study of science, the subjects chosen were machine construction and drawing, applied mechanics, inorganic chemistry, and steam. In order to obtain a full technological certificate it was necessary to pass in two of these subjects in addition to milling. W. Proctor Baker was appointed as examiner. Baker was a well-known miller, and was chairman of the trustees of a trade school in Bristol. When the first examinations were held in 1883, there were thirty-two candidates, twenty-two of whom were successful; two were examined at the School of Science in Gloucester, one of these being William Voller who was to play a prominent part in the development of milling education.[39]

Voller soon showed a willingness to take a part in the public discussion of milling education. Writing to Chatterton, he expressed concern about the requirement to study three subjects, and suggested that a candidate should receive 'a certificate for milling only, and if any did chance to go for science also, well and good; but have it plainly set forth that for practical milling a pass would be given'. He pointed out that milling literature was not generally accessible, that the recent candidates were likely to have been masters or foremen rather than operatives, and that 'Probably some hundred or more hands work in our local mills, and it would be safe to say that not a tenth of them know the why and wherefore of scientific milling – nor ever will they if our masters remain inactive'.[40]

During the first five years of formal milling education connected with the City and Guilds Institute's examinations and certification, from 1883 to 1887 inclusive, the total number of candidates was 173, and the total number of passes was 106. This stage was supervised by Proctor Baker, who was then succeeded by T. W. Hibbard and F. Ashby. Proctor Baker's reports to NABIM on the early efforts to promote technical education expressed concern at the small numbers of candidates, ignorance of the principles of machines and lack of skill in drawing. This last complaint was repeated: 'I trust that the Institute will use every influence to induce men of all grades in industrial occupations to learn drawing, as being an absolute necessity to all who desire to attain a power to advance themselves in manufacturing pursuits'. Those who were keen to improve their knowledge and their technical expertise needed access not only to the milling journals but to a full range of milling equipment. Proctor Baker commented:

> The best systems are to be found in large mills, and the work in large mills is subdivided into several distinct branches, and very few men have opportunities in acquiring a reliable knowledge of operations or of qualities of materials outside their own department. Small mills give men better chances of learning all branches of their trade, but in small mills the best machines of the day, and the best combinations of machines, are seldom to be found.[41]

There was an increasingly clear and insistent articulation by successive milling examiners of the need to understand the principles of the processes used in good milling practice. Against this advocacy there were expressions of indifference by operatives, foremen and masters, and the criticism by the President of NABIM, in 1887, that 'the existing examination was open to the objection that it was not so much a test of practical milling as an examination in the scientific technicalities of milling'.[42]

A Bill to provide for the extension of technical education was introduced into the House of Commons in 1888. *The Miller* welcomed it and the idea that instruction should be given in 'the principles of science and art applicable to industries and in the application of special branches of science and art to specific industries and employments'; the journal's view was that the teaching of 'mere practice' of a trade did not constitute technical instruction.[43] Several times the journal had criticised the nature of school education, reflecting the general strictures of the Royal Commission on Technical Instruction, which called for a unified system of elementary and secondary education in which the secondary schools could be the foundation of a system of scientific and technical instruction. At the fully vocational stage of education and training for aspiring millers there were practical problems of supply and demand: the organisation of technical classes and the availability of suitable teachers awaited each other. This problem applied generally in the sphere of technical eduation and was recognised by the National Association for the Promotion of Technical Education, which was founded in 1887. In the case of the milling industry, much depended on efforts made by a few individuals, while the general organisational structure and supervision were provided by NABIM. Discussion of difficulties and recruitment of examiners took place within the Association and leaders of the scheme were prominent members of the Association.

THE GLOUCESTER MILLERS' TECHNICAL CLASS

Significant initiatives for furthering the cause of milling education were taken by T. W. Hibbard, managing director of James Reynolds & Co. at the Albert Mills, on the dockside at Gloucester, and by W. R. Voller, who had joined the firm as wheat foreman in 1874 and had taken over the supervision of production in 1879. Hibbard was apprenticed in 1862 at the age of sixteen, and moved to the Albert Mills in 1869, to take charge of wheat buying and flour selling; he became a partner in 1872 and head of the firm in 1876.[44] Voller left school before the age of fourteen and worked in a water mill in Wiltshire, which ran three pairs of stones; he served two years as assistant to a stone dresser, and at sixteen, in 1871, took entire charge of the mill. Three years later Hibbard invited Voller to Gloucester. He became successively foreman, mill manager, a director and joint managing director of the firm.[45] Reynolds were the first to install a roller plant in the Gloucester district. There was an unsuccessful attempt to form a milling class at the Albert Mills at the end of 1883, but Voller stated that 'The ensuing year was one of remarkable activity in flour mills, in consequence of the rapid progress in roller milling. This, doubtless, had the effect of making men anxious to improve their knowledge with a view to being retained to operate the new fashioned machinery'.[46]

Figure 54.
Reynolds' Gloucester mill about 1892, with Voller at extreme right. (supplied by Reynolds)

Figure 55.
Marriages' Colchester
mill in the early
1890s. (supplied by
Marriages)

In the winter of 1884–85 about thirty meetings were held in the carpenters' shop at the Albert Mills, and in the winter of 1885–86 the work progressed so well that the Docks Coffee Room was hired and men from other mills were invited. Meanwhile Voller had qualified for a teacher's certificate. With Hibbard's support and collaboration, he took the leading part in conducting what became known as the Gloucester millers' technical class, the first such milling class in the country. Evidence of positive progress included Hibbard's statement in *The Miller* in 1885 that 'Soon after the class had been started I noticed a more intelligent interest was taken in the working of the different machines by the men who formed the class, which interest has gone on increasing'.[47] Voller frequently wrote to the journal, stressing the need for classes. Attendance rose to about twenty men and as the work developed the group was divided into elementary and more advanced sections. Voller was appointed as a staff teacher by the Gloucester Technical Schools' Committee, and classes were continued on school premises.

Through the correspondence columns of *The Miller*, advice was sought on how to pursue milling studies. Replies continued to make it clear that helpful and instructive reading matter was mainly to be sought in the journals and A. R. Tattersall in 1887 noted that 'there are few really helpful books in the way of milling technology ... Those noted in the City and Guilds syllabus are

Figure 56.
Marriages' Colchester
mill. (supplied by
Marriages)

in the German language, and no one has yet found it worth their time to translate them into English'.[48] Shortly afterwards he produced a pamphlet 'Helps to candidates for the milling examinations under the City and Guilds of London Institute', giving the regulations, syllabus, past papers and nine short essays on milling. *The Miller* deplored the lack of a suitable text-book.[49] The suggestion was challenged in the correspondence columns, but Hibbard, Voller, and Tattersall were strongly in favour of the idea. Hibbard, who had supported Tattersall with his small publication, asserted that

> A text-book is required wherein all the scattered information necessary to masters, foremen, and even milling engineers would be collected and assorted ready to hand, certain formulas and calculations which once made and verified, would always be available, as also experiments, in fact, a large mass of information the result of experience.[50]

Voller stated that 'the trade is demanding, and will have such a book – it is mainly a question of who shall write it'.[51] Eventually, Voller supplied it. He had been prompted partly by numerous requests for advice which he received from various parts of the country, and partly by a wish to develop his own personal teaching material into a more organised form; some of the content of his book had appeared as 'Notes for the milling examinations' in *The Millers' Gazette*.[52] In his first edition he said 'Very little has hitherto been done in the direction of giving definite shape to the vast amount of useful and instructive matter scattered broadcast by means of the press, and by lecturers, correspondence, essayists and others'.[53] His book, *Modern Flour Milling*, published in Gloucester in 1889, was the first substantial milling text by an English author. A thousand copies of the first edition were printed, a thousand of a second edition in 1892, and more than a thousand of an extended version in 1897. Voller's text was subtitled 'a handbook for millers and others interested in the grain and flour trades', and it gave readable descriptions of all the main aspects of British gradual reduction roller milling, including clear explanations of principles, discussion of problems of practical application, and variations in practice and opinion.

Friedrich Kick's text, *Flour Manufacture, a Treatise on Milling Science and Practice*, had been published in English translation in 1888, and Voller apologised for the appearance of his own book so soon afterwards, but the two were complementary. As Voller stated, Kick's work was not an exposition of English practice. By providing a review of the modern methods adopted in Britain, Voller's work enhanced the value of Kick's treatise as a source of reference. Voller's exposition not only gave shape to the vast amount of matter in the journals; it also provided a basis from which millers could study the flow of technical information. By this time, *The Miller* regularly had a page headed 'Books for Millers, bakers and kindred trades', obtainable from the journal office. The three substantial works on milling technology were Voller's, Kick's and the American Louis Gibson's *Gradual Reduction Milling*.

Voller had continually sought to encourage the spread of technical awareness and personal interest in proficiency, both within formal structures and informally. In the mid-1880s he had encouraged the sharing of knowledge through a correspondence circle, six years before R. W. Dunham advertised a scheme of correspondence classes in *The Miller*. Voller remained the clear leader in milling education until beyond the turn of the century; his earnest and constructive personality was evident in many public statements, including an article contributed to *The Miller* in the autumn of 1897, 'Self-improvement for young millers'. His introduction included: 'Winter in Great Britain is pre-eminently the season for all kinds of class and lecture work ... I will proceed to draft a few suggestions for the consideration of those of the trade who – during the coming winter – really wish to make some definite, if not rapid, progress in regard to mental or technical equipment'. This was followed by a series of suggestions for learning through experience, the improvement of practical skills, and discussion.[54] Voller calculated that during the first fifteen years of the City and Guilds scheme in milling, from 1883 to 1897, there were 562 passes, 182 being at the advanced level. By 1897, 107 of the passes in milling had been obtained by Voller's pupils.[55] The number of formal classes in the country in 1897 was six. He speculated on a future possibility of 500 candidates for yearly examination, eventually a realistic aspiration. The efforts that had been made were to the credit of individuals who took initiatives, and to the Association which provided the general opportunities.

CHAPTER NINE

Design and development

Convergence

The successful introduction of gradual reduction systems, using roller mills, depended on success at three stages of engineering design and development: (i) the mechanisms within the various machines, devised to carry out the basic milling operations, crucially the break operation; (ii) the main flour milling machines, incorporating those mechanisms; and (iii) the combination of the machines, the operations performed by them being complementary, to provide milling systems. The relationship between system design and machine design was potentially interactive, and engineering development depended on conjectures at barriers or thresholds. In successful development, system design was paramount, leading to overall improvement and quite quickly to system enlargement. Less successful development had the appearance of trial and error.

Roller mills were used on farms and in steel works. For flour milling, roller mills were disintegrators and grinders, evolved empirically, but with increasing refinement. A really effective break-roll pairing might seem to have become available almost suddenly, in the late 1870s, but there had been a lengthy period of experiments. Expositions by the Continental theorists Friedrich Kick and Gustav Pappenheim were at variance with practice established by Daverio and Simon.[1] Marston (1931) referred to a roller mill for grain processing in Britain in 1753, and listed the main features available in 1877, even though not combined and certainly not yet well executed:

> We have now the embryo of the modern roller mill, chilled cast iron rolls; differential speeds of three to one for breaks and nineteen to twenty-two for reductions; fluted surfaces; diagonal placing of rolls; roll scrapers; feed rolls and feed gate; and the introduction of helical gearing. All these were by different inventors, and it was many years before they were assembled together to form one accepted design.[2]

If a survey is made of British patents for variants of complete roller mills from 1874 to 1883 there may be thirty of general design interest, and twice that number if significant modifications are included (not minor improvements). Of these, some were illusory ideas and most others not of lasting consequence. Only specifications by Daverio; Gray; Mechwart; Turner, Turner & Carter; Simon; and Robinson were strongly influential or significant for UK application. In the long term the successful series of Bühler machines was supreme.

By the 1870s Daverio and others were putting together design components which would give good results, settling on chilled cast iron for the roll material. A saw-tooth break roll profile was adopted, rather than the alternative of

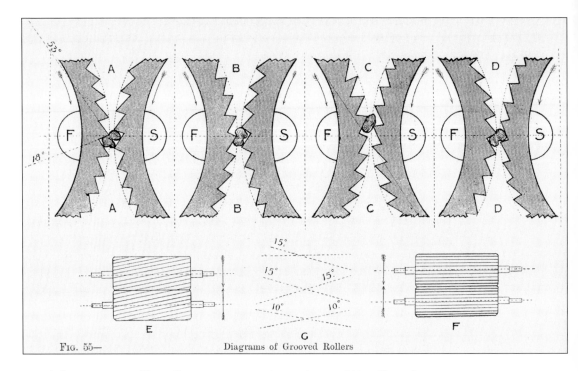

Fig. 55—   Diagrams of Grooved Rollers

rounded corrugations. Sharp fluting gave a cutting action, and literally a cleaner 'chop', contrasted with the squeezing effect of rounded profiles,. Simon (1879) dealt briefly with the detailed design of rolls, referring to 'fluted rollers of different degrees of fineness', to differential speeds as essential and to 'grooves or flutings' that were 'put on with a twist'.[3] Simon (1882) described the vital statistics of break rolls:

> The number of grooves to an inch of roller-surface varies according to the work to be done by the rollers; the best makers use from ten to twenty-five or even more grooves to the inch. With regard to the twist of the grooves, the angle adopted in ordinary cases by the Author is about 15 degrees ... The action of a pair of rolls with twisted [spiral] grooves is more scissor-like.[4]

An illustration showed that in each case of roll-pairing, the 'saw-tooth' profiles were arranged to act with sharp edge to sharp edge. Simon (1889) showed in a clearer diagram that the break rolls were run sharp to sharp, also that the saw-tooth was then not pointed; there was a small 'land' at each tip, to strengthen it and slightly reduce the severity of the cutting action.[5] Already in 1879 Simon had explained that progress was based on practical experiments:

> Some makers prefer to give the same circumferential velocity to each of the two rollers composing a pair; others prefer to run one considerably faster than the other, and thus employ what is commonly known as differential speed. Mr Daverio began without this differential speed, but prolonged experience taught him that conspicuously better results are certainly obtained with it. It stands to reason that without it, that is by more direct dead

Figure 57.
Diagram of fluting patterns discussed by W. R. Voller. (Voller 1897)

158

pressure, the flour is, so to say, forcibly pressed into the bran and consolidated into cakes, whereas with it a kind of shoving action, scraping or pushing the flour off the bran, is produced.[6]

It was left to later writers, particularly of text books, to describe a gripping action by the slow roll and a shearing action by the fast roll. Voller (1897) included a clear description but, as with most commentaries, analysis of the break operation was confined to the effect on grain, not the mixtures of material at break stages. Voller illustrated the four possible combinations of placing two saw-tooth profiles to act together, with his preferred arrangement of sharp to sharp to achieve the holding and shearing effects.[7]

Allocation of progressively finer fluting to successive break stages required initial assumptions about the relationship with grain size for the first break; there would have been doubt about gradation towards the later breaks. Cutting the flutes spirally was a sophisticated idea, and the preferred angle would have to be found, not calculated. Roll sizes were increased from an initial 12 inches length (and 9 inches diameter) to 30 inches length by 1882 and eventualy to 60 inches length (10 inches diameter). Simon (1882) commented on roll speeds:

> The number of revolutions of roller-mills vary a good deal. The Author uses for smooth rollers about two hundred [rpm] for the fast centre roller, and about one hundred and seventy [rpm] for the two slower rolls; and for grooved rolls, according to the work, from one hundred and sixty to about two hundred [rpm] for the slow roll, with a differential speed varying from two to three times that number or more for the two fast rollers.[8]

Many variations of the geometrical arrangements of rolls had been tried elsewhere, including a trail of discarded attempts. Orthodoxy was soon indicated by machines with four rolls in one frame, placed in horizontal or vertical pairings, but Daverio used three rolls, described in the specification (patent 2556 of 1879) as 'three rollers arranged with their axes in a nearly vertical line'. There were alternatives by Turners and Carter, and the Mechwart and J. Buchholz versions of the Ganz 3-roller mill. As expressed by Simon, one aim of the 3-roller design was the provision of a machine which required less power than the alternative of four rolls, both 3-roller and 4-roller mills being worked as two roll pairings. With cruder processing elsewhere, including Budapest, three pairs of rolls had been arranged vertically and used sequentially for three grindings without intermediate sieving. Some 3-roller mills were similarly applied (for two grindings) but when 3-roller machines were used to process separate streams of material there was the difficulty of guiding the two streams across each other. Simon described with enthusiasm Daverio's design of a 'cross-channel piece': 'With the application of this beautiful device the manufacture of three-high rollers became possible and successful'.[9] The Daverio 3-roller mill gave good service for a few years, but only by the standards of the early stages of innovation in Britain.

In addition to the principal mechanism for the break operation there had been careful attention to the design of bearings and the mechanism for adjusting the rolls. There was also provision for parting the rolls quickly and for stopping the feed. The means of guiding and controlling the feed to the nip of the rolls was an ongoing problem. In 1882 Simon referred to 'the Daverio mill, which the Author employs almost exclusively in the mills constructed by him in this country',[10] the close connection emphasised by Simon's promises to early customers that Daverio or Seck would start their plants. The system name was changed from Daverio to Simon-Daverio to Simon during 1879 to 1881. With many improvements to the continuously evolving system there was no need to call it anything other than the 'Simon system'.

During the 1880s there was the start of a long-lasting connection with Adolf Bühler at Uzwil in Switzerland.[11] It is well-known that Bühlers became manufacturers and suppliers of Simon roller mills, but there is a shortage of explicit information. Search of patent class 59: Grinding, Crushing &c reveals nothing by Bühler until 1902. *The Miller* frequently gave information and illustrations of Simon roller mills, but without comment about manufacture. There were machines with two, three and four rolls and then from the end of

Figure 58. Simon's source of roller mill manufacture. (*The Miller*, August 1885)

Supplement to "The Miller." August 3, 1885.

SIMON'S ROLLER MILL SYSTEM

H. Simon's ROLLER MILL Works.

H. SIMON

OFFERS

MILLERS

the following

ADVANTAGES

of H.S.'s Charge.

LARGEST and most experienced Sp

in Staff of Draughtsmen, Superintendin

xperts.

rove.

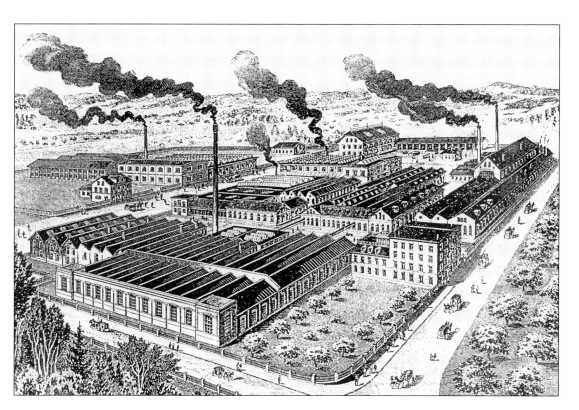

the 1880s the more impressive 'heavy pattern' four-roller mills. Roll pairings in two and four-roller mills used by Simon were arranged vertically,[12] with the exception of a design of 1883, which was soon followed by reversion to previous practice.[13] By 1886 there were new standards of 4-roller mills, Simon again enthusing 'The form and style of the machine is so correct that it resembles a first-class Whitworth machine tool'.[14] By comparing the English literature with Bühler publications it is clear that Simon roller mills came from Uzwil. The biggest roller mill of Henry Simon's own time, with rolls up to 60 inches long and shown in the 1898 catalogue, had an exact counterpart in Bühler's Modell A of 1897.[15] The 60 inch length was an approximation to an actual roll length of 1500 mm, the standard length in Bühler literature. A Bühler catalogue shows that by 1896 they had supplied 11,563 roller mills (*Walzenstuhle*) to a total of fourteen European countries and thirteen others, including Grossbritanien: 3860; Frankreich: 2495; Russland: 1865.

Simon's catalogue of 1892 included illustrations of workshops used for roller mill assembly and roll grooving, without saying where they were. Henry Simon's Circular of August 1895 was about 'the works in which my roller mills are made', presenting photographs of workshops, presumably at Uzwil. From 1881 there were references in *The Miller* to Simon's interests in manufacturing facilities: fluted rolls were manufactured 'at our own works'; there were 'extensive additions to my works'.[16] In August 1886 a journal advertisement included an external view of 'H. Simon's roller mill works'.[17] It strongly resembled part of

THE "SIMON" FOUR-ROLLER MILL
HEAVY PATTERN

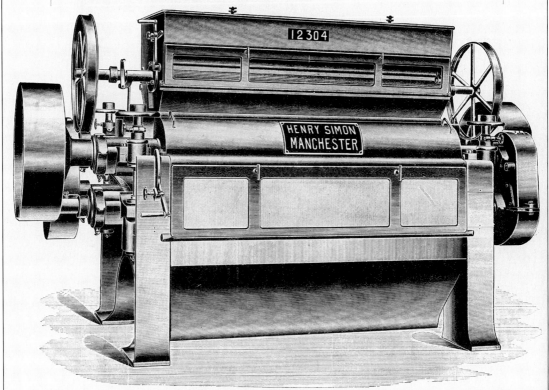

DIMENSIONS AND PRICES

Approximate Size of Rolls.	Extreme Length.	Extreme Width.	Extreme Height.	Size of Pulleys.		Revolutions.		Price.	
				Fluted.	Smooth.	Fluted.	Smooth.	Fluted.	Smooth.
In. In.	Ft. In.	Ft. In.	Ft. In.	In. In.	In. In.				
20 × 9	5 0	3 6	4 $3\frac{1}{2}$	16 × $5\frac{1}{2}$	20 × $5\frac{1}{2}$	375	220	£115	£100
24 × 9	5 3	3 6	4 $3\frac{1}{2}$	16 × $5\frac{1}{2}$	20 × $5\frac{1}{2}$	375	220	125	110
32 × 9	5 11	3 6	4 $3\frac{1}{2}$	16 × $5\frac{1}{2}$	20 × $5\frac{1}{2}$	375	220	145	125
24 × 10	6 0	3 $7\frac{1}{2}$	4 $4\frac{1}{2}$	16 × $5\frac{1}{2}$	20 × $5\frac{1}{2}$	350	200	145	125
32 × 10	6 8	3 $7\frac{1}{2}$	4 $4\frac{1}{2}$	16 × $5\frac{1}{2}$	20 × $5\frac{1}{2}$	350	200	160	140
40 × 10	7 4	3 $10\frac{1}{2}$	4 9	16 × $5\frac{1}{2}$	20 × $5\frac{1}{2}$	350	200	200	180
50 × 10	8 7	3 $10\frac{1}{2}$	5 $3\frac{1}{2}$	16 × $6\frac{1}{2}$	20 × $6\frac{1}{2}$	350	200	250	225
60 × 10	9 7	3 $10\frac{1}{2}$	5 $3\frac{1}{2}$	20 × $6\frac{1}{2}$	—	350	—	300	—

HENRY SIMON, LIMITED, MANCHESTER

a Bühler illustration of their works, published in 1927, and also a picture of the Bühler factory at Uzwil dated 1896.[18] E. D. Simon, who had been to Bühlers after his studies at Cambridge recorded informally in 1921 that 'machines were bought from Bühler and Seck', but Anthony Simon (1947) merely stated that Henry Simon 'had his machines built in Switzerland and Germany', not the full story.[19]

Henry Simon was certainly interested in the design of roller mills and it would be difficult to detach that from an increasing knowledge of manufacture. In 1883 he made a patent application for improvement of the mechanisms which controlled roll positioning and clearances. The surprising fact is that the general arrangement drawing showed unorthodox roll placements regarded merely as saving space: roll pairs were arranged diagonally, not one above the other, or side by side, but the chop would have been discharged towards the inside of the machine, not outwards which was to become the standard arrangement twenty years later.[20] In 1884 Simon communicated an application from abroad to his London patent agent for an improvement in the design of three-high roller mills; Simon was at Wiessbad in Switzerland.[21] There were others, not from abroad: in 1891, an improvement of the guide plates feeding material to the rolls; in 1897, an improvement in the gearing controlling roll speeds – in conjunction with Sidney Leetham of York.[22] These activities suggest that Simon was frequently in touch with roller mill design, and inescapably also with manufacture.

SIEVING AND SEPARATING

Simon commented in 1882, 'In England the introduction of centrifugal dressing machines during the last few years marched abreast with the introduction of roller mills'.[23] Centrifugals were designed to improve sieving efficiency, compared with the previous rudimentary dressers: bolters and reels, which were large cumbersome machines, which were rotated to tumble the meal round the inside of the cylinder. During separation of rough material in the meal, which was ejected at the end of the machine (overtailed), from the required product (throughs) which fell through the mesh, several grades of flour could be obtained, by covering a frame in sections with different mesh sizes. By contrast, centrifugals had rapidly revolving beaters within slowly rotating cylinders. The meal was thrown against the mesh. As the action was more forceful, centrifugals could be much smaller than reels.

For a short time, attention was paid to centrifugals from Nagel & Kaemp of Hamburg, but British firms soon moved into the market. Munden Armfield & Co. in Hampshire became specialists. Hind & Land at Preston were warning possible infringers increasingly sharply in 1881 about their recent patent for literally a new angle on their beaters.[24] There were many other British makers, and Simon commented again in 1882 'Numberless are the patents for different shapes and positions of these beaters'. He reported that Heinrich Seck of Frankfurt had 'invented a new centrifugal, combining both wire cylinder and silk in one machine'.[25] Simon was confident that the action was less severe than with other designs: 'The object of these inner beaters is to raise the

Maschinenfabrik und Giessereien

ADOLF BÜHLER, UZWIL (SCHWEIZ).

Gegründet 1860.

Neuester Vierwalzenstuhl

mit Walzen von 1250 und 1500 Millimeter Länge.

System Bühler.

Extra starkes Modell A. — Construction 1897.

Specielle Vorteile.

Platz- und Kraft-Ersparnis. Vereinfachte Bedienung.

Neue automatische Speisevorrichtung mit absolut gleichmässiger Mahlgut-Zuführung.

Einfaches Demontiren und Einsetzen der Walzen.

Bequeme Aspiration.

material … and throw it, in a gentle cloud, as evenly as possible, all over the surface' of the silk.

Henry Simon's advertisements referred explicitly to 'system' from 1879; J. Buchholz, Carter and Nagel & Kaemp proclaimed similarly from 1880, though only Carter was joining Simon in tangible progress to a full system. With other firms the accent was usually on individual machines. It was difficult to display the scope of 'system' in journal columns or in technical papers. Simon tried in 1879 with a diagram published in *The Miller*, showing opportunities for the use of centrifugals, rather than clear applications.[26] Simon (1879) referred in his lecture to NABIM to 'a mill recently established in Manchester', which must have been at McDougalls'. There was a claim that 'A large quantity of first flour' (break flour) was obtained, 'at least 15 per cent'. That was soon to be seen as a feature requiring change. In 1886 Simon was stressing that during 'granulation' an objective was to make 'as little break flour as possible'.[27]

Only as the reduction operation was extended, in coordination with fuller use of purifiers, could the even bigger conjunction be clearly seen: roller mills, centrifugals and, at that early stage, gravity purifiers. As systems were elaborated, the technical detail became so copious that expert knowledge was needed for even general interpretation of flow process diagrams. In his paper to the Civils, Simon (1882) included a simplified flow diagram, trying to preserve clarity by eliminating details.[28] Even so, it required several pages of the Proceedings to describe the flow, which represented a 'small plant of average completeness as suitable for small mills'. There were five breaks and centrifugals were used for scalping and for dressing out flour after reductions.

Intractable problems

As new machines were tried out in workshops and then in mills, followed inevitably by modifications, there were always uncertainties. The plansifter was for long a puzzling and hazardous design. The 3-roller mill was not an ideal design, though many were used until the mid-1880s, nor was the centrifugal found to be a fully effective all-purpose sieve and separator; it went in and out of favour, but had long-term usefulness. Gravity purifiers, long relied upon abroad, were being discarded in Britain in the mid 1880s. Milling systems became more aptly named when it was more fully recognised that the break, scalping, grading, purifying, reduction and dressing operations were not independent; they were linked not only when each operation was arranged to suit the next, but in more far-reaching effects throughout.

There were many topics for reconsideration, for instance when it was found that making flour at the break stages was unwise. From the first break the flour was inferior, containing dust or dirt or bran colouring or mysterious admixtures. It followed that the priority during scalping should be maximisation of semolina production with minimal reduction of particle sizes; it was necessary to be careful with the semolina and so there was concern that centrifugal action might be too severe. Flour production was to be the job of the reduction rolls, and purification needed to be an extended effort, carried out in relation to a

Figure 61.
Bühlers' advertisement at the Paris exhibition in 1900. (Bühler special catalogue)

lengthened reduction process. A good use for centrifugals could be at the flour dressing end of the gradual reduction process, rather than at the scalping and initial grading stages.

In 1886 Simon was claiming that his centrifugals had a more gentle action then others, so they could be used for scalping at all break stages. He discussed the requirements of what was 'generally regarded as a simple, rough operation', stating that 'to scalp properly is one of the most difficult and nicest operations in the whole process'.[29] Despite continued belief in the versatility of centrifugals, he was introducing a new method, using a rotary grading and separating machine. It had been adopted by 'two eminent firms, who have always been ready to accept improvements ... one of them has been running it for some time, and has reduced the quantity of break flour to about five per cent'. The new method which had been 'for a considerable time under consideration and experiment' involved gyratory motion applied to horizontal or slightly inclined rectangular sieving surfaces.

All the leading milling engineers produced what were called rotary machines but not meaning reels or centrifugals; movement was approximately in the plane of the sifting surface. The gyratory motion could be determined by some form of eccentric, crank or cam. There was scope for many design variations, including use of multiples of the basic sieving surface module. It was necessary to balance the oscillating masses, to minimise and preferably eliminate vibration. This could be achieved in relatively simple machines, but proved to be a daunting problem when larger and more elaborate versions were developed. Scott (1972) noted that at least some of the rudimentary ideas could be traced back to the 1770s and John Milne, from Aberdeen 'who settled in Rochdale and made wire birdcages etc and also bolting cloth'. Small plane sieves were tried at various times, quaintly named jogglers and dickeys, but the separations for which they seemed useful had defied mechanisation for large scale processing.

THE PLANSIFTER DILEMMA

A new theme started in 1888 with Carl Haggenmacher's patent specification for 'sifting, bolting, sorting or grading meal, middlings ... giving a swinging or swaying motion to the sieves'.[30] Haggenmacher was the proprietor of the Ofen Pesther mill at Budapest. His inventive step was to place laths along a sieve to form channels, and put smaller laths at right angles projecting into the channels, which forced the meal to advance; the swirling material was prevented from completing a loop by the cross laths, oddly called impellers, and so it moved along a channel, then back along the next one, greatly increasing the length of the sieving path. Haggenmacher's Plansichter (plane sifter) was taken up by Simon, initially for flour dressing, though there was continual confusion about the capabilities and limitations of all machines used to make separations. William Stringer's attempt to talk about the machine and its scope for application, when he addressed the Plymouth Convention in 1888, was tantalising and lacking in technical evidence; Simon's 'milling expert' took the risk of supporting a design that had not been sufficiently tested in UK conditions. His supposed title, in the absence of a paper from Simon or a practical demonstration, was

'Haggenmacher's patent scalper', but Stringer contended that 'it is not a scalper at all – it is a dresser'. His problem was the need to maintain the usefulness of his firm's rotary scalper. As Stringer said: 'Carl Haggenmacher put on his laths, and the stuff walked up and down from head to tail, and back again as often as might be necessary, or he could start in the middle of the sieve, and it would go round, like an army round the walls of Troy'.[31]

Participants in the discussion failed to obtain more details, so the new device was only notionally introduced. Stringer said: 'he had made many attempts to describe the machine on paper, but had failed'. Haggenmacher had written repeatedly to Simon, inviting inspection but 'never sent any description'. They had been too busy to go to Budapest, but 'the very day they saw the arrangement of laths on the sieve [possibly in the patent specification] he [Stringer] was on his way to Budapest'. Presumably the Convention audience was intrigued and puzzled. Voller protested that

Mr Stringer had told them that Haggenmacher's invention was destined to effect a revolution in dressing machinery; but, as other speakers had pointed out, he had not told them how this was to be effected … The essential thing to be told was whether the sieve would be a practical substitute for the centrifugals as well as for the reels'.[32]

Figure 62.
Haggenmacher's
plansifter of 1895.
(*The Miller*, November
1895)

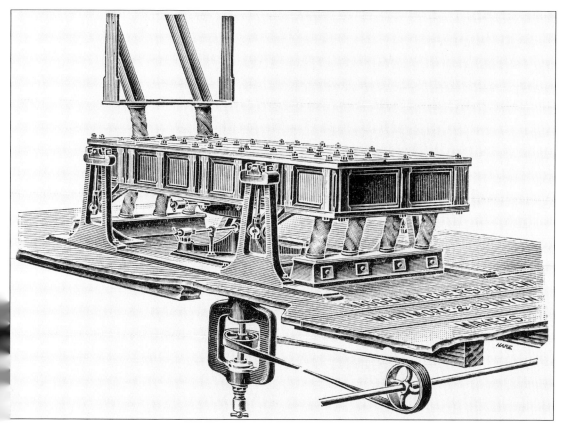

Stringer believed that he and Simon were on the verge of a breakthrough that would greatly simplify their system, and machinery requirements. Confronted with burgeoning technical competition between Simon, Robinsons and Carter, Stringer sought to reserve a place for Simon's sieving machine at the scalping stage and prepare for Haggenmacher's plansichter at the later stages of flour dressing. It was still a mysterious situation, as Frederick Kick referred to the 'Haggenmacher rotary scalper'. How versatile might it be? There was a shortage of news, as great expectations were followed by disappointments. During 1889 or soon afterwards there were technical difficulties and financial losses. It was said that sieve mesh became clogged with damp material, that the operation was hidden from view, and that there were alarming vibrations.

Eventually the plansifter was to become a sieving and separating machine for all occasions, with the establishment of all-plansifter mills, but such impressive system simplification depended on many design improvements, extending into the last third of the twentieth century. There was earlier usefulness in Europe, where the less varied materials-in-process and the drier atmosphere provided easier conditions but, even there, not without difficulties. In Hungary, application of the plansifter was more attractive as a replacement for laborious sieving procedures, and more easily tolerated during stoppages. In Britain, automatic systems required reliable machinery. William Stringer's too easy acceptance of Haggenmacher's early design was a costly mistake. It demonstrated clearly that system improvement depended on careful testing of machines in practical mill conditions, followed by close attention to details within the machine design, and to effects and requirements imposed on other parts of the total process.

Early in 1890 a meeting was held at Braunschweig, where four firms agreed to coordinate their dealings with Haggenmacher, mainly concerning trading areas and the stability of patent licence costs. The firms were Henry Simon, G. Luther, Ganz & Co., and Dobroff & Nabholz of Moscow. Simon was represented by Stringer.[33] In 1892 Simon and Stringer visited Braunschweig for discusssions with Luther, but Simon's contract with Haggenmacher seems to have been a hindrance to further development of interest in Luther's work on plansifter design. At the end of 1894 Simon made his difficulties public, through his regular communication to customers: 'Henry Simon's Circular'. Referring to 'rumours of an attempt to reintroduce into Great Britain a machine known as the Plansichter', he declared his position:

> Those of my clients who were induced on my representations to give it a trial, will admit that I put forth every effort and spared no expenditure to make it a success. It was in vain. All the skill of my engineering staff, all the experience of well-known millers, were fruitlessly employed, and after endless trials, endless alteration and endless expense, I was obliged to abandon further attempts to adapt the Plansichter to the requirements of automatic milling in Great Britain.[34]

He stated that he had paid £5,000 to cancel his contract with Haggenmacher, considering that the machine was defective; elsewhere he wrote that he had incurred losses totalling nearly £15,000. Luther also decided to cancel his agreement with Haggenmacher.

In 1895 'The Haggenmacher Plansifter' was announced boldly by Whitmore & Binyon, who had acquired an agency and responsibility for manufacture.[35] It had been 'introduced into this country some six years ago, but for some reasons was not then a success'! Optimistically, they suggested that 'oftentimes a first failure proves but to be a stepping stone to success'. They claimed that 'There is no system of reels or centrifugals for grading or dressing flour that will make such perfect separations as can be obtained by the use of the plansifter'. At the 1895 Convention in London, there was a paper on 'The Haggenmacher plansifter' by a representative of Whitmore & Binyon. The channels, along which material traversed the sieve surfaces, had been broadened to promote circulation, and were not sub-divided into series of squares. It was said that vibration problems had been dealt with. Voller was optimistic, but he did not think that the plansifter would have all-purpose applicability.

From 1895 Luther offered his automatic roller-plansifter system in Britain, through his agent in Liverpool, Emil Fiechter. Carter had a planesifter. Van Gelder of Leeds, who had experimented with plane sifters before Haggenmacher's machine became known, but had not thought of slats and impellers, became a sub-agent to Whitmore & Binyon. Hind & Lund of Preston, and Higginbottom at Liverpool, had other versions. Higginbottom stated that his design was 'fitted with an efficient mechanical brush and aspirating device. Is entirely without suspenders. Does not require peas and beans to clean the sieves'.[36] That referred to two awkward problems: how to support the sieve stacks, and how to keep the mesh open. In various machines large seeds were used to clear sieving surfaces by rattling about on them; they were gradually overtailed, separated automatically from the materials-in-process, and recirculated for repeated use. Alternatively, rubber balls were used as knockers on sieve surfaces.

Perhaps the most interesting alternative was the Common-Sense plansifter from Wm. R. Dell & Son, using a design patented by Bunge in Germany.[37] The sieves were circular, made up into a cylindrical stack, suspended from long thin rods. Advertisements included: 'No slats, no vibration, no beans … everybody astonished'. Luther suspended his plansichter by 'patent bamboo canes', a curious technique, which was to outlast many other design changes. Absence of slats gave freedom from the supposed force of Haggenmacher's patents. Although the aim of all plansifter designers was to mechanise the principle of the simple hand sieve, to bring large particles into upper layers and riddle small ones down through mesh of chosen aperture size, there was a surprising scope for variation of sieving effects. The fact that damper materials not only blinded sieve mesh, but hindered the free movements of different sizes of particles to appropriate layering positions, added to the difficulty that the process could not be watched, merely criticised afterwards. The perils of plansifter purchasers were increased by legal contests. Haggenmacher paraded five patent claims, assailed a Luther customer, and was defeated. Luther counter-attacked and two Haggenmacher patents were declared invalid. Simon returned to his

belief in the superiority of centrifugals, referring in 1898, in his last catalogue,
'to a curious reversion'.

SYSTEMS DEVELOPMENT

Renewed confidence was based on three aspects of extensive experience. *System enlargements*, with bigger plants at large port mills had given overall confirmation of principles. *System improvements*, involving individual machines, had been made continually, providing wide practical experience for the benefit of drawing office staff. Although the plansifter *v.* centrifugal episode was temporarily disconcerting, the reversion to previously preferred sifters was made after several years of successful work in *system extension*: wheat cleaning, washing and drying plants had been installed throughout the country, as shown on maps published by Simon each January. The better condition of much of the raw material led to reappraisals. Simon (1898) stated that improvement depended on gentle methods of scalping: 'Numberless machines were designed and constructed to meet this new demand, all of the sieve type, oscillating and rotary, with plane surfaces and conical surfaces, and with infinite variety in detail of construction'.[38]

Increased attention was paid to wheat condition, beyond obvious cleanliness or lack of it. Many devices were produced to remove seeds larger or smaller than wheat grain, and all too frequently dust, dirt and stones. But there was also growing awareness of what Voller called 'grinding condition' and methods of 'wheat conditioning', which he said was 'a term which is somewhat loosely applied'. In the 1889 edition of his text, he stated that 'To be fit for the mill working on a roller system, wheat should be nicely dry without harshness or undue hardness, it may incline to mellowness, but should not be soft or anyway damp'.[39] Some foreign wheats were flinty or brittle, and much English wheat was very damp, especially after poor summers and wet harvests. Millers had previously put a hard and a soft wheat together, in the hope of improving the milling quality of both. When silo storage became common the still vague aim was 'to enable some transference of moisture and assimilation of nature to take place', as expressed many years later by W. S. Thompson (1934).[40] With conditioning, the break operation could be carried out with tangibly greater satisfaction.

No finality

Engineering design thrived on searches for alternatives, influenced by commercial rivalry, and often expressed in patent litigation or threats of it. There was also a technical quest which generated its own momentum. A new period of purifier development from the mid 1880s seemed to indicate advance rather than solution of isolated problems. Although the study of all milling processes was empirical in nature, the new purifiers were more recognisably machines, in contrast to gravity purifiers in which an airflow acted on falling streams of stock to separate relatively pure and impure material. Simon possessed both the idea that there were technical boundaries, and also a belief that improvement would continue indefinitely. This helped him to survive and

Figure 63.
Reform purifier in
Simon's 1892
catalogue.
(Simon 1892)

THE "SIMON" PATENT
NEW "REFORM" PURIFIER.

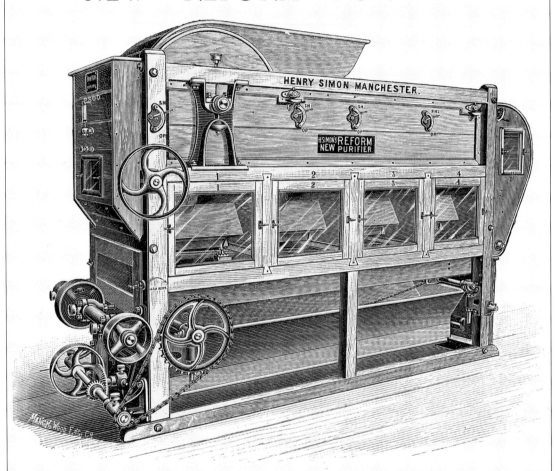

DIMENSIONS AND PRICES.

Size of Machine.	Extreme Length.		Extreme Width.		Extreme Height.		Driving Pulley.		Revolutions of Eccen. Shaft per minute.	Price.
WITH PATENT TAIL ASPIRATION.										
	Ft.	In.	Ft.	In.	Ft.	In.	In.	In.		
Single .	10	8	3	10	6	6	8 ×	3	450	£120
Double .	10	8	5	7	6	6	8 ×	3	450	150
WITHOUT PATENT TAIL ASPIRATION.										
Single .	9	3	3	10	6	6	8 ×	3	450	£115
Double .	9	3	5	7	6	6	8 ×	3	450	140

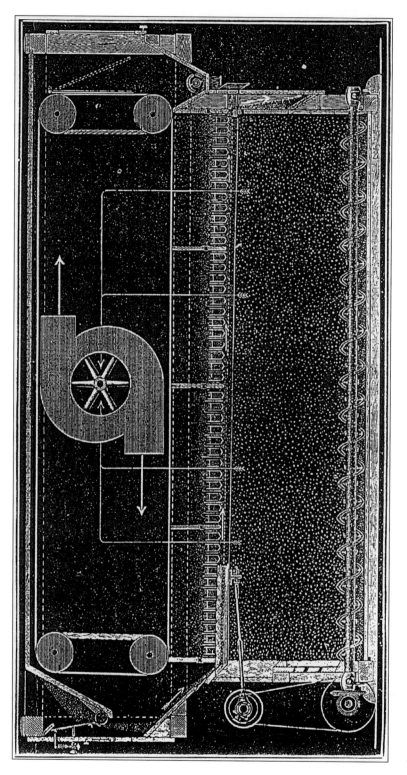

Figure 64.
Diagram of purifier
channels described by
Simon. (Simon 1890)

persevere, despite setbacks. He made a strong impact on the course of purifier design from about 1883 to the mid 1890s; there were three episodes: early experiments, machine development, and legal nuisance imposed unnecessarily by others, with competition between patents. From 1883 to 1892 Simon made at least thirty-three patent applications concerning milling machinery solely in his own name and at least six more in association with other applicants. Twenty-eight can be found in the volumes of Abridgements of Specifications, indicating accepted applications and, of these, eleven concerned purifier design. Amongst eleven applications not found in the volumes of Abridgements (therefore void) six dealt with purifier designs, presumably concerning work that was discarded or superseded.

Semolina was the attractive endosperm constituent, middlings the awkward part, bran the material to remove – in flakes if possible, but also the fragments and tiny particles wherever possible. So-called gravity purifiers varied in inner complexity and effectiveness. Particles which were less compact, especially if branny, were carried or deflected further by an airflow which was carefully regulated so that bran particles were channelled away from the rest. The devices were often intricate; Kick referred to 'tortuous air currents'.[41] From the mid 1880s they were steadily displaced in Britain by sieve purifiers which were more amenable to development. Simon announced the introduction of his patent Reform sieve purifier early in 1885 as 'An important & new departure'; he had a new method of dealing with the airflow and a selling point that it 'will purify the very finest stuff that no other machines can touch'.[42] With a series of modifications, the Reform purifier was shown to be comprehensively applicable and became a prominent feature of his system. The principle of the Reform series of designs was to draw an airflow up through the sieve, and then through a grid of channels in which bran particles were deposited as the air velocity decreased.

There had been sieve purifiers in Britain in the late 1870s; Voller (1897) called them 'old patterns'. Simon (1892) referred to allegations that the Reform principle and patent had been anticipated by 'so-called prototypes', claiming that they had failed 'the test of practical working'.[43] That did not apply to G. T. Smith's design, the best known before the Reform appeared, which Dells continued to offer until 1890. In 1883 Dells were issuing warnings: 'we beg respectfully to caution millers against purchasing machines which are infringements of the English patents owned in this country by the Geo. T. Smith Middlings Purifier Co. and the John T. Noye Manufacturing Co.'. Although Smith defended his position strenuously in North America there was no similar contest in Britain, perhaps because designs were becoming more sophisticated. Simon expressed his confidence by advertising in 1887 that 'The Reform improvement can be added to every sieve purifier on G. T. Smith and similar principles. Large numbers have been converted in England with great success, and no user of G. T. Smith purifiers should fail to have the Reform improvements added'.[44]

Kozmin (1917) attributed the design of the Reform purifier to Seck at Dresden and stated that it 'was evolved' from Smith's purifier, but his statement was an oversimplification. Kozmin was hindered by gaps in the literature available to him, complaining that 'the German authors do not give a broad scientific technical statement to their readers when they omit to mention English and American machinery'.[45] There were cultural and language difficulties. In 1896 Simon commented in personal correspondence that 'Made in Germany' was not in favour.[46] And often there were combined commercial and personal differences of viewpoint. Writing to Ingleby in 1894 Simon referred to difficulties in his dealings with Seck, but there was also an indication that Simon was always attentive to fresh ideas: 'the fact remains that for many years I have worked with him, that my attention was originally drawn to these channels by him'. Simon was giving instructions to Ingleby about discussions in Frankfurt concerning purifier design.[47]

The 'channels' formed the crucial part of the Reform method, distinguishing it from other techniques; the idea was expressed in Seck's patent 5155 of 1884, to which several Simon patents were related. Simon and Heinrich Seck collaborated closely until the firm of Simon, Bühler & Baumann was set up at Frankfurt in 1892. Henry Simon's telegraphic address was 'Reform, Manchester', and the word Reform exists in German with the same meaning. However, the many patent applications in Simon's name are indications of Simon's own activity. In 1890 he published a description of the Reform, which included a list of fourteen patent applications which he considered the most relevant up to the year 1887, including three by Seck and two jointly with Seck.[48] Simon was often abroad, sometimes for health reasons, sometimes on business. Six of the total of thirty-nine patents in his name from 1883 to 1892 were 'communicated from abroad' by him, including four concerning purifiers. No. 8542 of 1885 was sent from Hanover; others were submitted from Switzerland.

The introduction of the Reform purifier in 1885 had been closely connected with the experience gained during the firm establishment of the new milling methods from 1882 to 1885. Simon (1886) recorded that 'a machine was designed and built three years ago on an entirely different principle. This machine has been altered, improved, and perfected by practical experience, and this is the machine introduced by the author under the name 'The Reform''. At the same time he wrote about his increasing number of projects: 'one must not lose sight of the great amount of time and thought, and the number of practical experiments required, before these results could be attained. Very little has been done by intuition, and, as in every other branch of manufacture, the present comparative perfection has been attained by slow up-hill work'.[49] Gilbert Little (1887) commented on Simon's energy: 'it has been much to the advantage of modern milling that its greatest exponent has never believed in finality'.[50] The compliment was from the perspective of a competitor, previously with Harrison Carter. When Little made his comment the Reform was making news for the first time. It was reported to be in use in France, Belgium and Germany, but also in Austria-Hungary, and the appearance was already radically different from the rudimentary initial version. When Simon commented in 1892, there was again quite a new look, and it was that further move forward that led to a legal contest. Simon stated: 'For the engineer, as for the man of science, finality does not exist'.[51]

The distinctive feature of the Reform was the grid of channels placed closely above the sieve, running laterally; there were spaces betwen the channels. The slightly inclined sieve was oscillated to move the stock over several successive grades of silk cover, fine mesh near the head, coarser mesh towards the tail. The airflow drawn up through the sieve, combined with the shaking, produced a layering of the stock: pure middlings gravitated towards the silk, branny middlings rising, and small bran flakes coming to the top layer. Differences of particle size, density and air resistance allowed this sorting to be achieved. Pure endosperm passed through the silk. Endosperm particles of generally similar size, but with bran attached, and some separate bran flakes, were kept from the silk by the airflow and carried to the tail of the sieve. Bran particles and dust were lifted through the grid of channels. Dust was carried towards the fan, but caught in a filter or some other form of trap, while heavier components fell back into the channels and were shaken or brushed towards side troughs.

From around 1890 Simon advertisements included descriptions of improved separation of pure and reject material, contrasted with previous methods which had left impure middlings either amongst the endosperm or in the offal. An enthusiastic account of the action of the airflow through the grid of channels appeared in the small book by Simon (1890), which in 1894 became an exhibit and one of the few clear statements in the long drawn-out contest of Parkinson *v.* Simon in the High Court. The 'entirely new principle of separation' was described.

> Immediately above the silk is placed an apparatus which contracts the air current, increasing its speed and at the same time its sustaining power ... The action of the wind here is most peculiar ... the deflected currents of air (and impurities) when they meet in the open space between the channels pass up in one thin stream through the very centre of this space ... If the machine is examined when at work this peculiar action is most striking ... The intensified air having passed the channels emerges into an open space above them, where it expands, and consequently drops its load of suspended material.[52]

The shape of the channels described by Simon (1890) was different from the preference in Seck's patent 13141 of 1885, which appears less convincing. Comparison with the text by Lockwood (1945) shows that some basic principles remained valid for many years, using 'trays' or 'tins', as the channels became known. Lockwood summarised the overall complexity:

> medium sized pure endosperm particles had the same terminal velocity in air as larger endosperm particles with pieces of bran attached. Such stocks could only be separated by a combination of grading and aspiration, and this led to the development of the modern purifier, in which separations are made by a combination of sifting, shaking, gravity and aspiration; sifting and aspiration alone are not enough, because of the very slight differences between the stocks to be separated.[53]

In sieve purifier design the aspect of perennial interest was the airflow pattern.

After the small bran particles had been lifted from the stock on the sieve, it was necessary to alter velocities and directions of flow, in order to deposit the impurities. There were alternatives to the Simon-Seck channels device, one based on lengthy experience of inventing by Higginbottom, the other being the latest of Robinson's attempts to catch up. James Higginbottom of Liverpool was advertising a purifier as early as 1879, as part of an unorthodox assembly devised with Edward Hutchinson, the Liverpool miller: 'The best machine made. The air currents are applied uniformly to all portions of the vibrating sieve ... the machine has no internal baffle boards, valves, slides, or other clap-trap appliances'.[54] Higginbottom's method was to draw an airflow through nozzles in a tray above the sieve; subsequent expansion of the air currents resulted in impurities being deposited on the tray. Simon wrote to Seck in 1890: 'I regret to have to inform you that the history of the Reform patents increasingly takes on a more serious implication. If the indications which Higginbottom sent me are true ... [he] has been using our reform channels since 1879'.[55] That was not true, but there were complications. Simon sought to amend Seck's patent 5155 of 1884 and was opposed by Higginbottom, on the basis of his patent 14711 of 1888. Higginbottom's main interest was a point of detail: the nearness of the collecting surface(s) to the sieve. Consequences were that Simon's draughtsmen were hindered, and there was increased concentration on detail, not in drawing offices, where it was essential, but in rivalry which could lead too easily to lawyers' offices.

A much bigger issue was created by Robinsons of Rochdale as competition in the purifier market increased during the early 1890s. Robinsons had progressed from a design patented by the Case Manufacturing Co. of America to their new XL purifier based on an ageing Oexle patent and another from Jacob Holgate, a miller at Burnley. They made further progress with their Diamond purifier of 1886, in which U-shaped troughs were arranged longitudinally and described as 'the principal feature'; it seems surprising that it was not considered an infringement of the Reform, as the Seck patent 13,141 of 1885 stated that the 'troughs are arranged ... longitudinally or transversely above the surface of the rocking sieve'. Robinsons' next advance was opportunistic, and ironically resulted from Simon's personal mixture of enthusiasm with thoroughness. In 1889 T. & M. Parkinson, millers at Doncaster, were working on ideas for a new purifier and invited Henry Simon's participation. In January 1890 Simon wrote to them, expressing strong interest in acquiring exclusive right to manufacture and sell, though William Stringer had visited Parkinsons and reported that 'a great deal of further experimenting' was required.[56] In February Simon was writing about 'our new patent' and Parkinsons were confirming that dimensions of the sieve were being altered to incorporate suggestions from Stringer: 'The adoption of Mr Stringer's narrow track [sieve] idea has led to a further important development, viz.: side expansion spaces'.[57] The airflow was to be deflected, to deposit impurities on surfaces along each side of the sieve, Parkinsons' alternative to channels and nozzles, which would lead to trouble.

In March, Parkinsons reported that a 'representative of a very large mill-engineering firm' had visited them. It seems from his conversation that the

Victoria [Higginbottom's purifier] is a bugbear to this firm too'. Simon was not to be rushed: 'I have paid too dearly in the past, for introducing inventions before they were perfect, to make the same mistake again'.[58] Parkinsons' results did not seem equal to the performance of the Reform; prototypes were built at Doncaster and Manchester. Parkinsons asked 'How would the Narrow Gauge do for a name?', referring to the use of a narrower sieve suggested by Stringer. Simon replied that 'It is very difficult to find one [a name] that will, on the one hand steer clear of puffery, and on the other hand be sufficiently attractive and significant'.[59] In May, Ingleby warned Parkinsons: 'I am afraid that this thing you have has already been patented' and in June 1890 Huxley, head of Simon's drawing office, wrote on behalf of Simon: 'Mr Huxley distinctly remembers that this idea has been patented before, and published ... You will see the description of the purifier referred to above in the *Millers' Gazette* of April 28th', which was an advertisement for Higginbottom's Victoria design with a list of five patents clearly stated.

There had been hints that Parkinsons might also have a different version in prospect, but although in July Ingleby was still trying to maintain contact while critical of a lack of practical achievement, Parkinsons had already made a patent application. In August *The Millers' Gazette* proclaimed Robinsons' new Koh-i-noor purifier and in September reported that 'the invention of Messrs G. & T. Parkinson, the well-known millers of Doncaster, and its merits were so appreciated by Messrs Robinson & Son Ltd, Rochdale, that they at once paid a handsome sum for the sole right to manufacture it'.[60] *The Miller* produced a gem of puffery by calling the Koh-i-noor 'a diamond of even purer water'. Staff at 20 Mount Street in Manchester must have winced. Perhaps not many millers or journalists knew the whole story.[61] The specification for Parkinsons' patent 4176 of March 1890 included a distinctive feature of a narrow sieve, which could be either tapered or straight. The surfaces on each side of the sieve, on which impure material was to be deposited, had a larger area than the sieve. The geometry, especially the tapered sieve, was thought to be novel, but was not actually so. Progressive reduction of the width of the sieve by the tapering was an attempt to maintain an even depth of stock on the silk as pure endosperm passed through. However, it was not likely that a specific degree of taper would suit all conditions of raw material or grades of break stock; it relied on a one-off calculation, either too simple or naive.

Meanwhile development of the Reform continued. By 1889 advertisements declared that 'over 1200 of these are now at work.[62] Three hundred have been introduced in Austria-Hungary'. By 1890 there had been further modifications and in 1891 there was a 'New Reform purifer'. A main change was the elimination of the dust filter, without use of the old-fashioned stive room or dust-collecting chamber, or cyclone dust extractor. A major concern had been the fire hazard in flour mills. Simon had to weigh technical advantages and disadvantages, commercial trends, and customers' preferences. When asked to account for changing conventional wisdom in what seemed to be a commonsense matter of risk reduction, he replied 'The ways of insurance companies are inscrutable'. Instead of the travelling filter of woollen material there was a new device which was called a deflector in the specification for patent 12411 of 1891, with a collecting chamber above to collect residual dust. Later, Simon regretted that it had not been called a baffle, which would have prevented a confusion of lawyers, who argued that the Simon deflector was equivalent to a Parkinson deflector, though it was quite different in use and position.

LITIGATION: 'A TANGLED WEB' BUT SIMON VINDICATED

The Simon patent application was made in July 1891. In November he was advertising the 'New Reform Purifier – patent applied for', and there was another application in May 1892, to protect further ideas.[63] That September, Robinsons of Rochdale wrote to Simon alleging that he was 'manufacturing and selling purifiers which infringe Messrs Parkinsons' Patent No 4176'. Parkinsons owned the patent and thereby became the plaintiffs in the subsequent court case. On Simon's behalf, Ingleby replied 'Every detail of the machine was carefully considered, and I went fully into this matter with a view to avoid interference with any other person's rights. Therefore I am utterly unable to guess what points in my present machine you object to'. Robinsons had been issuing warnings to infringers, real or imaginary, in 1891 and already a statement had been published in The Miller that E. R. & F. Turner of Ipswich had agreed to pay a royalty on purifiers with side deposit surfaces.[64]

Patent litigation could be a parade of inappropriate comparisons, with convenient omissions, as plaintiffs tried to demonstrate overlap of ideas; defendants looked at differences. The legal tussle of Parkinsons v. Simon was an expensive example, with an initial action in the High Court, an appeal before the Master of the Rolls and two accompanying judges, and an appeal to the House of Lords before the Lord Chancellor and four more judges.[65] It began in February 1894. Simon's three counsel included Sir Richard Webster QC, MP and Mr Ernest Carpmael, who had conducted the successful defence in the trial of the Germ Milling Co. v. Robinson (the Deptford miller) in 1886. Parkinsons' four claims were for a tapering sieve with side deposit surfaces; a parallel sieve alternative; placement of deposit surfaces beside the sieve; and lastly, a combination of sieve and deposit surfaces with a deflector to direct the airflow sideways over the surfaces. It was alleged that Simon had infringed the Parkinson patent 'by manufacturing and selling sieves manufactured according to their [Parkinsons'] invention, or only colourably differing'. 'Colourably' was common parlance; it meant little but could be made much of. The defence thought they could rely on proving that the patent lacked novelty. Eventually they had to tackle the repeated and erroneous assertions that Parkinsons' arrangement and process had been a basis for the New Reform design.

Simon pleaded that he had not infringed, that the claimed invention was not new, and that there had been prior publications including specifications by Simon, Seck, and Higginbottom, also that the relevant machines had been supplied to many named prominent millers. On the third day, G. M. Parkinson was examined and Sir Richard Webster revealed the ill-fated liaison between Parkinsons and Simon, in which Stringer had been an active intermediary.[66] Stringer had died suddenly of a fever in 1893; otherwise there could have been

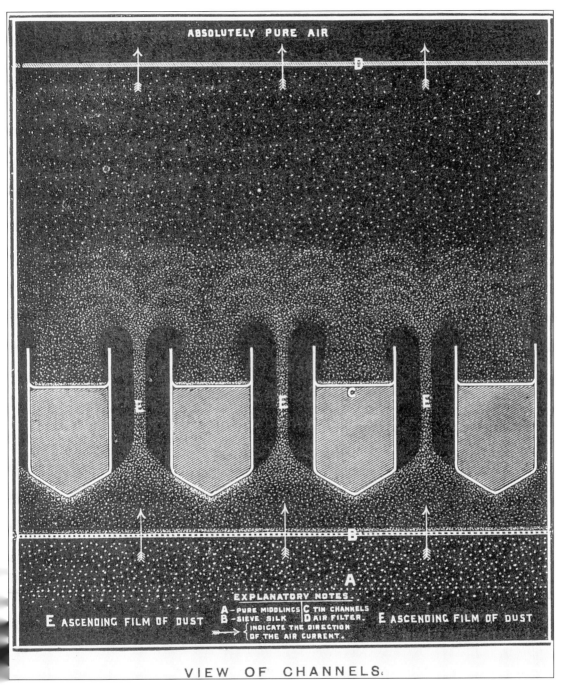

ABSOLUTELY PURE AIR

D

E   E   C   E

A

E ASCENDING FILM OF DUST

EXPLANATORY NOTES.
A — PURE MIDDLINGS   C   TIN CHANNELS
B — SIEVE SILK   D   AIR FILTER.
↦ { INDICATE THE DIRECTION
    OF THE AIR CURRENT.

E ASCENDING FILM OF DUST

B

VIEW OF CHANNELS.

Figure 65.
Diagram of grid of
channels and airflow.
(Simon 1890)

an interesting sequel in court. The account in *The Miller* was extensive and largely verbatim. It was reported that at the start of the fifth day 'we were again plunged into the labyrinth of deflectors, air velocities, eddies, grids, filter-cloths, side deposit surfaces, and the like exciting topics'.

179

During the fifth and sixth days Sidney Leetham of York was examined. Mr W. R. Bousfield QC, MP, counsel for the plaintiffs was abrasive, but Leetham remained polite despite provocation during an inquisition about diameters of pulleys. Carpmael, for the defendant, elicited from Leetham that as long before as 1887 Leetham had suggested to Stringer that the side troughs which received the impurities from the channels should be widened; in conjunction, there was a narrowing of the sieve. Ingleby appeared next. Bousfield tried to talk down to him, and beseiged him with questions about air velocities. Ingleby responded with insouciant politeness, and when it seemed that he might unwisely agree with some of Bousfield's propositions, he was assisted by the leadership of Mr J. F. Moulton QC, MP, the other counsel for the defendant, and possibly helped by Bousfield's loss of momentum: the pulleys and the air velocities had more adverse effects on the main practitioners of the adversarial method than on their opponents.

Henry Simon followed. Bousfield did not appear to have a clear idea of his technical target. Intending to show that Simon preferred larger sieve areas before the date of the Parkinson patent and smaller areas afterwards, he tried to fit statements in Simon advertisements into his argument. He tested Simon on whether he was 'scientifically accurate always in advertisements', to which Simon replied 'No, nobody I suppose is'. Bousfield made no more impact than with pulleys and air velocities. The most awkward aspect of the whole case was the failure to distinguish between the two 'deflectors'. It was ironic that Simon said that he preferred the term 'baffle'. In the New Reform it was a replacement for the filter. In the Kohinoor, in conjunction with the deposit surfaces, it was an alternative to the grid of channels of the Reform. The two deflectors were different in position, size and shape, and function; they were not equivalent.

Summing up for the defendant, Moulton 'submitted that the plaintiffs had stretched their net too far and wide, claiming things which were unquestionably old'. He pointed out that failure of any of the plaintiffs' claims to novelty would invalidate the whole. 'Their special deflector – their only evidence of novelty – was designed to do what the defendant did not need to do'. His conclusion was that 'The anticipations were all proved and showed no novelty whatsoever in the restriction of area'. In his judgement Mr Justice Kennedy found that none of the three separate claims in the patent were novel. He held that 'the combination claimed in the fourth claim of the plaintiffs' specification is an invention, and had that claim stood alone the patent for that combination would have been a valid patent'. He also stated that 'the defendant was entitled to improve his machine' provided that it was not by 'appropriation or colourable imitation'; there had been 'fair improvements'. The allegation of infringement failed.[67]

There was an appeal in June 1894; previous decisions were confirmed. The Master of the Rolls, Lord Esher, who presided in the Court of Appeal, said that 'the first rule of construction of a patent, as well as every other document, is that the Court must give effective meaning to every part of it, if it can'. Lord Justice A. L. Smith supported Bousfield's contention that in construing a specification 'you ought to read it as much in favour of the patentee, that is, of the inventor, as you can'. Lord Esher dealt extensively with the position, meaning, effect and comparisons of deflectors, with at least thirty-seven instances, yet higher authority was still not clear on the subject. Lord Esher also said that their practice was 'by everything we do to diminish litigation, and to put an end to disputes'. Simon concluded that it had been 'one of the most flagrantly and ridiculously hopeless patent cases ever conceived', but the contest was continued.[68] An Appeal to the House of Lords was heard in July 1895 and dismissed.[69] The Lord Chancellor was determined 'to pronounce no judgement' on the question of infringement. Counsel for the appellants were heard at length, but counsel for the respondents were not called. The fourth claim in the Parkinson patent survived, being allowed on its own by the Comptroller General in March 1897.

At the first appeal, Lord Justice A. L. Smith stated that 'the numberless plans and models mystify rather than explain'. Lord Esher had a similar reaction, saying that often 'on reading a Defendant's patent and on reading that alone, and reading the Plaintiff's patent alone, you can see that one is an infringement of the other without any further evidence'. The issue of infringement might have been settled more easily if Esher's principle had not been obscured by Bousfield detail. At all stages of the case, complicated word games clashed with sporadic attempts to interpret descriptions of apparatus, divorced from actual physical processes. The practice of construing got in the way, partly because legal procedures obscured the fact that few had the ability to read a drawing and then weigh differences of practical effect, a skill available in any good drawing office.[70]

The flow of patent applications needed to come up against a vetting system, to check for novelty and give general advice on ambiguity. Shortly after Robinsons had first threatened an action for infringement, Simon made some personal notes about differences in attitude to patent law in England, America and Germany.[71] He wrote that in England, searches for anticipations involved 'days and days' in the Patent Office, or heavy payments to agents. In Germany, there were official 'examinations into the novelty of inventions' which were 'in the truly continental spirit much more bureaucratic' and secretive. In America, trained specialist staff were available and the Patent Office 'delivers to anybody for a small charge complete official information as to the objections raised by the US Patent Office against the issue of a new patent'.

When the legal nuisance was finally over, design work on the Reform was resumed. In 1896 there was another patent to add to the series, and in Henry Simon's last catalogue of 1898 there was a 'patent new dustless purifier' based on a Simon patent of 1885. In 1894 Ingleby had said, in evidence, that they had sold '1600 Old Reform in this country, and over 3000, I think somewhere near 3500 if you take in the Continent and the Colonies'. The New Reform was a stage in a continual search for further improvement.

CHAPTER TEN

Henry Simon in business

Management and money matters

In the story of *The Simon Engineering Group*, E. D. Simon, son of Henry Simon,
recorded that there were only fourteen office staff in 1883. They were at St
Peter's Square in the middle of Manchester, from which Simon was extending
his activities in flour mill engineering while also interested in the construction
of by-product coke ovens for the iron industry. With expansion of his business,
bigger premises were needed and his series of journal advertisements show that
about March 1884 a move was made to Mount Street, which stretched from
near the gigantic and symbolic Victorian Town Hall ironically to Windmill
Street. The headquarters remained there until 1930. The longest serving member
of the firm was Joseph Ingleby, who described himself in 1894 as 'Mr Simon's
chief help for twenty-three years'. That set the beginning of their connection
as 1871, with Ingleby only twenty-two, seven years before the start of the
milling specialism.[1] His description of himself as chief help was based on length
and breadth of service, though when he said it in evidence at the Parkinson
v. Simon trial, he probably felt disappointment, as he confirmed that he was
not then a registered partner. Ingleby provided continuity, except that Simon
complained on two occasions that his manager was too often round the town
when he should have been in the office, saying 'There is nothing of a desirable
nature to be done in a place like Manchester during the day'.

In the 1920s there was still at Mount Street 'a severely austere room furnished
with Victorian desks and chairs except for two leather easy chairs which were
on each side of the fireplace'. That may have been Henry Simon's own office.
The setting is suggestive of formality, with friendliness as far as a reserved
nature would allow, and possibly of Ingleby sitting in one of the easy chairs.
Simon referred to the practice of having his technical literature 'generally
written out in my office and read to me, and discussed more or less with me'.
He indicated the extent of activity in 1894 by stating that 'I have about 50
clerks in my office'.[2] Obviously there had to be much delegation. He expected
to manage through the willingness of capable individuals. Although clearly
interested in many aspects of effective performance, he lacked a deputy chief
executive. Perhaps also, as he became increasingly interested in commerce,
there was insufficient inclination to stand by a drawing board and talk to a
draughtsman, which might have been better for his health. On Simon's death
in 1899 Ingleby was left in charge, his general experience then being invaluable.

To describe Henry Simon and his work in simple terms would be an injustice
to a complex character, his intensity of personal involvement, and the varied
contexts in which his actions can still be studied. Amongst a mass of information

Figure 66.
Portrait of Henry
Simon. (Clara von
Rappard)

the milling journals, on their brittle paper, still provide the most extensive
record but Simon's catalogues of 1886, 1892 and 1898, each with a long essay,
marked stages of commercial and technical progress. In addition, surviving
letters to staff and some other colleagues reveal personal interaction and
objectives. For more than ten years, Simon worried about his health, justifiably,
yet repeatedly he turned from a feeling that the pressure of business was
unendurable, to further effort and even more impressive achievements. In 1892
he gave a simple summary, referring first to the situation in 1886 when he had
given 'a short history of the revolution in milling methods then in progress'.[3]

Figure 67.
Henry Simon's offices
in Mount Street,
Manchester. (Simon
Ltd, *Occasional Letter*,
1921)

At the end of the 1892 essay he said: 'Five years were devoted to proving the broad truth of the principles propounded by the author in 1879 and the two succeeding years; five more have elapsed in elaborating the detail and practice of those principles. One period is ended, the other is endless'. The 1898 commentary confirmed the previous assessment.

Simon's three years of seeking a basis, 1879 to 1881, culminated in the year of the Islington exhibition, which was notable for the arrival on his staff of William Stringer and George Huxley. Stringer became his principal milling expert, described as such by Simon and by Ingleby, who had become the general manager. Simon supplied the drive and comprehension, Stringer the flair in process development; Huxley became head of the drawing office. Stringer may have produced ideas for improvements in purifier design, patented in Simon's name, but Huxley's work would have been essential for success at all levels of design from particular machines to mill layouts. William Stringer had served a milling apprenticeship with E. Shackleton & Sons at Carlow in Ireland, taking charge of the mill in 1878 at the age of twenty six.[4] Simon himself superintended the installation of a roller plant there in 1880 and was impressed by Stringer.

The status of milling expert which was soon accorded to Stringer was often given to individual entrepreneurs, also increasingly to members of firms. For the former it denoted energy in the promotion of new methods; for the latter, it suggested dependable knowledge. In Stringer's case, as also with Harrison Carter, there was talent for setting up new plants, making improvements, and working out alternative processing ideas. Both Stringer and the competitor Carter were star performers, enthusiastic, industrious and fallible. They had substantial practical experience, but were not professional engineers, nor members of the worthy class of engineer–draughtsmen.

Simon was on the other side of the obvious divide between millers and engineers, which somehow had to be bridged by combinations of evident knowledge and experience together with a vital intangible: insight. Simon was receptive to new technical ideas down to the level of mechanical engineering detail. He was bound to rely on some collaborators and delegate to others. Some of the design ideas for purifiers were clearly from Heinrich Seck at Dresden, some were evolved by the Manchester-based staff, amongst whom Stringer gave a lot of attention to the improvement of sifters and purifiers. The extent of Simon's personal participation in design discussions is still unknown; a memoir by Huxley or by Joseph Ingleby could have provided valuable information. Without that kind of record, Simon is still seen as a highly qualified professional engineer, an energetic technical manager and a forceful entrepreneur. His whole enterprise depended on continuous engineering development work, linking design to practice, as milling systems were improved and scaled up.

Figure 68. Joseph Ingleby. (1849–1916). (*The Miller*, August 1916)

A DIFFICULT YEAR: 1889

Between the first two signpost years of 1886 and 1892 the pressure built up: the halfway year 1889 was good for business and might have seemed a boom year, but there were problems. In 1886 there had been the approach to supposed but temporary depression. In 1892 there were the first hints of problems leading to the Koh-I-noor confusion. In 1889 there was the realisation that Haggenmacher's plansifter was a flop, a technical and financial tangle, though not yet widely discussed. Simon's personal correspondence shows that he felt hard pressed throughout the year, even when outwardly successful in business. In January he wrote at least five times to Stringer, trying to balance discussion of Stringer's preoccupation with income against his own risks and commitments. The mixtures of admonition and encouragement, in scrawly handwriting, may not have been closely read. Similar long lamentations had been directed to Ingleby, without lasting effect. Simon wrote to J. R. Radford at Melbourne, his main overseas traveller through three continents, asking 'Do you think it is to our mutual interests that you should stay out there?' He wondered about a possible return 'in case I might want your services in this country', and put his concerns in indirect terms: 'supposing that Mr Ingleby or Mr Stringer were to be at any time incapacitated from work through any illness, such as has recently happened to Mr Robert Buchanan who had to leave the mill in Liverpool for several months?' Simon, Stringer and Buchanan had become closely associated, Simon providing capital and Stringer the milling expertise, for a mill managed by Buchanan.[5]

In March there was an answer to Stringer: 'I herewith confirm that we have arranged for you to remain in my business for the current year against one-third of my net profits from the milling business, after paying Mr Ingleby his commission of twenty per cent'. In comparison, Huxley in the drawing office and Wilhelm Mehlhaus in the commercial office were on individual annual salaries with hopes of only modest increases. They conformed to the disciplined styles appropriate to their absorption in rational numerate activities. Even the two main UK travellers, J. W. Walworth and R. Witherington engaged in special pleading, which resembled demands – for bigger commission payments and guaranteed-minimum agreements. They may have made more money than Huxley and Mehlhaus. Stringer and Radford were accustomed to the most freedom of action and had a casual disregard for what Simon, in a proud moment, described to Sir Bernhard Samuelson as 'my personal generalship', and in anguish to Walworth as 'the disagreeable part of the business' in which 'all difficulties have to be thought over, worried over, and are disturbing our night's rest'. With direct family knowledge, Anthony Simon (1953) recorded that Henry Simon 'worried more and more about his business; he slept badly, with notebook and pencil at his bedside, and few nights passed in which he did not once or more turn on the light and make a note of some point that had struck him'.[6]

Ingleby had less scope for initiative, even during Simon's frequent absences, but in May he was writing to Radford at Melbourne: 'Mr Simon is still in the south of Europe for the benefit of his health but will return to the office in about 3–4 weeks'. Radford's future position was to depend on Simon's discussions with Ingleby and Stringer. There was then a new view of wider prospects: 'We have always been expecting here that the mills [in the UK] would get all fitted up and business drop off, but in point of fact we have more to do now than we have ever had ... Before all the mills are fitted up many of those first started will know so much more about the roller system ... that they will be inclined to increase or still further improve their plants'.[7] Simon was back by June and a few weeks later wrote another homily to Ingleby, telling him that 'you left an unwarrantable amount of work unattended to or on the shoulders of Huxley ... The want of a general manager's sharp eye shows in the office ... I had hoped to be able to withdraw more than ever from the business'. Simon then wrote to Radford: 'After my return from the continent I find that it is absolutely necessary to have more energetic help in my office'.

Simon oscillated between telegrams saying 'Return' and 'Don't hurry' and then wrote to explain, including 'from what I have seen of Mr Ingleby lately, and from what he says himself to me, he shows a certain amount of want of energy in his work, and I desire to have you here to possibly take a share ... the present amount of work is too much for Mr Ingleby'. Stringer had been pressing for a partnership, but Simon wished to avoid upsetting Ingleby who, although he had a decidedly good income, was aware that it fluctuated. Simon remonstrated 'You have had years up to £5,000 or so – clear profit – without even having risked one farthing ... I am deep in my sixth decade, and with a large family, must now earn more, or never. There are not many years left for me. You are in the best years yet and can well afford some more hard work'.[8] The profit and loss accounts included some surprising items showing Ingleby's commission for the years 1883, 1884, 1885 to have been £2,202, £5,022, £3,955. There was then a dip, but recovery to £2,961 in 1888. That was far beyond Huxley's increase in 1889 to £550, with £600 per annum promised for 1891! By October there was a possibility of equanimity, Simon writing cheerfully to Radford: 'We are going on well here, and I certainly wish we had you here to help us for the volume of business which we have on now is nearly overpowering'.

Then in November there was a flurry of communication to Sir Bernhard Samuelson, a machinery manufacturer at the Britannia Works, Banbury.[9] Simon was seeking partners. The first approach was in the hope that Samuelson might visit Didsbury in south Manchester, but there were no spare rooms so the message was sent 'Can easily reach my house by hansom either from Stockport or Manchester'. Then Simon wrote confidentially that on medical advice 'I must try to make arrangements to relieve myself almost entirely from the cares and anxieties involved in directing such a large business'. A sense of urgency prompted him to say that he was taking immediate action to turn his business into a limited Company. In December Simon was talking, with misgivings, about 'parting with this splendid business', but was not receiving a sympathetic response. The idea lasted until the following autumn when it became clear that he would risk losing control and earnings, but not responsibility.

By 1890 Simon was bouncing back. With the continuation of the second phase of innovation confirming Ingleby's forecast, Simon chided Stringer: 'We are distinctly under-manned in good millers at present, and it is absolutely one of your principal duties in the firm to procure these men'.[10] He was also seeking an 'engineer to work out any new machines that I may be constructing, inventing or trying to improve. I have a small works of my own for that purpose, and so far this part of my business has not been well looked after'. This was in reply to a candidate, Max Luzzato, who either could not see the potential of the job or somehow did not settle to it. In 1892 Simon was better pleased, writing to Ingleby who was convalescent at Las Palmas 'The Reform purifier seems now to be a real success, and Horsnail who is temporarily working as 'Inventor-in-chief' at our works has put a little arrangement to the sieves which renders it absolutely easy to get the stuff to travel on either side of the sieve. You will remember this has been our great difficulty. We are patenting the new idea'.[11]

The two prominent personalities in Simon's firm were Ingleby and Stringer but they can never be seen together. Stringer was forceful and persuasive. Simon said in a brief tribute when Stringer died in 1893, aged only forty: 'Mr Stringer's ability in roller milling was absolutely exceptional, his quickness of perception in setting right a large mill which might have gone wrong, amounted to genius'.[12] Impressed to that extent, Simon could forgive him for some errors of judgement, even big ones. Stringer allowed muddled situations to develop with Haggenmacher, Parkinsons and the miller Buchanan. In each case it was thought that there was opportunity for profitable business, but it might have been better to avoid all three. Simon was probably too much under Stringer's influence in dealing with other staff. In 1894 he recalled in a letter to E. L. Weigall, the chairman of the Rio de Janeiro Co.:

> I allowed Mr Stringer to send two of my very best men, viz. Mr Nicholls and Mr Shackleton, to Rio without one brass farthing's immediate profit to me. Mr Nicholls, who was an extraordinarily clever expert in purification, cannot ever be replaced; it had taken us years to train him, and we have the greatest possible difficulty in finding good men for the post.[13]

Nicholls had died, possibly of yellow fever. From about 1890 there was also Jacques Baumann,[14] apparently involved in practical milling. Simon wrote to Seck: 'Stringer looks with jealousy on Baumann and he underestimates him considerably ... It is sufficient that Baumann recommends something that Stringer loses interest in it. That makes the whole thing difficult. Stringer is strong-willed and sometimes he takes decisions too fast'.

Once Stringer had demonstrated his value to the firm, Ingleby was somewhat in the shadow of the slightly younger man, and was not released from that effect until Stringer died. The following year was marked by the Parkinson v. Simon case, with Ingleby and Simon both giving evidence, along with the miller Sidney Leetham who had maintained a long collaboration with Simon in technical matters. In his evidence, Ingleby stated that 'I understand the machines generally, and their action, and the results attributed to them ... I know how they work, although I am not a miller'. In addition to having responsibilities for general communication, though possibly without formal authority for coordination, Ingleby contributed to the work of technical presentation. He read Simon's first paper to the National Association, and seems likely to have been the author of some of the advertising copy, for which Simon did not take direct responsibility. Whoever controlled the journal presentations had an important task. Simon wrote in 1890 'It is by supplements in the milling papers that I have built up my milling business'.[15] He was referring to *The Miller* and *Millers' Gazette*. Supplements in *The Miller*, of two or several pages were far more impressive than any from competitors. They were direct communications, with strong assertions and bold illustrations. They must have focused attention generally, and reinforced ideas in the minds of regular readers. Much of the credit may be due to Ingleby, whose versatility was shown in Simon's note in 1890: 'It is understood that you will be good enough to continue to take a general supervising interest in the Luhrig business'. That concerned coal and ore dressing, one of Simon's troublesome diversified interests. Ingleby could be expected, during business in London, to call on a solicitor to discuss an unsatisfactory entanglement with a miller. In 1894 he could be sent to Frankfurt to discuss competing purifier designs and patent risks.

Simon's signpost dates of 1886, 1892 and 1898 were well chosen for retrospective and prospective review. All Simon's work can be studied and reappraised in relation to them. In 1886 he said 'The author attributes a great part of this success to the fact that all his best special engineers, experts and principal employees have remained unchanged'. In the previous October he had reported through *The Miller* that he was employing 'a staff of 15 experienced superintending engineers and leading hands, 200 joiners and millwrights, 12 experienced millers and roller men, besides principals, experts and a large staff of draughtsmen'.[16] In 1892 Simon again acknowledged the importance of skilled staff and their 'accumulated experience'. In 1894 he wrote to Weigall of the Rio Company, 'I am a Judge of character and ability and have known how to create and maintain a first-class staff'. It was not boasting, but in a context of mildly voiced complaint that the Rio Company had drawn excessively on his staff. Previously he had protested to E. B. Marriage, also of the Rio Company, that 'They seem entirely to forget that I do not work for the pleasure of the thing, but for reasonable and fair gain'.

Despite the presumed advantage of continuity, Simon often had difficulties with employees, and with colleagues elsewhere, who relied on his forbearance. He wrote to Seck in 1890, with Stringer's rashness in mind, 'One must appreciate the strong points of staff and forget their mistakes and weak points'. He was aware of limitations, including his own vulnerability to stress and his chronic heart trouble. Stringer repeatedly pressed for a greater share of the profits and wished to be a partner, a miller, or a consultant, without finding a clear focus. Always, Simon looked for ways to be accommodating, showing more consideration than he received. He observed to Professor Dixon of Owens College, when enquiring whether there might be collaborative study of explosions in mills, that Stringer 'has great powers of observation, and is an intelligent man, although without scientific education'. Simon had also pointed out to Stringer that there was involvement with Daverio, Bühler, Seck and Haggenmacher, but that 'Your want of knowledge of foreign languages renders it impossible for you to attend to this important class of business'. Two very important aspects of Simon's own contributions were the intellectual resources of his scientific background and his active communications within Europe.

The year 1892 was also marked by the start of Henry Simon's *Circular*, addressed to his clients and others. The frequent but not quite regular issues were of only a few pages, but on high quality paper, and with unusually clear illustrations.[17] Typical of Simon, the idea was constructive, to enable recipients to reckon that they were being kept in touch. In August 1895, 3,600 copies were sent out. From 1897 the title was changed to the *Occasional Letter* 'to millers at home and abroad'. Over a long period the main changes in the firm of Henry Simon Ltd were explained and senior members introduced. There were descriptions of major projects for well-known millers and news of many others. Issue number 180 was published in 1947. In Henry Simon's own time there were also commentaries on *causes célèbres* : Parkinson *v.* Simon, and the successful case against the manufacturer Van Gelder, who infringed a patent originated by the Knickerbocker company of Michigan. In contrast, the first of the series called *Occasional Letter* had a photograph of Simon (1835–1899) and his family of eight children, including E. D. Simon (1879–1960), three younger sons who as British army officers were killed in France, and three daughters of whom the youngest was age only four. In 1899 therefore, there was a gap to be filled in the direction of the firm, E. D. Simon being at Cambridge studying engineering.

Capital ideas

Henry Simon was closely involved in many projects, not all commercial, some distinctly altruistic. His technical work and the records of it also mask another kind of endeavour. From the mid 1880s he was increasingly attentive to opportunities for investment which could lead to greater scope and to an independence from bankers. Aiming to build up capital resources, Simon almost inevitably took commercial risks: Anthony Simon (1947) stated that 'at least once he narrowly escaped financial disaster'. As early as 1885 Simon was advertising that he was 'prepared to build at his cost flour mills in likely situations ... and lease them with option to purchase'. Whether that precise offer was taken up is unknown, but he certainly accepted deferred payment arrangements for new plant, including the machinery supplied for Joseph Rank's Clarence Mill at Hull in 1890.[18] He was patient with Weaver at Swansea, writing in 1893 that ' it would not be convenient to me to let you have the £5,000 very much longer ... I never contemplated letting you have that money for an indefinite period'; there was still £2,215 owing in 1899. Also during 1893 Simon was concerned about the possibility of financial loss on his large installation in London for Seth Taylor. *The Miller* , usually up-to-date with news of new projects, had noticeably little to say about progress towards commissioning. Simon was aware that Taylor had made large profits and large losses during wheat speculation, and enquired indirectly about the firm's recent purchases. At that time there was depression in the London flour trade.

Much earlier Simon had acquired close knowledge of commercial aspects of the milling industry, apart from engineering. He was particularly connected with the Rio de Janeiro Company and the Liverpool firm of Buchanan & Co., where he was actually the proprietor. In his paper to the Mechanicals in 1889 he referred to the Rio Company at length and to the Liverpool mill briefly, but solely in technical contexts. It is possible to study more fully the complexity of Simon's activity only by reading personal correspondence against a background of the technical literature. Surviving accountancy records add to the picture but would be a dull dimension without the correspondence. Simon described some of the main machines supplied for the Rio mill, for which he had been the consultant engineer. His focus on Rio was possibly to avoid UK examples of his current work and to provide a new approach to his subject. It may also have been because the Rio project was much on his mind. His personal correspondence files show his continued interest as a supplier of technical expertise, and that by 1890 he held £7,000 worth of shares in the company, also that he lost faith in the London-based managerial control.

When Simon mentioned the Kirkdale Roller Mills at Liverpool there was no reference to Buchanan & Co., the name of the milling business there. There had been a series of trials to try to establish firm data for the power requirements of typical milling machinery. A paper had previously been prepared by Simon, or under his direction, and presented at the National Association Convention of 1887.[19] The tests had been made by Mr Longridge of the Boiler Insurance Co., with Stringer collaborating. There was no textual content in the paper beyond the technical information of the literally run-of-the-mill tests. The fact that Simon was the principal partner of Buchanan & Co. was not widely known. Even the lively new journal *Milling*, published in Liverpool, appeared or pretended to be in the dark in 1893. Referring to the mill which 'formerly belonged to Mr James Radford, who obtained possession of it from Mr Molyneux', it was stated that 'it was bought by Mr Buchanan for the present company'. Within a journal series about local mills and millers, readers may have been puzzled by the statement that 'we are sorry that we are not able to describe more fully a mill which deserves a complete treatment in these articles'.

E. D. Simon stated in 1942 that 'My father took over a flour mill at Kirkdale as a bad debt; he handed over the management to Buchanan'.[20] Simon's balance sheet for 1885 showed £1,750 as 'Reserve against probable loss on Kirkdale Roller Mill Plant'. In 1888 there was expenditure on 'additions and experimenting' at Kirkdale. The Kirkdale Mill property then had a book value of £8,509 and from then until 1895 Simon's balance sheets showed the property valued at about £11,000. His profit & loss accounts showed that Buchanan paid him rent for the mill. At the end of 1888 Simon wrote to his solicitors Addleshaw & Warburton, suggesting a clause in a new partnership Agreement that required Robert and William Buchanan and Stringer each to put in £1,000 and build up to £2,000. His own capital in the Buchanan & Co. business was £15,316 in 1892. By then Stringer had suggested that they might rent another mill, and Simon wrote to Buchanan: 'The want of capital should, under ordinary circumstances, never be a reason for limiting our business. I am in a position and willing to find that to any reasonable extent'.

Ideas for expansion were linked to new formalities. In 1892 Simon wrote to George Nicholson, a partner in the firm of accountants he always used – Harmood, Banner & Co. at Liverpool: 'As you know it has for a long time been my desire to have the firm of Buchanan & Co. made into a limited Company. We now have an opportunity of placing the extension which our thriving trade makes desirable, in a very much better neighbourhood, viz., at the docks at Birkenhead, where communication with all the railways comes alongside the mill'.[21] Simon assumed it would cost £25,000 to build a new mill; in addition there would have to be working capital which he said he 'could easily find'. He then enquired 'Do you think you can obtain this money for us amongst Liverpool men, and other people whom you may know, without our issuing a prospectus and making it unnecessarily public?' By March 1893 Simon was assuring Buchanans that he agreed to find £12,000 to build the new mill and £13,000 for working capital. In the same month Buchanan & Co. Ltd was registered. Simon's shareholding increased gradually towards £16,000.

From 1893 to 1896 there was substantial progress, despite the loss of Stringer. Simon wrote to Buchanan in September 1894, in reply to the news that Vernons intended 'coming over to Seacombe' (Birkenhead), putting forward the idea that it might be 'to everybody's advantage to unite with them and make Buchanan Ltd and Vernons' present firm into one private company'.[22] The obvious alternatives were collaboration or competition, but Vernons may not have fancied the alliance. At the same time Simon reported to Buchanan that he was 'very pleased indeed' with their building project at Seacombe, though he suggested that arrangements for wheat handling 'would not be quite as economical as desired'. Simon's subsequent project at Seacombe for Vernons, completed in 1899, had a superior quayside site.

Simon's experience at Seacombe was dramatic. A fire destroyed the new mill for Buchanan & Co. Ltd, but a replacement was soon built and was in production by 1896, giving them a total capacity of 50 sacks of flour per hour for the two mills. Simon wrote to Nicholson, his accountant, saying that the replacement was 'in full swing, and I may say most satisfactory swing, being considerably superior to the mill that burnt down, we require more capital to be able to work the mill in such a way as to secure the greatest possible profit, viz. by buying complete cargoes [of wheat]'.[23] He was seeking a bank overdraft of £50,000. In November 1896 he wrote to J. K. Bythell, chairman of the Manchester Ship Canal Co: 'I am the principal owner of two flour mills in Liverpool and Birkenhead ... producing about one thousand sacks of flour per day. We are thinking of expanding'.[24] He was considering the possibility of a site on the canal, including the Trafford Park docks. He made other enquiries in 1897, with a view to concentrating at Trafford Park, but the basis of production remained unchanged. In November 1897 a new company was registered: Buchanan's Flour Mills Ltd. Simon's shareholding was shown in his own 1898 balance sheet as £57,881, less in his final assets of 22 July 1899. Complete sets of accounts are not available for any period and changes during the last few years make it impossible to unravel the complications of money movements.

Simon took the main financial responsibility for the Kirkdale and Seacombe mills and this extended to company organisation. When he wrote to Gustav Behrens in Manchester to recruit him as a director of the new company, he said: 'we have at last got everything ship-shape with regard to the getting of public money for Buchanan & Co. Ltd – the firm of flour millers in which I am so far the capitalist with financial liabilities of considerably over £100,000'.[25] After discussing financial arrangements and shareholding details for the change to Buchanan's Flour Mills Ltd, he said that milling output had been increased 'to seven times what it was when I began, ten years ago', which put the start with Buchanan at 1887. In his paper on 'Tests of the power consumed in roller mills' of that year, Simon had described the Kirkdale Mills as 'a first-class 8 sack plant on my system'. It would be surprising if the business relationship between Simon and Buchanan had remained unknown, yet the short obituary for Buchanan in *The Miller* in 1920 gave no hint; he was said to have been the 'Pioneer of the milling movement in Birkenhead'.

FURTHER AFIELD

Despite medical advice to reduce the strenuousness of his work regime, Simon's activity was still determined by his restless questing spirit. As the second major phase of innovation in the UK milling industry tailed off in the early 1890s, he turned his attention to opportunities abroad. Anthony Simon (1953) recorded that in 1892 Henry Simon 'set up a branch organisation in Frankfurt under the name of Simon, Bühler & Baumann; this business employing about 150 men in its own works, was one of the three leading milling engineering firms in Germany until its confiscation during the first World War'.[26] Contenders for the list would have been Luther at Braunschweig and businesses with the Seck name, either Seck Brothers or the apparently separate Heinrich Seck at Dresden. John Speight (1956) suggested that there was an initial stage when Simon's participation with Bühler and Baumann was not publicised, to avoid antagonising Heinrich Seck but, although Simon and Seck had collaborated technically and Seck supplied equipment to Simon, their potential as competitors was clear.[27] Surely Seck knew that Jacques Baumann, who was put in to manage the new Frankfurt firm, was from Simon's organisation? Simon was cautious for another reason, indicated in a letter to Baumann: there was an undefined financial risk (possibly political) in Germany, so that for a short time it was thought that Simon's name should not appear.

In May 1892 Simon had a mixture of hopes and misgivings spread across the range of the milling engineering business. Writing to Ingleby at Las Palmas, he kept his biggest worry till last. He was solicitous for Ingleby's welfare, after illness, and carefully sympathetic to Mrs Ingleby: 'I can quite feel for her as I am no great sailor', but he was relaxed about J. R. Radford's ocean-going prospects: 'The Argentine seems to be looking up and I have quite decided to let Radford have a go at it'. In the UK he was upbeat about a probable large order from Applebys at Blackburn, but cautious about becoming more of a miller: 'I am still in the throes of considering the Liverpool extension of Buchanan & Co. It is a most serious question for me, and I am inclining towards not proceeding with the new scheme'. Then after references to his own health and the weather in Madeira, Simon reached the subject of immediate concern. 'Today I expect Seck to discuss the establishment of Baumann at Mannheim. I rather dread the conversation, but the bull has to be taken by the horns'.

It was natural and convenient for Simon that he could write to some of his staff in German, to his cashier Mehlhaus, to Baumann, to Hahn (an engineer on the outside staff) and of course to Adolf Bühler in Switzerland. Copies of many outgoing communications in German have survived, but not the replies. Most are circumstantial, about inclinations rather than decisions, and about personal attitudes. In a letter to Herrn J. Hahn in Scotland, Simon said 'I need another factory in competition with Seck who is a very difficult person'. There were hopes of improving the standard of production obtained by Samuelsons at Banbury; details of their manufacturing connection with Simon are sparse, but in 1885 they had reported that they had 'laid themselves out specially for the purpose'. The problems with Seck and others demonstrate some of the effects of the continual search for resources and business profitability.

There were security risks. When Baumann and the partnership of Simon, Bühler & Baumann were clearly established at Frankfurt it was necessary to be careful about staff recruitment. Simon wrote in February 1893 about a Seck employee called Trettau who Baumann intended to take on: 'you would in him educate a most formidable competitor when once he has got hold of our diagrams and other information'. The clearest danger was that Trettau might return to Seck. In November Simon was advising Baumann that 'whether we like it or not we must bite into that sour apple of starting a small works especially for purifier building', but he was doubtful about cost effectiveness: 'What I am slightly frightened of is that at our own works a machine may possibly cost us more money than we think and that we will *nolens volens* be drawn into putting in more machinery to reduce the cost'.[28] The alternative of putting the work out to another firm was accompanied by a risk that designs and latest versions might be acquired elsewhere without agreement or recompense.

In July 1894 there was concern about business hostility between Seck and Baumann. Ingleby went to Frankfurt to advise about design and manufacturing policy, with a view to mollifying Seck. Simon, although critical of tactics used against Baumann, wrote to Ingleby: 'The simile of the big dog and the small dog and the bone, which Mr Seck uses, has really moved my heart in pity for him'. The big dog might have been Simon, or a particular shareholder in Seck's business, or a metaphor for the power of bankers and shareholders; Seck had recently adopted formal Company status. Simon regretted Seck's reduction of autonomy and profit share: 'I should not like to render his position worse under the circumstances as far as my own influence in the matter can go'. Simon also found Baumann difficult and informed Bühler that he (Simon) had 'lost pleasure in the Frankfurt business'. In 1897 he told Bühler that he might withdraw, but he had more important matters to consider in Manchester. Simon's own balance sheets showed that his capital investment in Bühler, Baumann & Co. was £492 in 1892. From 1893 the name was Simon, Bühler & Baumann, in which he showed £1,822 capital. It was a modest start, but by the doubtful year of 1897 he had put in £11,103. At the last count, in July 1899, Simon's capital there was £12,558, about one third of his capital in Buchanan's Flour Mills Ltd. It is only suggestive of relative importance; much more information would be needed before further comment could be made.

The most extensive distant market area was in Australia and New Zealand. Simon had employed J. R. Radford as his main agent there from 1887 to 1890 and described him as 'an intelligent man of business, brought up as a miller and corn merchant'. The start coincided with the beginning of the Simon-Buchanan connection at Kirkdale in Liverpool. It seems more than a coincidence that a James Radford had been at Kirkdale previously. The Australian business was put on a firm basis in 1893 with the establishment of an office and small works at Sidney, and Simon hoped that Radford would supervise the whole of the distant overseas market from Manchester, and voyage when necessary. Other opportunities were offered to Radford, all of which would have contributed to the strengthening of technical management: 'the introduction of new specialities, or the looking after conclusions of contracts and, in general, as a help to Mr Ingleby and to Mr Stringer'.[29] Simon asked for Stringer's opinion of Radford, adding that 'As usual, travelling in the colonies has somewhat unsettled him and probably given him rather high notions'.

Back in England after several more overseas trips Radford was unsettled, even though with the the loss of Stringer there was scope for managerial development. In December 1896 Simon wrote possibly the longest of his exhortations. There were many criticisms, often with comical aspects, for instance 'You remember that at one time we lost entire trace of you between Chili and San Francisco'. Radford still journeyed casually from Buxton and preferred seaside residence at Southport and Blackpool, arriving late and leaving early. J. W. Walworth had already queried Radford's remuneration, to which Simon had replied 'I do not at all like or desire to admit in my business a custom of comparing salaries between one person and another. The services of different employees are exceedingly different in their values and different in their kind'. Aware that some senior staff noticed Radford's 'leisurely way', Simon warned that 'comparative trifles are often sufficient to disturb the balance'. He ended optimistically: 'I would advise you to talk it over in a friendly way with Mr Ingleby who, from the beginning of the New Year will, after over a quarter of a century's connection with me, virtually be my partner'. J. R. Radford had become a central figure in Simon's dealing with the Rio company both in Rio and at formal meetings in London, Simon declining a seat on the board. In 1897 the Rio company acquired Radford's services full-time. Simon was dismayed and felt obliged to end the consultancy.

FOR THE FUTURE

Writing in December 1893 to Edwin Guthrie, a Manchester accountant, Simon had stated 'I intend forming my business into an absolutely private limited Company ... I desire to have as small a capital as possible seeing that the whole of my private capital and credit is at the disposal of the business'. In April 1894 he told Ingleby 'I have determined to make the milling branch of my business into a private Company in the course of this year'. He raised Ingleby's percentage and asked how much money he would like to invest. There was a delay, while he considered prospects at Liverpool and Birkenhead, and difficulties at Frankfurt, but in May 1897 the milling engineering business, based at Manchester, was registered as Henry Simon Ltd, six months before the formal step of registering Buchanan's Flour Mills Ltd. There was a tantalising sequel. Simon sought an amalgamation. He began: 'I ask pardon for writing to you without having the pleasure of your personal acquaintance, but I believe that an idea which has occurred to me may possibly be of the greatest advantage to your firm and mine'. He added that he 'would not dream of making such a suggestion to any other of my competitors'. A copy of the letter, not in Simon's own hand-writing, is nearly all legible, but the name of the addressee is not. It was to someone who had a 'machinery works' and the date seems to be 13 March 1898. After stating that his milling engineering business was 'as successful as ever', Simon referred to age, health and energy; 'I wish to perpetuate the firm. You are aware that most of my machinery, although made to my plans and patents is made by others'.[30]

The most important of those 'others' had been Adolf Bühler (1822–1896). He was succeeded by his son Adolf, who entered the private company in 1893, as a 24-year old engineer.[31] The partnership of Bühler Brothers was formed in 1901 and continued to be a vitally important manufacturer of machinery used by Henry Simon Ltd. It is unimaginable that Henry Simon could have achieved the speed of effective performance, which British millers needed, if he had been fully responsible also for machine manufacture. Throughout the 1880s he pioneered the route and thrust of innovation in British milling engineering. Afterwards, he might have reduced his diversity of activity, but he was a venturer and eager to engage in new areas which had an appeal of usefulness and profitablility. He was genial with collaborators and patient with those who conspired against. Not surprisingly, he was associated with individualists, and some character actors, but success definitely depended on him, no matter how many others joined in. Overall, he was a technical enthusiast who always aimed to encourage others.

When Vernons opened their impressive new mill at Seacombe, Birkenhead, on 30 January 1899 Simon was absent. It was his finest project, but he had to send a telegram: it began 'Exceedingly regret my doctor will not allow me to attend your celebration'. He referred to 'the great satisfaction … to my firm and our staff to conjointly plan and execute this probably finest mill now in existence in, or out of England'. A large party enjoyed what *Milling* called 'a very recherche lunch' on the White Star tender *Magnetic*, which had ferried the group across the wide expanse of water from Liverpool.[32] Simon's 1898 catalogue had included a modestly brief description and a simple sketch of a vast site by the standards of the time. Bennett & Elton (1900) gave a longer description 'of the latest and finest of the whole series of the splendid up-to-date mills of the period – that opened towards the close of the year 1899 at Birkenhead', stating that 'It adjoins the largest dock of the Mersey Dock and Harbour Board, and any vessel afloat can come alongside'.[33]

On 24 July 1899 *The Miller* carried a black-framed notice of Henry Simon's death, with a concise but well-judged biography; a fortnight later the journal presented a photographic portrait, with a further appreciation. In November there was a brief report about Simon's will, extracted from the *Manchester Guardian*, giving his full name Gustav Heinrich Victor Hermann Amandus Simon. It was stated that the 'gross value of the estate amounts to £176,306'. At the Seacombe opening Joseph Ingleby had represented Simon with George Huxley also present. These two took over the running of the Company, Ingleby as chairman, Huxley as managing director from January 1900.

With the loss of Simon's influence in coordinating the efforts of others, Ingleby had to consider what to change and how to continue. There was discussion with Vernons about the Buchanan mill, to explore a possibility of combination. Leetham had ideas for a larger amalgamation of interests; as Ingleby wrote to Gustav Behrens, a trustee for the Simon estate, it was 'a scheme they are now elaborating in connection with the large Hull and Cardiff millers'.[34] Mehlhaus, by then a director of Henry Simon Ltd, wrote to the other trustee Gustav Eckhard, requesting consultation as soon as possible. Ingleby wrote to Baumann, who was fretting about future arrangements, to explain that the executors 'are exceedingly full of work', and that Henry Simon Ltd would probably take Simon's place in the Frankfurt partnership. Relations with Baumann and Bühler and interaction with Seck occupied Ingleby extensively in the arts of diplomacy. By 1902 E. D. Simon was beginning to be involved, spending time with Bühlers at Uzwil in Switzerland; correspondence shows Ingleby as a conscientious guide, directly and through Eckhard, who was at Frankfurt to review policy there. Ingleby also demonstrated his ability to be 'fully *au courant*' across the range of industrial interests at Mount Street, just as Henry Simon had forecast, in discussions with Behrens in 1897.[35] In 1906 E. D. Simon joined the board of Henry Simon Ltd.

Part III

ↆ

Scaling up

CHAPTER ELEVEN

Combination and enterprise: 1888–1900

Combination

From 1888 onwards there was speculation and experiment in a new direction: combination. There were expansions and amalgamations, and also searches for a balance between port millers and inland millers, for ways to understand the connections between country millers' difficulties, agricultural conditions and national food supply. Combination embraced many forms of mutuality. In December 1888 *The Miller* reported on an alleged British millers' syndicate: *The Times* reported 'We hear that a syndicate of flour millers, whose operations are carried on over the district lying between the Humber and the Tweed, has been formed to associate all their mills in one vast concern'. This syndicate, trust or ring would arouse suspicion because it concerned the staple food which was price-sensitive, and because it was to do with production, which could, in theory, be controlled.

The Millers' Gazette estimated that there were twenty-five mills in the plan to form the North Eastern Milling Co. Ltd, and published a letter from Henry Leetham & Sons at York, the most prominent millers in the region: 'The object of this company is to unite under one management the business of the proprietors of the principal roller flour mills situate between the Tweed and the Humber, with a view of effecting economies not obtainable under separate ownerships'.[1] Leetham also suggested that 'Both the business and the district in which it [the scheme] is intended to be carried on are specially adapted to cooperative action'. That was at least ironic or possibly an unwitting incitement to the Cooperative movement. Although R. H. Appleton, past president of the National Association and also president of the Stockton Chamber of Agriculture, tried to assure farmers that the syndicate would not seek to reduce the price of wheat, nor advance the price of flour, *The Miller* and the *Millers' Gazette* reported rumours of monopoly and alarmed reactions.

At the end of January there was a conference at Newcastle where delegates from the Cooperative movement in the four most northerly English counties and north-east Yorkshire met to discuss 'the great flour ring'. The meeting was an expression of solidarity on behalf of a supposedly assured market of 'over 600,000 working-men members of our store system', but not without concern that some members or societies might be tempted to invest.[2] The threat was said to be from 'a wealthy ring of capitalists in London'; it was alleged that 'this ring has made a calculation that from 30,000 to 40,000 sacks of flour are used weekly in the northern district, in which the syndicate proposes to place its power of monopoly'. It was stated that there were 'thirteen cooperative mills, not counting those that formed part of the cooperative stores'. The possibility of building a Cooperative Wholesale Society mill in the Newcastle district had been discussed in 1883, and a site had been bought at Dunston on Tyne in 1886, where it was planned to build a mill with a capacity of 8,000 sacks of flour per week. Support for this large venture provided an opportunity for positive response to the syndicate, stimulating the previously hesitant Cooperative movement. The Dunston project progresssed, the new mill being opened in April 1891, with a designed capacity of 40 sacks of flour per hour.[3] A satisfactory market share was not easily acquired, profit not being shown until 1895. It was a prestige project for Thomas Robinson & Sons of Rochdale; a committee had decided to order the plant from them after 'a round of visits to flour mills of importance'.

There was over-reaction to the north-eastern syndicate. An article in *The Miller* in December 1888 suggested suspicion and disapproval of 'trusts'. *American Miller* picked up the story, and sought to correct the London journal's attitude, stating that 'our contemporary jumps on trusts, figuratively speaking, as an American importation ... Of trusts as they exist and are understood here, there

Figure 69.
Appleton's mill at
Stockton-on-Tees,
depicted in 1884.
(*The Miller*, July 1884)

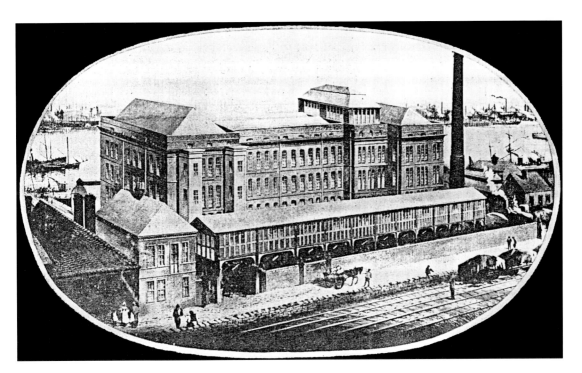

Figure 70.
CWS mill at
Dunston-on-Tyne, in
1891. (Simon Ltd,
Occasional Letter, 1951)

are probably as many of them in Great Britain as in the United States'. The syndicate did not reach beyond a thought experiment, but it was an exercise in thinking about territorial defence and trading area expansion, which would inevitably become more relevant.[4]

Concurrently there was a brief flurry of activity in company formation in Britain. James Tucker Ltd was registered in December 1889. *The Miller* reported that 'a number of influential and powerful capitalists had combined for the purpose of acquiring the extensive corn and milling business carried on by Mr James Tucker, at Cardiff, Swansea, Newport and Bristol'.[5] Their new mill on the East Dock at Cardiff, with an expected capacity of 50 sacks per hour, was opened in 1892. Much of the credit went to Whitmore & Binyon, to Carter's disappointment as he had acted as consultant. In 1898 ownership of the business which Tucker had established passed from the Cardiff Milling Co. Ltd to the New Cardiff Milling Co. Ltd. From 1902 Spillers & Bakers acquired control through the purchase of shares. In February 1890 there was a sequel to the over-ambitious Northumbrian scheme. Appleton, French & Scrafton Ltd was formed, the amalgamation of R. H. Appleton of Stockton-on-Tees and South Stockton, Thomas French & Co. of Stockton-on-Tees and Darlington, and Scrafton Brothers of Bishop Auckland and Middlesbrough. The group had a capacity of 9,650 sacks per week, but the venture was not successful. In 1898 in an application for the appointment of a receiver it was alleged that 'there had been large speculations which had turned out disastrously'; the directors had reported a substantial loss on forward wheat contracts. Cleveland Flour Mills Ltd, was formed to take over Appleton's mills.[6]

Figure 71.
Joel Spiller's mill at
Bridgwater, Somerset.
(*The Miller*, June 1936)

In March 1890 *The Miller* reported that 'another great amalgamation seeems imminent between Messrs Spiller & Co. Ltd of Cardiff and Messrs William Baker & Sons of Bristol ... The manufacturing capacity of the united mills ... would probably considerably exceed that of the Northumbrian firm, as the Cardiff mills have alone a capacity of some 10,000 sacks a week'. The amalgamation became effective during 1890. William Baker & Sons was a family firm, started in 1852. A larger mill was built in 1862. From 1867 the business was managed by Proctor Baker, and Arthur Baker who was President of NABIM in 1899. Spiller & Co. Ltd was a private limited company originating in Somerset. According to an outline history of Spillers in *The Miller* in 1933, Joel Spiller 'began business prior to 1830 in Bridgwater as a flour dealer and merchant'. He worked several small mills in Somerset and a steam mill at Bridgwater and formed a partnership with Samuel Woolcott Brown. Spiller sustained a fatal injury while inspecting the West Dock in Cardiff about 1854. Relatives of the original partners were brought into the business; after Brown retired in 1864, the firm traded as Spiller & Co. The nominal capital was £450,000 and there were thirteen shareholders. They had business offices at Gloucester and Bristol, and agencies at Newport, Merthyr, Neath, Swansea and Carmarthen.[7]

In April 1889 *American Miller* provided details of the Spillers mills at Cardiff. It was reported that 'The firm has four mills, known as the East, West, Bute and New Mills, having a weekly capacity of 11,000 sacks ... They employ in all about 400 persons'. There were details of machinery in two of the mills. The East Mill had forty-two Simon roller mills, nineteen of them used on a long system of seven breaks; there were G. T. Smith and Seck purifiers. In the

West Mill, there were seventeen Carter roller mills for the breaks and eighteen middlings roller mills, both Simon and Ganz types. There were G. T. Smith and Haggenmacher purifiers and four makes of centrifugal. There was a variety of machinery, rather than the use of a settled system or reliance on a regular adviser. When Simon referred to his work of 1891, he made the criticism 'that the easiest way for any miller to obtain a thoroughly complete and efficient plant is to decide which milling engineer deserves his confidence, and leave the designing and erection of the mill entirely in his hands'.[8]

During the 1890s Spillers & Bakers advanced, though not without difficulties. The annual general meeting in 1891 was informed that 'During the past year new branches of the grain department had been opened at Southampton and Plymouth, in both of which towns the initial difficulties having been successfully overcome, very good results might be confidently anticipated in the future'. In 1896 there was a new departure: John Davidson & Sons' Phoenix Flour Mills at Newcastle on Tyne were acquired.[9] There were logistical difficulties, indicated during the annual meeting of shareholders of Spillers & Bakers Ltd for 1897. Arthur Baker, as chairman, said that 'stocks and debts on either side must be expected to vary considerably, and no good could be derived from comparison of one year with another … however … the volume of trade had been greater this year than last, or indeed any previous year'.[10]

Just after the formation of Spillers & Bakers Ltd there was an amalgamation in Cornwall, to form Hosken, Trevithick, Polkinhorn & Co. Ltd, the first two members based at Hayle, the third at Truro; shares were offered for public subscription. There was another notable event in the south-west. At the start of 1892, Weaver & Co. Ltd was formed to build and operate a new mill at Swansea. Henry Simon described his project at Swansea for 'a large and powerful company, supported chiefly by well-known local capitalists'.[11] He also listed the features that were necessary for an up-to-date mill, which included 'the whole of the grain receiving, grain storage, grain cleaning, roller mill, warehouse, and accessory machinery, together with complete sprinkler and electric light installations'. Until Spillers and Bakers merged there might have been a tendency to regard an output of approximately 10,000 sacks of flour per week as a round figure of manageability, equivalent to 80 sacks per hour for a working week from 6 a.m. on Monday to noon on Saturday. Elsewhere that order of size could be exceeded by a few leading firms, whose capacity was concentrated on one or two sites.

Individual enterprise

JOSEPH RANK

In contrast with the combination movement, there was a miller whose individual vision and personal drive would be increasingly noticed: Joseph Rank. In January 1891 Joseph Rank's new mill was started at Hull; for the Clarence Mill(s) Rank had acquired a waterside site. He had been working on his own account since 1875, first with a windmill, then from 1880 a small steam mill which he leased. He had explored the south-west for a better prospect and visited roller millers, including Ingleby at Tadcaster and Moss at Salford, before deciding to commit himself to financing a new mill near the Alexandra Dock in Hull.[12] In 1885 he started the Alexandra Mill with a modest 6 sacks Simon plant, but Clarence Mills were initially equipped with a 20 sacks plant on the Simon system. By late 1892 the capacity had been increased to 35 sacks, and the Alexandra Mill could produce 12 sacks per hour. In the autumn of 1895, the actual output was at the rate of 65 sacks per hour, as observed by staff from *The Miller*; it was claimed that 10,000 sacks per week could be produced by working a full six days and nights.[13] Joseph Rank Ltd published *The Master Millers* in 1955, commemorating the eightieth anniversary of the establishment of the founder's business, describing progress from before the general introduction of roller milling. Rank had acquired personal experience in all the tasks of a traditional miller. Within ten years he advanced from possession of a fairly small roller mill to a position of strength in national terms. The opening of the Clarence Mills marked the big step forward.[14]

Joseph Rank's rapid technical progress coincided with the introduction of a new journal. G. J. S. Broomhall began *Milling* on November 6, 1891; he had started *The Liverpool Corn Trade News* in 1888. The first issues of *Milling* were slender, but style and content improved rapidly. The decade of the 1890s was a period of experiment in the columns of *Milling* and some loss of impact with

Figure 72.
Joseph Rank's
Alexandra Mill at
Hull in the 1880s.
(*Milling*, June 1904)

Figure 73.
Rank's Clarence Mills
at Hull in the 1890s.
(Milling June 1904)

the content in *The Miller*; the journals had many difficulties in trying to provide descriptions of mills and their processes as large installations were becoming too complicated to survey or describe except in general terms. Both gave Rank careful attention. In 1891 *The Miller* produced a lengthy description of the Clarence Mills. By December 1892 *Milling* could publish a lengthy article on Rank's progress. *The Miller*'s illustration suggested a dreary Victorian mill whereas *Milling*'s photographic version implied solid industrial action. When *The Miller*'s staff returned to Hull in 1895, they recorded the further progress inside the mill and building extensions. At this time, Rank was age forty-one, Broomhall was thirty-eight. In the milling industry especially, lasting success was often to depend on dynasties.

LIVERPOOL

During 1892 and 1893 *Milling* presented short descriptions of most of the Liverpool firms, though not with the technical detail which readers of *The Miller* would have expected, but with concentration on names, and dates of mill acquisitions. The series may have been partly to support the National Association convention held in Liverpool in 1893, but it would also have been publicity for Broomhall's new journal, published in Liverpool.[15] Data in the articles generally confirmed Simon's estimates of milling capacity.

The Miller applauded the decision to hold the convention at Liverpool, 'for not only is Liverpool a large milling centre, but it is the leading port in the United Kingdom and, as such, has built some of the finest warehouses and docks in Europe'. The new President was Edgar Appleby; in 1878 he and Arthur Appleby had succeeded to the business of Joseph Appleby & Sons, which had been developed from a mill at Enfield in Lancashire in 1841. They puchased the Carolina Mills at Bootle, on the Leeds and Liverpool canal, in 1886. In 1889 they purchased Sheppard & Pontifex's Bridgwater Street Mill in Liverpool; it was remodelled by Simon, to produce 20 sacks per hour. Their Daisyfield Mills at Blackburn were reconstructed during 1892–93, with a Whitmore & Binyon plant, to produce about 30 sacks per hour. Simon remodelled the Enfield mill to provide 15 sacks per hour.[16] The Carolina Mill was small, but Applebys' aggregate capacity then approached 70 sacks of flour per hour. *Milling* reported that the order to Whitmore & Binyon 'caused no little comment in the mill furnishing world', as it followed their contract for Tucker at Cardiff, when they had 'carried off the prize of the year in mill building'.[17] The returns of Joint Stock Companies for 1901 showed that Josh Appleby & Sons Ltd had been registered as a private company, one that 'does not issue any invitation to the public to subscribe for its shares'. Both Applebys and John Greenwood & Sons had mills at Blackburn and Burnley. In 1889 Greenwoods had been reported to have a total capacity of 14,000 sacks per week.[18] John Greenwood & Sons Ltd was registered as a joint stock company in 1891. Much later they acquired a base at Trafford Park docks in Manchester, but the Manchester Ship Canal was not available until 1894, by which time Applebys were established at Liverpool.

The name of Vernon was to become prominently associated with business leadership and with counselling roles within the industry. In 1847 John Vernon had purchased a small water mill at Fole, near Uttoxeter; in 1857 he retired and William Vernon took over. In 1888 William Vernon acquired his mill in Commercial Road, Liverpool, purchasing Jacobi & Co.'s plant there, and raising the output to 1700 sacks per week. He traded in Staffordshire, while gaining acceptance in the Liverpool area. It was suggested that the move to Liverpool was in recognition of the increasing use of foreign wheat. It was possibly also related to the increasing energy available as three sons joined William Vernon in the business. Having, as *The Miller* observed, 'secured a fair position in the local markets' and purchased Tonge & Sons' Toxteth Roller Mill (in Mill Street) in 1891, they overhauled it and enlarged the plant, to obtain an output of 20 sacks per hour.[19] With this acquisition there was 'a trade connection in South Wales'. In 1894 the Fole mill was burned out. Although the buildings were restored, it was decided that there should not be a refit. Instead, Vernons

Figure 74.
Joseph Rank
(1854–1943). (Simon
Ltd, *Occasional Letter*,
1904)

purchased J. C. Rivett's mill in Liverpool (in Seel Street). With their three Liverpool mills, Vernons then had 'an aggregate turnout of 6,000 sacks per week'. In about six years Vernons had made impressive progress from their previous situation at a modest country mill. The next step would be concentration on a major waterside site.

Another large family firm was founded by Edward Hutchinson, from Worsley near Manchester. In 1853 he moved to Liverpool to be foreman miller at Joseph Martin's mill (at Rainford Square). Soon they were both at the newly built North Shore Mills, but in 1857 or 1858 Hutchinson set up his own business. After working three small mills, Hutchinson built a replacement in 1876, the Mersey Mills (in Burlington Street). In 1892 *Milling* stated that 'There are few larger capacities in the kingdom than the Mersey Mills'.[20] In 1893 the output was said to be 60 sacks per hour and increasing. Simon roller mills were used for both break and reduction operations, but some of the equipment was devised by Hutchinsons. As late as 1898 *Milling* referred to the firm's continued use of their own processing ideas, notably their 'Mersey' gravity purifier.[21] In the report by *Milling* in 1893, Hutchinsons' machinery included sixty-two Simon roller mills, forty-one centrifugals, forty dressing reels and forty-one sieves.

The North Shore Flour and Rice Mill Co. Ltd was quite unusual, the business having been registered in 1857, and there was lengthy experience in one location. In the mid 1880s the company probably shared first place amongst British millers with Seth Taylor of London in terms of capacity. The practical operation was

Figure 75.
Applebys' mill at
Blackburn, depicted in
1893. (*The Miller*,
June 1893)

Figure 76.
Vernons' mill at Fole
in Staffordshire, now a
creamery. (Author,
1996)

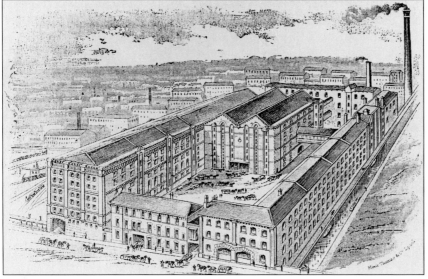

Figure 77.
The North Shore
Mills at Liverpool, a
drawing of 1892.
(*Milling*, December
1892)

in the hands of managers, not members of a family, but there was continuity in the directorate, which included commercial experience in the wheat trade.[22] The North Shore mill appears to have had a sound trade into the 1880s. Shareholders were receiving annual dividends of 10 per cent, but with the change to roller milling, during 1883 and 1884, there was disruption and loss of profitability. During the depression of 1886 and 1887 the company was adversely affected; there was no profit in 1886.[23] However, *Milling* reported in 1892: 'The mill proper is in reality an aggregation of three separate mills known as West, South and North Mills. South and North Mills were erected early in

Figure 78.
North Shore Mills
described in 1901.
(Milling December
1901)

the sixties, and the West Mill in 1887 to cope with the constantly increasing requirements of the trade'. In 1892 there was a capacity of 10,000 sacks per week, and in 1893 *Milling* stated that 'at present alterations are in progress, which will have the effect of still further improving the equipment of the mills'.[24]

There were other millers with well-established businesses in Liverpool. Thomas Leicester had bought a windmill in 1837, and later became known for his opposition to Bovill's blast and exhaust patents. He retired in 1888 and the firm was registered as Thomas Leicester & Sons Ltd. Carter had supplied a roller plant in 1883. When *Milling* reported in 1893, the company had a mill at Scotland Road and also possessed twenty retail bakery shops. George Lunt, included in Simon's list of Liverpool customers in 1884, also had his own extensive bakery trade. W. O. & J. Wilson of High Park and South End Mills at Toxteth produced both baker's flour and sizing flour. William Oldfield Wilson had moved from a previous mill in Liverpool to a windmill at Toxteth Park about 1847, later being joined in partnership by James Wilson. Their premises were in Grain Street and Bran Street. They entered roller milling in 1886. In 1894, J. W. Throop extended their plant, which *Milling* stated was 'owing to the great increase in their business'. Another incoming miller was Robert Buchanan from Glasgow, who later reached a prominent position at Birkenhead. He succeeded James Radford at Kirkdale, apparently at Grist Street.

LONDON

The London milling scene may have seemed strong in large, long-established businesses, relative to previous standards across the country, but there were few

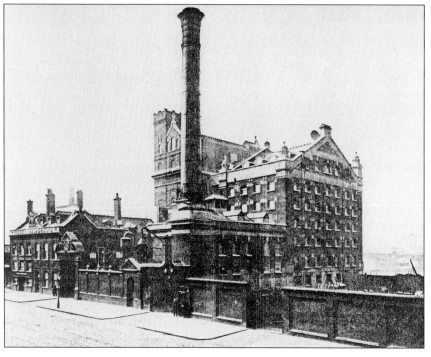

Figure 79. Robinsons'
Deptford Bridge Mill,
London, depicted in
1900. (*Milling*, March
1900)

Figure 80.
Mumford's Vauxhall
Mill, described in
1927. (*Milling*, June
1927)

big names, and they were not the first millers to adopt full roller milling systems. The prominent firms were all private ventures. Seth Taylor had succeeded his father at the Camden Town Mills in 1861. He also acquired the Blackfriars Mill and, with increasing trade, built new premises, as *The Miller* reported in 1887 'on a scale of the first magnitude ... the magnificent Waterloo Bridge Flour Mills, the construction of which was commenced in 1870'.[25] Taylor continued to follow traditional methods when he opened St Saviour's Mill in 1882 at Dockhead, Bermondsey, on the south bank of the Thames, but by 1885 he had arranged for both his large mills to be converted to the Simon system. He was described in 1887 as 'not merely one of the foremost millers in the United Kingdom, but also one of the largest importers of wheat'.

Other prominent London businesses were J. & H. Robinson's Deptford Bridge Mills; Peter Mumford's Royal Flour Mills on the Albert Embankment and Marriage, Neave & Co.'s Albert Bridge Mills. Robinsons had been millers at Lewisham, Henry Robinson joining his brother Joseph there in 1852, and in 1870 they built their mill on Deptford Creek. S. & P. Mumford worked small mills in the London area, one being at Lewisham, before moving to larger premises at Greenwich, adjacent to Robinsons' mill on Deptford Creek.[26] The son of the second partner, Peter Mumford (Junior) learned milling with his father, moved to Bermondsey to start his own business, and then in 1874 built on a larger scale at Vauxhall.[27] Mumford provided an interesting contrast for millers making visits during the London Convention in 1887 as he used the Hungarian Ganz machines, which enabled him to claim that 'The first roller flour made in London was manufactured at the Royal Flour Mills'.

Marriage, Neave & Co.'s Albert Bridge Mill at Battersea was opened in 1884, with machinery supplied by Thompson & Williamson of Wakefield.[28] One of the principals was E. Burgess Marriage, of the Colchester milling family, who later became managing director of the Rio de Janeiro Flour Mills and Granaries Co. Ltd. W. T. Bates, the prolific commentator in *The Miller*, moved from F. D. Collen's Albion Mills at Rotherhithe to take charge of the Albert Bridge Mill, which he apparently regarded as 'somewhat complicated'; he moved on in 1885 to take charge of Baxendells' Bee Mills at Liverpool. The opening at Battersea was celebrated with a crowd of visitors, a steamer trip, dinner at Richmond, and the accompanying band of the 1st Middlesex Volunteer Engineers. The account in *The Miller* was enthusiastic:

On Wednesday, July 9th, a party of about 120 gentlemen, including many representatives of the press, started in a specially chartered steamer from the Speaker's Steps at the House of Commons ... the magnificent mill which Messrs Marriage, Neave & Co. have been erecting during the last year or so now stands like a lighthouse on the east side of the spacious dock ... in the very heart of the rising suburb of Battersea ... Some time after five o'clock the inspection of the dock, foundry, and mill was finished, and ... the steamer made its way to Richmond, where dinner was awaiting the company at The Star and Garter Hotel ... Among the many objects of interest we passed on our way to Richmond, not the least striking was the building known as the Isleworth Flour Mills, which have a curious old-time look, and recall a time when steam boilers and roller mills were not.[29]

The Isleworth Flour Mills belonged to Samuel Kidd & Co., and were said to have contained 33 pairs of stones.[30] Successors continued as active members of the London Flour Millers' Association. Another well-known name was McDougall. Three members of the Manchester milling family moved to Millwall Dock about 1870, setting up a separate firm of McDougall Brothers.[31] Having only a small to medium capacity at that time, they gained recognition through specialist knowledge, firstly through their self-raising flour and later their practical experience with Indian wheat and their official investigation at the request of the Secretary of State for India.

Through the 1880s and 1890s the London Flour Millers' Association brought together the nationally well-known London millers with a group who were probably little known beyond the metropolis. Their discussions were often about transport topics, especially the costs of transferring imported grain within the Port of London; the extra costs which London millers incurred as a result of the double handling of grain from ship, via barge, to quay, were examined by the Royal Commission of the Port of London in 1902. London was undermilled; there was room for further capacity, and the Port of London received the biggest supplies of American flour. Not all of it remained in London, but if the threat of increased flour imports was to be countered then the London area had to defend on price and compete on quality. Continuing criticism of London bread implied complacency, though leading millers were not necessarily to blame; they did not supply the inferior foreign brands of flour, and they were probably not responsible for the bakers whose sales depended on providing the cheapest possible loaf to the poor.

District perspectives

The emerging milling centres had some similarities: the bigger mills traded further afield than local districts; they all needed supplies of foreign wheat; and they had to contend with increasing trade from a distance, both foreign and British. It is not easy to assess the main impact or the final effects of large supplies of foreign flour reaching particular United Kingdom ports, but much of the UK was affected.

The Miller regarded Dornbusch's Floating Cargoes List as authoritative.[32] That data showed the pressure of foreign flour supplies at the main ports; flour imported in 1892 was sufficient to supply 25 per cent of the United Kingdom population. The total quantity arriving at the Port of London was equivalent to more than half the requirement of the local population in 1891, and far more in 1892, though there were fluctuations; the apparent harmonious relationships between leading London millers suggest that pressure from the massive imports was not critical for all. Glasgow millers were certainly hard-pressed; imports could have supplied more than twice the local population in 1891, after which the situation worsened. Foreign supplies into Liverpool would have been enough for Liverpool itself and much of Lancashire in 1891. It was easy for critics to point to some of the big mills, but excess flour in the market was largely due to imports from America. Foreign flour could be shut out or curbed only through successful innovation.

Table 11.1. Imports of flour into the United Kingdom, taken from Dornbusch's Floating Cargoes List, published in *The Miller*, April 1913

	Imports of flour into the main ports 1888–1900 (thousand cwts)					
Year	London	Liverpool	Hull	Bristol	Glasgow	UK Total
1888	5642	3539	222	980	3709	16910
1889	4400	2830	86	706	3802	14672
1890	5028	3114	86	703	3809	15773
1891	5728	3490	163	823	3592	16723
1892	7683	4548	185	1313	4308	22106
1893	7206	3913	227	1116	3991	20408
1894	5802	4684	194	1089	3305	19134
1895	5459	4365	291	706	3728	18368
1896	6402	4690	607	923	3846	21320
1897	5721	3565	403	945	4127	18680
1898	7050	4507	270	1178	4325	21017
1899	7348	5144	550	990	4755	22946
1900	7610	4284	580	901	4310	21548

A prominent contributor to discussion of the supposed problems of over-production and overlapping was T. W. Hibbard of Gloucester, the immediate past president of the National Association, when he addressed the Liverpool convention in 1893.[33] He complained that large mills had been erected at Cardiff and Swansea and 'The consequence was an overcrowded market'. His Gloucester firm traded in South Wales. Hibbard suggested that a clearing house should be set up in what he called a 'zone' to deal with contractual agreements between millers and bakers. Copies of contracts for the sale of flour would be sent to the clearing house, whose staff would check that deliveries were made, accepted and paid for at the required times, and settle disputes. Forward selling without a written contract tempted bakers to refuse delivery on a falling market. To overcome the problem it was necessary to specify clearly both the prices and the conditions of sale, particularly the timing of deliveries, using enforceable contractual agreements. Otherwise, millers could not judge their raw material costs carefully in conjunction with expected income from flour sales.

The discussion after Hibbard's paper illustrated differences in outlook and conditions around the country, showing that it would be difficult to institute uniform sales practices. W. E. Nicholls of Spillers & Bakers supported Hibbard's plan.[34] R. H. Appleton of Stockton on Tees hoped that a clearing house would enable millers to avoid friction with customers, but a Scottish miller doubted whether 'a seller would escape obloquy simply by handing the matter over to the clearing house'. Across Scotland conditions varied: millers from Leith and

Aberdeen were confident of well-organised trading arrangements, but it was suggested that on the west coast every man 'paddled his own canoe'. It was pointed out that in Scotland 'they suffered more from importations of American flour than any other part of the United Kingdom – far more than in London, in proportion to the size of population'.

Of London millers, Peter Mumford considered Hibbard's scheme 'utterly impracticable', although he also said that 'coming from Mr Hibbard it deserved great attention'. Charles Brown of Croydon said that he 'had never had a signed contract' and he warned that 'If English millers bound themselves to a certain time [for completion of delivery] the Americans would have the trade entirely in their own hands'. He also stated that in London 'the American flour controlled greatly both the system and the price'. J. D. Taylor suggested that 'the struggle for life was much greater in London than in other places, and the principal consideration with people when buying bread was the price'. Taylor referred to quality: 'They had been accused of not educating the taste of the people of London, but the fact of the matter was that the people did not want to have their taste educated, so long as they could buy cheap bread'.

Hibbard's scheme was not carried out. Agreement could not be reached about penalties for not adhering to the proposed rules, for example offering inducements to customers who tried to renegotiate by obstruction. For millers of a district to cooperate, it was necessary to obtain allegiance of at least the majority in that district and for that group to be able to resist disruptive practice or external competition. Flour quality and commercial reliability provided further scope for competition. Hibbard's suggestion for combined action was not about price-fixing, but to establish standard conditions of sale related to delivery dates. The London flour trade was too large and diverse to be controlled and London millers had a basis of standard prices in the London Corn Exchange's regular quotations for English and foreign flours. Price agreements supported trade stability, rather than extra profit.

The bitter cry of the country miller

Competition within the industry was a subject of concern from about 1893, with increasing notice of the difficulties of inland millers. However, until 1893 there was enough optimism to encourage more millers to modernise, while the already experienced innovators strengthened their positions. The decreasing supply of English wheat handicapped country millers particularly. Most millers had expected to use some English wheat or even a significant proportion, but they were bound to drift away from that source of supply if the quality could not be improved. Contrary to general or popular opinion it was not only the price that mattered; the essential was milling quality, an increasingly used term.

British wheat growing had declined from 3.3 million acres in 1875 to 2.2 million in 1892. It dropped below 2 million in 1893 and below 1.5 million in 1895, after which there was a little recovery.[35] When Lawes and Gilbert published their investigation of 'Home produce, imports, consumption, and price of wheat over forty harvest years, 1852–53 to 1891–92', they made it clear that there had been a major reduction in United Kingdom wheat acreage and a very marked decline in price. They were mainly concerned with statistical results related to attempts to improve cultivation. They stated that:

> the less dependence on home, and the greater on foreign supplies, has been largely due to the increase of the population overcoming our capability of production; but, of course, largely due also to the reduction of area under the crop at home as a consequence of greatly increased production for export in other countries, and coincidentally great increase in our imports, and great reduction in price.[36]

That ignored the millers' problems, as also did much scientific and official discussion elsewhere, for instance in the reports of the Royal Commission on Agricultural Depression in 1894 and 1897. Obviously, the big national problem was the much lamented uneconomic state of agriculture. The first report of the Commission confirmed that there were tumbling prospects in terms of wheat acreage and production levels. In the final report there was attention to foreign sources of supply and to prices, but not to the usefulness of the grain produced, which was becoming a frustrating subject for the millers.

As early as 1890 the National Association had been trying to show that improvement was important. The Association annual report of 1891 said

> your Council decided that the time had arrived when an appeal should be made to every wheat grower throughout the country to exercise greater discrimination in the selection of the wheats used for sowing purposes. It was pointed out that certain wheats giving a large yield of grain and straw, but almost entirely unfitted for the mill, had gradually found more and more favour with farmers. In the interest of the farmers, as well as that of millers, it was deemed desirable that a circular, calling attention to the subject, should be issued to the press throughout the country.

Wilson Marriage drew up a circular, which 'was issued to and published by every important newspaper throughout the agricultural districts of the three kingdoms'. Unfortunately, nothing much happened in response.[37] *The Miller* provided extensive coverage of the Lawes and Gilbert report, which must have been of considerable interest to millers, but there was despair about the Royal Commission's work, which did not provide stimulus for progress amongst farmers: 'We have already called attention to this elaborate document, which, with all the pains and care that have been bestowed on its preparation, leaves us just where we were before'.[38] In 1896 Lawes and Gilbert contributed a paper 'On the world's wheat trade' to the Budapest Agricultural Congress. Again *The Miller* acted as a skilful intermediary with a succinct report, which could only have strengthened an impression that although overseas sources might vary in reliability, dependence on the outside world had been confirmed.[39] What would happen in time of war was to become a new focus for anguished reappraisal well before 1914, but the milling industry's hazards in the 1890s chiefly concerned inferior English wheat and cheapened American flour.

From the mid 1890s members of the country milling trade became increasingly anxious. In journal correspondence and comment columns they were encouraged to modernise, but the smaller their scale of operation the more they depended on proximity to good wheat-growing districts. Prominent as an encourager was W. T. Bates, who was still occasionally engaged in refuting traditionalist excuses. Simon was advertising roller milling equipment for as modest a capacity as one sack of flour per hour. W. R. Mallett of Exwick Mill near Exeter became a leading milling spokesman on the subject and did more to bring forward for consideration the difficulties facing country millers than sophisticated reports could do. Mallett addressed the Devon Chamber of Agriculture and the Exeter and District Chamber of Commerce in December 1893 on 'The future of English wheat growing', published as a small book. He continued with a paper to the Association in December 1895 on 'Our agricultural position'. Mallett's theme was recognised as a plea for government assistance. He claimed that there was a national financial loss due to reduction in wheat growing, not offset by alternatives but he regretted that the financial effect on the milling industry could not be calculated, which reduced his cause to a complaint. Mallett supposed that there were '3,000 mills, large and small, now working in the United Kingdom' and reckoned that there were about twice as many country millers as port millers; 'by the term 'country' I mean such mills as are situate away from a port of discharge – some near, some far, some with both canal and rail communication, some destitute of either; and by a 'port' mill such property as is situate at a port of discharge for sea-going craft'. Mallett assumed that '2,000 properties, large and small, come into the now undesirable catalogue of country mills', and that there was a contest within the industry.[40]

In June 1896 the Convention was at Southampton, when Wilson Marriage became President. W. R. Mallett presented a brief paper on 'Overlapping'. He offered an alternative term: 'perhaps I may more correctly say over-reaching'. Overlapping really meant that trading areas were not remaining separate; it was competition, but could be regarded as intrusion. Mallett described the increasing traffic in flour, to and from many towns, and he presented a long list, mainly immediately recognisable as the locations of well-known mills. He stated that flour was 'being sent into Plymouth from London, Liverpool, Cardiff, Swansea and Bristol', suggesting that some 'contributions' were sales below cost. Mallett introduced a dramatic image which could have increased a polarisation of opinion:

> It is admitted on all sides that trade is unprofitable; from the balance-sheets of large mills at our ports with but one or two exceptions, to the bitter cry of the struggling inland country miller, it seems a settled fact that the great business of feeding our fellow-countrymen with their staff of life is conducted without satisfaction to those engaged in it, and with most inadequate returns for the capital, the energy and the ability which is now more than ever necessary to carry it on.[41]

W. E. Nicholls responded on behalf of port millers, with good humour, though he said 'he would venture to give them the other side of the case', and also that 'he should like to know who was going to fight the foreign miller but the millers of the ports'. He referred to the amalgamation of his own firm with Messrs Bakers, when 'they had found themselves with a capacity of 18,000 to 20,000 sacks a week', and to 'their good friends the milling engineers who 'had there and then put up five other mills in the district with a capacity of about 12,000 sacks a week'.[42] The consequence was that South Wales was now producing from 26,000 to 27,000 sacks a week, while its actual consumption did not exceed 16,000 sacks'.

Towards twentieth-century perspectives

Mallett's rough impression of the structure of the industry, based on membership numbers of the National Association, which Wilson Marriage estimated 'was responsible for the manufacture of 70 per cent of the flour milled in this country', was over-simplified. In the industry as a whole there was increasing concentration at the ports, but many innovators were neither at major ports nor remote from urban areas. The term 'country miller' was an unsatisfactory label. Marriages at East Mills at Colchester and Humphries at the Coxes Lock Milling Co. at Weybridge would have been in sympathy with Mallett, but they had experience of both farming and the London area trading situation. Another miller present at Southampton, G. W. Chitty of Charlton Mill in Dover, probably regarded himself as a country miller; Charles Chitty certainly did many years later. The Association President in 1898, Henry Ibbotson of the Britannia Corn Mills at Sheffield, like many other successful town-based millers, fitted neither of Mallett's categories, although he had started at a small rural mill. A clearer description of the industry required something better than division into two classes, possibly businesses at major ports, in other large towns, in or near small towns, and in rural areas. An alternative would have been differentiation by output. Unfortunately, the labels of port miller and country miller became fixed.

The National Association responded to the emerging new structure of the industry, as milling concentrated productive capacity in larger size buildings, with more machinery and at favoured sites. There was discussion of ways of further enlarging the Association. Edgar Appleby's opinion was that the secretary should 'call on millers who were non-members here, there, and everywhere', but he and R. H. Daw were against an idea that the Association might try to organise district associations, which could be seen as interference.[43] A formula for a practical basis of action was elusive, though Mallett hoped that in each area millers would 'abide by whatever measures, whether in fixing prices or in terms of contracts, may be thought best in that district'. Twelve formal millers' groups existed in January 1894, but for several years their activites were not widely reported. In 1898 it was reported at the convention that 'no country associations were at the present time affiliated', but groups in Northamptonshire, Kent and the Liverpool district became affiliated in 1899.

A committee considered the possibility of setting up The Millers' National Trade Protection Society Limited, largely to assist members in legal matters, particularly concerning contracts, for example in disputes with shipping, dock, canal or railway companies, and in connection with rates or tax assessments.[44] A memorandum of association was drawn up in 1897 and there were numerous discussions, but the scheme was dropped; however it included an important feature: subscriptions were to be related to four categories of mill capacity in sacks per hour. It was followed by a group of suggestions intended to give the National Association a better standing in formal representation of the trade. One was that the basis of membership should be changed to be by firms or companies instead of by individuals, and that subscriptions should vary according to weekly output. It was also proposed that the National Association should become a Limited Company. Planning for this change of status for the National Association went ahead under the leadership of Arthur Baker, chairman of Spillers & Bakers, and President in 1899.

The official returns of registration of Joint Stock Companies indicate that progress towards more formal business organisation was significant from 1897 onwards. Table 11.2 shows basic data at the times of registration for many of the most prominent milling businesses that had acquired limited liability status by 1900:

Table 11.2. Extracts from tables of 'Companies formed and registered under the Companies Act, 1862, as Limited Companies', published in *Parliamentary Papers*.

Date registered		Company	Nominal capital £	Number of Share-holders
Oct. 1857	N	Liverpool North Shore Flour & Rice Mill Co.	90,000	
Dec. 1886		Rio de Janeiro Flour Mills & Granaries, London	250,000	129
Feb. 1887	N	Spiller & Co., Cardiff *	450,000	13
Oct. 1889		Pillsbury–Washburn Flour Mills Co., London	1,000,000	233
Dec. 1889		James Tucker, Cardiff	300,000	339
Feb. 1890		Appleton, French & Scrafton, Stockton on Tees	160,000	360
Mar. 1890	N	Hosken, Trevithick, Polkinhorn & Co., Hayle	250,000	451
Feb. 1891		John Greenwood & Son, Burnley	175,000	120
Jan. 1892	N	Weaver & Co., Swansea	200,000	448
Feb. 1892	N	Cannon & Gaze, Erith	100,000	7
Mar. 1893	N	Buchanan & Co., Liverpool	60,000	9
May 1893	E	Thomas Robinson & Son, Rochdale	120,000	78
May 1897	E	Henry Simon, Manchester	100,000	19
June 1897	E	E. R. & F. Turner, Ipswich	100,000	13
Nov. 1897	N	Buchanan's Flour Mills Ltd	185,000	161
Feb. 1898	N	Hovis Bread Flour Co., London	225,000	1,556
Feb. 1898	N	New Cardiff Milling Co.	165,000	536
July 1898	N	Rishworth, Ingleby & Lofthouse, Hull	165,000	536
Dec. 1898	N	Cleveland Flour Mills, Thornaby on Tees	100,000	7
Jan. 1899		A. & R. Appleton, Hull	80,000	12
Apr. 1899	N	Henry Leetham & Sons, York	575,000	847
May 1899	N	Joseph Rank, Hull	700,000	7
Dec. 1899	N	W. O. & J. Wilson, Liverpool	80,000	11
July 1900	N	James Fairclough & Sons, Warrington	100,000	7

Date registered		Company	Nominal capital £	Number of Share-holders
Sept. 1900	N	E. Marriage & Son, Colchester	60,000	9
Sept. 1900	N	Priday, Metford & Co., Gloucester	50,000	8
Dec. 1900	N	J. Reynolds & Co., Gloucester	80,000	53
Dec. 1900	N	J. & H. Robinson, Greenwich	100,000	7

* Not formed under the Companies Act, 1862.
N National Association member.
E Engineering Co

For registrations up to 1900 the tabulations provide easily accessible information about capital and shareholders. After 1900 statistical data for private companies was omitted, for instance for Applebys, who registered in 1901, and the Coxes Lock Co., in 1904. The National Association membership list for 1899–1901, when the basis changed from individuals to firms and companies, included about forty-three names of milling businesses with 'Ltd' attached. Some were private companies which did not invite the public to subscribe for shares. A few well-known millers had not acquired Limited Company status by 1914, including Seth Taylor and Peter Mumford in London, Hutchinsons at Liverpool and Vernon at Birkenhead and London.

When Henry Simon Ltd published *Modern Flour Mill Machinery* in 1898, with descriptions of major projects and a machinery catalogue, the continuing process of concentration was noted: a 'tendency towards the erection of large mills at seaport towns, and the decline of inland and small country mills, steadily becomes more marked and important'; causes included 'economies secured by discharging wheat direct from vessel or barge into the silo house'. There were recent Simon system projects 'on the water side' for Vernon; Weaver & Co.; Hosken, Trevithick, Polkinhorn & Co.; Buchanans; Rank; and Rishworth, Ingleby & Lofthouse. By far the most striking new project at the end of the century was W. Vernon & Son's new mill on the East Float at Birkenhead, where large ships could dock alongside the mill site; it was built and equipped at a cost of £200,000. There were two 30 sacks per hour Simon plants, with provision for doubling. The prestige of Henry Simon Ltd was enhanced, and Vernon's took a major step towards their future status amongst the leading milling firms. By 1901 the Birkenhead mill had an output of 10,500 sacks of flour per week.[45] A few businesses already had similar capacities, but Vernons' project represented a new phase of port mill development, which had to be recognised, accepted and included in any realistic appraisal of the state of the industry, which was on the verge of a period of dramatic change in structure. Simon had contributed enormously to the basic alteration of the technical form of the industry, which enabled innovative millers to survive and to prepare a basis for further achievement in the twentieth century.

CHAPTER TWELVE

Scaling up and relocation: 1900–1915

Dialectic

The years 1900 and 1901 marked the start of a new era in the history of the National Association. A revised constitution was agreed and an application was made to the Board of Trade for permission to omit the word 'Limited' from the title of the company, which was finally registered on 15 January 1901 as the Incorporated National Association of British and Irish Millers. There was a scale of annual subscriptions, related to mill (business) productive capacity, ranging from one guinea for capacities up to 500 sacks per week to ten guineas for capacities over 7,500 sacks per week.[1] The annual report dealt with the constitution, tax allowances for the depreciation of machinery, the Workmen's Compensation Act, and corn contracts. A paper was given on 'Motor haulage for millers'.

Debate within the Association was suddenly transformed at the Scarborough Convention in July 1900 through the initiative of the new President, Sidney Leetham of York. He introduced a dialectic approach, testing opinions during discussion. Following Henry Leetham, the founder of the firm, three sons had taken over. A personal collaborator with Henry Simon, Sidney Leetham was the technical miller and managing director.[2] *The Miller* reported that the firm had a total capacity of 112 sacks per hour; 100 sacks per hour continued to be an indicator of a very large business. Sidney Leetham had been active in an attempt to create a North-Eastern Millers' Association, so he had experience in studying the relationship between national and local collaboration. He advocated cooperation alongside competition, aiming to show the possibilities of one and the hazards of the other.

Leetham stated that the trade was 'dominated by the mills located at or about the four principal wheat ports', and referred several times to 'the balance of power'. He used the phrase 'survival of the fittest', which dramatised the changes due to technical advance during the previous twenty years.[3] During discussion of the supposed depression of 1887 Henry Leetham had used the evolutionary metaphor, but he thought competition 'stimulated them [the millers] to do the best they could for the public as well as for themselves'. In 1900 competition was increasing uncomfortably; it was partly but not completely due to imports. Neither of the Leethams was first to try to impress millers with

Figure 81.
Sidney Leetham of York. (*Milling*, June 1900)

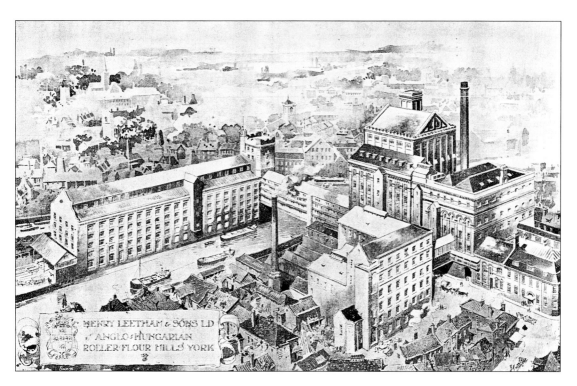

Figure 82.
Leethams' mill at
York. (*Milling*, June
1900)

the Darwinian analogy. Henry Simon had made an accurate forecast when he addressed the National Association in 1879:

> There is a growing tendency in many large industries or handicrafts, on the one hand, towards a reduction in the number of establishments, and on the other hand, towards a corresponding increase in their size ...
>
> This process is certain to make itself likewise felt in flour manufacturing, and smaller millers in particular will have to look out not to fall amongst the reduced or eliminated number. It will simply, like everywhere in nature, be that greatest and most unerring of philosophical maxims over again – 'the survival of the fittest' – that will rule in this respect.[4]

In contrast, Leetham sought a scheme to facilitate 'a community of interest, without curtailment of individual effort'. The journal summary of Leetham's main points was clear: 'Unregulated competition leads to loss, if not ruin, to the manufacturers, but by combination, which is possible, a living profit is obtainable from the consumers'. The vaguest item was 'Some form of association should be devised'. That was where most hopes for improvement were placed, and frustrated. These were not difficulties relevant only to millers as was shown by H. W. Macrosty in 1907 in *The Trust Movement in British Industry: a study of business organisation*. Two other terms were becoming familiar: combination and price-fixing. In other contexts combination was often a synonym for amalgamation, but in the milling trade it more often meant local coordination. The simpler term association was still most appropriate.

The term price-fixing was misleading. Millers had to set prices for their various grades of flour and they needed to alter flour prices in conjunction with wheat costs. If they agreed prices with other millers, this might be called price-fixing; in practice it was little more than price-setting. Weekly checks and adjustments might be made, but there were many public statements indicating that prices were more flexible, temporary or pushed down than fixed. A possibly desirable mechanism was price-regulation, following wheat costs closely, but otherwise seeking stability. Variations of conditions of sale and inconsistencies of purchaser behaviour amongst the many baker and grocer customers worked against simple price-regulating procedures. Commercial complications of the flour market, added to those of the wheat market, had prompted William Smith, President of NABIM in 1897, to ask 'Why is profit in flour milling dependent on speculative wheat buying?' Some millers remained concerned about overproduction: Hibbard had quoted a saying attributed to Joseph Chamberlain that 'if there was a demand for 50 articles and 51 were produced, the price of the 50 would be regulated by the price of the one'. In the 1920s A. E. Humphries used the same story with his own numerical preferences.

At the Council meeting in December 1900 Leetham emphasised that the flour market was being controlled by customers 'who pitted one mill against another and hammered down the price', presumably outwitting the travellers. He proposed to arrange a special two-day conference to try to reach 'a common understanding as to their system of transacting business'. At the following general meeting of the National Association in London, a range of attitudes was clearly shown. In Leetham's words: 'In various districts the trade has no very reliable understanding as to the terms upon which business should take place, and it occasionally happens that the competition is waged on such separate and distinct headings as cartage, sacks, discount, length of credit, forward selling and price. This is complexity with a vengeance'.[5]

A conference was organised for mid February in 1901 at the Palace Hotel in Buxton. *The Miller* reported 'The town being conveniently snowbound, and the air piercingly bracing, there was very little difficulty in keeping the members together'. Journal reaction, a few days later, was 'There is a general consensus of opinion that the Buxton meeting was by far the most important that British and Irish Millers have ever held'. In March *The Miller* presented a seven page report; 'This is the first great move that the National Association has made in a purely commercial direction'. The conference was carefully planned. Support had been canvassed and was assured. Buxton had been chosen as roughly central, with the railway station only a few yards from the large and impressive Palace Hotel. A preliminary document was provided, outlining principles intended as a basis for discussion, and a clear and energetic opening was provided by Sidney Leetham's address.[6]

Several forms of local organisation were put forward for consideration. Schemes could be temporary, rules could be modified, and it was possible to 'leave out price and simply control the terms and conditions of trade'. Ideas which Leetham presented were currently being tried by the North-Eastern Association. According to Macrosty (1907) 'One of the most interesting of all price associations was the North-Eastern Millers' Association formed at the end of 1899.[7] It covered the country from Newcastle to Grimsby, and included forty millers'. Macrosty stated that 'six local associations, which had occcasional understandings' had apparently agreed to recognise each other's prices. Joseph Rank regarded association as a means of improving understanding, but he also advocated independence and 'he thought it was better to be free in price than in any other way'. The concluding meeting was used to 'map out the country into districts'; nineteen were listed, including six with existing associations, the most prominent being the North-Eastern and the London groups, representing the most hopeful reformers and a much looser alliance with little appetite for further planning. The conference ended in general accord and optimism.

Rank spoke at length in May 1901 on the subject.[8] He was 'in favour of millers associating for the arrangement of terms and conditions of trade', but stated that it 'was a mistake to use association for the continuous regulation of prices'. A main point was that 'In arranging for fixed prices, it will be seen that the worst equipped and most unfavourably situated mills must be considered, and must, of course, make a profit; therefore, the larger mills must perforce work at such a margin of profit as shall, and indeed does, invite outside competition'. It was a rare reference to economy of scale. The scheme in the north-east was not effective: it was too legalistic. There was realism in journal comment that 'It is ever the case in times of drastic changes which make for the good of a community, that that community pitches its hopes too high at the outset, and has eventually to modify its aims', a hint of anti-climax after Buxton.

Leetham's most valuable contribution was his continuous effort to move investigation forward. He recognised that forward selling was a block to progress; price fluctuation could be considered only if forward selling practices were soundly based. *The Miller* continued to complain that 'The three great evils of the flour trade are forward selling, overlapping, and the cutting of prices',[9] though leading Association members knew that it was the tangle of terms of sale that was disruptive. It was also recognised that 'This system of overlapping cannot be avoided. No one has a right to say that mills shall only turn out the quantity that the immediate district requires'. In future, either demonstrable or supposed economy of scale would serve as a driving force for expansion, optimum sizes of operation being sought at higher capacities.

The Convention in June 1901 was at the Craigside Hydro in Llandudno. William Vernon of Liverpool opened the proceedings modestly: 'I confess I do not quite perceive that we have arrived at any very definite understanding as to the lines upon which the local associations and the National should be united'. He observed that the locals must be self-governing and the National Association was not 'composed of representatives or delegates of the millers, but of the millers themselves'. He viewed as attractive the idea of local associations extending 'all over the country, each looking after the interests of its own district'. Vernon discussed overlapping, explaining that his firm set ex-mill prices, to which their travellers added freight charges. He also stated that

Some members have complained that overlapping is brought about by over-production at the large port mills; but it seems to me that there can be no over-production in this country so long as we do not grind all the flour the nation consumes ... one-fourth of the entire consumption is ground in foreign mills; and until that large deficiency is reduced there can exist no such thing as over-production by British mills.[10]

When at Scarborough Leetham had sought 'unity and cooperation' as *The Miller* put it, he had explicitly rejected amalgamation. Vernon decided to examine the idea more closely. He did not personally advocate combination, but he presented the theoretical posssibility, expressing it as 'unification of capital and amalgamation of separate interests'; he invited Scott Lings, who had been Managing Director of the Fine Cotton Spinners and Weavers' Association, a combination formed three years previously, to address the Llandudno Convention on 'The formation of industrial combinations'. Scott Lings presented the main objectives as the purchase of raw materials more cheaply, the distribution of finished products more economically and the sharing of experience, to increase the general level of manufacturing efficiency.[11] He suggested that milling firms might combine by setting up a holding company, either without further functions or with control of buying and selling and possibly also finance. It was decided to consult the trade as widely as possible. Unenthusiastic response confirmed previous opinions about combination, for instance Joseph Rank had said that it was not feasible for the whole trade. Macrosty described Scott Lings' scheme as 'obviously fanciful'.[12] The optimism of the Buxton conference, when the country was mapped into provisional districts, was not maintained. Organisation could not be imposed from a central position.

Some impetus was lost when interest was diverted by the double disruption of the introduction of duties on imported wheat and flour in April 1902 and their removal in July 1903. Although the duties were only three pence per cwt on wheat and five pence per cwt on flour, the Council of NABIM was involved in discussion with the Chancellor of the Exchequer about the amounts of duty and payments on uncompleted contracts when the duty was introduced, and with the Board of Customs about rebates on stock held when the duty was removed, and about temporary bonding facilities for new supplies. At the annual general meeting of NABIM, in 1902, consideration of model rules for the local associations was dropped, in order to give more time to the discussion of the duty. The basic problem was not pricing but the establishment of clear terms and conditions of flour sale agreements. This was tackled energetically by successive Presidents, especially by W. E. Nicholls in 1905 and 1908.

Millennium

It is puzzling how British millers had retained confidence through the difficult 1890s, but there were hints from outside observers which might have helped them. In 1896 the cereal chemist and analyst William Jago wrote at length to

The Miller stating that British flour quality had improved while American flours were becoming less distinctive in their characteristics.[13] His overall view was encouraging for the prospects of the British industry. Storck & Teague (1952) attributed the eventual decline of the Amercan flour export trade to the successful development of British milling, admitting that American milling was not all profitable.[14] They referred to a statement in the *Northwestern Miller* in 1896 that 'In these times it is the exception, rather than the rule, for the miller to get out even on his export sales … The entire transaction is simply made in order to keep the wheels moving, in hope of something better in the future'. There were signs that it might be possible to act boldly: Vernons' mill at Birkenhead provided tangible evidence. Around 1900 there were occasional references at millers' meetings to the prospective 'arrival of the millennium', humorous asides especially when William Vernon was present; his top grade patent flour was called 'Millennium', an inspiration which he transferred to his Liverpool business from the tiny water mill at Fole in Staffordshire where the name was first used in 1892.[15] Millennium flour won many prizes, including a celebrated occasion of a contest against Hungarian brands.

By 1902 optimism was strengthening. W. T. Bates delved into statistics and concluded that 'It looks as if we had at last stemmed the tide of foreign flour competition'.[16] Although in December 1902 *The Miller* recalled that 'For more seasons than we care to count we have been at the mercy of those American millers who, regardless of cost, have flooded our warehouses with their surplus production', there was also better news: 'Many small millers have, during the year, taken heart and put their mills in better order, and there is a pleasant hum about things in general'. Further encouragement came from W. R. Voller

Figure 83. Vernons' Millennium Mills at London, described in 1913. (*Milling*, June 1913)

in 'A survey of the present position of the trade' for *Milling*: He stated that
the increasing availability of Canadian wheat made British millers less dependent
on American supplies, and his appraisal of changing conditions included

> American milling was not too flourishing as things were prior to 1902, and ...
> home millers could manufacture flour of satisfactory quality at so cheap a
> rate as to thin down the already attenuated profits accruing to American
> millers on their export business. Under the circumstances it caused no surprise
> when during the past year announcements came from milling centres in the
> United States, confirming opinion formed here, that flour selling had to be
> reorganised or cease to figure on the considerable scale of the past twenty
> years.[17]

For a year or two there was general discussion of tariff protection, although
there were few references to the fact that the United States, France and
Germany all protected their industries from foreign competitors. Within the
United Kingdom the subject was political, connected to economic theory or
supposed national interests, and obscured. *The Miller* had protested about hostile
criticism in English newspapers: 'Something was wanted to enable the miller
to live. Something was wanted to prevent a great industry from losing itself in
the vortex of foreign competition. Something was wanted to encourage larger
home production'.[18]

Joseph Rank thought that there was an unresolved matter of principle. As
the theme of his presidential address to the National Association at Harrogate
in 1904 he explained why he supported fiscal reform, to help various industries.
He was in favour of tariffs on imports, and later he argued his case as a member

Figure 84.
Ranks' Premier Mills
at London, illustrated
in 1904. (*Milling*, June
1904)

Figure 85.
Ranks' Atlantic Mills
at Cardiff, illustrated
in 1904. (*Milling*, June
1904)

of Joseph Chamberlain's Tariff Commission. Rank deplored the fact that 'as soon as Mr Chamberlain proposes to protect and encourage our agriculturalists, there is immediately an outcry'. Sidney Leetham addressed the York Chamber of Commerce on 'Free Trade Fallacies', criticising a 'one-sided system of Free Trade', and errors in economic text books: 'What a splendid dream it was – Universal Free Trade … But this state of things is not for us; it will come about the same time as the millennium'.[19]

Just after the experiment with import duties of 1902–1903, there was evidence of improving prospects and Voller's judgement was confirmed by the drop in flour imports in 1904, which is clearly shown in Dornbusch's data.

Table 12.1. Imports of flour into the United Kingdom (from Dornbusch's Floating Cargoes List, published in *The Miller*, 7 April 1913)

Imports of flour into the main ports 1900–1912 (thousand cwt)					
Year	UK total	Year	UK total	Year	UK total
1900	21548	1904	14723	1908	12970
1901	22576	1905	11955	1909	11052
1902	19386	1906	14190	1910	9960
1903	20601	1907	13297	1911	10065
				1912	10190

A combination of factors made the trade to Britain less profitable for American millers. According to Kuhlmann (1929) railway, steam ship and dock charges became less favourable for flour, compared with wheat cargo charges.[20] In 1904 *The Miller* referred to the lowering of wheat transport rates, to the advantage of British millers, and a new mood in the milling trade was indicated in such statements as 'The British flour trade is rapidly becoming the monopoly of the British flour miller. For nigh upon two years foreign competition has ceased to injure us'. The check on exports from America was maintained until 1914. As they found that American competitive pressure was weakening, the leading British millers gained further confidence for their expansion. Voller's hopeful appraisal in 1902 had substantially predated the actual downturn in flour imports of 1904.

If there were a millennium, it might be dated 1904. In September 1904 *The Miller* remarked that 'When the British miller found that America was no longer a competitor (with flour) he dropped out his American wheat from the blend'. After 1903 United States supplies of wheat to the United Kingdom plunged; India, Russia and the Argentine became the leading suppliers until 1912, apart from 1906. There was a brief rally in American supplies from 1906 to 1908, followed by a pronounced trough until 1912. Canadian wheat supplies became prominent in 1912, rising to major importance in 1914 along with a United States recovery. Wheat supply charts were a ragged picture of peaks and troughs, with Canada gradually coming into play.

The commercial expertise required by large businesses was considerable, as shown in the extensive report of the *Royal Commission on supply of food and raw materials in time of war*, published in 1905. J. H. Vernon, Seth Taylor and other prominent millers gave evidence; the chairman was Lord Balfour of Burleigh. During his evidence in June 1903 Vernon stated that his firm used no English wheat. He thought some port millers might use 10 per cent. An accidentally humorous Mr Chaplin interrogated Seth Taylor, not only a leading miller but also a major wheat importer:

2693 [Mr Chaplin] How many mills have you?
  Seth Taylor: There are two mills. It is a question of capacities; and you can hardly gauge them by numbers ...
  2698 You are aware of course that we have to rely enormously for our supplies upon foreign countries?
  Seth Taylor: Certainly.

There was a surge of innovative activity from 1904 onwards, when mill sites and mill interiors really assumed twentieth-century size and character. In 1904 William Vernon & Sons acquired a site at the Victoria Docks in London's Silvertown, where around 1905 W. A. Vernon, the principal's son, supervised the erection of a very large new manufacturing unit, equipped by Henry Simon Ltd with two plants giving a total capacity of 100 sacks per hour, named Millennium Mills.[21] By adding so substantially to their base at Birkenhead Vernons moved up through the group of the biggest milling firms. When W. A. Vernon became President of NABIM in 1913 *Milling* reported that 'The Millennium Mills throughout are built on a most extensive and handsome scale. In fact, if we were obliged to describe them in a single word, we would choose the word "palatial"'. With their arrival in London, Vernons became leaders there too, not necessarily in prestige, but certainly as innovators. Their capacity roughly equalled Seth Taylor's, but with a superior site they could provide for further technical development.

Joseph Rank's progress was equally dramatic and even more far-reaching. In 1902 he had visited America and formed a confident view of the quality of his own products compared with American flour. In 1904 he indicated this in an interview reported in the journal *Milling*: 'There is a large quantity of American flour consumed in London, and we think we ought to compete for some of it. London millers tell us that we shall find we have a very difficult task, but we think we shall be able to get some of the trade, even if a tariff is not put on'.[22] Joseph Rank's prominence was formally recognised in 1904 when he became President of the National Association. *Milling* described his career and current activity, with an account of the Clarence Mills at Hull with their three Simon plants, providing a total capacity of 100 sacks per hour, and illustrations of new projects at London and Cardiff. Ranks acquired sites for new mills at the Victoria Docks in east London and at Barry Dock at Cardiff. On the London site the first part of the Premier Mills was in operation by the spring of 1905, with a capacity of 30–35 sacks per hour.[23] In June the first part of the Atlantic Mills at Cardiff had been started with a similar capacity.[24] A second plant was in operation at London soon afterwards and a second plant was running at Cardiff in June 1906. By then both the London and Cardiff sites had 70 sacks per hour capacity, all on the current versions of the Simon system. The bold moves by Vernon and Rank between 1904 and 1906 showed that regional considerations were relevant to the planning of product distribution.

Although it was the most striking project in the north-west, Vernon's mill at Birkenhead, opened in 1899, had not been the only scene of activity in the Merseyside district around the turn of the century. *The Miller* reported on the North Shore Co.'s mills at Boundary Street in Liverpool, with a total capacity of 100 sacks per hour in 1899.[25] In 1901 *Milling* reported the replacement of the 20 sacks per hour plant by Thomas Robinson & Son of Rochdale, who installed roller mills with the new diagonal arrangement of the rolls.[26] In 1903 *Milling* reported the remodelling of one of the 40 sacks per hour plants, again by Robinsons.[27] Around 1903 Hutchinsons, the other very large business in Liverpool itself, acquired Walmsley & Smith's mill at Barrow-in-Furness; William Smith had been President of the National Association in 1897. The Barrow Corn Mills were enlarged in 1905–1906.[28]

Not far from the growing milling centre of Liverpool, there were opportunities for expansion on the Manchester Ship Canal, which had been opened in 1894. Richard Baxendell & Sons, who had worked a provender mill at Salford, and built the Bee Mills at Liverpool, decided in 1904 to expand their business with a large mill at the Manchester end of the canal.[29] Their Sun Mills were equipped by E. R. & F. Turner Ltd of Ipswich to have an initial capacity of 40 sacks per hour and started in January 1906. Almost immediately, Baxendells sold to the CWS, giving the Cooperative movement a large mill which they repeatedly extended. Positions around the Manchester Docks balanced the transport requirements for raw materials inward and the finished product outwards to more distant population centres. *Milling* reported that 'It would be impossible to improve the site, as not only is it all that is required for a Lancashire trade, but it is equally suited for business in West Yorkshire, the Midlands and the Black Country'.

Vernon, with his Liverpool site on the Great Float at Birkenhead, and soon afterwards also along with Rank at the Victoria Docks in London, looked further ahead as far as trans-Atlantic cargoes and ship displacements were concerned, but the docks at Manchester and Salford provided new locations for sound commercial investments. The Hovis Bread Flour Co. Ltd moved from the canalside at Macclesfield in Cheshire to a site on the Ship Canal at Manchester's Trafford Park in 1906.[30] About 1885 Richard Smith had devised his method of reintroducing germ into bread, and patented it, the final product being known initially as Smith's Patent Germ Bread. According to an official history, *The Hovis Jubilee* (1948), the name Hovis was derived from the Latin *hominis vis*, the strength of man. It was after Richard Smith's death in 1900 that the business expanded significantly, with the provision of the Trafford Park plant of 25 sacks per hour capacity, later increased to 40 sacks. This was only the beginning of a concentration of milling capacity in the area by others.

Around London there was an irregular distribution of medium size mills, several of which had principals who became President of the National Association, and obviously well-placed as far as information was concerned. The relative advantages of their sites varied. There had been Soundy at Reading (1884), and Wilson Marriage of East Mills at Colchester (1896). Successors

Figure 86.
Hovis mill at Manchester, described in 1906. (*Milling*, July 1906)

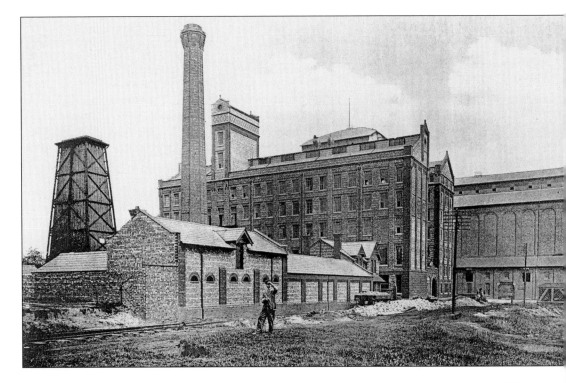

were Stephen Cannon of Erith in Kent (1903) and A. E. Humphries at Coxes Lock near Weybridge (1906). Robinsons of Rochdale, enlarged the Erith mill for Cannon & Gaze in 1902, to provide a capacity of 17 sacks per hour. Cannon had a Thames-side mill site, and wheat supply was by barge. In contrast, the small country mill at Coxes Lock was not quite on the Thames, but about a mile and a half up the Wey Navigation. The mill there had been rescued from closure in 1887 by A. E. Humphries and there were several stages of technical improvement and modest enlargement. About 1904 E. R. & F. Turner of Ipswich installed a 15 sacks per hour plant. Humphries devised the flow-sheet for the design of the plant.[31]

In the South-East, Marriages at Colchester were probably the best-known millers. Northwards the next medium-size mill was owned by Wm Marshall & Sons, Grimsby, Ltd, where there was some increase in capacity in 1904. At Ipswich, Cranfield Brothers, a firm founded in Huntingdonshire in 1860, extended their premises and installed new plant in 1906.[32] They then had a capacity of 18 sacks per hour on the dockside at Ipswich, with room for a possible doubling in the future. The East Mills at Colchester could take wheat from barges via the river Colne, but as demand for Marriages' flour increased they decided to build a new mill at Felixstowe, where work began in 1905; the East Anglia Mills, equipped by Simons, were completed in 1907.[33] Cranfields and Marriages were well-positioned to use English wheat. Most of the waterside mills in eastern counties, and at the Port of London, took in their foreign wheat from sailing barges. The mills at Felixstowe, Ipswich and Erith continued as medium size, though much bigger than very many others. In capacity they were comparable with mills at Gloucester and Sheffield and other large towns. But bigger businesses at main ports developed faster and much further.

At the turn of the century Spillers & Bakers were still possibly the overall leaders. In 1905 W. E. Nicholls, their managing director, became President of the National Association. *Milling* presented a profile of Nicholls and the early stages of the company.[34] Details of operation were unfortunately lacking. This might partly have been due to reticence, which had been suggested by Arthur Baker when accepting the Presidency in 1899: 'I shall be obliged to ask that no visit to our mills be included in the programme, as it is a rule with us not to allow our mills to be open for inspection'. In the case of Spillers & Bakers in 1905, *Milling* was able to provide information of a general nature. It was stated that Nicholls was 'the head of what is probably the largest milling company in the British Empire'. The company was said to have about 1,000 employees, a large number for an industry that was not labour intensive within production departments; the office and travelling staff was said to exceed 300 employees. The New Cardiff Milling Company, controlled by Spillers & Bakers since 1902, had become Cardiff and Channel Mills Ltd. In 1905 Henry Simon Ltd included Cardiff in a list of places where they had large new projects.

During the same period there were many new projects elsewhere. *Milling* reported in June 1904 that Messrs Henry Simon Ltd were 'unprecedentedly busy at the present time'. Of the twenty complete roller plants in course of erection, there were five with capacities between 30 and 45 sacks and five between 10 and 20 sacks per hour. They were also engaged in alterations and improvements at other places, including work at nine mills varying from 10 to 25 sacks, and in two larger mills, one of 60 sacks per hour capacity. They had current contracts in India, South Africa, Australia, New Zealand and South America as well as in the United Kingdom, which were the biggest plants. In October 1905 Simons were advertising that 'About two-thirds of the total amount of flour manufactured in the United Kingdom is produced by mills erected on this system'.[35]

Hoping for harmony

Concentration of milling capacity at the ports and in larger firms had been a subject of increasing importance through the 1890s, but it was a more striking development during the decade before 1914. The extent to which large firms were getting bigger became clearer from 1904 to 1906, and a significant fraction of the total national output could be assumed to be concentrated in several dozen businesses. The labels mammoth and leviathan were used to refer to the biggest mills and businesses, usually in good humour, and sometimes by candidates for those titles. The clearest impressions of change were to be obtained from reports of mill construction projects.

Milling made an attempt to guess the shape of the industry in 1901, including 'At the present time we believe there are over 1,000 complete roller system flour mills in the British Isles ... In all there are under thirty mills with over 50 sacks capacity each'.[36] The statistical unit was mills in 1901. In 1907, Milling estimated 'the number of roller-milling firms in the UK' : over 100 sacks per hour: about ten firms; from 50 to 100 sacks per hour: about twelve firms; from 16 to short of 50 sacks per hour: about forty-four firms.[37] Several of the firms in the largest category were advancing to a total capacity of twice or more times the nominal 100 sacks standard of very large businesses. The journal records should have been nearly as good as those accessible to the National Association or held by Henry Simon Ltd, particularly as the editor had a special interest in statistics. Medium size mills were also improved and scaled up; the journals warned that there could be too much scaling up.

Repeatedly there were statements about a division between port millers and country millers, so could there be a continuing shared sense of purpose? In 1905 W. E. Nicholls of Spillers & Bakers observed that 'it does not appear that we are ready for any elaborate community of interests'. Gradually the small rural mills had dropped out, partly through obsolescence, also affected by the drift towards town life, but there was not much margin to be gained by their further reduction. Businesses which kept up-to-date, increased their capacity, and ran their mills continuously, probably used up any spare market capacity faster than it became available. There was room for disagreement about aggregate national capacity: the mills were not all equally modernised and the industry could not be held still at an arbitrary point.

From 1905 to 1908 strenuous efforts were made to devise a standard and definite form of contract for flour sales. The lead was given by the successive

Presidents of NABIM: W. E. Nicholls, A. E. Humphries, W. R. Mallett and W. E. Nicholls again. The succession from Nicholls to Humphries was from the leader of the extensive business of Spillers & Bakers Ltd to the principal of the comparatively modest size business at Coxes Lock Mills at Weybridge; that from Humphries to Mallett was from a scientifically-minded miller, who was the pioneer in attempts to improve English wheat, to the leading advocate of the cause of country millers. The return to Nicholls showed that there was a basis for democratic interaction.

In 1905 Nicholls presented in clearer terms the millers' trading difficulties and his suggestions for improvement. His description of slack or unfair trading practices was direct: 'These methods take the shape sometimes of inferior flours adopting known brands, floating contracts, elastic discounts, rebates for haulages, own sacks, sack money, and secret allowances, which may be legitimate or illegitimate according to the views of the competitor adopting them'. Although he had been a supporter of attempts to devolve responsibilities to local associations, Nicholls stated that 'I consider the time for respecting local traditions has passed, and we must adjust our views in conformity with altered conditions'. He suggested that consideration should be given to the possibility of fixing terms and conditions of sale for the whole country and that the problem should be dealt with either by the National Association or by a sufficiently large number of millers to guarantee the success of whatever arrangement could be reached. He also suggested that there should be general recognition that the port millers had become the dominant partners. After studying about 140 different forms of contract then in use, Nicholls drew up

Figure 87.
Coxes Lock Mill, near Weybridge, described in 1906. (*Milling,* July 1906)

a suggested sale note, but there was little response when he circulated copies of it.[38]

Nicholls supported Vernon's argument that, while large amounts of flour were imported, it could not be held that there was overproduction in the British milling industry. Humphries cautiously admitted the possibility of overproduction, particularly if mills were enlarged further and if imports did not continue to decline. In 1907 he stated that milling capacity was increasing, without a corresponding increase in the consumption of flour. He then brought forward the idea of a general cut in output of up to 10 per cent and also, though possibly less likely, that mills could be bought out and closed, or that some might stand idle and receive compensation from the others. He invited discussion from the industry, but had to abandon the subject, which was too complex at the time.[39] Humphries' ideas would become relevant eventually. Appropriateness of the moment would depend not only on community of interest, but on judgements of realities, shared throughout the modernised industry. With perhaps a thousand mills, further concentration was a possible way towards a solution.

W. H. Mallett provided the first detailed estimates of increasing capacity at the ports. As President of NABIM he decided to investigate what he called 'the displacement of the locale of milling', presenting the results to the Exeter Convention in July 1907. The statistical basis was provided by G. J. S. Broomhall of *Milling*, who calculated that a total of 2,020 sacks of flour per hour could be made in 1906 at the principal ports, compared with W. E. Nicholls' estimate of 1,990 sacks per hour. Three-shift working was assumed at principal ports, based on 130 hours weekly for 50 weeks per year.

Table 12.2. W. H. Mallett's report to NABIM (from *Milling*, July 1907)

Source of flour	1890		1906	
A	Quantities estimated (in sacks)			
All UK port mills	9,847,500		19,662,500	
UK inland mills	16,852,000		13,947,000	
Imported	7,200,000		5,676,000	
B	% Total supply	% of UK Milling	% Total supply	% of UK Milling
All UK port mills	29	37	50	59
UK inland mills	50	63	36	41
Imported	21		14	
C	Output capacity at principal ports (sacks per hour)			
Liverpool	300		630	
London	300		540	
Bristol Channel	190		450	
Hull & York	140		400	
Total	930		2,020	

Mallett presented two main statistical comparisons: firstly, 'theoretical quantities of flour made' and imports in 1890 and 1906; secondly, increases in productive capability at principal ports. Contributions made by the various sources of supply are shown in Table 12.2. Sections A and C show the basic Broomhall-Mallett data, section B being derived from A. The quantities were, as industrial engineers would have said, 'guesstimates'.

Mallett's estimates suggest that the inland mills of the UK could have contributed half of the total in 1890, dropping to just over one third in 1906 with the port mills then contributing half. A full list of port mill sites was not given. The proportion of imported flour was shown as falling significantly, but Mallett's statement that in 1890 flour imports amounted to 7.2 million sacks contrasts with Dornbusch's estimate of 6.3 million sacks; there was precise agreement for 1906. If Dornbusch's estimate of imported flour in 1890 is substituted for Mallett's, the percentages in Table 12.2 are not much affected. The statistical results from Mallett and Broomhall seem fragile with respect to running hours assumptions and inland mills outputs, but robust with respect to alterations of imports. Mallett's 'theoretical quantities of flour' presumably referred to these uncertainties, but the results represented an unparalleled effort to focus on the effects of concentration at the ports.

By 1906 Liverpool had reached a position of marked leadership. In 1890 London was considerably undermilled and in 1906 was still undermilled. Millers in other port areas supplied flour well beyond their immediate neighbourhoods. There is limited potential for detailed analysis of industrial structure from available data in the Mallett-Broomhall efforts, Lawes & Gilbert's reports and Census of Production reports; data was severely lacking in the report of the First Census of Production of the UK (1907) which was not published until 1912.

Figure 88.
Marriages' mill at
Felixstowe, described
in 1907. (Simon Ltd,
1908)

237

In 1907 a group of principals of large firms decided to take the initiative in a new attempt to devise a national sale note. They formed the 'Port Millers' Committee' and obtained support from twenty-seven firms, another indicator of the approximate number of 'first division' members.[40] The basis for collaboration was to be national uniformity of form of contract, based on a universal standard sale note. It was not feasible to regulate prices. There were several kinds of separatists: those who already had some agreement with millers in the same area, for instance in London, and did not wish to adopt a different procedure; independent operators; and inland millers who did not wish be coerced by port millers. Another point of difficulty was enforcement of standard procedures. The Port Millers' Committe, later known as the National Millers' Committee, drafted an elaborate set of proposals.[41] An association was to be formed, with formal rules, and the members were to adopt their official form of flour contract. There was to be a council of eighteen millers, six of whom would be representatives of Buchanans Flour Mills Ltd, Edward Hutchinson, Henry Leetham & Sons Ltd, Joseph Rank Ltd, Spillers & Bakers Ltd, and William Vernon & Sons. The scheme was discussed at a meeting of the National Association in February 1908. There was strong support for general reform of trading arrangements, but not for the details of the National Millers' Committee's rules.

From 1908 to 1909 there was continual and exhaustive discussion of the new proposals at meetings of the National Association and of its Council, with W. E. Nicholls taking considerable responsibility for seeking a generally acceptable solution. There were some revivals of local associations, at least in the more populous districts of England, in the north, the midlands and the south-east; Nicholls attended many local millers' meetings. He also sent out enquiries to 767 firms, not only to test reaction to the National Millers' Committee draft sale note, but also to try to find whether milling capacity was in excess of requirements.[42] His tentative conclusion was that there was some evidence of overproduction, but that the extent of it was unknown. Shorn of the elaborate provisions of the proposed articles of association that had been drawn up by the National Millers' Committee, the main feature of suggested reform was a fairly simple national sale note for flour contracts, which the National Association decided to adopt.

The next step was to seek an agreement with the Bakers' Association, but in 1910 they would not accept a 'duty clause' in the conditions of sale. The clause provided that if a duty on wheat were to be imposed, repealed or varied, flour prices would be altered immediately. The reason for its inclusion was that there had been disagreements between millers and bakers about the timing of price alterations during the Government's experiment with duties in 1902 and 1903, and the imposition of import duties was still a subject of political debate. The large amount of work involved in trying to establish a standard form of sales agreement must have had long-term positive effects. All the difficulties were aired exhaustively. Like Royal Commissions, whose reports often gather dust and fail as exact recipes for action, they contributed to a significant change in the overall appreciation of problems, including implications of over-production.

While Nicholls was energetic in visiting, corresponding, and reporting to meetings, his aim was to try to promote cohesion. His enquiry to '767 firms of millers' dealt with more than the Association membership and probably represented most of the well-known businesses. For comparison, the Census of Production (1907) received 1254 returns, with some confusion between mills and businesses, of which 577 gave useful replies. Nicholls' remarked on the 'thinning out of the milling ranks'. Although that subject was often obscured by reminders of the thousands of small mills of the 1870s and 1880s, Nicholls referred more specifically to the falling numbers of country mills in active flour production during the previous few years. He indicated the rate of change in East Anglia:

> The position in the four counties, Norfolk, Suffolk, Essex and Cambridgeshire may be given as an illustration of what is probably going on throughout the whole kingdom. At the present time – 1909 – there are 116 milling firms situated within this area, whereas only six years ago – in 1903 – there were 352. Of course, those that have ceased to exist are those who were either not up to date or were unable, with the financial resources at their command, to turn out produce against their neighbours who were more favourably situated or were more possessed of this world's goods.[43]

It is not easy to extend Nicholls' information; Kelly's Trade Directories dealt with larger numbers of millers, as they included both provender millers and flour millers. For instance, Kelly's for Essex in 1906 listed 155. Directories show the decline of rural milling, and graphs for Essex, Kent and Sussex would look very similar, with a steady fall from the later 1870s, but Directory data obscures the rate of reduction in viability of rural flour mills. The Directories did not state capacities, but undoubtedly many of the mills listed in Kelly's columns, in the Census of Production crude data, and also in Nicholls' statistics were small production units, not destined to last much longer. There were still opportunities for 5 sack plants in small towns but, if a mill of that capacity was worked for 60 hours per week, production was enough for about 17,000 consumers of 5 lbs of flour each. Obviously some smaller mills could hope to stay in business, but could they be kept up-to-date?

No turning back

Opportunities had to be taken while it was thought they existed. The firm of F. A. Frost & Sons set examples of optimistic endeavour. It was the lot of J. M. Frost to succeed W. E. Nicholls as President of NABIM and present the proposed National Sale Note to the Association, and then report in 1910 that agreement could not be reached with the bakers.[44] Yet he regarded that frustration as postponement, rather than failure. At the Chester convention of 1909 there was earnest discussion but, despite trading difficulties, there was the usual pleasure programme of banquet, ball and excursions; a later President recorded that 'the ladies' hats resembled miniature flower beds'. At the smoking concert a quartet performed the ballad 'The Miller of Dee', an expression of a

Figure 89.
Frosts' mill at Chester,
described in 1909.
(*Milling*, July 1909)

miller's independence. Later, Frost presented the copyright of the musical setting to the Association. It was a good-humoured gesture from the best-known miller near the Dee. As Frost was taking on the tasks of diplomacy, his firm was engaged in further innovation.

At the Chester Steam Mills, on the Shropshire Union Canal, their machinery was developed to include a 20 sacks per hour plant, one of 12 sacks, and a testing plant of 1.5 sacks capacity. In 1909 they decided to build by the Manchester Ship Canal at Ellesmere Port, their plan being to move their larger and relatively new Simon plant to their new site, and remodel it to produce 30 sacks per hour.[45] *The Miller* reported that by the end of 1910 Simons would have installed the machinery to achieve the increased output. In anticipation of the completion of the move and remodelling, *Milling* stated that 'the milling capacity of Manchester, Warrington and Ellesmere Port will be about 250 sacks per hour'.[46] Both journals gave extensive coverage of Frosts' new situation, and both noted Simon's expertise in electrical engineering. There was a glowing testimonial to milling and engineering collaboration.

The big projects for Rank and Vernons from 1904 to 1906 just preceded a phase of reappraisal of processing details. On a smaller scale, Marriages' new mill at Felixstowe in 1907 also adhered to previous criteria. Frosts' new mill at Ellesmere Port was not orthodox by the technical standards of the middle of the decade. The capacity at Felixstowe was ignored in various accounts, thereby curtailing detailed comparison of two interesting firms: Marriages and Frosts, both of long standing and each moving out from venerable locations towards shipping routes. While many millers were wondering about commercial prospects and whether it would be profitable to improve their processes, Frosts represented decisiveness, which the CWS also demonstrated by steady expansion and Ranks soon confirmed by another bold move.

THE COOPERATIVE MOVEMENT

Between 1906 and 1914 the Cooperative movement rose to a prominent position in the milling industry. An official account of the development of the Wholesale Society was given by Redfern (1913) in which he described the full range of activity, including flour milling, from 1863 onwards. The CWS published fascinating descriptions of their work, as they became involved in the production and supply of food, clothing, furniture and general household goods, owning farms and tea estates, ships and coalmines, works for producing soap, boots and shoes, cocoa, jam; factories for bacon, butter, hosiery, corsets and shirts, amongst many other manufactures. Appropriately, the CWS Annuals were later called *The People's Year Book*.[47]

The Cooperative movement could trace its connection with corn milling to the foundation of the Hull Anti-Mill society in 1795. Benjamin Jones (1894), who wrote an extensive history of *Cooperative Production*, quoted the founders:

> We, the poor inhabitants of the said town, have lately experienced much trouble and sorrow in ourselves and families on the occasion of an exorbitant price of flour; that though the price is much reduced at present, yet we judge it needful to take every precaution to preserve ourselves from the invasions of covetous and merciless men in future.

Percy Redfern (1913) referred to 'thirty or forty cooperative corn mills scattered over the country'. Larger mills were built, notably for the Leeds Industrial Cooperative Society and the Halifax Flour Society mills in 1874, and the less important (except for the name) Rochdale District Cooperative Corn Mill Society mill of 1850. The Equitable Society and the Industrial Society at Oldham jointly supported the building of the Star Corn Mill in 1870. The Halifax, Rochdale, Sowerby Bridge & District, and Oldham mills had both individuals and societies as members. There were also mills owned by a society composed exclusively of other societies, such as the Derwent Society at Shotley Bridge and the Colne Vale Society at Slaithwaite. These were listed by Jones (1894), with a detailed account of different types of society and their progress; the larger cooperative mills were described, with technical detail, in *The Miller*.

The Cooperative Wholesale Society began business in Manchester in 1864, and by 1869 had premises in Balloon Street. Within the movement there was caution and rivalry about milling projects before the CWS opened their first mill at Dunston-on-Tyne in 1891, with an impressive initial capacity of 40 sacks per hour. A CWS flour mill was opened at Silvertown on the eastern side of London in 1900, with a modest capacity supplied by Robinsons, soon followed by major expansion. The CWS Annual (1914) described the area:

> Beyond the Isle of Dogs, between the river and the Victoria and Albert Docks, there is a railway-traversed factory-lined strip of shore, and that is Silvertown. If there exists anywhere a citadel of private enteprise it is here. Yet, with the CWS Flour Mill, Grocery Productive Factory, and new Soap Works, there is now to be found on this river bank a Cooperative settlement.

There were many conferences, hopes, doubts and disagreements before the CWS reached a stage of nationwide influence from 1906. In 1906–1907 the NABIM membership included the Barnsley British Cooperative Society Ltd, the Derwent Flour Mills Society Ltd, the Leeds Industrial Cooperative Society Ltd, and the CWS headquarters at Balloon Street, Manchester. There was contention between Liverpool and Cheshire Societies who wanted a mill on the Mersey, and north-eastern Societies who urged a case for a mill on the Humber. Anxiety about a possible large new non-CWS mill in the north-west led to negotiations and the CWS took over the Rochdale mill in January 1906 and the Star at Oldham in March. In April the Sun Flour Mill at Manchester was bought from Baxendells. By 1908 the Manchester mill was aptly titled in plural: the Sun Mills – 'the largest flour mills in East Lancashire'; 40 sacks capacity had been increased to 75.[48] In 1910 *The Miller* announced the opening of the Avonmouth Flour and Provender Mills: there were to be seven grades of flour, named

Figure 90.
CWS mill at Silvertown, London, illustrated in 1914. (*CWS Annual*, 1914)

Imperial, Empire, Extras, Double Supers, Supers, Fines and Households.[49] The CWS jubilee in 1914 was to be marked by 'the double Sun', which would be 'capable of producing the enormous quantity of 142 sacks, or 39,760 pounds weight of flour every hour', the latest news from Redfern who continued to record the history of the CWS up to 1938.[50] In NABIM's list of 1913 1914 there were also the Halifax Flour Society Ltd and the Leeds Industrial Cooperative Society Ltd. The CWS represented a growing milling group, which was further strengthened in 1915 when the Halifax mill and those at Sowerby Bridge and Colne Vale were taken over.

In Scotland also, where the pressure of imports had been severe, there were advances. The Scottish CWS opened their Chancelot Mills at Edinburgh in 1894, described by Simon in his 1898 catalogue as 'the finest block of flour mill buildings in the world' (it had a French chateau appearance).[51] In 1897 the SCWS bought the Junction Meal & Flour Mills at Leith. They purchased the Regent Roller Flour Mills at Glasgow from John Ure & Sons in 1903. Ure's mills had been built in 1889 and equipped by Simon. Ure had been President of NABIM in 1885; he died about a year before SCWS decided to increase production. Originally a 25 sack Simon plant, the Regent Mills were remodelled for the SCWS in 1905 by Henry Simon Ltd to have a capacity of 40 sacks, and again in 1913, with an increase to 55 sacks per hour.[52] The CWS Annual (1914) stated that the three Scottish mills had a total productive capacity exceeding 12,300 sacks per week, roughly equivalent to 100 sacks per hour.

Table 12.3. CWS mills

Mill	Date	Capacity at listed date (sacks per hour)	Capacity in 1914 (sacks per hour)
Dunston on Tyne	1891 opened	40	75
Star Mill	1890 rebuilt	20	32
Silvertown	1900 opened	12	50
Sun Mills	1906 acquired	40	140
Avonmouth	1910 opened	30	30

Redfern claimed that their modern mills would 'put the Wholesale Society probably in the position of being both the largest flour millers and the owners of the greatest individual mills in the United Kingdom. Night and day, at the rate of over 250 sacks hourly, this vast machinery works for the two million or so consumers who are its ultimate proprietors'.[53] The CWS Annual (1914) showed that Redfern's claims were being surpassed. Mills at Dunston, London, Manchester, Oldham and Avonmouth (Bristol) could produce well over 300 sacks of flour per hour. *The Miller* reported in March 1914 that work to double the capacity at Manchester was 'nearing completion'. Also plans were being considered to double capacity at Avonmouth. There was competition between CWS mills but they had enough scope within their separate regions, roughly corresponding to the major port areas.

The CWS helped to demonstrate that one overall authority, with other vast business interests, could coordinate a nationwide milling network. Organisational responsibility was presumably delegated, but the view to outsiders must have been instructive. In future, increasing scales of operation and wide geographical strategies would determine the principal characteristics of the milling industry. The cooperative retail shops, often to be known simply as 'The Stores' could provide for large numbers of the so-called working population of the north of England. Country millers in the south had more survival potential, but note had to be taken that the CWS mills, although never called 'leviathans' as others sometimes were, had gone to the ports. When in 1913 William Voller reviewed 'The Milling Trade of Today' for members of NABIM he was worried about a deficient Russian wheat crop, larger flour imports, increased working expenses, overproduction, and the Coop: 'Every thousand sacks made in Cooperative mills means a corresponding quantity less for the private miller'.[54]

ENTREPRENEURIAL ENTERPRISE

Joseph Rank's progress in mill development was impressively rapid during 1905–1906. In June 1905 *The Miller* estimated that the total output of Joseph Rank Ltd would reach 30,000 sacks of flour per week by the end of the year. In August *Milling* reported that the firm's output at Hull, London and Cardiff had already reached a total of 200 sacks per hour and that was before the order was placed for the second stage of the Atlantic Mills at Cardiff, which by the summer of 1906 was in operation. In June 1908 the capital was increased from £900,000 to £1,000,000. In 1909 a site opposite the existing Clarence Mills at Hull became available, and was acquired. It had 'railway accommodation and an extensive river frontage'. New buildings were erected and two plants installed, each of 50 sacks per hour capacity. When *Milling* described the 'History of the House of Rank' in 1933, it was shown that the Clarence Mills project of 1910 was an enlargement, not a replacement; 'the older mills being reconstructed and modernised, the complete capacity of the mills at Hull was then over 180 sacks of flour per hour'.[55]

The next big move was preceded by a mixture of news and speculation in *Milling* starting on February 17, 1912: 'Early in the week the news leaked out that the directors of an important mill on the Mersey were negotiating for the sale of the bulk of the shares of the company'. The company could be identified by 'a considerable advance' in the Liverpool Stock Exchange share price. It was next reported that 'rumours have been current for some time that the directors of the North Shore Mills, Limited, Liverpool, were negotiating with a large firm of millers for the sale of the mills ... The fortunate purchasers are Messrs Joseph Rank Ltd'. On March 2 *Milling* reported that 'Since the failure of the negotiations for the purchase of the North Shore Mills by Messrs J. Rank Ltd, there have been persistent rumours that this firm intends to build a large mill on the Cheshire side of the river. There had been opposition to the sale from two leading Liverpool millers, control of the North Shore Mills being jointly acquired by E. M. Hutchinson and Frank C. Wilson. There was a tiny report 'New flour mill for Birkenhead'. The Mersey Docks and Harbour Board had approved the lease of land on the south side of the West Float at Birkenhead

to Joseph Rank Ltd 'for the purpose of erecting a flour mill &c'. It provided deep water berthing for large ocean-going cargo boats.

In June 1913 *Milling* announced that the Ocean Mills were 'rapidly nearing completion'. Full operation was expected in about a month when 'employment will be given to 300 men'. In April 1914 *Milling* reported on a visit to the Ocean Flour Mills at Birkenhead, 'standing evidence of the latest enterprise undertaken by the huge milling firm of Messrs J. Rank Ltd'. The illustration was a general view across the water, stylish but not very informative. Rank (1955) said: 'The years preceding the first World War gave no hint of the shadow which plunged the world into four years of gloom'; also that 'May 1914 saw a further increase in the company's capital to £1,600,000 and all seemed set for a continuance of prosperity'. In the late summer, European events must have driven celebrations of a new giant mill out of the headlines. It is not clear which was the biggest milling concern in 1914, but Ranks, Spillers & Bakers and the CWS had forged ahead.

CHAPTER THIRTEEN

Feasibilty studies: 1900–1915

The involvement of chemistry

THE PUZZLE OF 'STRENGTH'

In 1890 and again in 1900 the National Association tried to interest farmers, agricultural societies and seedsmen in the possibility of growing wheat varieties that gave 'strength' to wheat and flour, which was still only vaguely associated with the protein substance called gluten at the stage of dough formation. In 1890 Wilson Marriage's circular was given widespread publicity, and in 1900 W. R. Mallett obtained the support of the Council of NABIM for a case to be made to the agricultural societies,[1] but farmers persisted in their policy of planting wheat varieties that gave high yield of grain and straw but did not provide strength. Mallett persisted with attempts to influence the farming community. Although the most prominent matters of debate at the time were about trade organisation, a new departure was made which had a different but longer-lasting value than was foreseen. During the period 1900 to 1908 the National Association took the initiative in trying to improve the milling quality of English wheat, which stimulated basic research in cereal chemistry.

In 1901 the Association set up a Home-Grown Wheat Committee, which soon found that the problems grew bigger. The members included Wilson Marriage, A. E. Humphries, W. R. Mallett, R. H. Biffen of Cambridge University and A. D. Hall of Wye College, London University. As both Marriage and Humphries had farming interests, progressive country millers were well represented. From 1902 onwards, selected wheats were grown in defined conditions at various places in south-east England. Humphries installed a small roller plant at his mill at Coxes Lock in Surrey in which he milled trial quantities, and the mill baker carried out baking tests. A. D. Hall, who became the Director of the Rothamsted Experimental Station, supervised laboratory analysis of the flours obtained and R. H. Biffen developed a programme of wheat hybridisation. Reporting to the 1903 convention of NABIM, Hall gave reasons in modest terms for the involvement in scientific laboratory work: 'We want to find out a little more knowledge as to why one wheat should be stronger than another. We want to get down to the cause of things. What makes strength? Why does the strength vary so much? We want to accumulate evidence to strengthen the practical judgement of baking'.[2]

In 1904 *The Miller* was complimentary about the work done by the committee, but seemed dismayed by the problems that had been found in the laboratory work: 'The upshot of all these careful and elaborate tests is that all the present known gluten theory is discarded, and we are plunged once more into acute controversy'.[3] Hall reported to the 1904 convention that strength did not depend simply on the amount of gluten. Gluten was believed to be made up of two proteins, glutenin and gliadin, and it had been supposed that the ratio of the two might determine strength, but the current research analyses did not support that idea. So far they had not found a laboratory method that could be used in general practice to estimate strength. In 1905 Humphries placed emphasis on the empirical definition of strength, rather than scientific explanation in terms of chemical constituents and behaviour. Even in that context, there was uncertainty of expression, as four versions were current, including the definition of strength as the quantity of water which a flour would absorb to make a dough of a standard consistency. Humphries supported the view that 'strength should be defined as a flour's capacity to make big well-piled loaves';[4] not only size was important but shape also. Attention turned again to baking tests with the hope that the already extensive laboratory work might lead to reliable methods of measurement.

In 1907 Hall reported that the chemical research was disappointing; a connection had not been found to link protein or nitrogen content with the results of baking tests.[5] At the same time, T. B. Wood, at Cambridge University, was investigating the effects on gluten of the chemical environment in which it might exist. Later work by Wood and W. B. Hardy developed the theory that gluten by itself had neither of the desirable properties of elasticity and toughness, those properties being impressed on it by surrounding conditions. When reviewing the development of cereal chemistry up to 1935, E. A. Fisher, the Director of the Research Association of British Flour Millers, stated that 'the modern chemistry of wheat and flour really began with the fundamental work and ideas of W. B. Hardy, T. B. Wood and A. E. Humphries'.[6]

Previously, it had been generally believed that strong foreign wheats always lost strength when grown in Britain. After trials with hundreds of samples of foreign wheat, it was found that a few appeared to maintain their strength under English conditions. Numerous trials were made, but after a period of optimism, notably around 1912, further difficulties were encountered; typical problems included low yields, variability associated with different soils and the non-homogeneity of some of the wheats used in hybridisation. The committee reported in 1913 that work was continuing in collaboration with the Department of Agriculture of Cambridge University and with the newly-established Institute of Plant Breeding.[7] R. H. Biffen, who was Professor of Agricultural Botany at Cambridge from 1908 to 1931, described how the problem of low yield persisted, but how the hybridisation work led, much later, to the production of varieties which gave good results in certain conditions.[8] The early analytical research in cereal chemistry revealed that the subject was more complex than had been expected.

FURTHER PRACTICAL PROBLEMS FOR CEREAL CHEMISTS

Between 1900 and 1914 there were other developments concerned with the chemistry of wheat and flour. The first of these was flour bleaching, which was started commercially in Britain about 1902 and came into prominence about 1905. Previously, all the operations of the main flour milling processes were mechanical separations. The only exception was in the preliminary process of wheat conditioning, in which the moisture content of hard brittle wheat was increased and that of soft damp wheat was reduced. Bleaching was a quite new departure.

In the 1890s there had been experiments with ozone: Jago (1911) referred to work by Frichot in France in 1898, but had tried a similar method earlier, to try to remove the very yellow colour of flour made from Oregon wheat. Both experimenters abandoned their trials because ozone imparted an unpleasant odour to the flour.[9] There were attempts to improve on Frichot's method, including a Leetham patent of 1904. In 1901 a provisional patent was obtained by John and Sidney Andrews of Belfast, for a bleaching process that used nitrogen peroxide obtained by the reaction of nitric acid and ferrous sulphate. The Belfast location was significant; there was a demand for very white flour in Ireland, possibly created by public liking for certain brands of American flour. Foreign flour had an advantage in that it aged during transit; ageing caused whitening. The complete specification for the Andrews process was accepted in 1902 but it had been opposed and, in order to meet further expected opposition, the Flour Oxidizing Co. Ltd of Liverpool was formed between Andrews & Sons and Ross T. Smyth & Co. There were numerous legal actions against infringers and a prolonged contest against Alsop Flour Process Ltd, holders of a patent taken out in 1903 for an electrical method of making nitrogen peroxide for bleaching.[10] In 1903 Jago produced a report for the Flour Oxidizing Co. which supported the effectiveness of their process and this was given bold publicity in the journal *Milling*. The subject of bleaching came to the general attention of the British milling industry during the next two years.[11]

From about 1904 Andrews were able to claim that they had a master patent and in 1906 the Comptroller of the Patent Office allowed Alsops to amend their specification to exclude an erroneous statement that their process increased the protein content of flour. The Alsop patent became one for treating flour without a specific claim to bleaching. Litigation continued, with Alsops failing in a case against the Flour Oxidizing Co. in 1908, in which they tried to fault the Andrews specification on various technical points of detail.[12] Andrews' position in their action in the High Court in 1908 against Carr & Co. Ltd was reported in detail in *The Miller*. Their contests with infringers culminated in an action in 1909 against J. & R. Hutchinson of Nottingham, whose defence was that the patented process was not useful for the specified purpose, the baking qualities of the flour were not improved, and the treated flour deteriorated as a result of the process. As Kent-Jones & Amos (1950) commented, 'The case thus became a complete investigation into the use of nitrogen peroxide as a bleaching agent'. The judgement upheld the Andrews patent. Mr Justice Warrington's conclusion, splashed in *Milling* as an advertisement for the Flour Oxidizing Co. Ltd was that 'the plaintiff has established the truth of the statement in his specification that no deleterious action on the flour is caused by the above mentioned treatment'. Bleaching experiments were also carried out using chlorine and several other substances,[13] but in 1911 Dr J. M. Hamill stated that nitrogen peroxide remained the only satisfactory agent. It might be added that judgements of permissible and impermissible chemicals and reactions could and did change. According to Hamill, electrical methods were then 'rapidly superseding chemical processes on account of their simplicity in operation and the greater accuracy with which the degree of bleaching can be controlled and overbleaching avoided'. Hamill also suggested that bleaching had not become universal practice, even amongst large firms.

In 1911 there were three publications of special importance to millers, including William Jago's text, *The technology of bread making*, which contained chapters on the chemistry of wheat, the strength of flour, flour bleaching and both detailed analytical and routine testing of wheat and flour, confirming his position as the leading industrial consultant concerned with laboratory testing and quality control methods for the milling industry. The two other notable publications of 1911 were of immediate importance to many millers. They were both by Dr J. M. Hamill. The first report was made to the Local Government Board on 'The bleaching of flour and the addition of so-called improvers to flour';[14] it followed representations to public analysts and general press publicity of objections to bleaching. A disturbing aspect for some bakers was that, whereas whiteness had been associated with high quality, bleaching introduced uncertainty; there were allegations that bleaching was used to conceal inferior quality, but against this it was argued that bleaching could not hide impurities such as bran specks and could make them more noticeable. Hamill's general conclusions were that there was usually only a small amount of bleaching, but that the process was not free from risk to the product and that the consumers did not obtain any compensating benefit. *The Miller* regarded Hamill's report as cautious expression of general concern: 'Scarcely ever has a mountain in labour produced a more ridiculous mouse; we refer, of course, not to the report itself, drawn up by its author with so much care ... but to the exaggeration and misrepresentation of the conduct of the trade by a certain portion of the Press'.[15]

In addition to bleaching to alter the appearance of flour, there were attempts to enhance the general baking properties and the strength of flour by the use of additives, so-called 'improvers', which included very small amounts of phosphates and persulphates. The work on improvers was connected with studies of the action of ageing of flour; it was known that ageing was accompanied not only by whitening, but also by improvement in baking properties. Hamill expressed greater apprehension about the use of improvers than about bleaching. In 1911 *The Miller* suggested that improvers were not widely used and was opposed to their use. Apparently *Milling* was not so exercised: 'we see no reason why a section of the trade should be debarred from practising science because another section has an objection to it'.

Also in 1911 Hamill reported to the Local Government Board on 'The nutritive value of bread made from different varieties of wheat'.[16] This enquiry was partly the result of public attention to a campaign which advocated the general consumption of 'Standard Bread'. A group of London doctors had issued a manifesto in which they had stated that white bread had inferior nourishing qualities and that all bread sold should 'unless distinctly labelled otherwise, be

made from unadulterated wheat flour containing at least 80 per cent of the
whole wheat, including the germ and semolina'. The campaign was supported
by the Bread and Food Reform League and was widely publicised by the Daily
Mail. Hamill's report appeared in *The Miller* in September 1911. He reported
adversely on the reformers' suppositions and requirements. Whereas they thought
that stone-ground flour retained the germ, that was often not the case. Their
special requirement for semolina was naive, as it was merely the name for larger
fragments or particles of endosperm, which all roller millers aimed to obtain,
free from bran.

Hamill found some virtue in wholemeal as food for children who lived in
poverty, those 'who live largely on bread, or bread supplemented only by jam,
sugar or other foods which add little to the available mineral matter, proteins,
organically-combined phosphorus or other substances which possibly may be
necessary for health'. But he stipulated that the bran should be finely ground
and generally he put more hope in the provision of better balanced diets, also
that 'It should be remembered that many children whose food consists largely
of bread do not get enough of it'. Standard bread would have required standard
wheat and standard processing and the production of a standard nutritive
content. The protein content and mineral content of wheats varied and the
inclusion of bran from some wheats would have made poor bread. The only
practical interpretation could have been to demand 80 per cent extraction,
which would usually have resulted in less palatable bread while failing to make
an improvement in food value.[17]

The annual report of the Chief Inspector of Factories for 1911 included the
sentence 'Mr Pedlar (South London) refers to an astonishing development in
the flour milling industry, consequent upon the "Standard Bread" boom – a
large number of old mills having been re-opened to cope with the demand for
stoneground flour'. In contrast, A. E. Humphries stated in a paper for the Royal
Agricultural Society in November 1911: 'we have seen the long continued and
apparently unsuccessful missionary efforts of the Bread and Food Reform League
taken up by an influential portion of the British press,' also that 'millers have
taken the greatest pains' to meet the demand for bread containing a large
proportion of bran, but 'even now the various forms of wheat meal bread do
not represent more than 3 or 4 per cent of the total bread consumed in the
United Kingdom'.[18] J. Reynolds & Co. at Gloucester made wheaten meal 'for
making wholesome and nutritious brown bread', but in 1908 they were also
using the Alsop flour bleaching process, to their considerable cost in payments
to settle with the Flour Oxidizing Co.

The misconceptions on which the previous wave of reformers relied in the
early 1880s were still present. There was a belief that valuable nutrient was
lost when roller millers removed the bran, but experiments in several countries,
notably in America, showed that the human digestive system could not extract
all the nutrient in brown bread. *The Miller* declared that 'Every now and again
it seems to be necessary to reiterate a few truths regarding the superior merits
of pure white flour'; whole meal 'is as valuable to the body as sawdust or
cocoanut matting'.[19] The belief that stone-ground flour had tasted better was

an expression of preference for English wheat flour, but the general public taste was not only for white bread but also for well-piled loaves of good texture. There was a large continued demand for qualities of white flour that could be produced from blends of imported wheats, or judicious mixtures with some English wheats, by gradual reduction roller milling, though for several years the standard bread campaign and the issue of flour treatment threatened jointly to cause some confusion.

However, during the summer of 1911 a movement developed against bleaching and the use of additives. A. E. Humphries proposed that 'wheaten flour sold as such without any qualifying designation should be the unbleached and untreated produce of properly cleaned and conditioned wheat only'. He also suggested that a 'Board of Reference' should be set up to consider whether flour treatment should be permitted and, if so, to what extent or in what way.[20] The Board would consist of 'physiologists, chemists, and business men', to be 'appointed by the Government'. W. E. Nicholls favoured a collaborative approach, which would include millers in any investigations. The National Association of Master Bakers and Confectioners appointed a committee and reported against all treatments. Robert Buchanan of Liverpool convened a meeting 'to promote legislation and to influence public opinion in favour of pure flour only being made, and to prevent bleached and treated flour from being imported'.

Jago maintained that 'improvers' could helpfully affect the gluten in the dough during baking. In 1913 he wrote articles on the subject for *Milling* and *The Miller*, stating in *Milling* that 'By general consent, the use of efficient improvers results in conferring additional strength on flour, causing it to handle better in the dough, to make larger and better piled loaves, and incidentally to increase the water-absorbing powers of the flour … By the employment of improvers the miller has been able to use a much larger proportion of English wheat in his mixture than he otherwise could have done'. He also claimed that 'the quantity of sulphates this introduced into bread is much less than that caused by many drinking waters … And beer contains four or five times as much sulphate as does bread made from flour treated by persulphate'.[21] Prejudice against chemical additives was gradually overcome. In 1913 Hull Corporation took legal action against a northern milling firm that was using potassium persulphate as an improver. The process had been patented by the Dover miller Charles Chitty, and William Jago. After hearing many expert witnesses the Stipendiary Magistrate held that the persulphate actually improved the flour and was not put in to conceal an inferior quality. According to Chitty, Jago, who was a barrister, conducted the defence, during which 'he dissolved some persulphate in some water and drank some to show that it wasn't dangerous'.[22] Kent-Jones & Amos (1950) gave an opinion that 'It is true that this case only established the permissibility of treatment with persulphate and when used at the rate involved in the case, but the decision was of importance in that it expressly showed that there was no legal objection to the use of improvers provided, of course, that these were harmless to health'.[23]

There were variations of attitude to flour treatment within the National

Association, as indicated in June 1913 by W. A. Vernon, then President. As an individual he was against bleaching: 'it distinctly takes away what, in my opinion, is the finest property of flour, its rich yellow bloom'. His judgement was that there would be legislation 'in the near future' dealing with bleaching and additives, but he recognised that there could be 'no jurisdiction over the method by which foreign flour was made', also that self-raising flour contained additives.[24] During times of controversy about what the public wanted and what was good for them, it was not surprising that some articulate members of the industry distrusted supposed chemical interference with the staple food. The Liverpool miller, William Buchanan, wished to move the industry clear of any possibility of criticism, and all millers work similarly, but it was thought unlikely that the effects on flour of natural ageing could be distinguished by laboratory methods from artificial ageing. Nicholls' attitude, in a series of extensive contributions to discussion, had been simply demonstrated in his suggestion to the 1911 Convention: 'I publicly invite the government authorities to allow their advisers to inspect our mills, and to ascertain in what way we call in science to the aid of the miller, and we will discuss every aspect of the question with them'.[25] What was needed was more knowledge of cereal chemistry, so that helpful evidence could be made widely available.

'No finality' in machine design

Henry Simon's words of 1892 echoed through the period 1900 to 1914: 'For the engineer, as for the man of science, finality does not exist'.[26] The words were often recalled, and applied to the whole span of engineering the milling process, as also to particular aspects of design, the sub-systems. In 1902 Frank Stacey, a frequent contributor to debate in *The Miller*, stated that 'there is no finality in anything mechanical'. He was reviving the controversy of 'plansifters *v.* centrifugals', and during the next ten years there was increasing awareness of the usefulness of plansifters, with various design improvements to try to overcome previous difficulties, but with apparently considerable further challenge. In 1905 Simon's words were applied to roller mill design, significant changes having been introduced during the previous few years.[27] It was no longer assumed that pairs of rolls should be arranged either horizontally or vertically. In 1908 *The Miller* was contemplating a tussle between a search for technical simplicity and fresh forms of elaboration, and commented 'there is not the slightest sign of any finality'.[28]

Both leading journals were carefully watching the stream of inventive activity and in *Milling* especially there was continual discussion of the operation immediately after the break: scalping, about which there was increasing puzzlement and extensive experimentation. There was a surge of interest in 'pneumatic' methods: could break flour be removed quickly and so kept away from attrition flour produced by the centrifugals and during transfer of material between operations? Attrition flour carried irremovable bran particles. In 1909 there was optimism following a rumour of a new bleaching method. In 1910 *The Miller* recognised that break roll profiles were regarded as standardised, but added that 'we do not believe that finality has been reached in roll fluting or for that matter in any other detail of a modern flour mill'. In 1912 *Milling* observed that there was 'no finality in the design and construction of flour milling machinery', the focus again being on plansifter design.[29]

ROLLER MILL CHANGES

Compared with the upheaval of the 1880s, many technical alterations could be regarded as details, though the journals did not take a complacent view, regularly urging millers not to be left behind. And although many ideas had discernible forerunners, there was often a subtly provocative aspect of novelty. In Britain, roller mill design was clearly altered during the first few years after 1900, following twenty-five years of gradual improvement from the rudimentary early versions. When Marston (1931) stated that many of the main features had appeared by the end of the 1870s, he added that 'it was many years before they were assembled together to form one accepted design'.[30] Often it must have seemed that change was mainly concerned with increasing size and general reliability. By 1897 break rolls up to 60 inches long were available from Simons. Reduction rolls did not usually exceed 40 inches in length, to avoid excessive mid-roll deflection and uneven grinding. Those lengths remained the normal maxima, and speeds of revolution remained approximately the same for many years. There were alterations and variations in other respects, including details of roll design, roll adjustment mechanisms and feed arrangements. After 1900 Simon heavy pattern roller mills, and other makes, were altered in external appearance, by 1904 decidedly so.

Departing from horizontal and vertical arrangements, new models appeared in which the two pairs of rolls in standard four-roller mills were arranged diagonally, the usual description for placement in planes typically at 45 degrees to the horizontal or vertical; there were variants at smaller angles to the horizontal. Robinsons were credited with an early decisive change from horizontal placement of two pairs of rolls. Earlier, Henry Simon had tried a diagonal alternative to his normal vertical pairings, but had not kept to it. Unlike the Simon experiment of the mid 1880s, the Robinson configuration had the lower roll of each pair nearer to the centre of the machine, so that the flow of material from the rolls was outwards and accessible for inspection; much then depended on the design of the feed to the rolls. Robinsons' new departure was experimental between 1897 and 1902, involving variations of the angle at which the roll pairs were set, and different roll diameters. By 1902 the change to diagonal placement was settled and in his text Halliwell (1904) stated that 'An innovation in the relative position of rolls has been introduced by Messrs T. Robinson & Son Ltd, Rochdale'.[31] Others followed the same scheme, which became the permanent standard arrangement, the basic geometry of the modern roller mill.

Simons' distinctly modern-looking design was patented in April 1904 in the names of George Huxley and Henry Simon Ltd.[32] Apparently the same machine was the subject of German and French patents by Bühlers in 1905. In 1902 Huxley had written about a prospective 'new standard pattern 4-roller mill, the

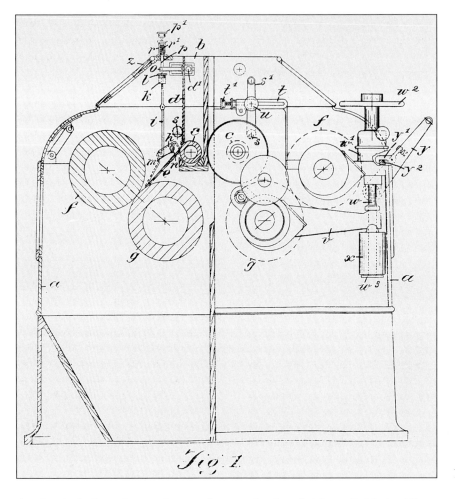

Fig. 1

Figure 92.
End elevation of
Simons' diagonal
four-roller mill of
1904. (Patent
No. 9704, April 1904)

details of which we have exhaustively considered with Messrs Bühler'.[33] There
had been several years of 'exhaustive experiments' before the settled version
was introduced into the Swan Mills at Hull late in 1904. *Milling* visited and
reported in December, commenting: 'New forms of roller mills seem to be the
order of the day'. The two pairs of rolls were set at 40 degrees to the horizontal,
with feed rolls at the level of the upper grinding rolls and feed plates arranged
to conduct material perpendicularly into the nip. This gave a lower and compact
configuration, without cramping the general arrangement. Instead of the
previously visible clumpy supporting structure, derived from earlier styles of bare
legs, the new four-roller mill was enclosed in a neat casing, which had an
added advantage of reducing clutter on crowded roller mill floors. There was
continual revision of control mechanisms.

Simons also designed a four-high roller mill and an eight-roller mill. The
first provided for three consecutive breaks and could be fitted with intermediate
scalping sieves 'when required'. It was intended for use in 'small country and
Colonial mills'. Their eight-roller mill was designed to provide a double

treatment on the first break. As with the standard four-roller mill, there were two separate mills placed back to back in the same frame: in each, there were two pairs of rolls arranged diagonally. The idea was to open out the wheat on the upper pair and make a heavier break with the lower pair.[34] Scalping sieves could be fitted below each pair of rolls or could be omitted from the upper position. The journals reported in 1910 that sieves were used only at the lower position in the eight-roller mills at Frosts' new mill at Ellesmere Port.[35] The patentees in 1908 were J. H. Trevithick, G. Huxley and H. Simon Ltd. Both these unusual machines were still offered in the 1914 catalogue. By 1930 there was a much simplified range of four-roller mill, two-roller mill, and Alphega system which had been developed by Briddon and Fowler.

There was a continuing background discussion about roll 'surface', meaning total length of roll contact. Milling engineers started on new projects by considering possible process diagrams, formalised to a greater or a lesser extent, and estimating the numbers of main machines needed to produce a stipulated flour output stated in sacks per hour. Halliwell (1904) and Amos (1912) both quoted 35 inches of break surface per sack as average practice. For a plant capacity of 20 sacks per hour a total of 700 inches of break roll surface would have been required. The next consideration was the allocation of numbers of roller mills for each break stage, sometimes an easy calculation, but not so simple when surface requirements varied between the stages and capacity was not large. There was general acceptance of four breaks, but occasional preference

Figure 93.
The Alphega method
of separating break
flour. (*Milling*,
December 1909)

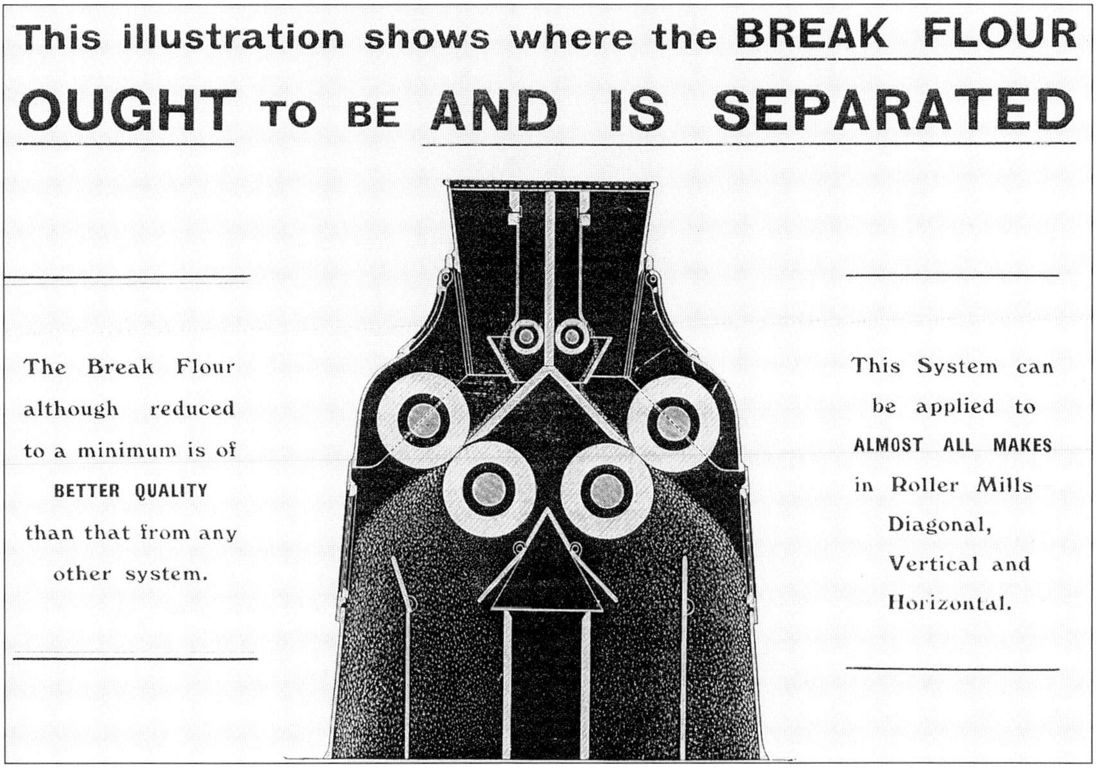

This illustration shows where the **BREAK FLOUR**

OUGHT TO BE **AND IS SEPARATED**

The Break Flour although reduced to a minimum is of **BETTER QUALITY** than that from any other system.

This System can be applied to **ALMOST ALL MAKES** in Roller Mills Diagonal, Vertical and Horizontal.

for five and some advocacy for three in smaller mills. The amount of roll surface depended on the current practice of individual milling engineers and the strength of views and financial resources held by millers. The extent of treatment through the reduction rolls also had to be considered, and the scratch system in which very finely grooved rolls followed the break stages, to remove remaining bran snips from the semolina. Amos stated that reduction surfaces ranged from 40 to 60 inches per sack.[36]

NEW SCALPING METHODS

Enclosing the space below the rolls might have seemed to be largely a stylistic alteration, but it facilitated other process changes devised by Briddon & Fowler and by Henry Simon Ltd. George Briddon had joined Henry Simon's firm in 1885 and became second to Huxley in the drawing office. R. J. Fowler began with Simon in 1889 and succeeded William Stringer as a milling expert.[37] In 1902 Briddon and Fowler decided to set up their own firm, producing a new range of machinery named Britannia, appropriate to construction at Banbury: Samuelsons had their Britannia works there. In 1908 they registered as Briddon & Fowler Ltd, and built up manufacturing facilities at Bredbury near Stockport.[38] Meanwhile Simons had succeeded Bailey & Garnett Ltd as owners of the Eagle Ironworks at Stalybridge and enlarged the works; since about 1898 some Simon machinery had been built at Stalybridge.[39]

Briddon & Fowler claimed that they were 'the first firm of milling engineers to popularise a roller mill with rolls placed diagonally'.[40] The word popularise was carefully chosen. They were better-known for their method of 'dealing with the break stock, whereby the break flour was separated [immediately] after leaving the nip of the rolls', with the aim of preventing contamination by bran powder. They were so pleased with their ideas, patented during 1906 and 1907, that they used the name Alphega system, as The Miller reported 'surely the alpha and omega of the break flour problem'.

The Alphega method was the simplest solution to a well-known but previously intractable problem. Pure or nearly pure flour was to be produced after scalping, grading and the withdrawal of fine particles, by careful purification of the semolina and middlings, followed by reduction to flour fineness by smooth reduction rolls. Millers worried about crease dirt, dust lodged in the crease of each wheat grain, which spoiled the first flour released. Many ways were tried to minimise the production of break flour and the presence of impurities in it, including rejection of the first flour released. Gradually attention shifted from talk of crease dirt; Voller completely rejected the idea; Bates called it a 'phantom' in 1892 and a 'will o'wisp' in 1910 – he was more worried about airborne pollutants with the use of air in milling processes.[41] The general adoption of wheat washing reduced the problem, but break flour was still regarded warily. The new scalping methods were attempts to prevent an admixture of inferior flour which had been made during energetic action through previous types of scalper and separator (reels, centrifugals or flat sieves), carrying tiny bran particles, dust and extraneous colouring matter. Fowler's design depended on the observation that heavier material leaving a pair of diagonal rolls was projected strongly from the nip, while break flour and other small particles dropped short. Vertical partitions were inserted below the rolls to separate the break flour, and the arrangement proved effective.[42] The idea was elaborated, to deal with vertical roll pairings, and even with horizontal pairs, by using a deflector to prevent the break products falling as a mass of undifferentiated components. A more complicated series of partitions was also tried, and the stock was teased out by use of a gentle air current. Simple partitioning was the basic idea, associated preferably with diagonal roll placement.

Many quite new methods of scalping were devised, particularly from 1905 onwards. There was an early scheme by Robert Buchanan, with a patent in 1900, and a further version in 1907. Buchanan's use of inclined sieves and an air current entitled him to credit as an early exponent of pneumatic scalping, a commonly adopted but possibly fanciful term.[43] Briddon & Fowler were able to advertise that well-known millers were using the Alphega system, also that they could modify other makes of roller mill, including Robinsons', Simons', and Gardners', each of whom had been developing other kinds of pneumatic scalper. Meanwhile Simons had also devised a method that was applied directly below the rolls and within the roller frame. Simons' method was a different way of separating out semolina and middlings. Two steeply sloping sieves were used, air currents assisting the withdrawal of specific components. The break flour was extracted through the upper sieve, the bulk of material overtailing to the lower sieve through which semolina and middlings were extracted. Material overtailing the lower sieve formed the feed to the next break stage. Three sets of rolls were placed on separate floors directly underneath each other, so the stock was spouted from each break to the next without use of elevators or conveyors; independent scalpers were eliminated.[44] In 1908 *Milling* described Simons' close association of the breaking and scalping operations as 'something new', and commented that apart from litigation about bleaching methods, patents which most interested millers in 1908 were for new scalping machinery and processes: during the last three years 'at least a dozen'. Simons were trying four new methods of scalping, while still offering centrifugals and their rotary plane sieves.

Millers faced continuous technical reappraisal. When Simons introduced their new four-roller mill in 1904, *Milling*'s judgement was that plants were 'immeasurably superior to those fitted up even five years ago'. In 1908 when Simons brought forward their new scalping system they had been experimenting with alternatives for eight years. Although *The Miller* started 1909 with the warning to the milling trade that 'Five-year-old methods are absolutely out of date and also costly', there was also awareness that a boom had finished. George Huxley's view in 1908 was that 'There will be a much reduced amount of work to be done in flour mills, millowners declining to spend any more money than they can help in alterations to plant'.[45] It is surprising that quite new technical methods were being devised. Perhaps Otto Moog had the key. In 'Four hundred years of the roller frame', published by *Die Muhle* in 1953, he suggested that 'When business is going well … modifications disrupt the work in hand. But in difficult times one tries to beat off one's competitors by innovation … these difficult times are therefore generally more fruitful in regard to technical advances'.

THE RIDDLE OF THE PLANSIFTER

The year 1908 was particularly notable for diverse innovative activity and technical debate. W. T. Bates helped to revive the 'plansifters *v.* centrifugals' argument.[46] Amme, Giesecke, & Konegen from Braunschweig seized on his statement that the flat sieve was 'the one and only correct principle of perfect separation'. They offered plansifters for both scalping and flour dressing. G. Luther, also at Braunschweig, advertised a similar plansifter design and had a longer experience. Wm. R. Dell tried again, with the advantage of being an English firm, but the disadvantages of round sieves and a foreign patent. Simons, Robinsons and others were still persevering with sifting and separating methods which involved the use of air currents, and therefore called pneumatic methods. Amos, in *Processes of flour manufacture*, published in 1912, included an illustration of a leading British design, by Robinsons, and made a clear appraisal, stating that progress was 'to the credit of manufacturers, who have steadily sought to improve it by careful and painstaking attention to all the details',

Figure 94.
Simons' plansifter in the 1913 catalogue.
(Simon Ltd, 1913)

hopefully a change from 1908 when it was said that 'The average operative looks upon the plansifter as a boxed up contraption'.

It was possible for the first time to make clear progress in Britain in plansifter design between 1908 to 1914, guided by practical experience in the mills, but the variety of raw material to be processed and the damp British climate meant that an early and general switch from centrifugals to plansifters was not yet possible. In principle, and increasingly in practice, plansifters could be used for scalping, grading and flour dressing. The required operation, and the number and sizes of component materials which were to be separated determined the arrangement of sieves in a particular stack; individual sieves within a stack could be set up to give a specific combination of routes and withdrawal points, with alternative options of sequential stages of flow or by-passes of stages. Stock was fed to the top of the stack and was progressively separated by either passing through sieve covers or overtailing.[47] The gyratory movement of the sieves and the progress of the stream of stock produced layering effects: finer, heavier particles gravitated to the underside of the stream and passed through sieve mesh of appropriate aperture sizes. Potential advantages included gentler treatment of the stock than with centrifugals, which were still often criticised for severity of action, the possibility of making a wide variety of separations or groupings of materials, and economies in space and power required.

To achieve a technical advance, it was necessary to solve a series of design puzzles, the way of transferring rotary motion of the drive shaft to gyratory motion of two stacks of sieve boxes being the basic objective. Other elements were the means of supporting the gyrating framework, and details of size and positions of pulleys, cranks, flywheels, balance weights and bearings. It was necessary to minimise vibration during normal running and eliminate erratic dynamic effects during starting and stopping. Adverse points which continued to be troublesome were doubts about thoroughly smooth running and the difficulty of ensuring that stock did not move unevenly; there was concern about the reliability of separations, which was dependent on the effectiveness of layering and on keeping sieve mesh completely clear. Mechanical brushes were introduced, to traverse under the sieves, and ventilation was provided; otherwise, damp or soft stock would not move freely and separate as required. Further improvements were needed: it was difficult to deal with blocked sieves, as easy access to any sieve in a clamped stack was not at first provided, nor satisfactorily worked out for many years.

In 1910 there was a mild sensation at the RASE show at Liverpool: Robinsons exhibited their own plansifter which they had patented in 1909. The journals gave detailed descriptions and *The Miller* reported that 'the fact that one well-known firm was exhibiting a British-made modern plansifter certainly caused millers at the show furiously to think'.[48] Publicity had started in the journal with a report of Robinsons' work on the new CWS mill at Avonmouth, for which the plant had been ordered in 1908 but the process design altered in 1910 to include plansifters. In 1911 Robinsons were advertising their Cyclo-pneumatic Plansifter System and Simons exhibited their Reform JN9a type plansifter at the RASE show at Norwich in June.[49] In August, Samuelsons

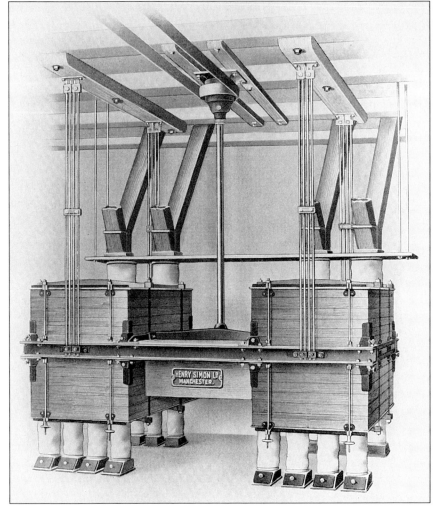

Figure 95.
Simons' free-swinging
plansifter in the 1914
catalogue. (Simon
Ltd, 1914)

put a large advertisement in *The Miller*, headed 'Plansifters *v.* Centrifugals', and announced provocatively 'The beginning of the end of the 3rd boom'; they had received an order to replace plansifters with centrifugals at a mill in the north-west of England.[50] Some readers may have wondered if a shot were being fired at Luther, whose agent was based in Liverpool, and who had stated in 1909 that 'all patented parts of our machines will be of British manufacture'.

Samuelsons' prophecy was unfulfilled. Turners at Ipswich had their own plansifter in 1911, neat in appearance and available in two main forms, either suspended on groups of canes or, as in earlier versions, supported from the floor on rocking pillars. In 1912 Turners used plansifters in a new Hovis mill at Vauxhall Bridge in London.[51] Strangely, their patent application of 1912 was not printed. Simons' 1913 catalogue showed two versions of the earlier type of flexible support, one being more impressive than the crude version shown at Norwich. Their 1914 catalogue included a more advanced form, the free-swinging plansifter, suspended and driven from above, accompanied by the statement that 'except under very special conditions, the Plansifter is the best machine for scalping, grading, and dressing the breaks'. Controversy continued but confidence, or at least familiarity, was growing. Simons' *Occasional Letter* in November 1913 contained the statement that 'we have been supplying plansifters and building plansifter mills on the continent for 15 years and in this country for five. We have during the whole of that time been testing and making comparisons and endeavouring gradually to come to some definite conclusions'.

Experimental work sometimes depended on the continuing enthusiasm of certain millers, not always much publicised. In 1910 Simons' new mill for Frosts at Ellesmere Port contained new ideas for the break and scalping operations, but not plansifters: Simon eight-roller mills were used in conjunction with Walpole scalpers.[52] J. E. Walpole had been a milling expert with Simons, but moved to Frosts to become head miller at Chester. In 1913 E. D. Simon presented a paper to the National Association on 'Analysis of the power required to drive a flour mill'. Extensive tests had been carried out at Vernons' Birkenhead mill, where scalping was still done on double centrifugals.[53] Simon included a consideration of the power that would have been required by plansifters. There was a curious reminder of Henry Simon's work, in 1887: E. D. Simon had not been able to find any similar record of tests. On the following day in 1913, Mr Amme of Amme, Giesecke & Konegen gave a paper on plansifters and predicted that 'the complete plansifter mill of today is unequalled and will be the mill of the future'.

PURIFIERS

So much attention had been devoted to early stages of the milling process that purifiers might have seemed neglected; there were even suggestions that purifiers might become less important, which became a familiar topic for W. T. Bates. In 1909 he inveighed about 'The inaccessibility of machines', which had relevance to purifier design, and in 1911 he ventured: 'they [purifiers] have been greatly overrated as essential machines'. He was critical of 'rows and tiers of machines which littered our mill floors in the past'.[54] Perhaps he had been re-reading statements by J. A. A. Buchholz on the subject of over-elaboration, or a journal forecast that 'simplicity will be the keynote of the future'.

Critical attention shifted to existing purifier designs, the basic features having survived from the early 1890s. At the RASE show at Norwich in 1911 Simons showed their patent MQ purifier, *The Miller* reporting 'an entirely new construction'. *Milling* reported that it 'makes visible the whole action of the purifier'. The old design had been called dustless, but was not; the suggestion was a confusion with the fact that there were dust-collecting chambers within the machine. In the new design there was no internal dust-settling apparatus, nor a fan on top of the machine; several purifiers were to be connected to a fan outside the building. For the MQ model it was claimed that 'The result of this arrangement is that the purifier floor can be made absolutely dustless', a strange statement when the so-called dustless version was still on sale.[55] The

MQ design was similar to its predecessor up to sieve level, but above that the enclosure sloped inwards, with windows in inspection doors along the whole length. Simons' 1913 catalogue stated that 'This arrangement renders possible what no purifier has hitherto permitted, viz. the easy observation of the whole work being done'. There had been complaints about previous purifiers, that it was 'impossible without a great deal of trouble to see what is happening on the sieves'. As with the new-look roller mill, there were new assumptions and a more modern appearance. The MQ purifier became the basis of successive Simon models until late in the 1930s.

While Simons were busy from 1911 onwards with their new machinery, Henry's son E. D. Simon was assuming responsibility for direction of the business. Ingleby had been chairman and Huxley was managing director during an interregnum after Henry. When E. D. Simon became a director in 1906 he was still a young man of twenty-six years, and it is tempting to wonder what might have happened if Henry Simon had lived longer or the personal influence of a professional engineer had been more sharply focused. In 1908 Joseph Ingleby resigned from the milling business, in effect bought out at considerable capital cost, and Huxley became chairman, with E. D. Simon as managing director. In 1910 Huxley resigned, planning to go round the world, and E. D. Simon took over as chairman. At the time of his paper in 1913, it was reported that

Figure 96.
Simons' MQ purifier
in the 1913 catalogue.
(Simon Ltd, 1913)

E. D. Simon had travelled widely. After his studies at Cambridge, and practical experience in England, Germany and Switzerland, he had voyaged to the United States, Canada, South America, India, China and Japan, and so had extensive knowledge of potential markets.

He regretted the loss to the firm of Briddon and Fowler and, although Simons remained leaders in the field after the boom years of 1904 to 1907, he was conscious of increased competition.[56] For many years the words 'The Simon System' had been a general assurance, rather than a nailed-down specification, but with confidence in the new roller mills and purifiers, and serious work being done on plansifters, 'Simon System' could continue as the firm's familiar advertisement. In 1915 Briddon & Fowler was absorbed by Henry Simon Ltd, the principals rejoining the Simon staff. Acquisition of the Bredbury talents and resources offset the loss of the Seck connection and the finish of the Frankfurt partnership, and provided new scope immediately. Despite the war Simons could report, in the *Occasional Letter* of January 1916, that an Alphega-Plansifter system had been installed at the King Flour Mills at Ellesmere Port. Kings had moved from Hanley in the Potteries to a new mill, completed for them in 1906, and so were well-established when Frosts started their new mill nearby in 1910. During wartime the production of munitions largely replaced milling machinery, but the Alphega-Plansifter system became a familiar combination in Simon projects of the early 1920s.

A cure for over-production?

In an article in *Milling* in May 1911, W. T. Bates referred to three phases of change in the milling industry: technical, commercial, chemical. He said 'we have passed through' the first two phases, yet in the Association's annual report, presented only a few days later, it was stated that the universal sale note 'was wrecked'. The bakers and confectioners' Association and the grocers' Federation would not agree, so after years of discussion and negotiation the hopes of the millers' official representatives were frustrated. If Bates was accurate in emphasising a new focus on chemistry, there was still also a mass of subjective opinion on the whole position of the industry, and basic concern about trading viability. According to W. E. Nicholls, in 1911 'in England and Wales we have as many as 720 millers, in Ireland 110, and in Scotland 20', a total of 850 recognisable millers, of whom 229 were said to be Association members. Many of the others must have had relatively small businesses: in 1914 the Association was said to comprise 'some 80 per cent of the output of all the flour milled in the Kingdom.[57]

Milling commented 'millers will have in the future to consider long and carefully whether some means cannot be found of bettering the status of the trade without undue interference with individual liberty of action'. In March 1914 an editorial item was headed 'The need of organisation'. There were references to overproduction and overlapping, but spread over two weeks' issues there was a trickle of what could have been interpreted later as advice to the industry in general, or for the benefit of particular groups. The journal was cautious in what was said, and also advised caution. Afterwards, it might easily have been claimed that nothing much had been said. Another heading was 'Resurrection of an old idea':

> It is strange how persistently the idea of a combination of millers, or a milling combine, as it is frequently termed, has been put before the public. No doubt the idea of a league of millers, banded together to regulate prices and to exploit the bread consumers to the utmost, is sufficiently terrifying to the man in the street, to say nothing of his wife at home ... It is just a quarter of a century since the London and provincial press was ringing with the details of a milling combine which was to come into existence, and to embrace all flour mills from Northumbria to Hull. It is a fact that a then well known company promoter had taken up the scheme with much enthusiasm, and spent much time and some – but not much – money on trying to get the northern millers into line.[58]

Next week, the heading was 'Trade organisation', which seemed vague, but would become a matter of increasingly clear focus in the 1920s. There was an intriguing sentence: 'We commented last week both on the benefit of organisation and the failure of previous attempts to form millers into a rigid, or indeed any kind of combination'. Again, overproduction was mentioned, with suggested remedies of the formation of an export trade, or 'the limitation of output'. This all represented an initial movement towards the feasibility of concerted reorganisation: eventually, rationalisation.

Another editorial topic was 'Position of the National Association', which was declared to be 'The natural vehicle for any scheme of cooperation or reform, with the statement: 'We think that attempts at reform will have a better chance of success if they are put forward through official sources'.[59] There was an underlying theme, aired tactfully. Council meetings of the Association had been held privately during 1913. Short summaries were supplied to the journals 'who had kindly given publicity'. In 1914 it was stated clearly in the annual report that many meetings had not been fully reported. The new era required new formalities, with opportunity for some debates to be pursued without the inhibiting influence of continual public comment on each step. Much later reports revealed that around the time of the Norwich Convention of 1914 a notional big scheme for reorganisation of the industry was being discussed, though not necessarily in official Association meetings; it became known as the O'Hagan scheme. Many millers must have known the main features, and many others would have heard something, but then it was largely lost to view. Its continuing merit was that it helped to break the mould of previous thought. *The Miller* commented in 1917:

> When some four or five years ago a scheme was afoot for a huge combine of British mills on the model of the Associated Portland Cement Companies we said little about it, partly because we were asked not to, but chiefly because we were quite certain that the great majority of millers were far too independent to be drawn in.[60]

In 1928 G. H. Ball, the secretary since 1919, wrote a paper 'The history of the National Association', published in *Milling* to celebrate the Association's jubilee. He referred to O'Hagan:

> The outbreak of war in August 1914 altered the whole trend of the Association's activities. For some time prior to this date Mr O'Hagan had been canvassing millers with a view to obtaining support for his organisation scheme, the main feature of which was an insurance policy to cover any decrease in output. He had made considerable headway, and had it not been for the intervention of the war, it is probable that he would have obtained sufficient support to bring about the inauguration of his scheme. The outbreak of hostilities, however, caused many things to go into the melting-pot, Mr O'Hagan's scheme among them, and the industry lost what would have been its most favourable prospect of organisation during the whole period of its existence.[61]

H. Osborne O'Hagan published his memoirs in 1929, called *Leaves from my life*, devoting a chapter to the milling industry. He had previously devised a plan for the cement industry, where he had a personal interest; it was the result of a long study of problems of combination without amalgamation, but the cement firms eventually preferred integration. He explained that control of purchases, output, prices, sales, and conditions of trade could pose legal problems as restraints of trade, also that penalties would be unenforceable. In seeking a solution for the cement industry, he had suggested the formation of an insurance company which would guarantee agreed outputs, based on previous performance, while leaving freedom of functional decision-making with the individual firms. Regulation would have depended on the registration of agreed outputs, with payment into a central fund for trading in excess, and compensation for shortfall.

O'Hagan related that in 1913 he was approached by several millers for assistance. At first reluctant, he agreed to devise a scheme for cooperative organisation within the milling industry. The basis would be the formation of a Millers' Insurance Company, to issue policies which guaranteed holders their output and sales, provided they adhered to various 'terms and conditions', with premiums related to capacity and actual output. O'Hagan stated that each miller 'could buy as he liked, mill and sell what quantities he liked, and on what terms he liked'. He also recounted that he was invited to meet 'a number' of millers, following which a 'committee was appointed, consisting of a dozen of the leading millers'. Later *The Miller* reported that meetings had been held at offices of cement firms, and O'Hagan referred to meetings at the Albany in London, and to visits to Cardiff, Manchester, York and Hull. He declared that 'We were making all our preparations to put the finishing touches on it when the Great War broke out and threw everything into confusion'.[62]

Even when the scheme was widely known it was probably also widely disregarded and may have been more tantalising than ultimately convincing. Those who had acquired relevant information and were readers of *Milling* could have noted that the editor was aware and dismissive. Obstacles would have included the acquisition of confidential information, setting a production datum for each firm, reaching agreement throughout the industry, and the arrangements for supervision. Despite O'Hagan's optimism, it probably needed the drawing together and the difficulties of war, and a recovery period, before radical reorganisation could be accomplished. The ideas of 1914 resurfaced briefly in 1917 and in the 1920s when the search for a rationalisation plan became more urgent.

CHAPTER FOURTEEN

Sea of troubles: 1915–1924

Wartime control and a new overview

THE GENERAL SITUATION

In April 1915 R. J. Read, the President of the National Association, referred to discussions about stocks of wheat, reporting that 'there had been a certain amount of purchasing of wheat by the Government'. W. A. Vernon stated that 'they were really interfering with the wheat trade of the country, and practically paralysing it. Mr Runciman at the Board of Trade sought ways to increase wheat stocks, but strategic thinking was not explained to the millers. There were discussions with Runciman in July 1915 and meetings with Lord Selborne, succeeded by Lord Crawford at the Board of Agriculture. This was the start of a period of confidentiality. General meetings of the Association were reported, but often the journals were required to keep information to themselves. Increasingly Council meetings had to be related to what was being said by officials, and closer involvement led to the proliferation of committees, and control of the industry which was to last until 1921.

So far, optimistic outlooks persisted. In 1916 *The Miller* had editorial items on 'Employment after the war' and 'National granaries' – not for immediate stocking but as a precaution for a more distant emergency 'after the war'.[1] A Royal Commission was appointed in October 1916 'to enquire into the supply of wheat and flour on behalf of His Majesty's Government, and generally to take such steps as may seem desirable for maintaining the supply'. In the first report, published in 1921, it was stated that 'by September 1916 it became obvious that the necesssary supply of foodstuffs from overseas was seriously threatened'.[2] As soon as it was formed the Commission took control of the importation of wheat; 'two firms of high standing in this country' were later reported (in 1921) to have 'entered into voluntary control', putting their organisations in Britain and abroad at the disposal of the Commission.[3] This provided the Commission with agencies in Canada, the United States, the Argentine and India.

In 1915 Oswald Robinson, son of Henry Robinson of Deptford Bridge Mills (the winner of the Germ Milling contest) had taken over the Association presidency and so became a member of the Royal Commission on wheat supplies, in addition to having the main management responsibility for one of the largest London mills, with a consequent breakdown in health in 1917. Through 1916 Robinson remained official chairman of the Association, with A. E. Humphries, the Vice-President, gradually taking over much of the work as the leading representative for millers throughout the country. In November 1916 the Association held an emergency meeting with Humphries clearly in charge. He described the first stage towards Government control of flour milling.[4] The Local Government Board had proposed that only straight run flour would be made, with a 76 per cent extraction rate. The use of many different wheats meant that the 76 per cent was to be an average, so awkward calculations had to be made to achieve the required result. The first milling order was issued from the Board of Trade and came into force from Monday 27 November 1916.

From December there was much increased activity. Lord Devonport was appointed as Food Controller, succeeded by Lord Rhondda six months later. The Commission instructed the National Association to devise more economical arrangements for transporting flour; the Council set up a Flour Distribution Committee with Humphries as chairman. Information was required from all merchant millers, replies being sent in confidence to a firm of accountants in London who made a statistical report, the general patterns being arranged on maps of England and Wales by the Association, showing by regions: flour requirements, production quantities, estimates of milling capacity, potential output from English wheat. From 476 returns which were supposed to state quantities of flour delivered, it was reckoned that an annual make was approximately thirty million sacks of flour. Capacity data suggested an excess of 30 per cent over requirements. By comparison Census of Production data was always sketchy and out of date. There was no table of numbers of mills of various capacities, confidentiality having been promised. In March, *Milling* showed for each district the estimated total milling capacity, and quantities of flour used, brought in, sent elsewhere. *Milling* gave more of the information in 1921, in anticipation of decontrol, showing distribution from the four main port areas, and production from home grown wheat. The results of the survey, though imperfect, continued as a portrayal of the industry as a whole.[5]

Figure 97.
A. E. Humphries of
Coxes Lock. (*The Miller*, July 1916)

The Flour Distribution Committee sent a scheme 'formulated to prevent overlapping in the distribution of flour' to the Ministry of Food and the Royal Commission. The plan was to distribute flour as near as possible to the mill where it was made. Each miller was required to set one price at any one time, to be charged ex-mill, with delivery charges shown separately on the invoice. Prices and charges were to be reported to the Food Controller. Presumably the mandatory delivery charges had a significant effect on distribution areas. Flours used in proprietary bread – Allinsons', Bermaline, Carrs' Malt, Daren, Hovis, Turog, were exempt from these regulations. After the first milling order specifying extractions averaging 76 per cent,there were soon three more orders. At the end of January 1917 extraction was raised to 81 per cent, either completely from the wheat or by inclusion of 5 per cent of diluents: barley, maize, oats or rice. A third order was issued in March, with 81 per cent definitely required from the wheat and further admixture that was to vary between 5 per cent and 15 per cent. In April a fourth order specified admixture between 10 per cent and 25 per cent.

CONTROL OF THE MILLS

A more drastic administrative step followed. From April 30 the Food Controller assumed control of all flour mills having a capacity of 5 sacks per hour or more.[6] Control was extended to smaller mills from 11 August.[7] The basic statutory rules and orders issued by the Ministry of Food explained little. There was a statement that any relevant 'factory, workshop or premises ... shall ... pass into the possession of the Food Controller'. On May 7 *The Miller* commented that 'doubtless the baker will before long have to accept his flour from the mills instructed officially to supply him'.[8] Later there was a regulation restricting delivery distances to a 100 mile limit. The Royal Commission reported merely that 'widespread organisations ... were set up to accomplish all the intermediate stages beween purchasing grain abroad and distributing flour to 40,000 bakers and 100,000 retailers of bread and flour'. Public discussion amongst millers focused on the word 'possession' in the statutory order. They had lost staff, been told what to make and could not have liked the look or taste of it and lost at least some freedom of trading areas; now there was apparent or imagined loss of ownership. Another worrying aspect was related to rumour that nationalisation might be imminent.

Across the country there was some unrest about uneven food supplies. In May the Food Controller made the Cake and Pastry Order, restricting amounts of sugar and flour used in cakes, scones and biscuits and curbing meals in tea shops. Beveridge (1928) referred to 'measures aimed by Lord Devonport at the pleasures of the table ... Their value, if any, was in making people uncomfortable so that they treated the problem of food seriously'. The order began 'No person shall after the 21st April, 1917 make or attempt to make for sale, or after the 24th April, 1917 sell or offer to sell or have in his possession for sale (a) Any crumpet, muffin, teacake or fancy bread, or any light or fancy pastries, or any other like article'.[9] In May the Flour Mills Control Committee (FMCC) issued a schedule fixing extractions to be obtained from forty-two grades and descriptions of wheat, revised the following month. Rhondda, Devonport's successor, was second of five controllers in four years. Devonport's resignation was associated with ill-health, and possibly personal criticisms. Beveridge stated that the War Cabinet 'sent him out at short notice across an uncharted sea of novel administration, and gave him neither definite sailing orders nor a free hand'. During the series of changes of Food Controller, the Wheat Commission provided much of the necessary continuity of executive action.

In May the journals could only speculate about the manner and extent of control of the mills. There was vague reference to Lord St Davids' committee. William Beveridge (1928) with experience as Permanent Secretary to the Ministry of Food, stated that:

the control of the flour mills was at first entrusted by Lord Devonport to an independent committee, under the chairmanship of Lord St Davids, having no organic connection with the rest of the Ministry. The committee was from the first rather shadowy and soon faded away, leaving the business in the firm and capable hands of the Wheat Commission.[10]

The FMCC included four millers: Robinson, Humphries, Joseph Rank, and Tom Parkinson for the Cooperative Societies; their presence could not really compensate for individual loss of autonomy. An attempt to arrange what Humphries called a better representation of millers was unsuccessful. If there were to be loyalty, it depended on millers who had become administrators continuing to sound like millers. Lord St Davids suggested that there could be a Consultative Committee of millers, which proved unwieldy and so a more compact group was formed called the Composite Committee.[11]

The FMCC formed sub-committees for finance, technical matters, grain grading, and insurance. Remuneration and other reimbursement was a basic part of administration and St Davids suggested that the millers should formulate a basis. Three methods were considered: payment on a gristing basis (quantities milled), on a capital basis, or a datum basis, which was the one chosen. The Finance (No. 2) Act, 1915 became relevant.[12] Millers were guaranteed remuneration related to their pre-war profits, and were required to work out a datum, which the Act described as the average profits of any two of the last three pre-war trade years. It was repeatedly stated that the datum was unsatisfactory: profits had often been poor before the war and various costs had risen since.

Figure 98.
W. E. Nicholls of
Spillers. (*Milling,*
September 1923)

Financial problems were not fully resolved even when the industry was decontrolled in 1921. Humphries acquired a wide-ranging authoritative position, becoming de facto chief executive for the industry. At the 1917 AGM Nicholls referred to him as: 'my esteemed friend who holds so many offices – he is really a Pooh Bah I am sure'. From the urbane Nicholls was it a wry remark? Humphries had been a talented musical performer at millers' banquets and Pooh Bah was the well-known Lord High Everything Else in The Mikado, Gilbert and Sullivan's comic opera.

In September the Food Controller fixed flour prices and discounts, and set a maximum price for bread: ninepence for a quartern or 4lb loaf. Exchequer subsidies as a result of these measures amounted to approximately £162,000,000 by 1921.[13] With wheat prices controlled, millers were squeezed. In 1917 general meetings of the Association were often only partly reported, while in the background there were many confidential or informal discussions. In November *The Miller* protested that 'no intimation has yet reached the trade as to the terms on which their mills have been taken over'. Some millers with small businesses protested to *The Miller*. A few wished for an inland millers' association and a Sussex miller complained about 'bureaucracy and absolutism'. But there was also cohesion. Whereas in June 1916 Oswald Robinson regretted that there were 'few live [local] associations', by November 1917 there were seventeen applications from local associations for affiliation to the National Association.

Reports of the AGM in July 1917 were packed with information about urgent activities at a critical stage of the war, and effective performance was repeatedly recognised by officials. It was desirable to enhance the new status by improving administrative arrangements within the Association. Humphries referred to his previous experience as President in 1906, when 'he didn't know exactly what the Association could do'. He appealed for collaboration and, though he did not express it in just one word: solidarity.[14] It was a prelude to the next item on the agenda, 'reorganisation of the Association'. W. A. Vernon had taken the lead in planning an up-to-date framework. New offices were available at 40 Trinity Square and a full-time secretary was appointed, succeeded in 1918 by G. H. Ball, a law graduate and an ex army captain. There was provision for an Executive Committee to assist the Council. Financial resources were to be improved through much increased subscriptions; full membership was to be for millers only. The new form of the Association was registered in September 1917.[15]

During the momentous months of 1917 there were contrasting subjects to consider. One was the national danger. In *The Miller* on May 7, under a heading 'Government control', mention of 'the U-boat menace' was almost incidental, as there were hopes of 'a successful counter', presumably the convoy system. That contrasted with a warning in *The Times* in January that the submarine campaign against British shipping could assume 'increased ruthlessness and intensity'. The danger was not only in terms of lost supplies, but also delays at congested ports and on busy railways. Just a few days failure of the bread supply would have been alarming. But also in May there were curious references to Lord St Davids, the chairmanship of the Portland Cement Company, and 'memories of the O'Hagan scheme'. In June, *Milling* was more definite, with a heading 'Permanent state control'. There were 'many vague rumours', and an item of substance: 'A scheme is being circulated by an anonymous individual under the title of 'The flour mills under state control". There was a tendentious proposal to 'ensure to the public bread at a fair price' and a supposition that it would be possible to close down mills that were declared to be uneconomic.

It was suggested that the new opportunism had 'doubtless been helped by free use of a certain much-discussed balance sheet'. The previous O'Hagan plan had been a remedy for unprofitability, the new application was a cure for imagined profiteering. The controversial balance sheet must have been the Spillers & Bakers statement of 1915, showing record profits. Hansard quoted a series of questions in the House of Commons on 28 and 29 April 1915, mainly repetitive; there was intemperate language. *The Miller* discussed 'Millers' profits' and thought that as 'prices of grain had advanced more than 50 per cent' there was a large paper profit. Nicholls was roused by allegations of 'robbing the poorer classes of cheap bread'. He quoted bread prices in London, Berlin, Paris, New York and Montreal, and declared 'I hurl back to these people the base accusation, with this rejoinder: Honi soit qui mal y pense'.[16] An interesting statement was made by Beveridge (1928): large purchases of wheat 'were made between November 1914 and February 1915, by a single firm of high standing, dealing on the market in the ordinary way of trade and without disclosing in any way the Government behind it'.[17]

It was then *Milling*'s turn, referring to the proposal 'to float a hybrid combination of a trust and a Government department'. It was believed that the scheme had reached the President of the Board of Trade. There was an attempt to probe the Association's attitude, with the assertion that 'if there is to be State purchase of flour mills it is obvious that as a trade the milling industry will come to an end, and there will be no more use for a National Association of British and Irish Millers than there is for a national association of British and Irish post offices'.[18] Tired of reconnoitring, in August *The Miller* decided to attack on a wide front. A circular letter was sent 'to all the trade', asking for opinions on the supposed proposal for 'one company under State control to take over all the mills and the purchase of British and foreign grain'. Few had heard much beyond rumour and journal comment.

A. E. Humphries was not amused, complaining to *The Miller*, and describing his own view in a letter to members of the Association.[19] He distinguished control from nationalisation, and gave a challenging forecast of conditions after the war: 'When the control of the mills reverts to our hands we [will] have to face the problems arising from over-capacity, uneconomic distribution in the face of dangerous competition, and a host of troubles associated with lack of organisation and exceedingly small manufacturing profits'. *Milling* claimed to have spoken first and shown restraint afterwards, but insisted that the scheme was not a side issue. The promoter was pretending to protect consumers, prevent profiteering and eliminate superfluous mills. The implication was that those notions might be absorbed into the process of control.

O'Hagan later (in 1929) described his scheme of 1917, in some ways an echo of his proposals of 1914, but with a quite different orientation as far as the millers would be concerned, and with oversimplification of practicalities. He claimed that 'the principal millers' had reacted favourably, which begged many questions. Prices and procedure would have been fixed, buying methods simplified and uneconomic mills stopped, in a non profit-making organisation. O'Hagan's conclusion was that 'before my scheme had been before the Board of Trade for three weeks, the Government were so ill-advised as to commandeer the whole of the mills'.[20] Many elements of the scheme became familiar in wartime, but would not have been viable afterwards. From 1917 to 1921 the Exchequer had to inject large amounts of money. Though the O'Hagan plan was regarded as fanciful or worse, Humphries would have been wary of a catalytic effect.

Government control turned out to be less drastic than O'Hagan's nostrum. On St Valentine's Day, 1918, Sir John Beale took a goodwill message to a meeting of the Association. As vice-chairman of the Royal Commission on wheat supplies and chairman of the FMCC he gave credible reassurance, by saying that he was 'no friend of the control of industry', and that 'We are anxious to keep the trade in such a position that they can resume their normal business as soon as possible'. The main purpose of the meeting was to study a draft of the millers' remuneration agreement, which was to be offered, but not enforced between three parties: the Food Controller, the Association, and each mill owner.[21]

Beale aimed to convince his audience that there was currently a serious food supply situation, and that it was essential that there should not be 'a state of uncertainty or disagreement between the milling trade and the government authorities'. Arrivals of grain imports had declined sharply during the autumn and winter of 1917–18. Wheat supplies from the Argentine and India had been restricted and from Australia had almost ceased. Severe winter weather in the United States had resulted in frozen harbours; railway routes had been blocked by blizzards. Beale required greater efforts in stretching supplies. There was much puzzling over the key relationship described in Humphries' statement: 'your remuneration is based on your datum, which refers to the pre-war period'. *The Miller* visited Somerset House, examined the financial statements of public limited companies, and found that 'they go to prove that the three years prior to the war were anything but a prosperous period for millers'.[22] The Association's solicitor warned that 'if this agreement is not accepted, you will simply embark on the sea of litigation', meaning that collective cooperation was preferable to individuals joining the queues at tribunals. The proposed agreement was not regarded as thoroughly satisfactory, but it was accepted.

For the milling industry, as for many other people, the period 1917 to 1921 required seemingly endless patience, without opportunity for Hamlet's proactive alternative of dealing boldly with 'a sea of troubles'. The leaders of the industry spoke frequently about patriotism, which mainly meant sending employees to France, and obeying the orders of the FMCC. Both Humphries and Beale used expressions of command, when clarity of direction might have been sufficient. There were unfortunate effects in the mills. In November 1917 Leetham referred to a 'train of disastrous fires and breakdowns' and complained about mill staffs 'whose capacities are as limited as their experience'. He also commented that 'the powers that be' did not realise that roller milling was a complex process. There were complaints elsewhere that some mill inspectors had no knowledge of milling, and a common grievance was expressed by a Sussex miller who wrote to *The Miller* that the FMCC had an 'insatiable thirst for returns which necessitate the small man spending an enormous amount of time in keeping records which are perfectly useless and unnecessary in a small business'.[23]

From the summer of 1919 criticisms of bureaucracy appeared more frequently in journal columns and records of meetings. An overall impression is of an industry excessively taken for granted by officialdom. The control arrangements were arbitrary in that there was supposed to be a review of agreements 'six months after the conclusion of the present war', but the millers were still waiting and hoping long afterwards, while wages and other costs of production were rising markedly. Also Lord St Davids had promised that de-control would be arranged in settled commercial conditions, for instance not during a period of clearly hazardous wheat market falls or fluctuations; unfortunately St Davids, who had encouraged collaboration, was not still guiding the administration. The milling industry was at risk of a rough passage.

Reconstruction

Sir John Beale proclaimed that food supply was 'really like a military operation'; he wanted the idea 'entrenched' in every miller's mind. In contrast, from 1917 there was talk of cooperation 'of all classes' after the war. Despite the continuing grimness of the national situation in 1917, the Minister of Labour had started to take advice from a Reconstruction Committee, chaired by J. H. Whitley MP. A. J. P. Taylor (1965) wrote that 'committees surveyed practically every aspect of British life'.[24] The Whitley Report was complete by March 1917. It was about the potential, participation, conditions and earnings of 'the workpeople', a term which by excessive use in the document clearly confirmed social divisions. The Whitley Report emerged as Industrial Report No 1 accompanied by a letter of exhortation from G. H. Roberts, the Minister of Labour, who was later to have a turn as Food Controller. It led to the formation of national joint industrial councils (NJICs), including one for the milling industry. A. E. Humphries and Ernest Bevin, acting respectively for millers and trades union members, formed a strong collaborative relationship; in 1919 Bevin was secretary of the Dock, Wharf, Riverside and General Workers' Union. The work of forming the NJIC for the milling industry, and demonstrating its soundness and usefulness, was regarded by informed observers as exemplary, though so-called Whitleyism was not liked by all the workpeople, nor by millers in country mill areas of eastern and southern England.

One aim described by Whitley was 'to restore the trade union rules and customs suspended during the war', but there were specific suggestions for formal negotiating arrangements in the future: the setting up of 'a triple organisation – in the workshops, the districts and nationally'.[25] This assumed that employers had or could soon devise procedures for collaboration amongst themselves and with union representatives at three levels of contact. In milling, wages had always been set by individual employers, and there were widely varying conditions. There were neither standard rates, nor external guidance. Overall, there were many difficulties, including the need for more than a simple differentiation between port and inland situations. Within the mills, there were many discernible levels or responsibility, with rollermen, purifiermen and silksmen clearly important, and not to be lumped with those in semi-skilled and labouring jobs.

In September 1917 James O'Grady MP, secretary of the National Federation of General Workers wrote to NABIM seeking formal industrial relations arrangements between the Association and the unions within his federation, which he claimed represented most mill operatives. According to L. H. Green, who became secretary of the Flour Milling Employers' Federation, O'Grady's claim was 'entirely repudiated' by the National Union of Millers.[26] In the NABIM annual report for 1918 there was a statement that the position of the Association had been misunderstood; the Association was 'not a central body to deal with labour matters'. Nevertheless, positive moves were made towards collaboration. It was a new activity, energetically pursued, in recognition of a changing mood of union organisation. As far as millers were concerned, there had not been much development over thirty years. In 1886 George Alexander of the London Amalgamated Trade Society had been hoping to form an Operative Millers' Union, but confessed his 'inability to construct or map out a programme; there were a few strikes, in 1911 at Hull, York and Cardiff.[27]

Early in 1918 the Whitley ideas were discussed within the National Association, and the local associations were regarded as the appropriate level for practical response; from their activity it was possible that a national structure could be built. Progress was then rapid despite the other pressures of wartime. By March the Association had decided to act on the proposals as soon as possible, and the Council appointed a Labour Advisory Committee to assist the local associations to set up works (mill) committees and district councils.[28] The Advisory Committee became the provisional board of the Flour Milling Employers' Federation, which adopted its constitution and rules in November 1918. The start of formal industrial relations precedures along Whitley lines was in January 1919, when a joint conference was held between the provisional board of the employers' federation and representatives of twelve trades unions.[29] There was a tangible result in an agreement to establish standard working weeks in the mills of forty-four hours for shift work and forty-seven hours for day work. The first meeting of the fully fledged NJIC for the flour milling industry was held at the Ministry of Labour in May 1919. Subsequently A. E. Humphries and Ernest Bevin served as chairman in alternate years.

By July 1919 there was confirmation that the arrangements were working, with an agreement about rates, based on a classification of mills according to location: Class A mills were 'in big milling centres, in large towns, or principal ports'; class B were others in towns or industrial areas; class C mills were 'situated in small country towns or in rural areas', and a further grading 1, 2 or 3 related to the extent of roller contact – a somewhat arbitrary measure used for insurance policies. Wages for first rollermen and general labourers were determined by the grade within a class. Wages for other operatives were to be set by district councils and with 'regard' to the classes and grades.[30] In August 1920 two intermediate classes were added and the grades were reduced to simply two. The Federation consisted exclusively of district associations, with no individual membership. General support built up quickly, and by March 1919 there were seventeen affiliated districts and 312 constituent milling firms.

When A. E. Humphries finished his two years as President of the Association in June 1919 he said that some millers thought he was 'too much of an official', but that elsewhere he was sometimes regarded as 'too much of a miller'. While he thought it appropriate occasionally to be an advocate, he said he could not be a delegate in relation to the FMCC or the Royal Commission, 'nor could he take instructions from the millers' Association or anybody else'.[31] In 1935 Ernest Bevin paid tribute to Humphries in the context of the work of the NJIC, including 'He held the scales fairly, and when disputed points came before the Council, his judgement was sound and given fearlessly'.[32] Presidents

certainly varied. Leetham was earnest. Nicholls spoke pleasantly about difficult
subjects. Joseph Rank said he 'did not like talking'; he had been active in
several sports, but suggested that none was 'as good a sport as business'.
Humphries seemed to prefer committee rooms to the mill at Coxes Lock, but
he also gave lectures to a variety of audiences explaining what millers were
trying to achieve.

From 1919 NABIM Presidents included J. A. Shone from Wilsons at
Liverpool, Samuel Armstrong from Cranfields at Ipswich, W. T. Carr from the
famous biscuit making and milling firm at Carlisle, Sir Herbert Brown who had
mills at London and Croydon, and R. Hutchinson from Nottingham. They were
all involved in seeking a post-war state of normality and wondering how to
improve the condition of the industry. Within the Association there were
preparations for peacetime before the last battles. Much of the visible activity
was committee making: in 1918 there were six main working groups, some tied
to wartime administration, but several with potential for moving on. In
November 1918 a Reconstruction Committee was appointed. Humphries
supervised and was enigmatic. In March 1919 he was asking members for
'suggestions with regard to post-control conditions', saying 'You can deal with
it from the one end of nationalisation to the other end of unified terms of
trading. There is a long range open, but I am not going to give any indication
of what is passing through my mind'.[33]

TRANSITION DIFFICULTIES

Whatever lay behind Humphries' teasing remark, there precisely was the starting
point of the main debate on rationalisation, which lasted until the Millers'
Mutual Association was formed in 1929. For several years there was no widely
supported plan or even a clear policy, but very many millers recognised that
some form of reconstruction was essential. There were many hazards; the Royal
Commission report listed four, including the 'acute freight difficulties of 1919'
when less shipping space was allocated to cereals than in 1918. At a more
sophisticated level private traders 'knew that on fluctuations of exchange alone
it would be possible to suffer overwhelming losses'. At a practical routine level
the report acknowledged that for merchants and millers the 'daily familiarity
with the changing conditions of markets at home and abroad had been
completely interrupted'. Also it was recognised that they were 'nervous of
Government intervention during the transitional period between control and
freedom'.[34] Partial decontrol was regarded by many millers as something to
avoid, even if the alternative had to be continued regimentation.

Through 1919 and 1920 it was difficult to build confidence. At the Association
AGM in June 1919 there was interest in the suggestion that 'decontrol was in
the air'. Four days later, the Food Controller served notice that he wished to
end control of the mills in December, but the Royal Commission intended to
retain control of the foreign wheat supply. According to J. A. Shone, the notice
was withdrawn 'through force of circumstances'. Beveridge, who had signed the
decontrol notice, explained in 1928 how circumstances had changed.[35] When
the bread subsidy had been introduced in 1917 the price of a 4lb loaf had

reached 12 pence and could have risen further. Just before the war the price had been roughly half that. Due to social unrest it was decided to peg the price at nine pence. In the autumn of 1919 the Government was hoping to withdraw the bread subsidy, and 'it appeared desirable that the mills would be under government control when the subsidy was ended'. Decontrol was postponed and so was the ending of the bread subsidy. It was risky to withdraw the subsidy until wheat prices were reduced and bread prices were thought likely to be held down by competitive trading.

Summertime sociability was resumed in 1920 with a NABIM convention at Felixstowe. J. A. Shone summarised the millers' interests: reconstruction, remuneration, decontrol. The Reconstruction Committee had considered several schemes, more than one involving a modified 'form of Government control'. Still not a vision of freedom, local associations were asked to consider 'which of the recent regulations they would like continued, which they would like modified, which they would like abolished and what new conditions, if any, they would like introduced'. Shone quoted a miller, who had stated in journal controversy 'that under control he was like a bird in a cage and he longed to escape', but warned members that if wheat were decontrolled at that time prices would be unpredictable and quality unreliable. There was little to report about remuneration. At the end of 1918, *The Miller* had begun to throw off some inhibitions: 'Millers have carried on under an oppressive amount of bumbledom … rather than be thought unpatriotic … officialdom has come to believe that they will stand anything'. By the summer of 1920 the tone was more severe, with allusion to 'obedience to the dictatorship of officialdom', and 'meddling by Government officials in trade technicalities about which they have little knowledge'.[36]

The latest annoyance was that in May the Food Controller had demanded 80 per cent extraction, a revision upwards after an easement since the autumn. *The Miller* made clear that 76 per cent was the maximum to obtain an approximation to pure flour, and called the change 'A sinister move'; a postwar version of the Bread and Food Reform League had been lobbying MPs. There was suspicion that the Food Controller had 'succumbed to the efforts of the food faddists', and a danger that an 80 per cent extraction rate might be enforced after decontrol. The journal tried to counter misinformation: chemical analysis might show the food value of hay and straw for grazing animals, but not for 'man, who would starve in a field where a cow or a sheep would fatten'. The Bakers' Association reported complaints about poor quality flour from all over the country, and particularly from the large industrial areas. The Ministry of Food told them that 'those who are responsible for the distribution and supply of wheat and flour are in a much better position than the general public to know the exact facts of the case'.[37] A letter on behalf of Lloyd George told them that 'The leading medical opinion is unanimously in favour of flour containing from 80 per cent to 90 per cent of grain'. As Samuel Armstrong took over the Association presidency in June 1920, he acknowledged that there were hopes that he could inform the public that millers were not responsible for current flour quality and the 'debasing of the loaf', adding: 'The amount

we should have received from the government for moral and intellectual damage
is incalculable'.[38]

Armstrong lamented: 'we have had nothing but meetings for the last five or six years, and some of us are very tired of it'. At the end of Humphries' second year of office it was reported that he had attended 150 out of 157 meetings and during the same period 1918–19 there were eighty-six millers attending Council or committee meetings.[39] Armstrong looked out from Felixstowe at 'the great and wide sea' and said they needed a holiday. He played tennis, and the following week he outplayed the officials in London. The Earl of Crawford and Balcarres invited him to join the FMCC 'with the cordial assent of Mr McCurdy'. With elaborate courtesies Armstrong negotiated his freedom to concentrate on Association work; his 'predecessor in office and esteemed colleague Mr Shone' agreed to renew his membership of the FMCC and his commuting from Liverpool. So Armstrong avoided the danger, noted by William Irish, that 'when a man became a Government offical he became a new creature'.[40]

Immediately after the Felixstowe gathering the Association was warned that a notice of decontrol was imminent. The Miller commented that for the second time the official policy was 'first issue the notice and discuss the wisdom of doing so afterwards'. The foreign wheat market was not in an assuredly stable state. Rising bread prices would lead to criticism of the milling industry and the Government. In October 1920 the notice was withdrawn, with the statement that the decision to control the price of the 1920 crop of home-grown wheat 'would appear to involve the continuance of financial control of the flour milling industry for the present'. The NABIM annual report for 1920–21 stated 'Muddle is the only word which describes the policy pursued by the Government in connection with home-grown wheat'.[41] Two problems defied them: forecasting price movements, and relating home grown supplies to foreign wheat. There had been 'alarmist reports' of world shortage, which The Miller correctly refuted, concentrating fire on the 'lugubrious forecasts of this disciple of hypochondria', the Food Controller. Milling referred to 'uncertainty created in the minds of farmers'. Wheat acreage plunged and did not recover until the mid 1930s, despite strong advocacy by NABIM that home-grown wheat was clearly important for the nation and essential for country millers.

A third decontrol notice was issued in December, but J. A. McCurdy, the last of the Food Controllers, sought agreement for termination on March 31, 1921. For country millers the best date would have been at the start of the next cereal year. McCurdy offered £1,500,000 compensation to the industry as a whole. The Wheat Commission assisted transition to normal commercial practice by taking full responsibility for the supply of foreign wheat in April and providing 20 per cent less each month until August, after which the trade took full responsibility. More than 400 of the Association's 481 members met in London in March to discuss the Controller's proposals. Although there was only a week available for further consideration, it could not be assumed that there was a general predisposition to accept. Samuel Armstrong presented a persuasive case for acceptance, clearly supported by Joseph Rank. A resolution to accept was carried, and a formal poll of all the members confirmed the decision – just in time.[42]

Another Irish observation was that the official financial negotiations needed 'gingering up', which led to the introduction of 'Mr Armstrong's pig'. In the autumn of 1920 Armstrong had told the story of 'the old woman who wanted to get her pig to market'. She had to beat her dog, so that it bit the pig, and persuaded it to go over the stile and then to market, where there were further delays and doubts about its size.[43] The moral was that everything that could be done to move the financial negotiations on had been done; no further gingering up was conceivable. Armstrong beguiled his colleagues with variations of the theme at a series of meetings, the last one in March 1923. Though the journals were not impressed with the pig and its prospects, and Armstrong knew that it had been called a mouse, light relief was helpful. The millers obtained some financial improvements, including a modest allowance for depreciation of machinery. Armstrong's sense of humour, allied to his firmness of purpose, probably helped the Association members to reach decontrol with hopefulness.

RECONSTRUCTION IN THE BIG GROUPS

While flour distribution was controlled some businesses lost customers and others gained trade. Following decontrol it was obvious that losers would aim to regain territory and the others would try to hold their position. For millers on London committees there was a particularly vivid image of the practical aspects of reconstruction. On Saturday January 20, 1917 *The Times* reported that 'an explosion occurred this evening at a munitions factory in the neighbourhood of London'. On Monday there was more news: 'A chemical factory, a flour mill, and a number of smaller workshops and storehouses were destroyed ... Fires were caused in neighbouring warehouses and factories, one of the largest of which was an important flour mill'. The explosion was at the Brunner Mond factory at Silvertown; the mill destroyed was Vernons' Millenium Mill at the Victoria Docks.

From the early 1920s, Spillers and Ranks were the strongest influences on the future of their industry, each with a distinctive tradition, both with fresh impetus. Vernons' plans for reconstruction became generally known when *Milling* reported in February 1920 that Spillers Milling and Associated Industries Ltd had been arranging an amalgamation with Wm Vernon & Sons. Vernons were registered as a private limited company with a capital of £1,500,000.[44] By 1919 there was a general reorganisation. Spillers Milling and Associated Industries Ltd was set up as a controlling and shareholding company; there were fifteen subsidiary or affiliated companies. The flour milling company was registered in June 1919 with the familiar name of Spillers & Bakers Ltd and a nominal capital of £1,500,000. Vernons' Millennium Mill was reinstated and was in operation just in time for Sir William Edgar Nicholls to report to his AGM in May 1921. The prestige of Millennium flour had been lost with the explosion, and could not be revived until the industry decided to cancel a transitional agreement to continue making only one grade of flour. Spillers' own mills on the Bristol Channel and at Newcastle, together with Vernons' position at

Figure 99.
Advertisement by
Seth Taylor Ltd of
London. (*Milling*,
September 1923)

Birkenhead and the potential of the up-to-date London mill, provided a strong
basic network, from which to extend in the north-east, the north-west and the
midlands.

During 1921 the Spillers group acquired four other well-known businesses,
including F. A. Frost & Sons Ltd at Chester and Ellesmere Port, and Watson,

Todd & Co. Ltd of Birmingham. Nicholls announced a new policy: 'we shall as an economic factor create zones to be supplied primarily by the mills within these zones'.[45] Preliminary agreements had also been made with Rishworth, Ingleby & Lofthouse Ltd of Hull and John Jackson & Son Ltd of Manchester and Bolton, and they too joined the group immediately. Nicholls stated his 'concept' of the future for the Spillers Industries group, which was 'to occupy a place in national commerce which will not take second place to any competing house'. In 1924 Nicholls reported that Spillers Industries owned the entire share capital of seven milling companies, including Cardiff & Channel Mills Ltd, also Spillers Victoria Foods Ltd, Uveco Cereals Ltd, Spillers Nephews Ltd and Turog Brown Flour Co. Ltd. In addition to the main flour production they made oatmeal, ship biscuits, self-raising and packed flours, feedstuffs for the farming industry and dog biscuits. They owned the Spillers Steamship Co. Ltd, and Spillers Grain Co. Ltd, claimed to be the largest distributor of imported grain in the UK.[46]

The official commentary by Joseph Rank Ltd (1955) showed that the other contender for leadership of the industry regarded reconstruction as an opportunity to move forward, an effort to regain trade lost during the period of government control, and a counter to the renewed threat of flour imports. In 1920 Joseph Rank, with an organisation strongly represented in the four main port areas, decided to increase capacity and regional presence. The business of John Herdman & Sons Ltd at Edinburgh was acquired, and also the smaller firm of Kirbys Ltd at Selby, followed in 1921 by the acquisition of John Ure & Son and the Riverside Milling Co. Ltd at Glasgow. In the same year Buchanans Flour Mills Ltd at Birkenhead was purchased, considered as a base for provender milling; the availability of the site followed the demise of William Buchanan in 1920. In 1923 the businesses of W. Sutcliffe & Sons at Manchester and T. Hanley & Sons Ltd at Doncaster were acquired.[47] Rank's overall national status was clear to everyone.

There was another major grouping in 1921. Associated London Flour Millers Ltd was formed as a holding company to acquire seven well-known businesses:[48] J. & H. Robinson Ltd, Cannon & Gaze Ltd, Samuel Kidd & Co. Ltd, The Medway Milling Co. Ltd, S. P. Mumford & Co. Ltd, Sun Flour Mills Co. Ltd, and a new company to be formed to take over the business of Seth Taylor, who had died aged eighty years in 1917. Taylor's St Saviour's Mills continued in the old premises on the south bank of the Thames, below Tower Bridge; Vernons had purchased his Waterloo Mills in 1918, for use as a warehouse. The new group had a nominal capital of £1,750,000. Each constituent company traded separately under its own name, hoping to preserve individuality. The reasons for the formation of the group were explained by J. H. Robinson of Deptford at their first AGM. There were common structural and commercial problems: a national 'surplus of manufacturing capacity', narrow profit margins and increasing costs. Flour imports were again a threat to business viability; quantities increased markedly in 1918 and remained substantial until 1923, and London was particularly vulnerable.[49] Two long-established firms which remained outside the new group were Peter Mumford & Sons at the Royal

Flour Mills at Vauxhall[50] and Charles Brown & Co. at Tower Bridge Mills and Croydon. Charles Brown & Co. Ltd was incorporated in 1922 and acquired the Vauxhall mill in 1926.[51]

Trade organisation: not plain sailing

Encouraged by the National Association, local associations met in groups, often with Sidney Leetham as chairman. Post-control arrangements included a general agreement to keep to straight-run flour, at least for a few months. Terms of trading and prices were to be settled within the local associations. Armstrong's advice was that 'we have had in a sense to become our own controllers'.[52] While some millers were inclined to continue with a samely product, others wished to get back to flour divides and the production of patent grades. Amongst the bakers there were many who purposely produced lower price bread. The imported flour trade was freed form control in January 1921, prompting a surge of supplies from overseas before the UK milling industry was decontrolled. That presented an increasing threat to the home-milled flour trade, so that a return to flour grades was inevitable. Recognising that the trade was reaching that decision, Joseph Rank Ltd wrote formally to the Association in July to declare his firm's position: 'we feel strongly that the time has arrived when both the question of price and quality must be decided by each particular firm in relation to the foreign competition it has to meet'.[53]

Samuel Armstrong presided at the Keswick Convention in 1921 amid statistical challenges. He hoped for progress with the collection of 'statistics for the manufacture, stocks and deliveries of flour', so that reports of the state of trade could be supplied to Assocation members. Requiring more immediate comment was a Bill that was being rushed through parliament. In future, millers would have to buy wheat and sell flour in hundredweights (112 lb); otherwise there would be no contractual basis. The National Farmers' Union, the Central Chamber of Agriculture, the Central Landowners' Association, the Agricultural Policy Sub-Committee and the *Church Times* were all in favour. The corn trade, the millers and the bakers had not been consulted. Between 1887 and 1898 there had been four attempts to bring in legislation to set standard weights and measures, but since then 'measures' had ceased to be important, and customary units of weight for wheat, barley and oats were used with practical advantage. Earlier, there had been efforts by J. H. Chatterton, the first NABIM secretary, and by Liverpool millers to encourage the use of the cental (100 lb) in place of the then existing chaotic geographical variations of practice in corn-dealing. Armstrong contended that in thirty years experience he had never heard a farmer wishing that the corn trade dealt in hundredweights. In exasperation he declared: 'The country is being reconstructed to the devil'.[54]

W. T. Carr succeeded Armstrong and tried to promote the sharing of information. In March 1922 the Association's Executive Committee suggested that a Trade Organisation Committee should be formed. The work would be to study the statistics, enquire about output from British mills and about flour imports, and 'to put forward practical ideas for improvements in the conditions

Figure 100.
The NABIM
Convention of 1922
at Dieppe. (*Milling*,
June 1962)

of trading'. Carr commented that the Association's Reconstruction Committee had 'succeeded in reconstructing nothing'.[55] The new committee was suggested eight years to the day after the journal *Milling* proclaimed the title 'Trade Organisation' and called for improvement. During the 1920s adverse profit and loss accounts became a chronic complaint. The Association's leaders spent seven anxious years wondering how to proceed and what might be agreed. The scheme to obtain weekly statistical returns from members lasted six months. In conditions of sharpening UK competition, it could hardly be expected that millers would tell all. However, totals and regional patterns were known more clearly than before, so that quantities produced could be compared with overall capacity and related to national requirements.

Carr presided at Dieppe, succeeded by Sir Herbert Brown, who had suggested the unusual venue for the 1922 convention, taking his cue from *l'entente cordiale*, and arranging the banquet at the casino. Some Association members needed reassurance about the passage from Newhaven to Dieppe, but the elderly Wilson Marriage sailed from Brightlingsea in his ketch. Secretary G. H. Ball achieved clearer recognition than his predecessors, complimented on the style and increasing content of the Association's annual reports, which were so voluminous that the journals could no longer give more than excerpts. From about that time, therefore, the full official record of the Association receded further from general public view.

The Trade Organisation Committee completed a preliminary report by July

1922. The potential capacity of the mills of England and Wales for the year 1922 was estimated as just over 40 million sacks of flour, the quantity required as just over 30 million sacks. The potential capacity was on a basis of three shift working of 127 hours per week for fifty weeks per year, and could be expressed as about 6300 sacks per hour. (Consumption was reckoned as 4.3 lb of flour per person per week.) The supposed surplus capacity was about 1500 sacks per hour, and could be expressed as very roughly a quarter of the total available, or as an additional third above requirements.[56] Leetham suggested that 500 sacks per hour could be considered as a necessary operating margin, and he called the other 1000 sacks per hour 'damaging excess'.[57] It was suggested that the 'remedy appears to lie in making the quantity of flour offered bear some reasonably close relation to the quantity required', which implied that there should be tighter control of sales practices. The tactical interactions of bakers and competing travellers made it seem that there was a substantial surplus of flour. Flour prices were talked down when travellers accepted hearsay, and matched or undercut their adversaries. Travellers were sometimes allowed to send in 'pocket orders' (undated contracts) several days after an advance in wheat prices. Leetham called the situation 'trading on the ragged edge of nothingness'. The pervasive term was 'troubles'.

In the report there were two radical proposals: a 'scheme for insuring output' (O'Hagan's scheme), and another for 'purchasing superfluous mills', the theory being that, if production were concentrated in the mills that could be run most economically, the pressure of imports could be resisted more effectively. There was an implication that mills that were not technically up-to-date were unlikely to prosper. Into this contentious area between port and country mills there was scope for complaint, but not yet an immediate prospect of a unifying solution. The O'Hagan scheme was said to have 'a simplicity of plan that is astounding', and that was still true. For an initial premium of six pence or possibly one shilling per sack of registered capacity, and continuing premiums of three pence per sack of each sack of flour delivered, each policy holder could insure his output. There would be a central authority, to collect information from each firm, circulate reports to members, and regulate national aggregate output when necessary. No price controls were involved. The objective was to make available the amount of flour that the market required and would take, to be well-informed about changes in demand and to try to avoid overproduction. Leetham provided ideas for buying out 1000 sacks per hour of capacity at a possible cost of £2,000,000, perhaps to be raised as a charge on manufacturing.[58] More than thirty millers, with an aggregate capacity of about 300 sacks per hour, had approached G. H. Ball, offering to sell.

All members of the Association received the report in the form of an explanatory paper, with discussion of problems of overcapacity and overproduction, together with a copy of the O'Hagan scheme of 1914. Members were asked if they approved the basic ideas for a scheme to insure output and to buy out superfluous mills. The results were discussed without much detail in March 1923. Although there had been positive replies, there was insufficient overall support and Sir Herbert Brown's way of reporting disappointment was by saying that 'it is essential to obtain some sort of favourable verdict from the large groups'.[59] Avoiding public discussion of recent information, Humphries referred in detail to the Census of Production report for 1907; as there was excess capacity then, he merely confirmed that it was a familiar condition. He was also sceptical of the popular theory of reducing unit costs by increasing output: it was a 'misleading will o'the wisp'. Whereas Brown spoke for many, in stating that there was 'far too much milling capacity' the most clearly visible problem was still overlapping, which had been increasing for thirty years. O'Hagan (1929) wrote of 'the whole host of travellers who were tumbling over each other',[60] pre-war or post-war. A more vivid description was Leetham's expression: 'hatchet competition'.

Keeping flour prices down helped to keep flour imports out, but there was a significant supply from overseas even after the post-war surge had been checked. It was not possible to find room for an expansion of UK flour production by much further reduction of the flow of foreign flour, by exporting from the UK, or to more than a moderate extent by catering for increases of population. Leetham's opinion was that the trade was 'non-elastic', and the members already knew that there was little prospect of immediate action unless all the big groups were involved. The only other possibility was to persuade the public to eat more bread, words which became a slogan and an advertising message. In April 1923 *Milling* gave news of similar efforts in the United States, where there was an energetic campaign. Publicity was a new phenomenon. *Milling* was enthusiastic: 'Advertising experts know full well that if the product were advertised sufficiently well, the public would eat brown paper. Even G. H. Ball, when replying to newspaper criticism of the Trade Organisation report, referred to the 'eating capacity of the nation'.[61]

Figure 101.
The 'Eat More Bread' campaign of 1923. (*Milling*, September 1923)

As so often happened, Leetham made a memorable statement: 'You cannot make people eat more bread than they want, and it is not a social thing to say to a man come and have a bread loaf'.[62] *The Miller* was doubtful about the value of an advertising campaign. There were indications that the demand for bread might be declining; Voller was concerned about 'various breakfast foods, which are imported into London, Liverpool and Bristol in enormous quantities'. The bakers asked the millers to 'cooperate with them in an extensive advertising campaign, with the object of persuading people to eat more bread'. It was estimated that £150,000 or more would be needed, but it had not been possible to work out how to raise that amount. *Milling* was optimistic and announced 'the first move in the publicity campaign', by helping to sponsor an 'Eat more bread' poster competition.[63] There were plans to display the results on roadsides and at railway stations, and to advertise in trial towns, but by the middle of 1924 there was a recognition that there were no practical results.[64] The only potentially long-lasting item was a special issue of *Milling* in September 1923 on the theme 'Buy home-milled flour', with contributions from Nicholls, Humphries, Voller and Jago, together with many fascinating advertisements.

The convention in June 1923 was at Buxton. *The Miller* contrasted the expectations of social togetherness with earlier gatherings when 'whatever pleasures were indulged in were, after the supposed English fashion, taken somewhat seriously'. Sir Herbert Brown was completing a difficult year. He hoped that there could be consultation between Joseph Rank and Sir William Nicholls. Mutuality required a sense of participation by businesses of varied size and background. If the biggest firms had taken a clear lead, there would have been scope for allegations of monopoly; there were numerous possible sources of opposition: country millers, bakers, wheat growers, political activists, and members of the Cooperative movement. Some of these did complain about ideas for reducing productive capacity. Brown reported that for several months there had been a sustained and apparently concerted campaign of hostile criticism, using 'hundreds of papers in various parts of the country'. The Association had been called a federation; there was mention of a trust, and rumour that surplus capacity was to be 'abolished' by closing country mills. By July, *The Miller* had collected many press cuttings which were so alike that the conclusion was that 'they all emanate from an identical source'.

The Miller's conclusion was that a plan to buy surplus mills 'never had a ghost of a chance' and that is was not surprising that the proposal was 'misunderstood' by some innocent people and misrepresented by others less simple'.[65] Humphries later commented on the idea of buying what he called redundant mills: 'The thing broke down with its own weight. The job was too big, the difficulties were altogether too great and therefore that lapsed'.[66] Obstacles included the large amount of capital required, and the problem of appointing decision-makers. There were more than fifty members of the Council, representing all parts of the industry; it was their task to consider whether further proposals were well devised and might be universally acceptable. *The Miller*'s appraisals varied from a recognition that a curtailment of production had been 'ruled out' to a criticism of 'the predominance of the 'almighty maximum' of three-shift working.[67] *Milling* suggested that 'the single aim [of trade organisation] should be to employ and not to curtail capacity and output', which was consistent with continued support for the 'eat more bread' theme.

Research: a glimpsed horizon

There was another uncharted venture. In 1919 the Association started to explore possibilities for scientific research, in conjunction with the Department of Scientific and Industrial Research, which could supply funds for five years in approved cases, provided an industry matched the amount granted by the DSIR. W. A. Vernon and A. E. Humphries investigated, and the Education Committee of the Association worked out how to proceed, under the leadership of J. L. Williams. A report was presented to the Association council and local associations were consulted. An early idea included provision of a milling school attached to a major college, and acquisition of a mill for practical work, especially experiments with new machinery. By 1921 the concept of a Research Institute had come to the fore. Soon there was an appeal to Association members for support for a proposed Research Association for the industry, to include laboratories, facilities for an information service, and arrangements for collaboration with the work at a demonstration mill.[68] An idea for an associated training centre disappeared during 1922. *Milling* reported with surprise and disapproval that the NJIC might take over responsibility for technical education in the milling industry. *The Miller* referred to a 'somewhat startling proposal' and doubted its wisdom. The change had been initiated by the City & Guilds Institute and became official via the Ministry of Labour. The Whitley Council report had included technical education and training among the wide range of functions conferred on the NJICs, and also industrial research;[69] both were dubious perceptions, the latter being farcical. By 1923 the transfer of responsibility for technical education was a *fait accompli*, which left the Association with a clearer task of establishing a research organisation.

Figure 102.
C. W. Chitty
(1874–1979). (Chitty,
1972)

Meanwhile the Association's Research Committee had reached a stage of actual plans. New Barnes Mill near St Albans was to be leased and initial support had been canvassed, though there was the first of several set-backs: so far, the large firms did not wish to join. Many of them had their own laboratories and Williams reported that a similar division existed in other industries. It was thought that more than thirty industries were expecting to set up research facilites, but the DSIR had stated that active support was from medium and small firms. There was optimism in journal columns that the millers' formal research organisation might be a unifying influence; clear absence of enthusiasm by any sector of the industry was therefore a double disappointment. The Research Association was registered in September 1923, with a membership of seventy-nine firms, and British Flour Mills Ltd was registered in January 1924 as a private company, to engage in 'the business of flour milling for research and other scientific work'. The Director of Research was E. A. Fisher, with lecturing and research experience in agriculture and textile chemistry.[70] His first public appearance in his new field was at the Folkestone convention in June 1924. Stating that 'in agriculture and the textile trades, the scientific study of processes, as distinct from products, has barely begun', he asked if millers and milling engineers understood the milling processes, and also said: 'I do not think I am going too far in suggesting that milling machinery has not been designed on the basis of any real, intimate and fundamental knowledge of the work it is called on to perform, but rather just built'.[71]

A. E. Humphries was more absorbed in the search for wheat varieties of good milling quality, and the possible promotion of an all-English loaf, than with

Figure 103.
Chittys' mill at Dover,
illustrated in 1931.
(*Milling*, February
1931)

mechanical engineering intricacies, but he appeared to be making a sweeping generalisation in the comment that 'we should seek for precise knowledge, instead of working on haphazard lines, punting about in the dark'. E. D. Simon, chairman of Henry Simon Ltd, who had diversified into politics, missed Fisher's olympian discourse, but hurried from Westminster to join the discussion. He countered Humphries' assertion, stated that his firm had been employing chemists for fifteen years, and referred to the continuing opportunity 'to make out what strength means', administering an adroit corrective: 'Mr Fisher will be a very lucky man if he spends the rest of his life at it and gets in sight of a solution'.[72] With the escape from the uncertainties of 1921 and 1922, there was a need for scientific reappraisal, but commercial problems remained predominant, and Fisher was soon to discover that work of immediate practical relevance should be given priority.[73] A suitable subject was wheat conditioning, and E. D. Simon had already given a paper to the Association, a special contribution at the 1923 convention, when he said that for twenty years the subject had been 'the most interesting and important as well as the most controversial technical question before the milling industry'.[74] Attention was also required to practical problems in mill or bakehouse. Millers who did not have extensive laboratory facilities often needed assistance from an analyst and consultant.

D. W. Kent-Jones became the most widely known cereal chemist. Soon after

Figure 104.
D. W. Kent-Jones
(1891–1978). (*The Miller*, October 1938)

the war he was engaged by Charles Chitty at Charlton Mill in Dover, to take charge of a growing business in flour improvers. Their first main product was a chemical additive, sold as Salox, and marketed by Henry Simon Ltd. Later, Kent-Jones introduced a heat treatment method. Chitty had studied engineering, but not chemistry; his early guide and colleague was William Jago.[75] Charlton Mill had an 18 sacks per hour plant, remodelled in 1922 by Simons.[76] Chitty considered that his location at Dover, but not at the docks, was unfavourable. However he was well-known and one of the six members of the Association's Research Committee. Kent-Jones took an increasingly intense interest in the many factors affecting wheat, flour and dough which might be investigated scientifically. He developed test procedures and equipment, and provided the classic text *Modern cereal chemistry*, first published in 1924, which in the later editions became an essential work of reference.[77] His work was still necessarily in an empirical field, but represented a new level of scientific knowledge spreading within the milling industry. Later, he invested in his own laboratories and set up as an independent analyst.[78]

Rationalisation and a new era: 1925–1939

Backwards or forwards?

In a decade of political uncertainty, the years 1925 to 1927 were particularly challenging for millers. In January 1925 *Milling* was closely attentive to the activity of the Royal Commission on food prices and newspaper perception that wheat merchants, millers and bakers might be profiteers: 'The Prime Minister [Mr Baldwin] apparently fell a victim to this suggestion, as he promised some months before he was returned to office that in the event of his party being elected to power, he would cause an enquiry to be made into the cost of living'. The Royal Commission was appointed in 1924 despite the anticlimax of the recent Linlithgow report on similar ground, and reported formally in May 1925, dealing with wheat supply, the flour milling and baking trades and the meat trades; *Milling* called the elaborate compilation 'a damp squib' as the public had been 'grossly deceived' about profits.[1] In June *The Miller* declared 'The mountain has laboured and brought forth a mouse', referring to the creation of a Food Council 'with a watching brief over the operation of the food supply, and vaguely inquisitorial powers of interference'.[2] The National Association of Master Bakers used some similar phrasing. Leading dailies varied in satisfaction and lack of it.

The Commission, chaired by Sir Auckland Geddes, included Sir Henry Rew, who as head of the statistical branch of the Board of Agriculture had provided evidence for the Royal Commission on supply of food etc in 1905. He was one of several exponents of the official style of interrogation, used to dissect evidence but not necessarily leading to systematic understanding. Rew was an interventionist, more so was W. R. Smith, whose objective was full state control. T. H. Ryland was against it, with clear reasons. The report dealt with proposals for and objections to state trading in food, reacting to pressure from representatives of socialist causes. The Commission considered economic theory, acquired copious statistics, and looked for cheap bread. Their 'Description of the milling trade' began 'It is not within our province to examine the highly technical process of milling wheat, and we propose to confine ourselves to a consideration of the broad outlines of the trade, paying particular attention to the costs of the milling processes'.[3] A better beginning would have been to visit some mills. Major P. R. Reynolds and Dr A. E. Humphries gave evidence about the milling industry. After war service, Reynolds had been a technical adviser to the Royal Commission on wheat supplies, before returning to the chairmanship of milling businesses at Wakefield and Grimsby.

The first stage of the whole commercial process from wheat field to baker's shop – the complex subject of wheat supply – was considered extensively, but not in close relationship to the millers' practical situation. G. J. S. Broomhall described the 'mode of collection and publication of grain trade statistics' and reviewed world supply. W. E. Nicholls described the Canadian context, from a basis of current practical experience; Spillers had become financially interested in grain supply and milling companies in Canada.[4] Nicholls warned the Commission against the idea of Government involvement in grain trading. Lord Crawford, who had been chairman of the Royal Commission on wheat supplies, gave reasons against state interference in wheat trading or control of milling and baking. He tried to explain that the 'logical outcome' of controlling the price of bread would be a requirement for standardized flour, with all mills provided with similar quality and cost of wheat; 'ultimately 40,000 bakers, and probably 100,000 retailers of flour, would have to be state controlled'.[5] Presumably few millers read the report from the Commission on food prices, but the journals gave extensive coverage. In January 1925 *Milling* had a headline 'Lord Crawford and Sir Wm Edgar Nicholls oppose state control'. After that it was obvious that the industry needed to think harder about implications of action and inaction.

In his statement of evidence to the Commission, Reynolds showed that overseas wheat sources were chiefly the USA and Canada, followed by the Argentine. After 1927 United States supplies faded away gradually and then sharply. Australian wheat was an important additional resource, reaching second place around 1931. Indian supplies were small after 1924, and Russia sent only tiny amounts during the 1920s. As the pattern of available sources and varieties of wheat changed frequently, committees or Government departments would not have found it easy to regulate supply. Sir Henry Rew observed that the price of bread varied across the country, and asked if it would be 'a standard loaf in each case'. He repeatedly suggested that the price could be fixed. Humphries replied that interference would result in being 'driven to go the whole hog' of complete control.[6] Rew persisted: 'You do not think therefore it would be practicable simply to fix the price of the loaf leaving all the play of free trade in the literal sense of the term all along the line?' Humphries tried to explain that overseas conditions and results varied, ending 'Unless you have control throughout the world which nobody could have, the price of the loaf must vary according to the price of wheat'. In response to quibbling, Humphries commented on the variety of taste and customer preference, adding 'I do not see why you should seek by fixing the price of bread to set up uniformity … why should you interfere with the freedom of the subject?'[7]

Humphries was concerned to clear up confusion between millers conferring and acting in combination; he stressed that 'No such thing as a Trust exists in the industry'. Several Commission members had been imagining cost savings if the mills formed 'one big combination', which was an uncomfortable though unspoken hint of O'Hagan, or even of nationalisation. Humphries protested that Reynolds had been questioned in a way that suggested local associations 'were something in the nature of a combine', which might have the power to dictate prices, declaring 'it is absolute moonshine'.[8] He stated that millers set a price for 'one grade [of flour] as an index and were at liberty to sell other grades at whatever difference they can get', but at that point he did not stress that meetings were informal, and that there was not strict adherence to set or quoted prices. A remark late in the interview was probably the best answer to Geddes: 'In ordinary times the miller's net profit represents, say, one eighth of a penny per 2lb loaf, that is to say, a farthing per quartern of bread, and in recent years even this has not been obtained'.[9] Although Royal Commissions might be expected to be objective enquiries, Geddes presided over a confrontation.

The Commission passed responsibility to the Food Council, to consist of twelve members: four nominated by Government ministers, four with business experience including a Director of the CWS, four to represent consumers (two being nominated by the TUC and two by Local Authorities). The Council's overall responsibility was 'to maintain continuing supervision over the staple food trades'. Concerning the milling industry, the Council was to 'watch the operations of price fixing associations and intervene if necessary'. In the bread trade, the Council was to investigate overlapping. The Commission had noted that 'in towns it is usual for a number of bakers to deliver from door to door in the same street' and they suggested 'the allocation to particular bakers of exclusive areas of operation'. In his minority report, W. R. Smith went further. He claimed that 'The chief protection which the consumer now enjoys is afforded by the Cooperative movement'. He recommended that 'The government should take open responsibility for the supplies and prices of the food of the people', that 'The milling industry should be formed into a statutory corporation', and that 'Local Authorities should have power to open municipal bread and meat shops and to require the licensing of retailers'.

T. H. Ryland produced an additional report. He regarded the Food Council as a proposal for 'a definite advance in the direction of State Socialism', involving 'irritating interference with business by bureaucrats and amateurs'. He objected to an assumption that 'those engaged in the food trades should adopt for commercial purposes principles of philanthropy and self-denial which are not expected of other businesses, trades and professions'. Reviewing the composition of the Council, he scorned its lack of competence. Ryland disputed that the Council could 'grapple with a single one of the root causes that have led to a higher level of commodity prices generally'. He pointed to the arbitrariness of trying to 'assess reasonable rates of profit' and declared 'Profiteering is a delightfully vague offence, which always relates to another man's profits'.[10]

In the summer of 1925 Milling called the Food Council a 'twentieth-century political frolic', and thought the members' qualifications would have delighted W. S. Gilbert. For variety, Lewis Carroll was invoked, with a skit: 'Alice in Commissionland'. The Miller had stated that the 'decline in the number of baker bankrupts' had been used by the Commission 'as an argument to prove profiteering. Could any argument be more grotesque?' Miss Drapper of the Council sought data on bankruptcies in the baking trade, but apparently did

Figure 105.
Vernons' rebuilt
Millennium Mills.
(*The Miller*, June 1936)

not know where to look. In 1925 NABIM president J. G. McDougall criticised the Food Council 'composed almost entirely of amateurs' and Nicholls referred to 'people who know nothing whatever about the large trades which have to provide the food of the country'.[11] In 1926 NABIM president P. R. Reynolds reported that relations with the Food Council were 'entirely friendly up to the present time', a gloss on a policy of diplomatic cooperation, but at a tactical level the Food Council harried the London Flour Millers' Association, seeking information from which they hoped to discover how to rule a relationship between flour and bread prices: in 1929 the London Association was still protesting about misleading bureaucratic statements.

The mistaken impression that millers met conspiratorially persisted. Although local groups had tried to set prices to maintain a 'millers' margin' against a trend towards its complete disappearance, it was a fragile arrangement. Until the middle of 1925 there were hopes that a network of commercial communication would survive, but W. E. Nicholls warned the Harrogate Convention in June that 'we are always on the edge of a chasm, upon which some individual or individuals will take the view that coordination is not in their own particular interest'. By the end of the month regulation of prices and trading terms had been abandoned. In 1926 Leetham stated forcefully that 'any scheme which has to do with regulation of prices is out of date'.[12]

While the Royal Commission was deliberating, *Milling* produced a constructive idea, and in January 1925 launched *Milling and the National Baker*, giving the existing journal a new look and expanded coverage, with a monthly issue of 'mutual interest' to millers and bakers. This new trade literature included articles to encourage smart retailers by describing 'The baker and his window', to answer the question 'What is a good loaf of bread?', to describe some of the impressive large bakery firms, and to provide 'The truth about bread wrapping', which from a start in the UK in 1920 had soared in popularity. Cookery recipes were included, with a surprising diversity for Christmas puddings. Leading millers had whole page advertisements: Mark Mayhew at Battersea had artistic assistance while advocating 'London's premier flour is Silver Belle', and W. Vernon & Sons had good clear style, supporting their 'Millennium' as 'The purest flour the world has ever known'; Vernons had the cachet of a Royal appointment crest. J. Reynolds (Voller's firm) had counted 192 gold medals awarded to bakers using Reynolds' wholemeal. Edward Hutchinson had a blank page except for names in small print: from Liverpool five 'Golden' brands were offered: Crown, Sheaf, Grain, Light and Ring, contrasting with the fashion for super whiteness; from the Barrow mill the two lowest flour grades were called Community and Equity. E. Marriage & Son called their top grade British Oak. Clearly there was scope for advice. Mr J. R. Curry, an ex-President of the London Master Bakers' Protection Society, regretted the prevalence of 'all kinds of lazy foods', and he commented on changing hours of work and eating habits: the loaf was no longer prominent on breakfast tables and flour foods had been 'almost banished' from the dinner table. He observed that 'the bread baker gets a look in at tea time, sharing the business with the confectioner, biscuit baker, and packet cake mixture manufacturer, and a few others'. Mr Curry also missed 'the old style boiled puddings, the beef pudding, the roly-poly, the apple pie, the cut-and-come-again open tart'. His suggested cure was for 'a widespread publicity campaign to restore flour foods to the important position they formerly held in the domestic life of the nation'.[13]

The National Association Convention was held at Harrogate in June 1925, with the Yorkshireman P. R. Reynolds presiding. Reynolds proposed a return to the strategy of trying to stimulate demand. W. A. Vernon described himself as 'an apostle of advertising', and made a plea for suet dumplings. Reynolds introduced the possibility of advertising. A long address by the advertising consultant Thomas Russell was a quite unusual event, meriting inclusion in any anthology of modern 'Millers' tales'. He described advertising as 'the assistant to the economic task of distribution' and he dealt with the biggest obstacle to collaborative advertising: cost. He tried to shift attention from budget to target: 'there is an inevitable question. Will it pay? One thing is quite certain; it will not pay if you do not do it'. Russell's illustrations were humorous: he started with tomatoes and soap. British tomato growers had been concerned about imports from Holland, but had advertised so successfully that Dutch growers wished to contribute to the campaign. He said 'our consumption of soap is the largest in the world – even America with the multiple bathroom does not approach us'. He thought that effective advertising was demonstrated by the growing market for 'Shredded Wheat, Grape Nuts, Quaker Oats, Post Toasties, Kellogg's corn flakes and Brown & Polson's cornflour'. Examples of cooperative advertising in other industries included campaigns for gas, paint, Scottish tweeds, milk and fruit.[14]

Russell could not find new ideas specifically for flour; more toast might be eaten and 'the good old-fashioned bread-and-milk habit' might be revived. He recalled that in commercial hotels 'it was a common thing to see quite a bunch of travellers sitting in the smoking room at night having a bowl of bread and milk'. Russell had three better ideas, including the use of 'perfectly mouth-watering posters'. He added that the millers 'might induce the bakers to make their bread a little better'; there was also 'another effect of advertising – it will improve your cordial relationship with each other'. The AGM at Harrogate instructed the Association's Council to consider and act, though in the vaguest terms. Responsibility was passed to a Trade Development and Improvements Committee.[15] A circular was sent to members, asking for financial support. The estimated required budget was about £100,000 per year but, although individuals and firms could have worked out that it was equivalent to the modest amount of one penny per sack of flour produced, the circular did not say that; W. A. Vernon noticed in March 1926, but by then the proposed publicity scheme had been blocked. The 'great majority of the larger millers' were in favour, but some firms stipulated that all branches of the trade should contribute, including the CWS who decided not to participate. The circular was sent to 365 members; eighty-five replied, so frustration could not be blamed solely on the CWS, though that proved tempting.

In 1922 the CWS had eight flour mills, having decided in June to close the Halifax mill.[16] CWS official statistics for 1922 show that 3,144,755 sacks of flour and wheatmeal were produced during the year, equivalent to 495 sacks per hour for 127 hours per week and fifty weeks. In 1925 *Milling* had a brief report which indicated a higher output, along with a comment that the Cooperative movement was 'certainly spreading and growing' and the forecast that 'It will in all probability buy or build more mills'. The Cooperative News copied the assessment, with satisfaction, and *Milling* recopied for emphasis. Since 1923 there had been signs that the increasing strength of CWS milling would confirm a strategic separation from the rest of the industry. There were frequent reminders that although the CWS mills might have some disadvantage in selling only to Cooperative shops, there were advantages, within the movement, of a privileged tax position. It was also alleged that Coop grocery shops used low bread prices as inducements, to draw in customers to the habit of buying various goods on the same premises, or nearby, and counting on 'divi' or returned margin, at the end of each trading quarter. During the mid 1920s it became necessary for the Association to consider how to move on independently.

A waiting game

The industry between mid 1925 and mid 1927 had returned to harder trading conditions. Successive Presidents of NABIM took responsibility for trying to devise a reorganisation scheme and for negotiations with constituents: the largest firms, the port millers in general, the country trade, the local associations, and the CWS. *The Miller* reckoned that by 1926 there had been 'nine separate and distinct schemes for a revival of the trade'. In 1927 Lieut. Col. F. K. S. Metford took over the presidency from Reynolds. Metford was reminded of Sisyphus in Greek literature, who had to roll a stone uphill; always it rolled back down and his punishment was to repeat the task. For many millers news of schemes was scanty and knowledge of Sisyphus limited; they could observe only an apparent state of impasse. Association members were sent annual reports of about 400 pages, records rather than news. Council, committee and local association meetings were not usually recorded very extensively, though there were fuller accounts of some important committee subjects. Each year the journals reported the main spring meeting, the AGM, and the Convention proceedings. When a member suggested that the presidential address should be printed and circulated, Metford replied that 'every word I have uttered this morning will be reported in *Milling* on Saturday morning without any deletion or alteration'.

Amongst the biggest firms Joseph Rank Ltd was still a private company. Joseph Rank reached seventy-two years of age in 1926; neither he nor W. E. Nicholls, who retired from the chairmanship of Spillers in 1926, were engaged in the formalities of the Association. Their occasional public statements were noted carefully and studied for signs that they might be able to initiate moves towards a scheme that would work. At the end of 1925 *Milling* had asked Nicholls to write an open letter of encouragement: he obliged, and warned that a 'new attitude of mind must be attained'. Joseph Rank repeated his well-known view that orders should not be taken which did not yield a profit. In June 1926 Reynolds reinforced Rank's principle: each business should say 'Does that transaction leave me a margin?' Leetham varied Nicholls' line with 'The only way to get a change of mind is by a change of concept'.[17] 'Mutual confidence' had been sought by Reynolds. The change of basic idea had to be towards a clear recognition of 'mutual interest'. Metford confirmed Reynolds' surmise that excess capacity was the most basic difficulty, and reported that 'schemes' had focused on regulation of output and removal of redundant mills. Details of individual situations continued to block progress towards acceptance of each notional scheme. Metford tried to move attention towards practical cost accounting and suggested that NABIM should study 'the practicability and usefulness of establishing a unified costing system for the whole industry'.[18]

The only milling company that provided a substantial public chronicle of policy, problems and overall financial position was Spillers and Associated Industries Ltd, with a record continued from Spillers & Bakers. As a holding company, Spillers summarised group activity, without details about individual mills or milling technology. Nicholls' statements were extensive and, though he referred to the need for discretion, surprising facts emerged.[19] For the year ending January 1925 even Spillers' position was precarious: he reported that 'one sixth [of the group's profits] was obtained as flour millers and five sixths as merchants'. In the following year the group made a loss of £429,392. Ordinary dividend had been high in 1924 and 1925, but fell to 2.5 per cent in 1926. The values of shares dropped dramatically. Sir Gilbert Garnsey of Price,

Waterhouse & Co. was consulted. He recommended that trading operations should be centralised under one organisation. The holding company was replaced by a trading company, and a central board supervised milling managements in four regions. Activity in Canada was reduced. The reshaped milling business was named Spillers Ltd, with E. A. V. Baker as chairman. The new scheme of management came into effect in February 1927. *Milling* commented on the report to Spillers' next AGM, observing that millers had little information beyond their own experience from which to judge their prospects as 'reports of flour milling companies are few and far between'. Flour manufacture was seen as 'a gamble, a deplorable fate for an indispensable industry'. The Spillers' AGM of 1927 mentioned that their mill at Birkenhead, built in 1915 adjacent to Ranks' new mill, but left empty, had at last been started up. Robinsons of Rochdale had supplied the machinery.

After the war, there was a short period when mills required refurbishment, but then it was necessary to look for orders overseas. Henry Simon Ltd needed to reconsider their facilities. E. D. Simon had noted in 1921 that 'we now manufacture everything ourselves except roller mills, for the milling department'.[20] In 1923 it was decided to build a new works, particularly in response to the importance of the export trade. An initial plan was to build in the Manchester residential district of Fallowfield, but there were objections from landowners, residents and allotment holders. Sir William Milligan observed that 'people connected with the Infirmary, the University and the Manchester Girls' High School lived in the neighbourhood ... it would be penny-wise pound-foolish to drive them away'. Although the City Council approved 'provided that the works were electrically driven and that no smoke or noise or smell were emitted', Cheadle Heath was considered and chosen, and the new works opened in 1926.[21]

Reviewing his company's trade during 1926, E. D. Simon reported that the total value of orders received was 'the best in the history of the company, with the exception of the boom year of 1920', even though business in the UK had been depressed. Henry Simon's old headquarters at Mount Street continued in use until 1930, when the drawing office and commercial office staff moved to the works. The works at Stalybridge and Bredbury were not adequate for long-term planning and modernisation, but there had been a waiting time until sufficient capital accumulated. The long relationship with Bühler Brothers at Uzwil finished, and they extended their own market for milling machinery. Machine design, manufacture, and system development had all benefited from interaction between several firms, notably with Bühlers. Until at least 1930 E. D. Simon retained a personal interest in studies of the basic milling operations. Simon wrote later about the successive 'generations' of the firm:[22] the first was clearly Henry Simon's creation, the third would be moulded by younger managers; in between there was transition, and an appropriate time for new planning.

There was an irony in E. D. Simon's continuing interest in 'the physical science of flour milling', the title of a text published in his name in 1930. In 1924 E. A. Fisher, Director of the recently formed Millers' Research Association, had said that milling machinery was not designed on a basis of fundamental knowledge but 'just built', but at the end of 1925 he reported that it was 'not practicable at present to study, for example, the theory of breaking or the action of purifiers'! [23] His scope was reduced further when it became clear in the middle of 1926 that the demonstration mill had failed financially. About the same time the new laboratories at St Albans were ready for use. The work there passed scrutiny by the Department of Scientific and Industrial Research (DSIR) Inspection Committee in 1928 and a basis was formed for sophisticated investigations and for the establishment of a practical advice service. Expansion of resources, including more staff, depended on recruitment of more members. In 1929 the Research Association had a membership of sixty-two firms. From an inauspicious start the laboratories and the information service developed to a position of usefulness and importance. When he addressed NABIM for the first time Fisher overemphasised a contrast between empirical and scientific investigations. Concurrently, at the more modest end of the scientific and technological spectrum, efforts were being made to modernise technical education. Within the new NJIC structure, the first conference of teachers of flour milling technology was held in 1925, and during 1926 there was much debate about a new study syllabus; as usual, there was some agitation against scientific aspects.

The prominent miller on the NJIC was A. E. Humphries, with his leading role in strengthening industrial relations, and a keen interest in technical education. He was also a leading member of the Research Association, hoping to see progress in the study of wheat. Another member of the small research committee was Charles Woodland Chitty; his experience at his mill in Dover, combined with early experimental work at Woodlands laboratories there, gave him a wider perspective than some colleagues possessed. Woodlands Ltd, founded in 1912, was extended in size and influence in the 1920s by the innovative chemist D. W. Kent-Jones.[24] Chitty, Kent-Jones and E. D. Simon all had experience of empirical methods and empirical knowledge, in Simon's case both from his background in professional engineering and also from a long collaborative relationship with Woodlands. A common interest was the application of flour treatment processes, a subject of serious concern amongst millers during the 1920s, emphasising the gap between remote aspirations at St Albans and current challenges. Kent-Jones wrote common sense articles, and included up-to-date appraisals in the second edition of his text *Modern Cereal Chemistry*; in 1927 a review in *Milling* referred to 'extraordinary advances in cereal chemistry', even since 1924.[25] His expositions on bleaching and flour improvers, and on the nutritive value of bread related to two major current issues. Food faddists again had been making accusations and journalists had assisted campaigns. The public were alarmed, confused or not listening, in unknown proportions.

A Departmental Committee of the Ministry of Health was asked to study flour treatment: the use of bleaching agents and improvers. P. R. Reynolds and A. E. Humphries had given evidence before the end of 1924 but, to the inconvenience of the industry, the report did not appear until 1927. In 1923

Neville Chamberlain, then Minister of Health, had appointed a committee to enquire into the use of preservatives and colouring matter in food. Encouraged by the NABIM Flour Committee, the Departmental Committee agreed to consider whether flour treatment would in future be regarded as permissible or might be restricted. Reynolds reported at length to the Association in March 1925 and explained that the official investigations were 'really in continuance' of discussions with the Local Government Board in 1911. Reynolds stated that flour bleaching was 'purely a matter arising from the public taste', meaning the demand for white flour. There had been allegations that some treatments masked the presence of bran fragments. Kent-Jones and others rejected the idea that bran specks could be hidden. It was maintained that improvers did improve flour and help the bakers; Kent-Jones stated that 'it must not be forgotten that the baker uses them also, and perhaps to a more marked degree'.

In a new campaign against white bread, the New Health Society provided a base for Sir William Arbuthnot Lane, who *Milling* described as 'devoting his life to the exaltation of brown bread, chiding millers for giving bran to pigs and the public for consenting to it'.[26] A white bread versus wholemeal bread contest developed. Most of the polemic could have been countered from old evidence, but there was also a new suggestion that millers were devitaminising bread, and that white bread was deficient in vitamin B. It was still held, and by an increasing number of available academic experts, that white bread was a valuable food and that in wholemeal the bran acted as a deterrent to the process of digestion and the function of assimilation. From NABIM G. H. Ball sent questionnaires to more than 1,000 physicians and found that most of them ate white bread. Rear Admiral Beamish MP, a director of Henry Simon Ltd, tried to induce Mr Chamberlain to comment on the 'periodic denunciation of this staple article of diet'. Chamberlain replied 'I do not pretend to give opinions on scientific subjects'.[27]

The Departmental Committee reported in March 1927. They were 'not prepared on the present knowledge available' to recommend that the bleaching agents and improvers then in use should be prohibited, though they hoped that 'improvement' might be effected by physical means. The report was described at length in *Milling* in March and the same issue carried a brief statement that Chitty and Kent-Jones had patented a method of heat treatment. The committee thought manufacturers and millers should make declarations to customers about bleaching agents and improvers, with information about substances used and quantities. A. E. Humphries wrote to several newspapers, stressing that the report was a 'masterly document'; as its title was the 'treatment of flour with chemical substances', Humphries also tried to show that the word 'chemical' could cause difficulties: many foods contained chemicals, salt was sodium chloride, and some soups contained calcium phosphate from the natural ingredients, which as self-raising flour was useful for cakes and scones.[28] There was no further official action at that time. Kent-Jones (1939) stated that 'the report stands merely as a recommendation. No regulations, based on the report, have so far been issued'.[29]

A group of physiologists and physicians, three of them at London University, wrote to *The Lancet* to refute the faddists. They stated that it was 'difficult for a European to omit essential quantities of vitamin B from the diet which perhaps ignored variations in economic and social conditions, but there was a common sense point that 'Important and frequently overlooked factors in the selection of a dietary are palatability and appearance'. In 1927 Kent-Jones wrote a forceful but humorous article for *The Miller*: 'When the brown bread exponent gleefully announces that white bread kills rats, he might truthfully say that wholemeal bread kills guinea pigs. All such statements are only misleading'.[30] Yet he took seriously the work of Professor R. H. A. Plimmer on the sensitivity of pigeons to absence of vitamin B, and concluded 'The more we know about vitamins and the nutritive value of foods the better'.

Vitamins were still a mystery to millers and most other people in the early 1920s. Successive editions of Kent-Jones' text show gradually increasing understanding of their functions and complex molecular structures. Storck & Teague (1952) referred to social and occupational contexts of changing nutritional ideas in the 1930s, from 'energy-giving characteristics of foods to their protective aspects';[31] the result was the adoption of a new practice of enriching flour. Winifred Cullis, a Professor of Physiology at London, told a *Daily Express* reporter that 'we do not eat bread mainly as a source of vitamins, but as a food. Vitamins are not a food'. She also suggested that 'The brown bread fanatics should learn common sense'. Thomas Russell would have approved her description of white bread as 'a magnificent food'. Many people liked brown bread, but they did not represent a large proportion of the population. In 1926 the chairman of Hovis Ltd had reported that in Great Britain '95 per cent of the sales of bread were in respect of white bread'.

A rational solution

F. K. S. Metford addressed the NABIM spring meeting in 1928 with many practical problems in mind. He welcomed the constructive tone of some leading newspapers, especially the *Daily Express*, but warned that the danger of recent attacks on the trade, in effect the white bread scare, was 'not that the public would turn from white bread to brown, but that they would abandon bread altogether in favour of pre-packed foods'. Another worry was that some politicians had ideas for reorganisation of the milling industry. At Association meetings the millers had always avoided reference to politics, but the general strike in 1926 had been unsettling. Largely through the personal accord between A. E. Humphries and Ernest Bevin much had been achieved within the NJIC to establish mutual trust in industrial relations practice.[32] At the end of 1927 L. H. Green, secretary of both the Flour Milling Employers Federation and the Joint Industrial Council for the Flour Milling Industry, stated that 'the general strike came as a great shock'. He did not mean that there had been no prior anxiety, but that the pioneering work of the NJIC was jeopardised; it was fortunate that there had been joint interest in non-contentious subjects, particularly the successful development of technical education. Humphries and Bevin moved quickly to restore a basis for collaboration, issuing a joint statement that the trades unions concerned would not in future instruct members to strike without exhausting negotiation procedures.

In the wider contexts of the milling industry's external connections with the public, with official bodies, and to a changing political climate, the leaders of the Association needed more urgently to form a policy for decisive action. Other important industries had excess capacity and dwindling profitability, so the millers were not peculiar in seeking an improved form of commercial organisation. However, some of the supposed basic principles were in doubt. W. A. Vernon, who had put faith in advertising, had been convinced that the demand for flour was diminishing, and others agreed. Humphries was adamant that although demand for bread might be less, the requirement for flour remained fairly constant.[33] Voller was concerned about increasing sales of confectionery, which should not have been alarming unless he did not like cake, especially if Humphries was correct in asserting that aggregate flour demand was steady. Humphries also reckoned that in 'any period exceeding a few weeks the quantity of flour made is the quantity sold and delivered'. Overproduction was a complicated flux of regional imbalances, accentuated by salesmen's efforts to drum up trade, so creating a pseudo-excess production situation. Several leading millers decided that the basic problem was over capacity, and that became the general conclusion. As capacity was merely a potential to produce, output was the active ingredient. In large businesses idle plant might not have been easily tolerated, and there could have been a simple policy of keeping output up and then exerting sales pressure. Amongst medium size businesses, Humphries, Voller and the west country miller Charles Richardson advocated two-shift working. Humphries' argument was that an increased cost per sack for two-shift running should be weighed against losses incurred in accepting cut prices on at least some sales.[34] But many millers would have been wary of reducing output if there were a consequent risk of having a low datum in an eventual rationalisation scheme.

An increasingly noticed method of reducing national capacity was to close as 'redundant' mills where there was out-of-date machinery, or site or location drawbacks, or firms that might agree to close down if compensated. For some southern millers, candidates for closure were thought to be in the north. When Bristol millers suggested that there should be a scheme for the regulation of output, Reynolds said that there were as many ways as there were members of the Trade Development and Improvements Committee. A new vocabulary was needed and a new orientation. John White, ex-secretary of NABIM and member of a well-known Scottish milling family, wrote a series of articles for *The Miller* between 1926 to 1928.[35] He supported regulation of output, confirmed that production should be related to consumption and, like Leetham, differentiated between regulation and restriction. Metford deduced, perhaps incorrectly, that the Liberal Party had connected rationalisation to rationing, if only of valuable resources and energies. Many people must have wondered what rationalisation really meant, or what it might turn out to be.

There was an emerging topic of 'rationalisation or nationalisation', relevant also to other industries. White wrote that he was convinced that 'if the leaders of the industry do not move quickly the Labour leaders will do so'. At the Liverpool Convention in 1928 Leetham added to the vocabulary for change: 'Each member appears to have about the same amount of trade as he had two or three years ago. Consequently I do not think that there is the same trouble of arriving at a quota'.[36] The new President was James Voase Rank. Rank's address was read by G. H. Ball, but there was a dramatic item. Active members knew that in May 1927 a meeting of representatives from the local associations had decided to approach Joseph Rank Ltd and Spillers Ltd, asking the two companies to meet and try to formulate proposals for reorganisation of the trade. In 1929 J. V. Rank stated that 'we found it very difficult to evolve any set of principles which the trade as a whole would accept'. *The Miller* had already hinted at 'deadlock'.

The year 1928 marked the National Association's golden jubilee. *Milling* celebrated with a special issue, including G. H. Ball's historical review. Joseph Rank wrote about his early experience and frugality; the journal added merely that he was Governing Director of his company, with a manufacturing capacity of more than 700 sacks of flour per hour. Henry Simon Ltd advertised '50 years of progress' since the installation in 1878 for McDougall at Manchester, and described the Cheadle Heath works as 'certainly the most modern, and, we believe, the best equipped flour milling engineering works in the world'. At the Liverpool Convention E. D. Simon presented a paper on 'Flour milling research', describing attempts to calculate costs and benefits of innovation. He also suggested that tests should be devised to determine how much bran powder was present and how much was made by attrition during specific milling operations. Larger bran particles could be removed from the flour during processing, but bran powder could not be extracted. If a test for bran powder could be developed and standardised, attrition could be studied throughout the milling process. There was a research project at Simons to devise a testing technique which might show where process changes were needed and then detect whether progress was made.[37] This raised the question of how far might it be possible to go towards precision of description and measurement in the engineering science, and also in the more abstruse field of cereal chemistry.

Simon observed that 'there is today no recognised means of recording scientifically the quality and sizes of the particles of a given stock'. He also noted that Fisher had 'stated that there is no scientific definition of strength except the power to make a dough which the baker likes and a bread which the consumer likes'. Fisher, Humphries and Reynolds did not welcome someone else talking about research, and responded unconstructively. Together, they shifted the paper out of the spotlight, and it was left to Kent-Jones to provide light relief and a warning that large bakeries in America had chemists who specified requirements to millers in terms of quantitative test data. An opportunity had been missed in not inviting him to provide a paper on a cereal chemist's puzzles: the tangle of argument about strength, his own experiments with colour assessment, and the mysteries of an important but frequently overlooked variable – the flavour of bread. It must have become clear throughout the milling industry that lack of early momentum in the St Albans project was largely due to absence of a philosophy of inclusiveness.

The *Corn Trade News* was first with the sensational announcement in September 1928 that Spillers Ltd and Joseph Rank Ltd, acting together, had bought H. Leetham & Sons. *Milling* referred to 'mutual arrangement', *The Miller* to 'mutual understanding'; might Ranks and Spillers have further joint purposes? It was reported that there had been rumours for more than a year, but when Sidney Leetham met his shareholders he said that negotiations with a view to selling were begun by H. E. Leetham in 1922.[38] The business had been built up to include seven other smaller firms, the combination having a total capacity of 215 sacks of flour per hour. Spillers acquired H. Leetham & Sons at York, Roger Shackleton & Son at Leeds and Messrs C. D. Mills at York, with an aggregate capacity of 140 sacks per hour. Ranks acquired Cleveland Flour Mills of Thornaby-on-Tees, A. & R. Appleton at Hull, Elland Flour Mills, and Wm Metcalfe & Sons at Malton. There were poignant events later: Sidney Leetham's demise in 1929, a fortnight before the formation of the MMA was announced, the dismantling of Leethams' Hungate Mills in 1931 and their simultaneous destruction by fire.

In 1929 the tone of Association meetings changed. Without public commentary, restrained hopefulness replaced the previous frustration of division. At the spring meeting, J. V. Rank hoped that members would not think that he had been idle. On 31 August 1929 *Milling* broke the big news 'Rationalisation of the flour milling industry', with the admission or boast that it had 'been known for some time in the best informed circles that negotiations were going on to place the flour milling industry on a sounder basis, and latterly market gossip has been confirmed by a certain amount of circumstantial evidence'. An official statement was issued from the Association offices that 'A new organisation, called "The Millers Mutual Association" has been formed'.[39] Price fixing was 'definitely excluded'. Some 'redundant mills in uneconomic positions' would be closed down. An output quota was allotted to each member, the quota being related to the previous volume of trade. If a quota was exceeded an extra premium was required; for a shortfall there was compensation, but not without limit. G. H. Ball was appointed secretary of the MMA.[40] There was effective communication with trades unions, newspapers and the editors of bakery trade journals, resulting in general acceptance and approval. The CWS did not join the MMA, but in terms of the flour output of mills throughout England and Wales 95 per cent of the rest of the industry soon became members. The initial intention was that the MMA should operate for ten years, but the scheme continued, with modifications. In June 1929 the Purchase Finance Co. Ltd was registered, to deal with the purchase and closure of redundant mills; the directors were J. V. Rank, Samuel Armstrong of Ipswich, E. A. V. Baker of Spillers, J. K. S. Metford, W. H. Paul of Birkenhead, P. R. Reynolds and B. C. Robinson – chairman of Associated London Flour Millers Ltd.[41]

James Rank received the plaudits for finding ways round the obstacles, launching the MMA and ensuring that it became established. The journals hoped that they would soon be able to publish full details of the MMA arrangements. Reasons for reticence included the incompleteness of membership, vulnerability to speculative opinion, the need to gain initial experience, and a reasonable right to at least some privacy. National economic conditions were hazardous. *The Miller* had an editorial in May 1930: 'Mill nationalisation soon?' Political concern had been aired by A. E. Humphries at the annual dinner of the Flour Milling Employers Federation in April 1929, but cheerful news was received at a similar event in April 1931, when Miss Bondfield, the Minister of Labour, commended the employers: She approved progress in industrial relations provisions during rationalisation, including helpful measures to deal with employee redundancy, and a pension scheme. 'You have, I think, been hiding your light under a bushel too much. You should have your good works blazoned on the house tops'.

Political difficulties

The MMA may have been essential for commercial stability. NABIM was indispensable in reforming ill-conceived Government plans. Previously, political comment had been avoided at main millers' meetings, but bureaucratic interference from March 1930 to November 1932 could not be ignored, despite a Minister of Agriculture's statement that impositions aimed at the milling industry were the 'Government's affair and nobody else's'. A threat was contained in new uses for the word 'quota'. Initially it meant a protective device for the compulsory use of home-grown wheat, adopted in much of Europe from 1928 onwards. Soon it denoted also a sellers' market in wheat, promoted by Canadian politicians. Millers thought that they would all have to use some English wheat and, as there was also talk of an import board to control overseas supplies, the overall impression was of official meddling. NABIM President Savory described proposals for an English wheat quota as a 'death knell of the country millers', a dramatic phrase from a genial miller, who probably envisaged raised costs of English wheat at a time when state-subsidised Continental flours were already affecting the country milling trade.

A. E. Humphries, the leader of the cause for English wheat growing, thought it unnecessary to 'resort to compulsory powers' but the Government objective remained a demand that millers would use 15 per cent of English wheat and also 55 per cent of Dominion wheat. Sir Malcolm Robertson, chairman of Spillers Ltd, wrote to *The Times* at the end of 1931 that the quota scheme was 'cumbersome, uneconomic, and unworkable'. The Government refused to consult, but eventually returned for advice and accepted guidance, particularly from Samuel Armstrong of Ipswich, long regarded as the Association's expert on political difficulties. The Wheat Act of May 1932 was milder than feared, at least in effect, though Robertson was purposely undiplomatic about 'the art of word jumbling' by Parliamentary draftsmen. Nicholls wrote that it was 'utterly wrong to make wheat growing a charge upon the milling industry'.[42]

Lord Peel was appointed chairman of the Wheat Commission, to control the working of the Act; he made a radio broadcast, giving a neat summary of the unnecessary legislation. The 84,000 wheat farmers would register with merchants,

2,000 of whom would issue certificates; there were fifty-four local committees to hear appeals.[43] Each year, the average price of English wheat would be deducted from a standard price of forty-five shillings per quarter of 504 lb of wheat, the result being the deficiency payment for each grower of millable wheat. The Commission was to levy two shillings and three pence (later increased) on each sack of flour produced by every flour miller, 1,800 provender millers being exempt. As Nicholls pointed out, a simple tariff on imported flour would have helped all millers, raised employment prospects, and provided more wheatfeed (rejected milling products) for livestock farmers. The quota principle remained as an estimated six million quarters of English wheat per year which would be subsidised.

Conferences were held in London and Ottawa to encourage imperial preference in commodity trading, with particular attention to wheat. There was an absence of reciprocal attitudes: a suggestion to exchange surpluses of coal and wheat was not welcomed. The situation was affected by the development of state-aided wheat pools and that became a major problem for the British milling industry. An early tactic had been to hold up supplies of Manitoba wheat and complain when alternatives were used; from 1928 onwards, Argentine supplies were strategically important. The trade analyst Sydney Gampell explained repeatedly how Canadian leaders sought domination of wheat supplies to Britain, which implied ultimate and not very distant control of prices and of the British milling industry.[44] The Canadian Premier hoped to increase a notional Dominion quota of 55 per cent of British imports to 70 per cent, a 'tied house' as *The Miller* made clear. The complex subject of wheat supply was the most obvious topic in the journals from 1930 to 1933, but many warnings and Gampell's exposure of political and commercial manoeuvrings were not officially recognised. Only strenuous efforts by NABIM President Norman Vernon and colleagues at a fateful meeting in Ottawa ensured that the plan to impose a quota was abandoned. The Ottawa Agreements Bill of November 1932 placed a duty of two shillings per quarter on non-Empire wheat imported into Britain and 10 per cent on the price of non-Empire flour. Vernon reported that the British Government 'seem very loath to give us a square deal by safeguarding us against dumping and unfair and subsidised competition'.

New confidence

The year 1930 was one of unrelieved gloom, when *The Miller* observed that 'the MMA entered its second year with the world in a topsy turvy state', and the chairman of Associated London Flour Millers Ltd (ALFM) reported 'extreme severity of competition'. There were fluctuating and falling markets in wheat, flour and wheatfeed. Continental countries continued to dump state-subsidized flour in Britain. In 1931 it was estimated that flour imports into London had been equivalent to 225 sacks per hour of milling capacity, or more than the output of two very large mills, or the Leethams group on three shifts. The ALFM Sun Mills at Bromley-by-Bow were temporarily shut down, yet by July 1931 ALFM had decided to build a large new London mill at the Royal Victoria

Docks, which would facilitate rationalization within their group. The new site was just to the west of the Millennium and Ranks' Premier Mills.[45] Fortunes varied around Britain and Carrs Flour Mills Ltd celebrated the centenary of the arrival of J. D. Carr at Carlisle in 1831, but modestly, acknowledging both the loss of the chairman, ex-NABIM President Theodore Carr, and the current national economic difficulties.

With the subject of quotas still much in the foreground, and concern increasing, the industry started towards a remarkable resurgence. Spillers exemplified the trends. Early in 1930 it was known that Spillers had acquired Marshalls' Victoria Mills at Grimsby, apparently with involvement of the MMA. There was anxiety at York and Grimsby about employment and associated effects. Leethams' mill was closed; there had been a continual disadvantage of bringing in wheat via the River Ouse, and the York mill needed remodelling. Spillers' Cardiff & Channel Mills also received attention, one of the three mills on the East Dock being modernised by the introduction of the Simon Alphega-Plansifter system. Boardroom changes followed mistakenly adventurous trading in maize. The new 'independent chairman', Sir Malcolm Robertson, was an ex-diplomat and recently ambassador at Buenos Aires.[46] He took charge late in 1930 and his first AGM review, in May 1931, was regarded as 'masterly'. He reported that Spilllers had abandoned speculative grain dealing and were relying on manufacturing which was, in effect, a hopeful endorsement of the rationalisation processes.

At Spillers' AGM in 1932 it was announced that sites for large new mills had been sought at Cardiff's Roath Docks and at Avonmouth.[47] Both sites

Figure 106.
Spillers' Roath Mills
of 1933 at Cardiff.
(A. Simon, 1947)

would provide deep water port facilities, and would lead to the replacement of out-of-date mills in their south west regional organisation. By the autumn two long-established businesses at Glasgow had been acquired, the Scotstoun mill from John White & Sons Ltd and the Craighall Mill. Spillers' dividend on their ordinary shares was 15 per cent, described by Robertson as 'a bumper year'.[48] Ranks were busy with large construction projects, the Pacific Mills at Belfast, and the Solent Mills at Southampton.[49] Also in 1932 they acquired Josh Appleby & Sons Ltd with their Carolina Mill at Bootle and Daisyfield Mill at Blackburn, and an aggregate capacity approaching 80 sacks per hour.[50] In November there was a rumour concerning ALFM and then news about the clearest step towards concentration since Vernons' amalgamation with Spillers in 1920 and the purchase of Leethams in 1928: a controlling interest in ALFM had been acquired by Ranks, the whole of the issued share capital being acquired during 1933.[51] In December 1932 *The Miller* reported the extent of issued capital by ALFM Ltd £1,530,256; Joseph Rank Ltd (still a private company) £4,206,500; and Spillers Ltd £3,803,674, those valuations being by various entries in *Milling*, appropriate to a new financial awareness. London Stock Exchange prices for shares in milling companies became a feature of increasing interest from 1934.

Figure 108.
Spillers' Avonmouth
Mills of 1934.
(A. Simon, 1947)

In November 1933 Ranks became a public company, acquiring the whole of the issued share capital of Joseph Rank Ltd. The journals carried an unprecedented and identical feature, a summary 'history of the House of Rank'. It included a listing of mills and capacities, including mills built by Rank totalling 580 sacks per hour, ALFM capacity 220 sacks per hour, and other acquisitions from 1920 onwards with a total capacity of 390 sacks per hour, all together 1,190 sacks per hour.[52] Only the first stage of the new Belfast mill was included; the Southampton mill was not ready and not included. Although there would have been many remodellings, there was confirmation elsewhere of an aggregate of more than 1,200 sacks per hour. A revised valuation for Ranks Ltd was £7,295,600; average profit for the three years ending July 1, 1933 was reported to be £829,743 per annum, a return on capital of a little over 11 per cent if reckoned simply on the current revaluation. A minority of the shares was sold; control of the business was unchanged.

The Miller referred to the 'new milling plants of colossal proportions' and reported that there were remodellings and extensions 'throughout the kingdom', though there was comparatively little published information. Ranks waited for trade to improve after installing a 40 sacks per hour plant at Southampton. The latest versions of the Simon system were celebrated in a publication from Cheadle Heath showing Empire, Avonmouth and Roath projects, each for 100 sacks per hour.[53] Much of the structural engineering for Spillers was reinforced concrete, also the wheat storage silos for all three, not an aesthetically attractive material but in several cases adding to the powerful appearance of the modern mill. Layouts and looks of the big mills varied, but together they represented another stage of modernisation. The machinery for Ranks Pacific and Solent Mills was largely from E. R. & F. Turner. At the Empire Mills some Robinson machines were incorporated, but the latest mills were so extensive that it was difficult for the journals to provide full descriptions. 'Britain's largest mill' was the title claimed in 1934 by the CWS for their vast long-established and

Figure 109.
Applebys' Carolina
Mill at Bootle about
1930. (Author's
collection)

therefore old-fashioned looking Sun Mills at Manchester's Trafford Park, with a capacity of 240 sacks per hour.[54] In 1933 and 1934 all three of the mills there were modernised, two by Thomas Robinson & Son, who were also responsible for remodellings at other CWS sites. At Trafford Park Simons dealt with the other mill, providing a complete refit with new plant. Soon the CWS were conjuring with ideas for a giant mill at the Port of London which would 'eclipse' all their previous projects.

When Spillers started planning their mill at Roath Dock in 1932 it might have seemed that their remodel at Cardiff's East Dock in 1930 was wasted, but the earlier work was a large-scale experiment to assess the latest version of the Simon system in comparison with the performance of their existing mills nearby. Five breaks were tried, in contrast with Spillers' previous use of short systems of three breaks. The normal standard and Simons' preference for four breaks was adopted for Roath. Simons had been increasing the number of rolls used and the number of stages of reduction, to provide a main feature in new work of 'long [extended] roller surface', emphasised by E. D. Simon (1930).[55] He also stated that 'classification and purification of the stocks have been substantially improved', the overall advance being 'the elaboration and perfection of the diagram' – the processing scheme, showing the flows of stocks from each machine to others. In the latest projects roll surface (total of the lengths of roll pairs used) was increased to appreciably more than 100 inches per sack of flour per hour. A modest 20 sacks plant might require 50 inches of surface for breaks plus scratch rolls, and 70 inches for reduction, using possibly a total of thirty or more double roller mills. Without even mention of the purifying operation, the elaboration was apparent to designer and customer. Long roller mill surfaces had been used before but J. F. Lockwood, Simons' chief milling expert, stated in 1936 that there had been a steady increase 'over the past thirty years and the outcome of an increase has always been a marked improvement in the quality of the flour'.

The current objectives were to grind more gently and make less bran powder, also to keep the stock cool and minimise evaporation loss. Water cooling of the rolls was also included at Roath, a 'vogue' of the 1930s, according to J. H. Scott (1972); a member of Simons' technical staff, Scott had been enthusiastic, including a relevant chapter in his text *Flour milling processes* of 1936. E. D. Simon (1934) summarised a general aim: it was necessary to keep the stock dry enough to obtain efficient sifting and separating, and moist enough to ensure that the bran was not unnecessarily broken.[56] Overwarm stock sometimes 'sweated', a continuing challenge to designers seeking to extend the usefulness of plansifters, which were used as scalpers after the first three breaks at Roath. As E. D. Simon (1930) stated, most milling machines were still being

Figure 110. Empire Mills at London in the mid-1930s. (Simon Ltd, 1937)

Figure 111.
CWS Sun Mills,
Manchester, 1934:
largest capacity in
Britain. (*Milling*,
December 1934)

Figure 112.
Cranfields' mill at
Ipswich in 1935. (*The
Miller*, December 1936)

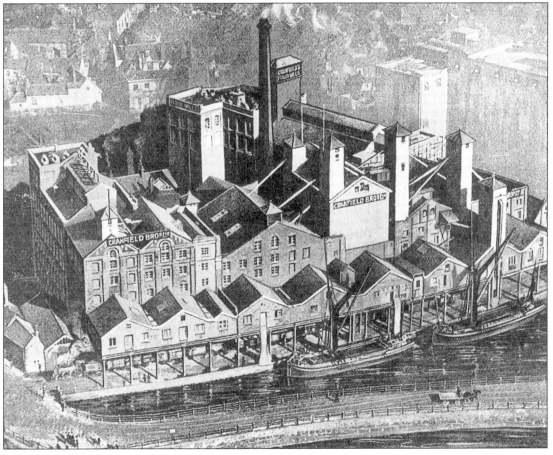

designed 'on a purely empirical basis'; his text, which benefited from assistance by several members of staff, was an attempt to try to encourage discussion of technical difficulties. Dr Fisher retained his lofty attitude to 'rudimentary knowledge', criticising the book for lack of mathematical equations. Lively argument and distinct approval appeared in journal columns, and the inclusion in the text of Simon's previous paper on conditioning was continually relevant. An obvious gap was an exposition on rolls: their speeds, fluting details, and performance; much was still standard practice from long before, but Scott (1936) provided a substantial exposition of current practice.

Simon dealt with processing puzzles, avoiding overlap with straightforward information, much of which was presented in the NJIC series of technical education pamphlets, sold for sixpence each, and intended for a wider audience in the mills, but Scott's text was needed as a review for technologists. Technical education was thriving: at the end of 1934 the NJIC reported a total of 630 students enrolled in formal flour milling classes at twelve centres, including 224 students at Liverpool.[57] As a general resource and for use by students remote from main centres a comprehensive text was required, and supplied by Leslie Smith, who had served an apprenticeship under Voller, managed Ranks' mill at Barry Dock and was later with Robinsons at Rochdale.[58] Smith provided an extensive correspondence text, dispensed via *Milling*, and reprinted in inexpensive book form by Robinsons in 1936. A more sophisticated exposition was by J. F. Lockwood, the modern classic *Flour milling* of 1945; Lockwood

Figure 113.
Simons' Cheadle Heath works, opened in 1926. (Simon Ltd, 1930)

succeeded R. J. Fowler as chief milling expert at Cheadle Heath from 1934. Fowler had joined Henry Simon in 1889 and acquired a high reputation as a technical authority, also the amused regard of a chief accountant, who described him as 'a personage'; he went to Silloth near Carlisle to manage Carrs' mills. E. D. Simon, who became Sir Ernest in the new year list of 1932, wished to devote himself to public work; he resigned the chairmanship of the company

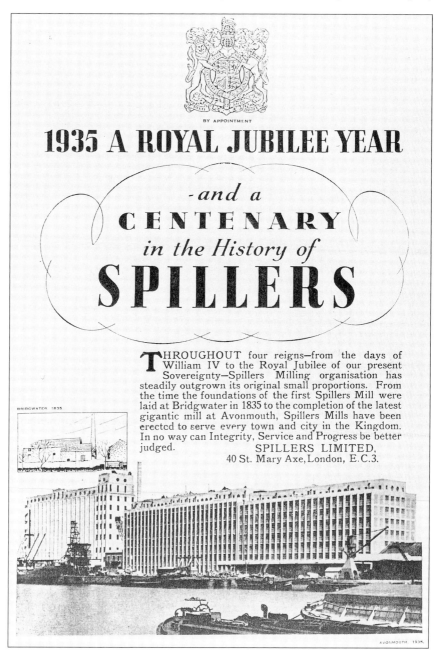

BY APPOINTMENT

1935 A ROYAL JUBILEE YEAR

-and a

CENTENARY

in the History of

SPILLERS

BRIDGWATER 1835

THROUGHOUT four reigns—from the days of William IV to the Royal Jubilee of our present Sovereignty—Spillers Milling organisation has steadily outgrown its original small proportions. From the time the foundations of the first Spillers Mill were laid at Bridgwater in 1835 to the completion of the latest gigantic mill at Avonmouth, Spillers Mills have been erected to serve every town and city in the Kingdom. In no way can Integrity, Service and Progress be better judged.   SPILLERS LIMITED,
40 St. Mary Axe, London, E.C.3.

AVONMOUTH, 1935.

Figure 114.
Spillers' 'Centenary'.
(*Milling*, April 1935)

313

and was succeeded from 1934 by Cecil Bentham, who had planned the Cheadle Heath works. Lockwood and three other senior staff joined the board in 1935.[59]

The NABIM President in 1934 was Alexander Dence, chairman of Hovis. Having acquired Marriage Neave & Co. Ltd at London and Humphries & Bobbet at Bristol during the 1920s, and with plans for remodelling at Manchester, Hovis had a capacity of about 160 sacks of flour per hour,[60] possibly next in size after the three leaders of the industry, and had a specialist market position. Dence was nicely placed to assess difficulties in other sectors: loss of export opportunities, a surge in flour imports from Europe, and continuing change in dietary preferences. The Irish Free State prohibited flour imports from England, previously a million sacks a year, an unfortunate loss of trade for millers in north west England. During the early 1930s the country millers' most obvious adversaries were not the port millers, but Continental suppliers who sent state-subsidised products at prices far below the cost of production and transport. The grades sent approximated in quality to much of the English wheat flour production, on which many country millers relied for business with the packet flour and biscuit trades.

Dence, Armstrong and colleagues, including a petitioning group of seventy-nine country millers, tried to convince government officials that the dumping was flagrant.[61] Perhaps the Import Duties Advisory Committee looked at flour imports data for a long time span and decided that the industry knew how to survive and make profits. Dence and the seventy-nine petitioners considered the situation alarming; they and F. K. S. Metford at Gloucester expected more closures of country mills. Refusal to defend country millers against disruption from abroad mocked official pretence of support for English agriculture, but officialdom compounded previous political interference with indifference to the consequences. Changing social and domestic conditions, even at a time of national economic stringency, made an impact everywhere in the industry.

The bakery trade was increasingly mechanised. Sliced bread had been known in London since 1929, waxed bread wrappers became popular in Britain in the early 1920s. These were additional moves towards convenience foods.[62] In the magazine *Punch*, the humorist A. P. Herbert described bread 'not as a staple food of man but as the principal condiment. It is an admirable adjunct to almost every food'. It was 'the perfect platform for an egg' and 'for mopping up delicious gravy its value [was] undeniable'. His message was that 'Bread has no independent existence of its own' and his least humorous contribution was 'The people do not want bread'.[63] In 1934 A. E. Humphries informed the NJIC that 'we have to face up to the fact that consumption [per head of the population] of flour, as well as of bread, has gone down materially'.[64] Advertising was essential. The MMA, appropriately as an industry-wide organisation, diversified into that area of responsibility. Bread weeks were launched in selected towns: posters, displays paraded on lorries, exhibitions, literature, cookery demonstrations. The Arsenal footballers 'testified to the energy value of bread', and so did the Oxford and Cambridge boat race crews. The prominent slogan was 'Bread for energy'. Feminine attention to fashion and figure consciousness was not helpful, but in America 'bread energy for vitality' was a response, with inspiration from glamour photography. Although the Kodak camera was widely available, visualisation was not yet a universal habit in Britain, so the energy theme was preferred to Thomas Russell's possibly better notion of 1925: 'You can have such perfectly mouth-watering posters'. Some of the nation's energy was used to celebrate the reign of King George V. Much was written in the journals about milling and engineering achievements, expressed with optimism. There were large advertisements including '1935 A Royal Jubilee Year and a centenary of the history of Spillers'. *The Miller* definitely had a claim to fame – sixty influential years.

By 1935, there was a clearly modern flour milling industry in Britain. According to J. F. Lockwood in 1936 there was 'a mild boom in mill construction', a modest statement for readers of *American Miller*;[65] Henry Simon Ltd continued as the prominent British milling engineers and there were further large projects at Newcastle-on-Tyne and Avonmouth. Simons' new work for Spillers at Newcastle was completed in 1939 and at about the same time they finished a large installation for Hosegood Industries Ltd at Avonmouth. Spillers acquired a controlling interest in Hosegoods and that Avonmouth site was still in use at the end of the century, lasting longer than their slightly earlier and much celebrated Avonmouth mill. In 1937 Spillers decided to concentrate production at their newer mill at Beaufort Road, on the south side of the deep water West Float at Birkenhead, in preference to the old Vernons' site at Dock Road, on the north side of the East Float at Seacombe. The CWS intention of moving their London area production to a deep water site at the Victoria Docks, with room for further expansion, led to another Simon contract, with frustrated attempts to complete during wartime. In contrast with this vigorous activity there were some areas of contraction during the later 1930s, notably in the northwest and partly due to loss of trade with the Irish Free State. In 1938 Ranks obtained control of John Greenwood Millers (1934) Ltd, the large Lancashire business founded at Burnley in 1825, extended at Blackburn, and also in 1912 at Manchester's Trafford Park. In 1938 there was an end of an era in Liverpool: it was reported that the Millers' Mutual Association had purchased the goodwill of the flour milling part of the North Shore Mill Company's business, though trading was to continue, particularly the provender business. The North Shore site at Boundary Street was the location of Henry Simon's largest early installations. The Vernon site at Seacombe had been the scene of his last major project.

Part IV

☙

Epilogue

CHAPTER SIXTEEN

The later twentieth century

The earlier history of the flour milling industry could not be written without the massive resources of the journals, but the later twentieth century has no similarly comprehensive main sources. A detailed history of the industry from the 1940s to the millennium requires a team of commentators: miller, engineer, chemist, administrator, food scientist. Milling, milling engineering and cereals science have become increasingly sophisticated, and there are at least three obstacles to comprehensive appraisal: the large milling companies have complex financial and commercial contexts; background knowledge in chemistry and biology has advanced well beyond simple non-scientific terminology; and it has not been feasible for the various journals to provide detailed records and interpretations of the whole scene. In these ways, as for many industries, an outline can be presented, but expertise and actuality can be appreciated fully only by those within or close to the action. There are problems of technical and commercial sensitivity which a team aspiring to write the fully detailed history of the last fifty years will find difficult. It is hoped that this outline might tangibly assist further work, to record continuing hazards and achievements.

The widespread destruction of 1939–45 was followed by massive reconstruction projects, continuing through the early 1950s. During the next twenty years there were radical alterations in the organisation of the industry. In the 1980s the principles of automation were increasingly applied, and during the 1990s there have been further technical developments, accompanied by dramatic commercial change. The most striking structural changes in the industry are described here, including in text and illustrations the fate or after-lives of some earlier roller milling firms. The record is on-going, never complete and inevitably unsatisfactory for all who wish to find more. It is notable that aspects of recent practice may be traced back to precursors between 1875 and 1935.

Destruction and rebuilding

Many port mills were severely damaged during wartime bombing, including in 1940 Ranks' Solent Mills, and in 1941 their Ocean Mills at Birkenhead and Buchanans' Mill. Paul Bros' mill was destroyed. Ranks' Clarence Mills at Hull were burned out.[1] At London's Victoria Docks, Ranks' Premier Mills were destroyed, also Spillers' Millennium Mill. Nearby, the new CWS mill remained unfinished but escaped disaster. Ready for use in 1945,[2] it was curiously similar in general appearance to some of Le Corbusier's Unité d'Habitation designs of the next five years; much earlier he had described 'American grain elevators and factories [as] the magnificent first fruits of a new age'.[3]

Between 1945 and 1954 there were massive reconstructions at the ports. Spillers' projects included Pauls' mill at Seacombe, that business and the Homepride flour brand having been acquired in 1945, and the rebuilding of another wartime casualty: the Swan Mills at Hull where the separate firms of Rishworth, Ingleby and Lofthouse had amalgamated in 1900. A new Millennium Mill was built at London's Victoria Docks. At the opening, Wilfred Vernon of the leading dynasty of millers within the group said 'I think it is important that industrial buildings, which may last a century, and which must be functional, must not be eyesores'.[4] The latest large port mills were architecturally impressive but they were not all destined to reach the next millennium.

Just before the war Ranks had been preparing a new site at Gateshead; the construction of the Baltic Mills there was the start of their post-war programme of modernisation. The Solent Mills were rebuilt and new Clarence Mills constructed. Robinsons supplied the machinery for Southampton and J. V. Rank described the mill as 'the finest possible development of scientific and practical milling capacity'.[5] Of Joseph Rank's three sons, James succeeded to the chairmanship of the company in 1943, Rowland had been independently based at Mark Mayhew Ltd at Battersea, and J. Arthur Rank, both a miller and a prominent film-maker, became chairman in 1952. Production was resumed at the rebuilt Premier Mills in 1954. Rowland Rank's son Joseph McArthur, joined Joseph Rank Ltd in 1936 and Ranks' board in 1948, becoming joint managing

Figure 115.
CWS new mill at Silvertown, London, completed in 1945.
(A. Simon, 1947)

director in 1955 [6] and chairman in 1969; he was the last of that milling dynasty and retired in 1981.

Many of the large installations were Simon plants, including a new mill for Hovis Ltd at Manchester's Trafford Park in 1953. Illustrations in *the Simon Engineering Group* by Anthony Simon (1953) show that at Hovis and elsewhere pneumatic handling of mill stocks was accepted practice. Seemingly a secondary feature amongst many aspects of technical improvement, pneumatic handling of materials-in-process was actually a significant advance. It was pioneered by Bühlers in Switzerland and introduced in the UK by Spillers on the initiative of Vernon and C. P. Rishworth.[7] For many years grain had been transferred from boat to mill silo pneumatically, but within the mills the movement of mill stocks had been through conveyors, elevators and wooden spouting. The new method moved stock in airflows through sleek metal tubing, removing the nuisance of moth pest and consequent cleaning problems; materials in transit between operations were cooler, reducing the problem of moist components blinding sieve covers. This contributed to a more general acceptance of plansifters, and the approach to the 'all-plansifter mill', with rolls and purifiers of course, but at last marking the obsolescence of the centrifugal as an old relic.

Even before post-war reconstruction was fully effective, J. H. Scott (1949)

Figure 116. Coxes Lock mill prior to conversion into flats. (Author, 1986)

had noted that machines were 'smoother externally, streamlined' and 'often simpler and more easy to control', also a 'tendency to adopt built-in or individual motors' and 'increasing use of electrical controls'.[8] That was the position in many industries and would lead gradually towards the so-called age of automation, often proclaimed speculatively but prematurely. Scott considered the possible characteristics of 'flour mills of the future' in a series of articles which were themselves innovatory, as a fashion for detailed forecasting of technical futures was not prevalent until the early 1960s. He raised the possibility of a 'radically new method of obtaining flour from wheat'. The idea of producing creaseless wheat, not much mentioned since the 1920s, was not often regarded seriously until the end of the century. Scott paid more attention to a supposed desirability of a 'more compact' break operation, and in shortening the reduction process, and those were good shots at a distant target. He judged correctly that pneumatic conveying would be successful, expected that mill interiors would have 'harmonies of colour with everywhere shining cleanliness and most striking of all, very little noise'. Mill environments were improved, but when processing requirements included faster throughput and more robust treatment of materials-in-process, the big modern mill became noisier. Scott was accurate in anticipating 'a certain amount of getting together of mills and bakeries', and that became the most pervasive factor governing later developments and the structure of the milling industry.

Supply – or demand for white sliced bread?

Normality in the sense of release from governmental control was delayed after the war, with many forms of stringency: restrictions on building and even bread rationing from 1946 to 1948. The government decided to retain control of wheat buying, so the Liverpool Wheat Futures Market could not reopen. International trade was transferred to the Chicago Market and not recovered later.[9] By 1953, with much reconstruction accomplished, it became possible to take more far-reaching initiatives. Recognising the changing methods and structure of the baking industry, Spillers and Ranks decided to acquire plant bakeries. Allied Bakeries Ltd were expanding a plant bakery and retail shops business, based on a preliminary stage in the 1930s, when Garfield Weston extended his bakery business from Canada and the United States to Britain. By 1954 the company had seventy UK plant bakeries and acquired sixteen more and hundreds of bakers' shops by 1958.[10] As Spillers and Ranks consolidated their integration forward into baking, Allied Bakeries Ltd integrated in the other direction, the group entering the milling industry in 1961, the management divisions for milling and baking then being governed by Associated British Foods Ltd; between 1961 and 1963 ABF Ltd acquired thirty mills.

There was another major long-term influence on the baking industry, facilitating further mechanisation and automatic control of large scale bread production methods. Commercial bread making had involved a long process of dough-mixing, dividing, proving, moulding, baking and cooling. In 1961 the Chorleywood Bread Process was introduced commercially, in which a short

period of intensive mechanical working of the dough replaced the traditional lengthy fermentation period: weaker flour could be used, yielding more loaves, which were expected to keep better. Research staff at the British Baking Industries Research Association at Chorleywood reported the commercial and technical advantages, stating that bread made by the new process was softer and whiter and that taste panels had concluded that flavour was similar to conventional products.[11] Industrial planning was conducted in a climate of exhortation to pursue 'economic growth', a subject of renewed interest in the 1950s and increasing prominence through the 1960s. But scaling up and modernisation in any industry depended on market potential and availability of capital.

Response varied from tactical action to resignation. Millers in Kent, east of the Medway, provide examples. The Charlton Mill site at Dover was bought by G. W. Chitty & Co. in 1865, before which they had worked several windmills near Deal. Charlton Mill was burned out during the 1939–45 war as a result of shelling from the French coast and Charles Chitty decided not to rebuild even though he had intended that his nephew should take over the business. Most of Chitty's flour trade was with small bakery businesses, which he described as 'on the way to extinction. We should have had to find almost all our customers among the big plant bakeries'.[12] Mill capacity had been 18 sacks per hour since 1922, but trading prospects were always uncertain. Some form of

Figure 118.
Marriages' mill at
Colchester, converted
to a hotel. (Author,
1995)

business collaboration was continued until 1957, followed by sale of the goodwill to Charles Brown & Co. Ltd of London and Croydon, that company being acquired later by Spillers.

There was also at Dover the flour milling partnership of W. & E. Mannering, at Buckland Mill from the 1870s, with earlier family milling activity nearby since 1836 and experience of four watermills. A frequent contributor of reminiscences to *Milling*, John Mannering wrote in 1957 that on 'June 6th of this year the feed ran off the breaks for the last time'. He recognised that in the nineteenth century 'five and eight sack plants in many a country town turned a blind eye upon the windmills which, one after another were standing motionless upon the hills', and concluded that 'the vast changes in the pattern of the baking industry will inevitably leave many a country mill silent by its stream'. John Mannering was still philosophical twenty years later, the mill emptied of machinery, the unchanged office still a place for good-humoured conversation.[13] The Dover mills were not on a dockside, nor was the Isle of Thanet Mill at Ramsgate, owned by C. J. Hudson Ltd, with a milling tradition started in the eighteenth century. All three were in coastal towns, but even a 5 sacks per hour mill, as at Buckland, needed a substantial customer base when merely on day work and not working weekends, possibly requiring 15,000 flour consumers. During the war continuous working was needed to make up for the losses at the major ports, but by the mid-1950s trade for many small town millers had dwindled.

At Chatham, W. Hooker & Son Ltd hoped to expand. Wingent & Kimmins Town Mills on the edge of the Medway had been idle for several years during the 1920s. Herbert Hooker moved from the family firm in Canterbury, to renovate the Chatham mill. The Hooker family had progressed from a rural windmill and a small water mill near Canterbury. At Chatham there was a remodelling by Simons in 1928. Pneumatic conveying was introduced in 1956 and the capacity raised to 13 sacks. At about that time there was an amalgamation with Hudsons at Ramsgate to form Hooker & Hudson Ltd. In 1959 E. Marriage & Son Ltd of Colchester and Felixstowe took over Hooker & Hudson. In 1960 Hovis McDougall Ltd acquired E. Marriage.[14] In 1962 Ranks Hovis McDougall was formed, Hooker & Hudson being taken into the group. The Chatham mill was dismantled in the mid-1970s. The ex-Hudson Isle of Thanet Mill continued, also Hookers' other competitors, H. S. Pledge & Sons Ltd at Ashford, where the Victoria Mill, built in 1890 for the Pledges, was run from 1910 to the mid 1980s by successive members of the Garnham family. An elderly Mr Garnham attributed continuation of the business to his son's interest in practical milling. They described the firm as 'Independent millers of quality flours'.[15] In Essex, Marriages' East Mills at Colchester, remained in production until the mid 1970s; their East Anglia Mills at Felixstowe continued through the 1990s. With these changes, more family names of independent millers were displaced. In the south east, two names had the distinction of representation on the celebrated visit of millers to Vienna and Budapest in 1877, when Wilson Marriage was the leader and George Chitty the eldest of the party.[16]

There were some unifying influences. The National Association was instrumental in bringing together individual millers and executives with varying business interests within a formal organisation and on social occasions. In addition to administrative tasks the staff of the Association were to be increasingly concerned in the gathering, analysis and dissemination of official information, often related to EC regulations. As milling and baking became more closely connected there was another development to provide background support for all millers. The big groups had their own research departments, and the Research Association of British Flour Millers, founded in 1923, moved from St Albans to Chorleywood to join the British Baking Industries Research Association, formed in 1946.[17] The combination continued there as the Flour Milling & Baking Research Association (FMBRA) until 1995, when the Campden & Chorleywood Food Research Association was set up; at Chipping Campden there had been experimental work on food preservation since 1919.

Three big groups

From the 1950s to 1960 the number of UK flour mills decreased steadily or markedly, capacity was concentrated and old plant discarded.[18] Between 1957 and 1961 the Millers' Mutual Association purchased the goodwill and plant of forty-four firms, including in 1959 Edward Hutchinson Ltd at Liverpool and Barrow-in-Furness, previously amongst the most prominent Lancashire milling businesses. In the mid 1960s the production units, which evolved as Allied Mills Ltd, encompassed twenty-three milling companies. Some were relatively small concerns, but there were familiar names within the group: James Fairclough & Sons Ltd at Warrington, the Coxes Lock Milling Co. at Weybridge, Healings at Tewkesbury, and Reynolds at Gloucester. Spillers referred to their eleven milling branches, mainly at the ports, their consolidated network developed over a long period of experience through amalgamation, absorption, construction, and rationalisation of their accumulating resources. Many branches had traditional roots in previous family milling firms, most prominently the Vernon family. In 1965 Sir Wilfred Vernon was succeeded as chairman by Sir Archibald Forbes who handed over to Michael Vernon in 1968. Beyond milling, Spillers developed their second national organisation, United Bakeries. They extended their interests in provender and other animal food products, followed by moves into a variety of agricultural and food industry businesses.[19]

Ranks Hovis McDougall Ltd (RHM), the holding company formed in 1962, encompassed five trading divisions or management companies, two of them becoming the largest milling company in the UK and the largest bakery enterprise. Ranks' earlier notable acquisitions had included the previously sturdily independent north west millers Buchanans, Applebys and Greenwoods, and in 1933 the group of well-known firms which had constituted Associated London Flour Millers Ltd. Hovis McDougall Ltd had been formed on 1st January 1957. The subsequent merger with Ranks gave greater prominence to a range of well-known brands: Hovis flour was sold throughout the country and McDougall's self-raising flour was familiar to most household cooks. J. Arthur

Figure 119. Leethams' mill building at York, converted into flats. (Author, 2000)

Rank presided over both the far-reaching moves into baking and this broadening of the milling base. He and his nephew and successor Joseph extended the group's interest into agricultural merchanting and to well-known brands of grocers' goods. To mark their centenary in 1975 Ranks published a booklet *RHM 1875–1975*. Their official history of the first eighty years had been neatly composed in 1955. The centenary memento commented on recent progress, up to 1969: 'In 20 years the company had changed almost beyond recognition. With products ranging from flour, bread and cakes, salt and gravy powder, cereals and crispbread, spaghetti and biscuits, soups and tinned foods, it could justifiably claim that every larder in Britain held at least one RHM product'.[20]

Leadership amongst the big groups was liable to change or at least to be contested. The CWS may have aspired to the title before 1939 and possibly until 1951, but as the other big milling groups progressed in the 1960s the policy of CWS milling changed from forceful independence towards supposed advantages of combination, though optimism was followed by a seemingly fading presence. In 1971 CWS milling and baking interests were merged with those of J. W. French & Son Ltd, a subsidiary of J. Lyons & Co. Ltd, to form J. W. French (Milling & Baking Holdings) Ltd. Spillers' milling, baking and animal feeds interests were merged with that new amalgamation to form Spillers-French Holdings Ltd;[21] the financial structure of the increasingly linked milling and baking industries was becoming more complex. The involvement of the CWS might have seemed surprising, as within the Cooperative movement it had been claimed that the CWS mills were a safeguard against monopoly and that Cooperative bakeries ensured modest bread pricing. In 1971 the CWS hoped to 'capture a far greater part of the national bread and flour market as well as to gain essential economies of production'. It was reported that the CWS and Lyons shared control equally in the first amalgamation and that Spillers Ltd 'owned' 75 per cent of the larger combination.

Also between the mid 1960s and 1973 the milling resources of the ABF group were modernised and rationalised. A majority shareholding in Chancelot Mill Ltd at Edinburgh was obtained from the Scottish CWS. New mills were built at Tilbury and Liverpool. In 1972 the well-known firm of Cranfield Brothers Ltd at Ipswich was acquired. Other plants were remodelled and fourteen mills were closed. The structure of the milling industry was being simplified by concentration of capacity, and was also more complicated in relation to the diverse activities of the largest organisations. There was increasing awareness of 'the big three' milling and baking groups: ABF, RHM and Spillers.

On 1 October 1973 the Department of Trade and Industry referred the 'Supply in the United Kingdom of wheat flour and of bread made from wheat flour' to the Monopolies and Mergers Commission (MMC), whose investigation ended with their report on 14 July 1977. The journal *The Miller* had ceased publication in 1950; otherwise it might well have called it 'a damp squib'. *Milling* managed a few column inches, headed 'Bread and flour – nothing wrong!' The journal's conclusion was: 'The Commission habitually used the phrase "not against the public interest" when its investigations find nothing wrong. In the

Figure 120.
Cranfields' mill at
Ipswich, closed in
1999. (Author, 1996)

cases of these two inter-linked industries it might have been fairer to say that their nationally vital activities were "in the public interest".[22]

The structures of the 'big three' milling and baking groups were investigated in considerable detail. The Commission discovered 'a modest level of profitability' and many instances of losses, especially on an inflation adjusted basis. This was described as 'not surprising since the price of bread is severely limited by statutory controls'. The bread industry was supposedly freed from controls in 1956, but intervention and regulation continued in various forms. Millers, bakers, retailers, bureacracy and the public were involved in a complex web of commercial interaction. Estimates were made of consumption and expenditure from information obtained in surveys. From 1956 to 1976 weekly domestic consumption of bread decreased markedly. Consumption of household flour decreased to 1967 but then increased moderately. Estimates of consumption of bread plus flour suggested that in 1956 there was still more than 3.5 lbs consumed domestically per person per week, in 1967 less than 3 lbs and in 1976 about 2.5 lbs; these calculations did not include bread consumed non-domestically. Bread and flour were still important foods, but not so prominently the universal source of energy and protein. Bread was not an expensive commodity. Between 1956 and 1974 average household expenditure on bread and flour was a small proportion of total food purchases, estimated as approximately 7 per cent.[23]

As with previous official enquiries the duration was a nuisance and the activity curiously zealous. However the report did contain interesting data. For instance, it was stated that 'At least 75 per cent of all bread is now baked in plant bakeries by the Chorleywood Bread Process', and that whereas 'there were 24,000 bakers and confectioners in Britain in 1935' the number of master bakers who were producing bread in the UK in 1975 was approximately 5,500.[24] The big groups were said to 'account for about 80 per cent of the supply of flour and 60 per cent of the supply of bread' in the UK. The numbers of flour mills operated by the groups and by thirty-nine independent millers were tabulated to show variation of size expressed as sacks per hour capacity. The number of hours worked per week ranged from 60 hours for some of the smaller mills to 160 hours.

Capacities in sacks per hour	Numbers of mills operated in UK[25]			
	RHM (1973)	ABF (1976)	Spillers (1976)	Others (c. 1976)
100 or more	7	2	4	4
80–99	1	1	5	2
60–79	6	2	2	6
40–59		4	4	5
less than 40	7	12	2	30
Totals	21	21	17	47

In 1978 Spillers decided to withdraw from bread baking. It was reported that thirteen bakeries were sold, and the remainder closed; three flour mills were closed. Also in 1978 the National Association reached its centenary; *Milling* commemorated the achievement. In 1979 it reported that it was 150 years since Joel Spiller started a one-man business at Bridgwater in Somerset, and there was up-to-date news: Dalgety Ltd, an international trading company, had acquired control of Spillers.

During the last years of the twentieth century there have been surprising rearrangements of industrial structures and ownership. In 1985 the milling engineering company Robinsons of Rochdale was sold, and in 1987 became the Thomas Robinson Group Plc, which purchased the Simon milling engineering business in 1988, forming Robinsons Milling Systems Ltd. The flour milling engineering interests of the Robinson Group were purchased by the Satake Corporation of Japan in 1991.[26] In 1998 there were several reorganisations among prominent milling companies. The MMC had stated that previously 26 per cent of total UK flour production was by Allied Mills, 24 per cent by Rank Hovis, and about 13 per cent from Spillers, so that more than a third of output was from the rest of the industry. The Kerry Group Plc of Ireland acquired the Spillers milling business from Dalgety, and soon afterwards Tomkins Plc acquired six of the seven Spillers mills from Kerry. The DTI (Department of Trade and Industry) referred the situation to the MMC; as a result of their report,[27] Tomkins were instructed to sell four of the Spillers mills, which were bought by Archer Daniels Midland Co. (ADM) of Illinois. It was reported that 'ADM Milling is North America's largest flour milling company, operating twenty-nine mills in the United States and eleven in Canada'. ADM acquired mills at

Newcastle, Liverpool (previously Wilson King), Avonmouth (originally Hosegoods), and Tilbury (once CWS). Large milling businesses include Smiths Flour Mills (Northern Foods Plc), Heygates Ltd, Wm Nelstrop & Co. Ltd and Carr's Flour Mills Ltd. Other millers include specialists in the wholemeal trade. One large capacity mill produces flour for starch and gluten production. In July 2000 the *Financial Times* reported that Tomkins had 'confirmed the sale of RHM' to 'the private equity group Doughty Hanson'. Apparently there had been plans to demerge RHM for 'more than a year'.

Interactions

The machinery used in flour mills has been modified and hopefully improved many times. In comparison with small or medium mills that were occasionally or only partially remodelled, a fully modernised large mill of the later 1970s was a revelation, the smart appearance of the machine rooms often allied appropriately with an attractive brochure illustrating a variety of bread and flour-based food; millers' advertising was becoming freed from previous confinement to flour brand names. An up-to-date mill of the 1980s represented another considerable advance, and the technical design options of the 1990s increased markedly. In 1996–97 white bread was still the predominant end-product, using 55 per cent of UK flour; wholemeal bread plus brown bread used 9 per cent. Now three-quarters of the UK bread supply is sold through the grocery multiples. The closer commercial connections between milling and baking and the scaling up of production units have led to a stronger interaction between milling requirements and engineering possibilities; either can propel the other. The large scale flour customer specifies flour quality more precisely than previously, and the large scale flour maker is a potential customer for technical improvements if they are likely to be profitable, not a new relationship, but with much greater impact on capital expenditure and commercial prospects than previously.

The whole supply-demand chain from wheat growers to bread eaters, with milling engineers having to study all the links, was altered by a surprising increase in the use of English wheat. Everything, and certainly the field of engineering design, was affected. Until the 1970s most British millers reckoned that strong Canadian wheat was essential for white bread flour. H. L. Garnham of Ashford said 'You can't make a loaf of bread for the English public out of English wheat. It would be soggy. It wouldn't be appetising'. He had tried using English wheat up to a proportion of 40 per cent but frequent complaints obliged him to revert to 20 per cent. In many mills, wheat purchases were two-thirds Canadian, and in large port mills there was little call for English wheat, even of supposedly improved varieties. English wheat could be used for cake and biscuit flour. Several factors combined to bring English wheat into favour: the availability of improved varieties; EU regulations imposing import duties on non-European wheat; widespread adoption of the Chorleywood Breadmaking Process; the addition of gluten in the milling process to make up for the lower protein levels of English wheat. By the 1980s home-grown wheat provided about two-thirds of the UK supplies and during the 1990s more than 80 per cent. One obvious effect would be that inland sites would gain importance if in largely urban regions, near them, or near eastern county wheat growing areas.

Figure 122.
Carrs' mill at Silloth in Cumbria. (Author, 2000)

332

Figure 123.
Nelstrops' mill at
Stockport. (Author,
1989)

English weather was once a crucial factor and may again have some influence. Canadian wheat, which was previously essential, is still an important commodity. Future patterns of wheat supply might be affected by the condition of British agriculture and policies in middle Europe.

Inside the mills progress from 1950 to the end of the century might be considered in two phases. Up the 1970s there were significant advances in machinery design within established milling practice. Many improvements in the complex interaction of processing operations were forecast by J. H. Scott, and in more controversial style by John Speight.[28] Speight was a miller who had managed Marriages' mill at Felixstowe. Before the war, he produced ideas that would make a distinct impact on plansifter design. Speight changed a long-accepted geometrical arrangement, facilitating access to the sieves, which had always been a problem. He dispensed with impeller slats previously required to move stock along the sieves: an ingenious device became unnecessary gadgetry. Scott assessed the new effects and approved. Speight's design was successful in the mills, but was superseded when design was focused on increased capacity requirements. A non-technical visitor to a modern mill might regard the plansifter as a rumbling box but, as with the purifier, it is possible to separate materials into different components and sizes with remarkable discrimination. Speight often wrote as if he despaired of the gradualness of overall technical progress, but in the 1950s he described his effort to change just one aspect of plansifter design with the comment that at one stage 'the task appeared to be almost impossible, until ...'. He then turned the sieves at right angles to the customary alignment and other alterations followed. Scott (1972) stated that the development of machines for 'all the diverse stock separating, grading and dressing operations in the mills has involved immense ingenuity'.

Purifier design also improved markedly from the later 1950s. Following ten years of post-war work in their R & D department, Simons produced their type S machine. They had listed nine design principles including economy of space and elimination of 'gadgets'. The outcome was neatly stylish, no longer a bulky container for contraptions such as tins or channels, or nozzles and trays, all devices to remove smaller bran fragments: . The new versions from all purifier designers again extended into series of new models, typically incorporating double sieve decks to improve purification. Reversions or revivals were also possible. During their very earliest experiments Robinsons of Rochdale had tried the Excelsior purifier from America, in which small free-roving rubber balls were used to clear sieve mesh. Automatic brushing replaced those and other strange devices, and became the standard, though still much criticised. The Excelsior type device may still be seen in revived and improved form, with plastic balls that bounce, hover, dart and collide again with the purifier mesh, fascinating to watch.

Principles and details were frequently reviewed, including the importance of the purifier: the sharpest question was 'are purifiers necessary?' *The Miller* had warned against misuse and disuse, but had itself disappeared in 1950. The journal *Milling* encouraged conjecture about all parts of the process and in the 1960s Speight observed that a purifier-less mill could produce flour from soft wheat, or a single grade for special purposes. Scott confirmed the need for

Figure 124. Ranks' modernised mill at Manchester. (supplied by Rank Hovis Ltd)

purification to obtain high grade flours, suggesting that more definite data of the effect of purifiers on flour colour should be sought; he hoped the millers' Research Association would investigate that 'old and much debated milling question'.

Even the roller mill was challenged and in the 1960s Speight asked 'Will it survive?'[29] He wrote: 'this simple machine, often described as a superior metal roller, double differentially speeded mangle, housed in a metal framework, has defied all attempts to replace it', but he considered that even the modern 'streamlined affair' still had a relatively low capacity. Some of Speight's criticisms and implied exhortations were echoes of J. H. Scott's post-war views: Scott moved from Simons and was not so bound by collective technical assessment. He had a possibly unequalled knowledge of the chronicle of design changes. Speight, like W. T. Bates long before, drew on practical experience to support a skill as a controversialist. But there were serious puzzles, such as the optimum rate of flow of grain to the break rolls. An old suggestion to photograph the action had been too difficult to accomplish, but by the 1960s evidence from high-speed photography confirmed that fluted rolls had much more free surface space than coverage with grain. Scott (1936) already knew that from his own calculations, but had regarded the margin of space as desirable. The contrast with the perception of a substantial curtain of stock falling from a pair of rolls may have provoked fresh discussion, and would have been a lively topic in drawing offices. However, implications were that capacity could be increased, flow sheets possibly simplified and fluting should be studied further, though there were other problems to consider, including the feed of material to the rolls and the possibility of air turbulence created at the approach to the roll nip. The mechanical science of flour milling machine design involved far more intricacy than would be imagined by a casual observer.

The roller mill has had an amazing history of change through hundreds of variants, many notable mainly for novelty, and some would be candidates for a collection dedicated to Heath Robinson, the artist who delighted in contraptions. An early one would be Smith, Dell & Stewart's combination of rotary motion with transverse reciprocating motion. In contrast, there have been revivals of previous unusual configurations. Between 1900 and 1914 there were several unusual designs, including Simons' 8-roll mill, with a pair of rolls in diagonal placement above another pair, the four reflected on the other side of the machine; wheat passed through two pairs, with or without intermediate sieving. In an old catalogue the design looks ponderous, and nearly Heath Robinson, yet a sophisticated version of the 8-roll mill is an important feature of some of the most modern UK mills, part of a more compact process of faster throughput and greater intensity of action.

There are varying requirements across the UK milling industry, making generalisation difficult, but the number of roller mills required for the break process in large modern UK mills is now often markedly less than twenty years ago. Then, the total break surface (total length of roll pairs) was often in a range 40 inches per sack of flour production per hour, plus or minus 5 inches; for a stipulated mill capacity, the number of roller mills required can be deduced. Now, there may be an allocation of 5mm per kg of wheat ground in 24 hours (rather less for short systems), and that is equivalent to 8 inches per sack per hour in the previous units. With this decrease by a factor of five or more, milling plants clearly may be more compact, and when 8-roll mills are used for the first two breaks, the trend is reinforced. Roll speeds, material feed rates and applied pressures have been altered appropriately, and effects of new processing criteria have rippled through the entire system.

When Scott and Speight and others had wondered about alternatives to the roller mill and the whole system, Speight thought 'a new concept will arise' and Scott stated that a new development might 'render present milling methods obsolete virtually overnight'. The notion of creaseless wheat was a question for botanists, not yet for geneticists. They reviewed other long-familiar speculations. Could the bran be removed by a chemical treatment? Was it possible to peel or abrade the bran from the grain? During the 1990s there has been renewed interest in what is now known as debranning, and accumulating experience with alternative techniques in particular mills. Wilkinson (1996) has referred to the 'Tkac' method in use at Goole for E. Timm & Son.[30] B. C. McGee (1995) has described the 'Peritec' process and its application,[31] developed by the Satake Corporation, which Nelstrops at Stockport are using. The break process in conventional practice still normally comprises four or five stages, but might that be altered radically? There is a hint of expectation in the currently changing milling vocabulary, where a recent term 'traditional milling' no longer refers to millstone practice, but has alternatives of 'conventional' or 'classic', with the implication that a new modernity is coming.

During the last twenty years, automatic process control represents the biggest technical change in milling. As in other industries, there was a period of gradually increasing experience of remote control of starting, stopping, and routine procedures and sequences, using electric relay switching circuits; the states of production activities and general plant conditions were indicated by lights on diagrammatic displays. That methodology was a useful preliminary to the development of control systems based on miniaturised electronic components and logic circuits. Control of milling processes, using PLC (programmable logic controller) microprocessors was introduced into UK mills from the late 1970s. Advance depended on more sophisticated instrumentation techniques for use on-line, to test materials moving through the system and adjust processing operations. There was renewed incentive to review machine designs, to achieve greater functional precision, and ensure effective operation at higher capacities.

Before automatic process control was developed product quality tests were made in control laboratories, and research results also were evaluated away from the machinery: there was a barrier to progress. On-line instrumentation was the key to control of system variables, through measurement, the initiation of adjustments to the process, and the provision of data to monitor performance. J. Watson (1984) referred to 'crude on-line instrumentation' of the early 1980s,[32] but there was then tangible progress and the development of integrated control systems, using several or more PLCs to regulate parts of the milling process, with a master microprocessor in a position of overall supervision and control. Monitor screens, grouped together, allowed continuous scrutiny of the whole process. Input of instructions at microprocessor keyboards provided centralised command of process changes, material flows and plant adjustments. Hierarchies of controls were developed to increase scope for interaction between parts of the process, with the possibility of moving beyond a repertoire of standardised responses towards a regime that could include anticipatory regulation. J. Watson (1984) discussed the dependence of mill control on the prior control of wheat blending and conditioning, to ensure consistency of the grist. Control of raw material specification was accompanied by refinements through the process. Roll adjustments were controlled automatically and more accurately than Scott (1972) had believed possible. The milling operations were regulated to ensure specifications were met for moisture levels, protein content and the extent of flour extractions. Flexibility of controlled flour blending procedures made it possible to meet customer requirements that were stringent and urgent – a 'just-in-time' basis of production. Complete organisation and predictable results were required for a whole plant to operate for an extended period without close personal supervision; when achieved, another new term entered the vocabulary: 'lights out plants', although they were not completely unattended.

In 1985 *Milling* described the Rank Hovis mill at Trafford Park with its modernised Simon plant, stating that 'An impressive level of automation has been achieved'.[33] There were further installations by Satake UK Ltd, which had absorbed Simons, and in 1994 it was stated that 'The process control system at the Manchester mill is at least as comprehensive and technically advanced as that in any flour mill in the world'. In 1997 production started at the Allied Mills Coronet Mill, also at Manchester, which the American journal *World Grain* later described as part of 'One of the largest flour mill and modernization programs in North America or Europe, if not the largest – the £100 million Project Apollo of Allied Mills Ltd, England'.[34] The project has been based on Bühler equipment including the now clearly established eight-roller mill. The chairman and chief executive of Allied Mills stated that 'we have built flour mills to be run by millers, not computer-driven factories as some might think'. In a series of articles in the British journal *Cereals International*, Gavin Owens (1997) has also been philosophical: 'judgements and skill as well as experience are required to make informed decisions. The future of the miller is safe for some time to come'.[35] The full effects and reactions to so-called automation are not yet clear. In Continental Europe there is much more variation in conditions: in 1998 France had 673 flour mills and Germany had 515,[36] but elsewhere there is growing emphasis on international perspectives.

Whatever happens next in the UK, in large scale production many processing actions are more efficient within automatic control regimes. There may be advances in instrumentation techniques. High grade flours are expected to look good and to meet various quality stipulations. In the early days of roller milling 80 per cent extraction indicated a rough product. Now, extraction ranges from the previous standard 72 per cent to about 80 per cent. Processing is more precise, but many millers and bakers need to know how much bran is present. E. D. Simon (1928) discussed the difficulty of measuring the amount of bran powder in a given stock, in order to assess machine performance. Scott (1962) suggested that 'more accurate colour grading and other test equipment' could be used to determine the effect of changes in the purifying process. Improved testing techniques are now applied through the sequence of milling operations, contrasting with the more rudimentary methods familiar to Simon and Scott. A possible application is in the 'Branscan' range of instruments, using image analysis. The contribution of dark particles, contrasting with the light endosperm background in a digitised image is automatically measured and recorded. The on-line versions of Branscan, which provide continuous monitoring of flours or blends, are available for incorporation into process control systems to optimise profitability and product quality.[37]

A significant advance which affects the milling process is the combination of the chemistry and biological science of wheat and flour. From the 1960s a growing field of research has progressed from topics that would once have appeared obscure to many millers and milling engineers. There is now so much applicability that the field of investigation known as 'technology of cereals' guides all modern milling practice. Kent & Evers (1994) stated that 'The complexity of cereal proteins is enormous', determination of the structure of gluten, which 'is responsible for the dough-forming capacity of wheat flour',

Figure 126.
Huffkins, craft baker
in Burford,
Oxfordshire. (Author,
2000)

being a formidable problem.[38] The statement preceded lengthy discussion, which is a reminder that expert knowledge is not easily represented in everyday language, without over-simplification, as in the current comic caption 'organic flour'. Official reports have often included curious comments about milling. The MMC report of 1977 referred prematurely to 'the highly automated port mills'. An MMC report of 1998 stated that flour milling 'is a relatively low technology process and technical advancement has been confined to automation, quality control and the speed and scale of milling plants', remarks oddly reminiscent of John Speight in a whimsical mood. A gulf exists between practical referential experience and public perception.

The text book literature of the British milling industry, dealing with the mechanics of processing, began with Voller's first edition of 1889 and seems to have finished with Lockwood's last edition of 1960; since then it has been increasingly difficult to bring together the principles of diverse subjects and clear insights into intricacies without extensive detail. NABIM has devised a way of assembling basic technical information, moving from a gap-filling provision in the late 1970s to a flexible framework and smart format of Open University style study units.[39] The course is followed by 1000 students, half in the UK, half overseas, showing that, although there has been a trend towards concentration of UK milling capacity, a substantial force of technical millers exists in Britain.[40] It is difficult for contemporary milling journals to describe whatever is typical without appearing at least partly out of date, and this detaches the industry and the actual milling situations from the general literature. As the extensive record contained in older journal volumes survives in only a few libraries, and sometimes in brittle condition, there is a danger that knowledge of routes to the present will be lost.

Many previous suggestions about future technical changes have proved to be realistic, but forecasters might have been surprised by the inter-relations. The newest era of modernisation poses problems in relating future prospects to very expensive capital investment programmes. Prices of ordinary bread are extraordinarily low. Forecasts usually concern trends but there are also less easily discerned interactions. Perhaps Henry Simon should be remembered again for his view that 'there is no finality'.[41]

Notes

Notes to Introduction

1. There were frequent acknowledgements of usefulness and dependability from NABIM and individuals. Also the wealth of material provides many cross checks.
2. Their experience ranged from rural and small town businesses to involvement with a very large firm, and included knowledge of national issues. From this start through their suggestions an extensive network of contacts and sources of information evolved.
3. Henry Simon's statement, *The Miller*, January 1895, supplement.
4. Report of special committee of NABIM, *The Miller*, July 1887, 186–88; *Milling*, October 1901, 228.
5. Final report: first Census of Production of UK (1907), published 1912 [Cd. 6320.]
6. W. R. Voller, 'Events of the past year', *Milling*, December 1909, 700.
7. 'The gluten theory', *The Miller*, June 1904, 181, referring to attempts to improve home-grown wheat.
8. Kent-Jones & Amos (1950), 134.
9. Extensive reviews, both April 1935.
10. With metric units, the equivalent of 1 sack per hour of flour is 4 tonnes of wheat processed per 24 hours at 75% extraction. Calculations are commonly based on 100 kg of wheat per 24 hours; plant capacities in tonnes of wheat per day.

Notes to Chapter 1: A revolutionary change

1. Simon (1886), 6; *The Miller*, April 1879, 86. From August 1880 Simon's statements and advertisements in the journal were often in supplements.
2. Simon (1889), 148.
3. J. H. Clapham, *An economic history of modern Britain* (1932), 89, dealing with industrial change 1850–86; W. Ashworth, *An economic history of England, 1870–1939* (1969), 83; A. E. Musson, *The growth of British industry* (1978), 234; W. Smith, *An economic geography of Great Britain* (1961), 545.
4. W. R. Voller, 'Five decades of flour milling' in "Home made flour", *Milling*, September 1923, 27–33.
5. 'Modern flour mill machinery', *The Engineer*, April 1887, 317.
6. Commentary on the census, *The Miller*, December 1883, 754; February 1894, 520.
7. *The Engineer*, February 1875, 91, 92, 98; February 1873, 95–8
8. There were financial difficulties. The site was still disused in 1890. *The Miller*, June 1890, 140–41.
9. In building projects, leading London millers confirmed their prominence, but they were not yet equipped to counter imports.
10. 'The late James Wood', *The Miller*, October 1887, 357.
11. 'The half-high grinding system', *The Miller*, July 1877, 221–26. John Ure: *The Miller*, July 1885, 453.
12. NABIM AGMs, *The Miller*, June 1881, 292; June 1882, 268.
13. 'The President's speech', *The Miller*, July 1885, 423–25.
14. A. B. Childs & Son: *The Miller*, January 1878, 530 and February 1879, 762.
15. *The Miller*, September 1877, 351; May 1880, 183.

16. David Cecil, *Max* (1964), 4.
17. 'William Dunham', *The Miller*, December 1894, 785–86. Their wide range of equipment was indicated in *The Miller*, January 1876, 335.
18. Dunham's statement: *The Miller*, March 1885, 48.
19. Broomhall's activities: *George Broomhall's Corn Trade News 1888–1938*; also 'G. J. S. Broomhall', *Milling*, June 1938, 801–2.
20. *The Miller*, December 1894, 785–86.
21. Edward Martin, 'Looking backward and forward', *The Miller*, May 1929, 165–66.

Notes to Chapter 2: New processing ideas

1. Lockwood (1945), 31; Voller (1897), 17.
2. NABIM, *Wheat* (1991), 8, Fig. 5.
3. Kick (1878 & 1883, translated H. H. P. Powles, 1888), 212.
4. George Rieger, 'The milling industry at Buda Pesth exhibition', translated for *The Miller*, November 1885, 666–67.
5. 'A pioneer roller mill', *The Miller*, May 1890, 98–9.
6. Oscar Oexle, 'On roller mills', *The Miller*, March 1876, 13.
7. Rhys Jenkins, 'Roller mills: a historical sketch', *The Miller*, July 1887, 200–5 and *The collected papers of Rhys Jenkins* (1936).
8. Oexle, 'On roller mills', *The Miller*, April 1876, 53–5; July 1876, 172. In two series of articles in *The Miller*, starting March 1876 and March 1878, Oexle described the difficulties of rudimentary uses of roller mills.
9. Storck & Teague (1952), 227–28.
10. George Rieger, translated for *The Miller*, December 1885, 709–10.
11. Fourteen mills were listed in *The Miller*, March 1876, 357. Oexle stated in *The Miller*, March 1878, 18 that 'Rollers were used up to 1874 only in two or three mills, and only extensively at the Pesther Walzmühle'.
12. Friedrich Kick, 'Austro-Hungarian high grinding', lecture in Prague translated for *The Miller*, March 1878, 19.
13. Kuhlmann (1929), 125.
14. G. T. Smith, 'The origin of New Process milling', *The Miller*, February 1881, 877. Storck & Teague (1952), 211–15.
15. Storck & Teague (1952), 254; Kuhlmann (1929), 131.
16. Storck & Teague (1952), 207.
17. Scott (1972), 243.
18. Kick (translated Powles 1888), 199.
19. G. T. Smith, *The Miller*, February 1881, 877.
20. Kuhlmann (1929), 118.
21. 'Mr George T. Smith', *The Miller*, November 1883, 665–66 and March 1921, 34–8; works described in April 1884, 114–15.
22. *American Miller*, 1876, 107–8, 140–41.
23. *The Miller*, March 1921, 34–38.
24. Kuhlmann (1929), 125–27.
25. Kuhlmann (1929), 121; Storck & Teague (1952), 229, 235; *American Miller*, July 1876, 48; *The Northwestern Miller*, March 1936, 814.
26. *American Miller*, March 1876 and May onwards.
27. Storck & Teague (1952), 245.
28. *The Northwestern Miller*, March 1936, 814.
29. Storck & Teague (1952), 236–37.
30. W. D. Gray, 'About roller mills' for the *United States Miller*, extracted in *The Miller*, April 1881, 99–103.
31. *The Miller*, May 1876, 166; June 213–17; 226–27.

32. Storck & Teague (1952), 247.
33. Storck & Teague (1952), 246.
34. *The Northwestern Miller*, March 1936, 814.
35. Gibson (1885), 24.
36. Dedrick (1924), 97 stated 'Only in a few cases did American millers attempt to adopt and carry out the full Hungarian system'.
37. *The Miller*, September 1880, 498. Storck & Teague (1952), 252. Hibbard, *The Miller*, September 1880, 489; August 1880, 421–22.
38. Kuhlmann (1929), 131–32; *The Miller*, December 1881, 746–48.
39. Storck & Teague (1952), 254; *The Miller*, December 1883, 743–44.
40. 'The two milling capitals', *The Miller*, January 1886, 761–62. Capacity stated by George Rieger, *The Miller*, November 1885, 710.
41. Kuhlmann (1929), 130–38, 293.
42. NABIM special report on apparent depression in the UK milling trade in 1887.

Notes to Chapter 3: New ideas in Britain

1. *The Miller*, August 1876, 212–13.
2. *The Miller*, March 1877, 45 for instance.
3. G. A. Buchholz made tentative experiments from 1862 onwards.
4. Corcoran became a prominent opponent of roller milling.
5. Clarke & Dunham advertised a wide range of milling equipment.
6. *The Engineer*, October 1875, 300–1.
7. A group photograph was printed in *The Miller*, July 1899, 309.
8. *The Miller*, September 1877, 349–52.
9. *The Miller*, February 1876, 357.
10. *The Miller*, May 1879, 191; April 1880, 103; August 1881, 438–39; April 1882, 121–23.
11. Pekar's report to the Hungarian Government: comments and translation. *The Miller*, September 1881, 511; April 1882, 130, 134–35; May 1882, 190.
12. *Ganz Kozlemenyek*, March 1931, communications bulletin kindly translated by Mr Neumann of Ganz Machinery Works Holding Ltd in 1996. *The Miller*, August 1887, 261; July 1889, 191: letter from Ganz & Co.
13. 'Gustav Adolf Buchholz', *The Miller*, February 1889, 502–3.
14. *The Miller*, October 1875, 193–95; June 1895, 231.
15. Marston (1931), 10–11; *Milling*, November 1963, 505–6.
16. Patent 229 of 1870 referred to 'ripping and cutting rollers'.
17. Bennett & Elton, vol. 3 (1900), 304 6.
18. *Proc.I.Mech.E.* (1872), 225–35.
19. G. Little, 'Modern milling', *The Engineer*, July 1887, 41.
20. *The Miller*, August 1883, 462; October 1883, 567.
21. *The Miller*, September 1881, 507; Simon (1882) 229–30.
22. Storck & Teague (1952) 228–29.
23. *Proc.I.Mech.E.* (1889), 175.
24. *The Miller*, March 1887, 7–8.
25. *The Miller*, October 1887, 357.
26. *The Miller*, July 1877, 221–26.
27. Patent 2560 of 1875.
28. Simon (1886), 5.
29. J. A. A. Buchholz, son of G. A. Buchholz, briefly agent in the UK for Ganz.
30. Wegmann Patents 823 of 1874 and 4571 of 1876, from abroad. *The Miller*, June 1905, 189.
31. *The Miller*, January 1877, 417; February 1877, 464.

32. *The Miller*, April 1881, 81; A. B. Childs, May 1887, 95–6.
33. *The Miller*, January 1879, 708.
34. Kick (translated Powles 1888), 162 and supplement 32–4; Kozmin (1917), 212; Scott (1972), 168, 176–77.
35. *The Miller* gave extensive coverage in 1879: January 708–15, April 115, July 384–88, August 475, December 775.
36. *The Miller*, May 1878, 154.
37. Marston (1931) 12–14; Simon (1882), 201–2 explained basic mechanical aspects.
38. Henry Simon, 'Daverio's system', paper to first NABIM annual meeting, June 1979, *The Miller*, July 370–73.
39. *The Miller*, May 1880, 194.
40. *The Miller*, August 1880, 393. The attempt to spoil the market for chilled iron rolls was exemplified in November, 121.
41. *The Miller*, September 1879, 527–29.
42. For instance, typical advertisements in *The Miller*, April 1881, 81; *Proc.I.C.E.* (1882) 268–70 also exemplified Wegmann pseudo-science.
43. *The Miller*, July 1884, 387; January 1892, 463.

Notes to Chapter 4: Challenges to British millers

1. *The Miller*, March 1890, 2.
2. For instance, in 'The present condition of the baking trade, No VIII', *The Miller*, March 1878, 32, and *Annual Reviews*.
3. 'The British baker', *The Miller*, September 1878, 435–36.
4. Simon (1882), 194.
5. *Proc.I.C.E.* (1882), 167.
6. J. H. Carter, *The Miller*, January 1880, 829–35.
7. '1879', *The Miller*, January 1880, 847.
8. Royal Commission on supply of food and raw material in time of war (1905); *The Miller*, September 1885, 575.
9. RASE paper, also reported in *The Miller*, starting August 1893, 215.
10. Royal Commission (1905), 361. Statement by R. H. Rew.
11. For instances *The Miller*, January 1882, 835; January 1892, 466.
12. 'James Walker Rush', *The Miller*, December 1909, 645.
13. *The Miller*, August 1890, 221.
14. *The Miller*, January 1884, 837.
15. *The Miller*, April 1887, 51–3.
16. NABIM Council, *The Miller*, April 1887, 41–4; Report of the committee of enquiry in *The Miller*, July 1887, 186–89.
17. *The Miller*, December 1885, 715.
18. *The Miller*, December 1887, 433.
19. Voller (1889), 59–63.
20. 'Testing flour No. 1', *The Miller*, August 1881, 454.
21. Professor Graham, 'The chemistry of bread-making', five lectures for the RSA, extracted by *The Miller* between February and July 1880.
22. *The Miller*, January 1885, 908.
23. Kent-Jones & Amos (1950), 134, quoting Jago (1911), 291.

Notes to Chapter 5: British millers search for answers

1. Storck & Teague (1952), 245.
2. Simon (1882), 195.

3. For instance NABIM meeting reported in *The Miller*, May 1880, 181.

4. *American Miller*, 1889, 389.

5. *The Engineer*, July 1887, 4.

6. Scott (1972), 167.

7. *The Miller*, January 1879, 719; January 1882, 837; John Ure, President of NABIM: July 1885, 453; January 1884, 838.

8. NABIM meeting, not reported in detail. *The Miller*, May 1880, 181.

9. Chancery Division, April 11, 1878; *The Miller*, May 1878, 162.

10. Simon was optimistic about splitting grain along the crease, for instance. Simon (1889), 160. Voller (1889), 83, was dismissive.

11. Friedrich Kick, 'On novelties in roller mills', specially contributed to *The Miller*, May 1880, 173.

12. *The Engineer*, April 1887, 317; June 1887, 484; July 1887, 4.

13. The first claim referred to Patent 1262 of 1883; the second was mistaken. *The Miller*, June 1890, 151 gave personal details.

14. 'Abbey mills, Reading', *The Miller*, December 1881, 740–42; 'The Cleveland steam flour mills', *The Miller*, July 1884, 371.

15. Patent 4033 of 1878, illustrated in *The Miller*, September 1879, 552.

16. NABIM meeting, paper by H. J. Sanderson, *The Miller*, August 1882, 442–44.

17. *The Miller*, May 1883, iii; June 1901, 209–10.

18. 'J. W. Throop', *The Miller*, May 1879, 193.

19. W. D. Gray, 'About roller mills', *The Miller*, April 1884, 99–102, also June 1879, 278, May 1882, 216–17.

20. *The Miller*, April 1883, 96.

21. *The Miller*, January 1884, 839; June 1887, 136–38.

22. 'The Reliance iron works', *The Miller*, June 1884, 284.

23. Patent 2050 of 1877. Also described in *The Miller*, July 1879, 357.

24. *The Miller*, July 1880, 312.

25. *The Miller*, February 1885, 1018; August 1883, 462; March 1884, 20.

26. 'Rounds sectional roller mill', *The Miller*, July 1883, 344.

27. *The Miller*, October 1883, 567 showed the Odell alternatives.

28. 'The works of William Gardner & Sons', *The Miller*, August 1895, 410–12.

29. NABIM meeting, *The Miller*, August 1882, 434–40; also July 1882, 361–62.

30. S. G. Chisholm's paper, *The Miller*, August 1882, 437–38.

31. *The Miller*, April 1886, xi; September 1886, xiii; November 1884, 696.

32. 'James Higginbottom', *Milling*, October 1931, 407; Patent 1722 of 1878, and *The Miller*, February 1879, 788–89; May 1879, 235.

33. *The Miller*, November 1883, 693.

34. *The Miller*, January 1886, xxiv, September 1886, 308.

Notes to Chapter 6: Success

1. Anthony Simon (1947), 1.

2. The Pendene Press, Leicester (1997).

3. Anthony Simon (1947), 1.

4. Patent 2556 of 1879 was the most important: Daverio's roller mill.

5. 'Henry Simon', *The Miller*, August 1899, 376–77; 'G. Daverio', 378.

6. *Proc. I. Mech. E.* (1889), plates 41 and 42.

7. 'Daverio's system' to NABIM, June 1879; to I. C. E., May 1882.

8. *100 years of Bühler Brothers* (1961), the official history.

9. *The Engineer*, August 1887, 167.

10. Simon (1882), 216.

11. Simon (1886), 6.

12. *The Miller* printed bold advertisements, often as journal supplements, for instance in August 1880. Heinrich Seck's centrifugal, Patent 1542 of 1879 was also described in *The Miller*, September 1879, 553.

13. *The Miller*, 1881: May, 183; June, 273–74; September 507.

14. Particularly through papers to NABIM and the I.C.E.

15. *The Miller*, January 1895, supplement.

16. Anthony Simon (1953), 12.

17. Simon (1889), 151.

18. *The Miller*, April 1882, supplement.

19. For instance, editorial in *The Miller*, August 1884, 459.

20. Simon (1889), 148–92 including the current mapping.

21. 'Bernard Hughes', *The Miller*, February 1879, 775–76; 'Edward Hughes', *The Miller*, November 1893, 373–74; 'Model flour mills, Belfast', *Milling*, December 1911, 668; 'North Shore mills', *The Miller*, March 1886, 12; *Milling*, December 1892, 285.

22. *The Miller*, November 1884, supplement.

23. Simon (1886), 8.

24. Rearrangement of tabulation in Simon (1886), 69.

25. Joseph Rank Ltd (1955), 28.

26. 'J. Harrison Carter', *The Miller*, May 1906, 159; *Milling*, April 1906, 361–62.

27. *The Miller*, February 1894, xxxvii.

28. Carter's paper to NABIM, *The Miller*, January 1880, 830.

29. Turner's works at Ipswich, *The Miller*, June 1885, 321–26; *Milling*, July 1937, 40.

30. *Proc.I.C.E.* (1882), 240.

31. *The Miller*, February 1936, 103.

32. NABIM at Dublin, *The Miller*, June 1886, 130–31.

33. *The Miller*, January 1885, ii.

34. Patent 1423 of 1881. There were many alternatives.

35. 'West Gore Street mills', *The Miller*, August 1883, 423–24; 'Frederick Moss', *The Miller*, February 1911, 732.

36. *The Millers' Gazette*, June 1884, 181–82 also gave a list.

37. Davidsons' Phoenix mills: *The Miller*, December 1885, 699–702.

38. *The Engineer*, March 1888, 191.

39. *The Miller*, November 1884, 693; January 1885, 879–82; November 1889, 396; *The Millers' Gazette*, December 1884, 625–26.

40. *The Engineer*, July 1887, 4.

41. *The Engineer*, November 1887, 404.

42. *The Miller*, January 1908, 734.

43. Carter's paper: *The Miller*, April 1891, 54–9.

44. *The Miller*, January 1894, xxxvii.

45. *The Miller*, December 1888, ii advertised the handover to Turners.

46. 'J. Salkeld Robinson', *The Miller*, August 1892, 243; 'Thomas Nield Robinson', *The Miller*, July 1909, 295; *Milling*, February 1893, 330–35.

47. D. W. Povey, to Rochdale Literary and Scientific Society, 1962.

48. *The Miller*, November 1883, 667.

49. Voller (1889), 82–83 and (1897), 195–96.

50. By 1885 Robinsons had an orthodox double horizontal roller mill, with two independent pairs of rolls, and vibrating feed.

51. Report of special committee 'to investigate the present depression in the milling trade', NABIM, June 1887.

52. Lawes & Gilbert (1893), 118–19 gave estimates of wheat usage for food. R. H. Rew gave estimates to the Royal Commission (1905): Minutes of evidence, Appendix 2, 95. Data supports estimate of flour consumption of about 5 lb per person per week.

53. NABIM special report, June 1887, general conclusions.

54. NABIM annual report, 1889, referring to the 'revolution'.
55. Henry Simon (1892), 3.
56. *The Miller* supplement, showing impressive range of activity.
57. *Henry Simon's Circular* number 8.
58. *The Miller*, July 1897, supplement.
59. Simon annual advertising statement, as journal supplement.

Notes to Chapter 7: Resistance to change

1. Miss M. Yates to the editor: *The Miller*, December 1880, 720.
2. Bread Reform League conference: *The Miller*, January 1881, 788–90.
3. Journal editorial: *The Miller*, January 1881, 808–10.
4. Professor Graham, 'The Bread Reform League', *The Miller*, February 1881, 880.
5. *The Miller*, August 1881, 452.
6. *The Miller*, March 1881, 39–40. Commentaries contained memorable quotes.
7. Discussion after Carter's lecture, *The Miller*, January 1884, 817–22.
8. W. T. Bates described in *The Miller*, April 1914, 83; April 1924, 117.
9. Corcoran's business: *The Miller*, October 1885, 608; April 1887, xlvii; April 1890, 48; March 1901, 22; April 1901, 77–8.
10. *The Miller*, September 1880, 509–10.
11. Carter's paper to NABIM in December 1879; Corcoran's paper to London lodge of Amalgamated Millers Trade Society in September 1882.
12. Carter's paper, initiating a formal aspect of the rollers versus millstones controversy, a substantial contribution to the acceptance of technical change.
13. Bates became the most prominent advocate during the controversy.
14. Corcoran's exposition of millstone practice , his arguments ill-founded.
15. Paper by Voss: *The Miller*, December 1882, 773–78; 785.
16. *The Miller*, March 1883, 27–34; 39–40.
17. *The Miller*, November 1884, 693–95, 711; January 1885, 879–82; December 1884, 808–10.
18. Corcoran rejected statements by Carter and Moss about power requirements but contest through journal correspondence columns weakened his position.
19. Henry Simon to the editor, *The Miller*, November 1880, 666.
20. Simon paper to NABIM, *The Miller*, July 1887, 195–98.
21. T. W. Hibbard's paper to NABIM: *The Miller*, July 1886, 185–88.
22. *The Miller*, December 1881, 742; April 1886, 55.
23. For instance, *The Miller*, November 1881, 716.
24. Report to NABIM AGM, *The Miller*, June 1882, 267.
25. J. H. Chatterton to the editor, *The Miller*, April 1886, 55.
26. NABIM annual report in *The Miller*, July 1886, 180.
27. The Germ Milling Case, in detail: *The Miller*, July 1886, 217–26; Court of Appeal: *The Miller*, December 1886, 454–58.
28. Journal appraisal: *The Miller*, December 1886, 462–64.
29. Defence Association, *The Miller*, December 1883, 768; March 1884, 22.

Notes to Chapter 8: The National Association

1. *The Miller*, December 1875, 276.
2. Carter to the editor, *The Miller*, February 1876, 361.
3. *The Miller*, September 1877, 351.
4. 'Millers organization', *The Miller*, December 1877, 500–1.
5. *The Miller*, February 1878, 603.

6. Meeting to establish NABIM: *The Miller*, March 1878, 22–25; draft rules: *The Miller*, April 1878, 86; Inaugural: *The Miller*, May 1878, 150–52.

7. J. H. Chatterton, appreciation in *The Miller*, March 1928, 40–41.

8. Council meeting, *The Miller*, January 1889, 445. Amended NABIM rules: *The Miller*, June 1879, 280.

9. *The Miller*, July 1879, 364–73.

10. Editorial: *The Miller*, March 1880, 39–40.

11. 'The National Association': advice from *The Miller*, June 1880, 266–67; November 1883, 674–75, referring to the editorial 'What is the good of it?' of October 1880, 579–80; editorial, the importance of committees, *The Miller*, May 1882, 207–8.

12. NABIM, October 1883, including 'Practical milling' by James Higginbottom.

13. Each January, with the annual review, *The Miller* published details of local millers' associations. In August 1881 and September 1882 full lists of members were published, but not afterwards in the journal.

14. Annual report of NABIM, *The Miller*, September 1889, 284.

15. Coucil meeting, *The Miller*, October 1890, 317–19.

16. A summary of early exhibitions appeared in *The Miller*, March 1881, 17.

17. From 1878, the increasingly impressive journal advanced with general progress.

18. Kilburn show, *The Miller*, June–September 1879.

19. Dell's candidate for a 'Heath Robinson' collection of mechanical ingenuity was described in *The Miller*, July 1879, 357; Patent 2050 of 1877.

20. Carter to the editor: *The Miller*, August 1880, 433–34 and editorial 427–28.

21. Editorial: *The Miller*, October 1880, 578–79; February 1881, 864–66.

22. *The Miller*, May 1881, 175–88; June 1881, 257–82, 286–90, 298–301.

23. Simon (1886), 69.

24. Simon (1886), 6.

25. Voller, 'Five decades of flour milling', *Milling*, September 1923, 28.

26. Annual reviews: *The Miller*, January 1882, 837; January 1884, 838.

27. *Proc.I.C.E.* (1882), 162–270.

28. NABIM, *The Miller*, November 1883, 657–63.

29. Simon, *The Miller*, July 1887, 195–98.

30. *The Miller*, July 1884, 357–58; Stansfield: 358–60.

31. *The Miller*, August 1888, 221–29.

32. Glasgow: *The Miller*, July 1885, 439–42; Dublin: June 1886, 130–36; London: June 1887, 135–40.

33. 'Exit the milling exhibition': *The Miller*, October 1896, 587.

34. Report of AGM of NABIM: *The Miller*, July 1879, 379–80.

35. 'Milling technology', *The Miller*, November 1880, 657.

36. Chatterton to the editor: *The Miller*, January 1881, 794.

37. 'The City and Guilds of London Institute', *The Miller*, August 1881, 451.

38. NABIM, *The Miller*, August 1882, 433.

39. *The Miller*, August 1883, 449.

40. Coucil meeting, *The Miller*, November 1883, 655–56.

41. First NABIM Convention, annual report, *The Miller*, July 1884, 342–43.

42. Council meeting, *The Miller*, February 1887, 535.

43. Bill for promotion of technical instruction, 1888, following report of a Royal Commission in 1884. 'What is technical instruction?', *The Miller*, July 1888, 189

44. T. W. Hibbard: appreciation in *The Miller*, July 1892, 199–200 and July 1907, 295.

45. W. R. Voller: appreciation in *The Miller*, April 1900, 78 and *Milling*, February 1923, 147–48, also *The Miller*, October 1930, 796–97.

46. Voller (1889), 243; *The Miller*, December 1886, 473.

47. T. W. Hibbard to the editor; *The Miller*, August 1885, 536.

48. A. R. Tattersall to the editor: *The Miller*, January 1887, 499.

49. 'Millers and milling technological examinations', *The Miller*, November 1884, 713.
50. T. W. Hibbard to the editor: *The Miller*, September 1887, 307–8.
51. W. R. Voller to the editor: *The Miller*, September 1887, 308.
52. *J. E. Beerbohm's Corn Trade List: the Millers Gazette*, January 1888, 523–24 to May 1888, 63–66. Second series December 1888 onwards.
53. Voller (1889), 2.
54. *The Miller*, October 1897, 571–72.
55. Voller (1897), 463–66.

Notes to Chapter 9: Design and development

1. Kick's early commentaries, amongst a variety of roller mill ideas, left him encumbered with by-ways in design. Pappenheim's text was similarly cluttered with soon obsolescent break roll details; see *The Miller*, October 1879, 605.
2. Marston (1931), 19.
3. Simon's paper to NABIM, *The Miller*, July 1879, 372.
4. Simon (1882), 206.
5. Simon (1889) Plate 41.
6. Simon to NABIM, *The Miller*, July 1879, 371.
7. Voller (1897), 207. Birch (1930) treated design in detail.
8. Simon (1882), 205.
9. Simon to NABIM, *The Miller*, July 1879, 371.
10. Simon (1882), 203.
11. In *100 years of Bühler Brothers* (1961), 5 the company recorded their start in roller mill production in 1876.
12. Simon (1889), Plate 41.
13. Patent 1179 of March 1883, described in *The Miller*, April 1884, 107.
14. Simon (1886), 21.
15. Bühler special catalogue, 1900.
16. *The Miller*, supplements: March 1884, December 1884.
17. Journal supplement on very brittle paper.
18. *Milling*, July 1927, 58; and a depiction in a Bühler catalogue of 1900; commemoration of Adolf Bühler by the company, 1897.
19. Anthony Simon (1947), 18. According to *The Miller*, December 1885, 725, Sir Bernard Samuelson & Co at Banbury manufactured machinery for Simon.
20. Marston (1931), 27–29 described the design.
21. Patent 9856 of July 1884, communicated to J. Imray.
22. Patent 14756 of August 1897.
23. Simon (1882), 220–21.
24. For instance, *The Miller*, December 181, 788.
25. Simon to NABIM, *The Miller*, July 1879, 372.
26. *The Miller*, April 1879, supplement.
27. Simon (1886), 12.
28. Simon (1882), 232.
29. Simon (1886), 14.
30. This was mechanization of the basic hand-sieving procedure, a combination of movements familiar to cooks and gardeners, described by Simon in *The Miller*, July 1888, supplement.
31. Stringer's address to NABIM: *The Miller*, August 1888, 224–227. Kick decribed the action of Haggenmacher's plansifter in *Dingler's Polytechnisches Journal*, reproduced in *The Miller*, March 1889, 27–28.
32. Voller: *The Miller*, August 1888, 226.
33. Simon letter files: Agreement recorded in German, 6 February 1890.

34. 'The plansichter', *Henry Simon's Circular*, November 1894, also June 1895 and February 1897.
35. *The Miller*, January 1895, xi and supplement. W. J. Perrett paper to NABIM, *The Miller*, July 1895, 312–14. Voller's general appraisal of plansifter problems, *The Miller*, June 1895, 238–39.
36. Voller (1897), 18. Voller described Haggenmacher, Higginbottom and Luther plan-sifters: 302–317. Carter exhibited at the RASE at Darlington.
37. Voller (1897), 304–5. Halliwell (1904), 101–3. Both described the unusual Bunge design, also Kozmin (1917) 354–56.
38. Simon (1898), 8.
39. Voller (1889), 75.
40. Thompson (1934) (mill manager to G. W. Chitty & Co Ltd, Dover).
41. Kick (1878) translated by Powles (1888), 200.
42. *The Miller*, February 1885, supplement; April 1885, supplement.
43. Simon (1892) 14–15.
44. *The Miller*, November 1887, supplement.
45. Kozmin (1917), 410 and Preface, v.
46. Henry Simon to Colonel Sadler, August 1896.
47. Henry Simon to Joseph Ingleby in Germany, 25 July 1894.
48. Simon (1890), 38–39.
49. Simon (1886), 8.
50. *The Engineer*, August 1887, 167.
51. Simon (1892), 22.
52. Simon (1890), 10–14.
53. Lockwood (1945), 349.
54. *The Miller*, September 1879, 512.
55. Henry Simon to Heinrich Seck, April 1890, in German.
56. Henry Simon to T. Parkinson & Sons, 4 January 1890. Record of Court of Appeal Parkinson *v.* Simon, House of Lords 1895, 382–83 of bound proceedings.
57. Parkinsons to Simon, 21 February 1890, Appeal Record, 386.
58. Simon to Parkinsons, 10 March 1890, Appeal Record, 390.
59. Ingleby to Parkinsons, 30 May 1890, Appeal Record, 395; also Huxley to Parkinsons, 27 June 1890.
60. *The Millers' Gazette*, September 1890, 373–75.
61. *Henry Simon's Circular* gave details in April and September 1894.
62. *The Miller*, July 1889, supplement.
63. Simon (1892), 66 showed the new design, also *The Miller*, August 1892, supplement, and a description September 1892, 280.
64. *The Miller*, October 1891, ix. Turner's latest purifier had been described in *The Miller*, March 1891, 10–11; Higginbottom's latest design 12–13.
65. *The Miller*, March 1894, 13–20 in extensive detail. Judgement: April 1894, 100–1. The full verbatim account was included in the official record after the House of Lords appeal stage. The first appeal was reported in *The Miller*, July 1894, 331–35, the House of Lords appeal in August 1895, 408–9, 428.
66. Stringer had given practical advice to Parkinsons, described in House of Lords appeal record, 382–95.
67. House of Lords appeal record, 342–49, especially 344, 347.
68. *Henry Simon's Circular*, September 1894.
69. *The Miller*, August 1895, 408–9.
70. The Koh-I-Noor purifier was described in *The Miller*, September 1890, 272–74 and *The Millers' Gazette*, August 1890, 272–75. The Reform purifier was described basically in Simon (1890), *The Miller*, November 1890, 365–60. The design specified for Patent 9768 of 1892 was described in *The Miller*, September 1892, 280.

71. Henry Simon 'Notes re Patent Laws', December 1892, item 445 in personal file.

Notes to Chapter 10: Henry Simon in business

1. Joseph Ingleby: appreciation in *The Miller*, August 1916, 334.
2. House of Lords appeal: Parkinson *v.* Simon, 322, 325.
3. Simon (1892), 1.
4. William Stringer: *The Miller*, December 1893, 425.
5. William Buchanan moved from Glasgow to Liverpool. Prototype stage designs for several machines were tried at Buchanan premises, including Glasgow, also at Leethams' at York.
6. Anthony Simon (1953), 5.
7. Ingleby to J. R. Radford, 12 May 1889.
8. Simon to Ingleby, 14 September 1889.
9. The first approach was via Ernest Samuelson, 27 November 1889.
10. Simon to Stringer, 13 February 1890.
11. Simon to Ingleby, 11 May 1892.
12. *Henry Simon's Circular*, November 1893.
13. Simon to E. L. Weigall in London, 19 January 1894.
14. From 1892 Baumann managed Frankfurt for Simon and Bühler.
15. Simon to W. Schroller at London, 22 October 1890.
16. *The Miller*, October 1885, 640.
17. Copies of the *Circular* and the *Occasional Letter* were conserved in an archive at Simon House, Eaton Gate, London by the Simon Engineering Group, later the Simon Group. A substantial collection of Henry Simon's correspondence and other records was also preserved.
18. Joseph Rank Ltd (1955), 33–34.
19. *The Miller*, July 1887, 195–98.
20. Notes on the history of the company, made by E. D. Simon.
21. Simon to George Nicholson at Liverpool, 12 March 1892.
22. Vernons amalgamated with Spillers in 1920.
23. Simon to Nicholson, 19 May 1896. The two mills were the earlier mill at Kirkdale together with the new Seacombe mill.
24. A clear statement of his involvement in milling apart from mill engineering.
25. Simon to Behrens, 16 November 1897.
26. Anthony Simon (1953), 12.
27. John Speight in *Milling*, March 1956, 254–55, containing errors.
28. Simon to Baumann at Frankfurt, in English, 28 November 1893.
29. Simon to J. R. Radford, 20 March 1891, indicating Simon's senior staff problem, lacking someone to support the established executives. Ideally, Ingleby needed a stronger technical background and a resourceful assistant.
30. Pages 1000–2 of letter book.
31. Bühler (1961), 6.
32. *Milling*, February 1899, 55–56. A long account of the Vernons' progress and the project at Birkenhead was published in *Milling*, April and May 1912.
33. Bennett & Elton Vol III (1900), 308–15.
34. Ingleby to Behrens, 25 August 1899.
35. Simon to Behrens, 16 November 1897.

Notes to Chapter 11: Combination and enterprise

1. *J. E. Beerbohm's Millers' Gazette and Corn Trade Journal*, December 1888, 467; also other reports and comments: December–February.
2. *The Miller*, February 1889, 489–91, 507–8.
3. *The Miller*, May 1891, 91–3.
4. *American Miller*, January 1889, 46. There was also a short-lived prospectus for an amalgamation of Yorkshire and Lincolnshire millers, to form the United Steam Millers Co Ltd, noticed in retrospect in *The Miller*, January 1892, 449.
5. *The Miller*, January 1890, 471.
6. *The Miller*, March 1890, 22.
7. *The Miller*, March 1890, 5; June 1890, 150. Previous information about Spiller & Co: *The Miller*, March 1887, 11. 'The story of Spillers': *The Miller*, November 1933, 988–89; December 1933, 128–29; February 1934, 124–26.
8. Simon report for journal 'Trade Items': *The Miller*, January 1892, 474.
9. Described in *The Miller*, December 1885, 699–700.
10. *The Miller*, June 1897, 283.
11. Simon report for journal; *The Miller*, January 1892, 473. Company information: *The Miller*, February 1892, 493; October 1893, 327.
12. Joseph Rank: *Milling*, June 1904, 469; Joseph Rank Ltd (1955), 27–8.
13. *Milling*, December 1892, 276–77; *The Miller*, April 1891, 44–6; November 1895, 715–16.
14. Joseph Rank Ltd (1955), chapters 3–6.
15. *Milling*, September–December 1892; May–August 1893.
16. *Milling*, May 1893, 398–402.
17. Tucker's mill: *The Miller*, April 1892, 55; the company: January 1890, 471.
18. *The Miller*, November 1889, 396; capacity about 100 sacks per hour.
19. William Vernon: *The Miller*, May 1901, 145–46; July 1919, 424. *Milling*, April 1912, 355–57, 382–84; May 418–20.
20. *Milling*, September 1892, 202.
21. *Milling*, January 1898, 10–12; October 1931, 308.
22. North Shore Mills Co: *The Miller*, September 1884, 537; March 1886, 12. About the management: *The Miller*, October 1887, 357; *Milling*, December 1892, 285–86.
23. Annual meeting: *The Miller*, September 1886, 347.
24. *Milling*, July 1893, 490.
25. Seth Taylor: *The Miller*, July 1887, 225; mill premises: October 1886, 359; June 1887, 135–36; September 1882, 536 and *The Engineer*, February 1873, 95–6.
26. Robinsons: *The Miller*, October 1878, 489–90; June 1887, 136–38.
27. S. & P. Mumford: *Milling*, April 1923, 404. P. Mumford: *The Engineer*, February 1875, 91–2; *The Miller*, June 1887, 139–40; June 1895, 253; *Milling*, June 1927, 691.
28. Marriage Neave: *The Miller*, November 1884, 702–7; June 1887, 138–39.
29. Albert Bridge mills: *The Miller*, August 1884, 453–55.
30. *The Miller*, March 1876, 17.
31. *Milling*, June 1924, 638–39; May 1935, 527.
32. About Dornbusch: *The Miller*, September 1881, 511–12.
33. T. W. Hibbard, 'Forward sales', *The Miller*, July 1893, 164–65; on 'The clearing house scheme', *The Miller*, May 1895, 180–81.
34. Nicholls was prominent in the search for trading equilibrium through to the 1920s.
35. J. Percival, *Wheat in Great Britain* (1948); B. R. Mitchell & P. Deane, *Abstract of British Historical Statistics* (1971).
36. *Journal RASE* (1893), 77–131, also *The Miller* from August.
37. NABIM annual report: *The Miller*, August 1891, 228; January 1894, 468: 'the farmer declines to adapt himself to his environment. He sows wheat for quantity when quality is his best chance of profit'.

38. *The Miller*, September 1897, 511.
39. Lawes & Gilbert report: *The Miller*, March 1897, 9; May 1897, 163.
40. *The Miller*, January 1896, 852–58.
41. Mallett was said to have conveyed 'the bitter cry of the country miller'.
42. *The Miller*, July 1896, 342–45.
43. *The Miller*, August 1895, 406.
44. *The Miller*, October 1895, 586; May 1898, 155; February 1898, 905; July 1898, 300–1; July 1899, 292.
45. Simon (1898), 9; *Milling*, April 1912, 357, 382; *The Miller*, May 1901, 146.

Notes to Chapter 12: Scaling up and relocation

1. *Milling*, April 1900, 272–76.
2. Leethams: June 1892, 137; *The Miller*, June 1900, 225; August 1900, 352.
3. NABIM at Scarborough: *The Miller*, August 1900, 351–57, 361–69, particularly summary 367–69.
4. Henry Simon paper: *The Miller*, July 1879, 370–73.
5. *The Miller*, January 1901, 709–12.
6. *The Miller*, February 1901, 770, 817–20; March 1901, 2–12.
7. Macrosty (1907), chapter viii, particularly 219 onwards.
8. NABIM AGM: *The Miller*, May 1901, 168–69.
9. *The Miller*, February 1901, 817 and December 593 editorials.
10. Vernon's address: *The Miller*, July 1901, 277–80.
11. Scott Ling's address: *Milling*, June 1901, 452–57; *The Miller*, July 1901, 284–89.
12. Macrosty (1907), 226.
13. William Jago: 'American flour', *The Miller*, November 1896, 638–40.
14. Storck & Teague (1952), 272.
15. *Milling*, April 1912, 355–57 described the Vernon mills, including Fole.
16. W. T. Bates, 'Prophecy and facts', *The Miller*, September 1902, 371.
17. W. R. Voller, *Milling*, December 1902, 45.
18. *The Miller*, May 1902, 123 deplored 'the little boats of fancy phrases' used in the press to the disadvantage of the millers.
19. *The Miller*, March 1904, 12–13.
20. Kuhlmann (1929), 294–95, 312–15. Kuhlmann also referred to British expertise in wheat mixing.
21. Millennium Mills: *Milling*, June 1913, 608–9.
22. *Milling*, January 1904, 32. See also *Milling*, June 1904, 469 and illustrations.
23. Premier Mills at London: *The Miller*, June 1905, 190–91; *Milling*, June 1904, 538; June 1905, 421–22; August 1905, 149.
24. Atlantic Mills at Cardiff: *Milling*, June 1904, 538; June 1905, 453; July 1906, 148.
25. North Shore Co: *The Miller*, August 1899, 393–94.
26. *Milling*, December 1901, 400 and illustrations.
27. *Milling*, December 1903, 547–48.
28. *Milling*, September 1892, 202; January 1898, 10–12; May 1911, 534–35.
29. *Milling*, July 1893, 487–88; October 1905, 301; June 1908, 562; *The Miller*, June 1906, 218–19; March 1914, 21–2.
30. Hovis Ltd, *The Hovis Jubilee* (1948); *The Miller*, March 1884, 24–5; *Milling*, July 1906, 72–4; September, 407.
31. Coxes Lock: *Milling*, July 1906, 8–12.
32. Cranfields: *Milling*, July 1906, 64–6; *The Miller*, December 1936, 1152–54.
33. Marriages: *Milling*, December 1907, 794–97.
34. Spillers & Bakers: *Milling*, October 1905, 284–85 and illustrations; June 1908, 529; *American Miller*, April 1889, 207.

35. *Milling*, October 1905, supplement.

36. *Milling*, October 1901, 228–29.

37. *Milling*, March 1907, 290. During 1907 Broomhall of *Milling*, was involved in estimating capacity throughout the industry; see *Milling*, July 1907, 126.

38. NABIM AGM: *The Miller*, July 1905, 235–37. At the Convention in 1908 Nicholls summarised the commercial debate since 1893: see *The Miller*, July 1908, 293–94.

39. *The Miller*, August 1906, 355–56; February 1907, 771. About A. E. Humphries: May 1906, 148.

40. *Milling*, July 1907, 127–28; *The Miller*, August 1907, 369–71.

41. *The Miller*, March 1908, 1–3, 10–18; May 1908, 160–63; July 1908, 293–98.

42. NABIM general meeting: *The Miller*, March 1909, 7.

43. Extensive expositions by Nicholls to NABIM were reported in *The Miller*, July 1908, 293–95; March 1909, 6–9, particularly 7.

44. Universal flour contract: *The Miller*, May 1910, 129–30; July 1910, 260.

45. J. M. Frost: *The Miller*, July 1909, 292–93; mills: *Milling*, July 1909, 22–6; December 1910, 590–96.

46. *Milling*, March 1910, 219. *Milling* gave estimates of milling capacity in the Liverpool area inn January 1911, 82.

47. CWS, *The people's Year Book* (1930), 69–72 gave a summary of 'landmarks in CWS history', including dates of mill acquisitions.

48. *Milling*, June 1908, 562; December 1934, 670–74 described the Sun Mills as 'Britain's largest mill', capacity 240 sacks per hour.

49. *The Miller*, April 1910, 386; also June 1921, 288–92.

50. P. Redfern, *The story of the CWS* (1913), 237–38. Redfern also compiled *The new history of the CWS* (1938) and W. Richardson continued with *The CWS in war and peace* (1977).

51. Simon (1898), 41–2.

52. *Milling*, October 1905, 305–6; December 1926, 757–60.

53. Redfern (1913), 238.

54. NABIM general meeting: *The Miller*, May 1913, 131–35, particularly 132.

55. *Milling*, November 1933, 610–11; *The Miller*, November 1933, 1035–36, 1043; at the end labelled 'ADVT', it was a surprising statement of Rank's progress.

Notes to Chapter 13: Feasibility studies

1. NABIM annual report: *Milling*, July 1900, 13; Mallett, *The Miller*, July 1901, 282–83.

2. Home-grown wheat committee: *The Miller*, December 1901, 646–47.

3. Editorial: 'The gluten theory', *The Miller*, June 1904, 181. *Milling* indicated emerging complexity: June 1903, 414–115; November 1907, 578.

4. A. E. Humphries, 'The improvement of English wheat', Convention in Paris, *The Miller*, November 1905, 490–95; December 550–54; January 1906, 619–23.

5. Humphries to British Association: *The Miller*, September 1907, 444–47, including 446: statement by A. D. Hall.

6. 'Sixty years of cereal chemistry', *The Miller*, April 1935, 374–78. See also T. H. Fairbrother, 'Cereal chemistry', *Milling*, April 1935, 430–35. Kent-Jones & Amos (1950), 136–37 summarised early research stages.

7. NABIM annual report, *The Miller*, July 1913, 261.

8. *The Miller*, April 1935, 365–66.

9. Jago (1911), 375.

10. Sidney Andrews, *Nine generations*, ed. John Burls (Isaac Andrews & Sons Ltd, 1958), 165; Jago (1911) 376–77.

11. Jago's report for The Flour Oxidising Co: *Milling*, June 1903, 428–30. Voller (1923), 29; *The Miller*, November 1905, 487–90.

12. Jago (1911), 377; *Milling*, June 1904, 483; *The Miller*, May 1908, 176.
13. *The Miller*, March 1908, 22–6; Jago (1911), chapter 17, particularly sections 507–9; *Milling*, June 1910, advertisement. Kent-Jones & Amos (1950), chapter 10.
14. Hamill's report: *The Miller*, May 1911, 141–48, particularly 143.
15. Editorial: *The Miller*, May 1911, 127–28.
16. Hamill's second report: *The Miller*, September 1911, 397–405.
17. Jago (1911), 553–61. Hamill also described gradual reduction milling at length: *The Miller*, September 1911, 397–99. Standard bread: see editorial 391–92.
18. A. E. Humphries paper, JRASE vol 72, 1911 (reprint), 1–6, 13.
19. 'In praise of white bread', *The Miller*, October 1908, 475.
20. NABIM Convention: *The Miller*, June 1911, 210–14.
21. Jago on flour improvers: *The Miller*, June 1913, 609–12; also November 1913, 532.
22. Conversation with C. W. Chitty (1975).
23. Kent-Jones & Amos (1950), 249.
24. NABIM Convention: *The Miller*, July 1913, 263–64.
25. NABIM discussion: *The Miller*, June 1911, 210–14, 239–40, particularly 239.
26. Simon (1892), 22.
27. Editorial: *The Miller*, October 1905, 413.
28. Editorial: *The Miller*, October 1908, 473; also used in 1908 in 'Editorial notes' of January and August, a year of technical reappraisal.
29. *The Miller*, April 1910, 62; *Milling*, November 1912, 442.
30. Marston (1931), 19.
31. Halliwell (1904), 57.
32. Patent 9704 of 1904; also *Milling*, December 1904, 541.
33. G. W. Huxley to Ernest Simon, 17 October 1902.
34. Simons' 1914 catalogue, 61; Patent 6993 of 1908.
35. *The Miller*, November 1910, 536–39; *Milling*, December 1910, 590–96.
36. Amos (1912), 151 and 198.
37. R. J. Fowler: *Milling*, November 1933, 584.
38. *Milling*, June 1903, 443; December 1903.
39. Simon (1953), 14; *The Miller*, September 1914, 454–56.
40. Briddon & Fowler 1906 catalogue; *Milling*, May 1905, 406.
41. *The Miller*, April 1892, 77; February 1910, 767.
42. *The Miller*, July 1906, 286; *Milling*, July 1906, 76; Patent 739 of 1906.
43. Buchanan: Patent 14,019 of 1900, Patent 1317 of 1907.
44. *Milling*, May 1908, 389; Simon 1908 catalogue 44–5; Amos (1912), 152.
45. Huxley became chairman of Henry Simon Ltd in 1908.
46. *The Miller*, January 1908, 734; April, 89; September, 417 onwards in correspondence, especially October, 476–78 and in 1909.
47. Illustrated in Voller (1897), 309–12; Amos (1912) 168; Lockwood (1945), 320–22.
48. *Milling*, June 1910, 664–66; *The Miller*, July 1910, 253, 280.
49. *Milling*, May 1911, supplement; *The Miller*, July 1911, 281.
50. *The Miller*, August 1911, xxv.
51. *Milling*, June 1913, 727.
52. *The Miller*, November 1910, 538–39; February 1906, 683–84.
53. E. D. Simon to NABIM: *The Miller*, July 1913, 267–72.
54. *The Miller*, October 1911, 520–21.
55. *Milling*, May 1911, 592.
56. E. D. Simon's notes in 1921.
57. NABIM Conventions: *The Miller*, June 1911, 212; June 1914, 295.
58. *Milling*, March 1914, 292.
59. NABIM annual report: *The Miller*, July 1914, 291.

60. 'A pretty scheme': *The Miller*, July 1917, 208–9; J. Hutchinson in *Milling*, April 1935, 414; B. C. Robinson, *The Miller*, May 1937, 474.
61. G. H. Ball, *Milling*, June 1928, 647–48.
62. O'Hagan (1929), 322, 328 and generally chapter 68.

Notes to Chapter 14: Sea of troubles

1. *The Miller*, March 1916, 3.
2. [Cmd. 1544] of 1921, unlike most Royal Commission reports, an account of actual administrative arrangements.
3. Royal Commission first report, 1921, 3.
4. NABIM emergency general meetings: *The Miller*, December 1916, 586–90; February 1917, 715–19.
5. NABIM special notice: *Milling*, March 1917, 212–13 and mapped data, also in February 1921 and *The Miller*, June 1928, 658. NABIM general meeting: *Milling*, March 1917, 234–39.
6. Statutory rules and orders 1917, No 377 [Cd. 8556.]
7. Statutory rules and orders 1917, No 774 [Cd. 8708.]
8. Editorial 'Government control', *The Miller*, May 1917, 111–12.
9. Statutory rules and orders 1917, No 372, also in Royal Commission report, appendix 21, 53.
10. W. H. Beveridge, *British Food Control* (1928), 96. Beveridge's account, the Commission report and the NABIM records in the journals provide a mass of information on the period. A. E. Humphries provided a summary of 'War-time control of breadstuffs' for *The Miller*, April 1935, 379–86.
11. NABIM AGM, *Milling*, July 1917, 57–76; the most basic source of information related to the millers and the official procedures in wartime.
12. 'The public general Acts', published 1916, 292–93.
13. Flour and bread (prices) order 1917; Royal Commission on wheat supplies (1921), 12.
14. AGM: *Milling*, July 1917, 71; Humphries; *The Miller*, May 1906, 148.
15. *Milling*, July 1917, 64; Memorandum of Association: *Milling*, October 1917, 290–91.
16. Spillers & Bakers Ltd AGM: *Milling*, May 1915, 480–84; editorial 'Millers' profits', *The Miller*, May 1915, 123–24.
17. Beveridge (1928), 13.
18. 'The state control scheme': *Milling*, July 1917, 1–3, continuing the topic 'Permanent state control', June 1917, 517–19.
19. Humphries' comments: *The Miller*, August 1917, 315 and *Milling*, August 1917, 159, 162; *The Miller*, September 1917, 327–28.
20. O'Hagan (1929), 332.
21. NABIM information on committees and financial problems: *Milling*, September 1917, 2, 46–50. Meeting with Beale: *The Miller*, March 1918, 4–6.
22. 'The remuneration agreement', *The Miller*, March 1918, 1–2.
23. 'The voice of the trade', *The Miller*, November 1917, 453.
24. A. J. P. Taylor, *English history 1914–1945* (1965), 93.
25. Reconstruction committee, chairman J. H. Whitley, 1917 [Cd. 8606.] 4.
26. L. H. Green, *The Miller*, April 1935, 399.
27. George Alexander to *The Miller*, August 1886, 254.
28. NABIM Council: *Milling*, March 1918, 268.
29. Industrial relations agreements: *The Miller*, March 1919, 36–38; June 1919, 304–10.
30. *The Miller*, August 1919, 510–12; August 1920, 562–64.
31. NABIM AGM: *The Miller*, July 1919, 396–419.
32. Tributes to A. E. Humphries, *Milling*, October 1935, 406–8.

33. NABIM general meeting, *The Miller*, April 1919, 118–130.

34. Report of the Royal Commission on wheat supplies, 16

35. . Beveridge (1928), 299–300.

36. 'Official interference', *The Miller*, June 1920, 313–14.

37. Ministry of Food to the Bakers' National Association: *The Miller*, May 1920, 238.

38. S. Armstrong to Felixstowe Convention, *The Miller*, July 1920, 450.

39. NABIM AGM: *The Miller*, July 1919, 406.

40. *The Miller*, August 1920, 546; Irish comments: April 1920, 136. W. Irish was manager of Marshalls' mill at Grimsby: *Milling*, April 1923, 403.

41. NABIM annual report: *Milling*, June 1921, 778.

42. NABIM general meeting: *The Miller*, April 1921, 108.

43. Irish on 'gingering up', *The Miller*, April 1920, 136; Armstrong on the story of the pig, October 1920, 756. See also July 1922, 392: 'Mr Armstrong's pig'.

44. 'New companies': *The Miller*, July 1919, 447; number 155962.

45. Spillers Milling and Associated Industries Ltd AGM, *Milling*, May 1921, 571–74.

46. Letter from Sir Wm Edgar Nicholls, *Milling*, November 1924, 532–34.

47. Communication from Ranks, *Milling*, November 1933, 610–11. Joseph Rank Ltd (1955) dealt with big projects, and general growth.

48. Associated London Flour Millers registered June 28, 1921, *The Miller*, August 1921, 503. See also *Milling*, July 1922, 84.

49. ALFM first general meeting; *Milling*, July 1922, 84. Reports continued to 1932.

50. Mumford's Vauxhall mill, *Milling*, June 1927, 691.

51. Charles Brown & Co Ltd, *The Miller*, December 1932, 1162.

52. Armstrong's address at Keswick, *Milling*, June 1921, 773.

53. Editorial, *The Miller*, September 1921, 539–40; Rank, *Milling*, July 1921, 129.

54. Keswick Convention: *The Miller*, July 1921, 370–74. *Milling*, June 1921, 777–80; *The Miller*, July 1921.

55. W. J. Carr and Silloth: *The Miller*, May 1911, 140; June 1921, 278–80.

56. Carr listed basic committees: *The Miller*, July 1918, 214. Trade organisation was added in 1922. See *The Miller*, April 1922, 122, and Dieppe Convention, *The Miller*, July 1922, 382; also editorial, September 1922, 559–60.

57. 'Mr Leetham's scheme' and national capacity: *The Miller*, April 1923, 110; first NABIM general meeting with lengthy 'Trade organisaation' discussion.

58. Pursuit of output as a 'will o' the wisp', *The Miller*, April 1923, 114.

59. Sir Herbert Brown's appraisal, *The Miller*, April 1923, 108.

60. O'Hagan (1929), 331.

61. Advertising: *Milling*, April 1923, 394.

62. 'The question of output',, *Milling*, March 1923, 310A.

63. 'Eat more bread competition', *Milling*, July 1923, 67.

64. Advertising campaign reports, *Milling*, March 1923, 307; April 1924, 366.

65. 'That milling trust', *The Miller*, July 19223, 376.

66. NABIM Convention, *Milling*, June 1927, 722–32 surveyed the industry's difficulties: see F. K. S. Metford and A. E. Humphries;, also Royal Commission on food prices, report vol II, 70: evidence by Humphries.

67. *The Miller*, editorials, June 1923, 288; July, 376, 380; August, 475–76.

68. Cereals Research Station, St Albans, *The Research Association of British Flour Millers 1923–1960*; *The Miller*, May 1920, 472; December 1921, 798, 824; April 1922, 126; May 1922, 204; January 1923, 940–44; *Milling*, January 1923, 36–40.

69. 'Industrial reports No 1, Industrial Councils', Ministry of Labour (1917) 13 viii; Reconstruction Committee: 'Joint standing industrial councils', Ministry of Labour (1917), [Cd. 8606.] 5 viii.

70. Company and director: *Milling*, January 1924, 90, 96; report to NABIM, April 1924, 368–69. St Albans laboratories: *The Miller*, November 1926, 684–92.

71. E. A. Fisher, 'The field for research in the milling industry' at NABIM Convention: *Milling*, June 1924, 708A–711.

72. E. D. Simon, during discussion of Fisher's paper: *Milling*, June 1924, 742–50.

73. Fisher's reports: *Milling*, March 1925, 328–30; June 1928, 666A–67; and annual meetings: December 1925, 911–12; November 1926, 562–64.

74. E. D. Simon, 'The principles of wheat conditioning' to NABIM Convention: *Milling*, June 1923, 738–40, 772–75.

75. Conversations with Charles Chitty (1975).

76. 'G. W. Chitty & Co Ltd', *Milling*, December 1930, 700–1, 710.

77. Successive editions, including Kent-Jones & Amos (1950) became authoritative.

78. Conversation with D. W. Kent-Jones (1975) and many papers by Kent-Jones in the milling journals of the 1920s.

Notes to Chapter 15: Rationalisation and a new era:
1925–1939

1. *Departmental committee on distribution and prices of agricultural produce: cereals, flour and bread*, Cmd. 1971 (1923), Ministry of Agriculture report, known as the Linlithgow report.

2. 'Breadstuffs traders vindicated', *The Miller*, June 1925, 271.

3. *Royal Commission on food prices*, Cmd. 2390 (1925), vol. 1, 47.

4. Broomhall of *Milling*, a recognized authority on trade statistics.

5. Evidence by Crawford and Nicholls: *Milling*, January 1925, 136–37.

6. Royal Commission evidence by Humphries, vol 2, 71.

7. Also vol. 2, 74, Humphries: 'The British public, myself included, are not in love with bureaucracy'.

8. Royal Commission, vol. 2, 74–5, particularly 75.

9. Vol. 2, 75. P. R. Reynolds had been examined, vol. 2, 61–7.

10. W. R. Smith: Commission report 182–99; I. H. Ryland 173–81.

11. NABIM AGM, *Milling*, June 1925, 802–10A.

12. NABIM conference, *Milling*, June 1926, 712. Regulations of output or encouraging consumption were alternatives.

13. J. H. Curry, 'Popularity of prepared foods', *Milling*, April 1925, 420.

14. Thomas Russell, 'The expansion of markets at home and abroad' to NABIM Convention, *Milling*, June 1925, 843–48; *The Miller*, July 1925, 396–406.

15. Resolution by F. K. S. Metford after Russell's paper.

16. 'The CWS', *Milling*, December 1922, 754; CWS, *The People's year book* (1930) gave dates of main mill openings and closures. 'Growth of the CWS', *Milling*, September 1925, 451.

17. Leetham's theoretical proposition: London conference, *Milling*, June 1926, 712.

18. F. K. S. Metford's address, *Milling*, June 1927, 728–28A.

19. There were extensive reports in the journals, particularly AGMs from 1921 onwards, in *Milling*, each May, also an appreciation of Nicholls in February 1926.

20. E. D. Simon: informal notes; *Henry Simon Occasional Letter*, November 1921.

21. New works at Cheadle Heath, *The Miller*, August 1926, 432; *Henry Simon Ltd Occasional Letter*, June 1928.

22. Introduction to Anthony Simon (1947).

23. Research Association second AGM, *Milling*, December 1925, 912.

24. 'Woodlands Ltd', *Milling*, June 1925, 750–52. Conversations with C. W. Chitty and D. W. Kent-Jones (1975).

25. Detailed review: *Milling*, October 1927, 414–15; 'K-J is obviously none too happy about the existing numerous definitions of strength and reviews them at some length'.

26. *Milling*, October 1926, 495. From 1923 there had been campaigners against white

bread, referred to as faddists, bran mashers and wholemealers. *The Miller*, March 1923, 5–6 opposed 'The vilification of the white loaf'.

27. NABIM enquiry: G. H. Ball's letter to doctors, *The Miller*, February 1927, 938; results March, 34. Beamish and Chamberlain: *Milling*, November 1926, 655.

28. Departmental Committee (Ministry of Health) report in detail in *The Miller*, April 1927, 110–20 and *Milling*, March 1927, 296–303; Humphries 332. See also April, 384.

29. Kent-Jones (1939), 330, Kent-Jones & Amos (1950) chapter 10 provided extensive discussion of bleaching and flour improvers. See also Kent-Jones on physical methods, *The Miller*, July 1927, 378–87.

30. Kent-Jones, 'Brown and white bread', *The Miller*, October 1927, 602–4.

31. Storck & Teague (1952), 304.

32. Ernest Bevin, *Milling*, October 1935, 408; April 1935, 418–23.

33. Vernon and Humphries at NABIM meeting: *Milling*, March 1926, 416–17.

34. Humphries to NABIM AGM, *Milling*, June 1927, 728B–729.

35. An extensive review of trading problems by John White for *The Miller*, continuing from April 1926 to March 1928.

36. NABIM Convention, *Milling*, June 1928, 788.

37. E. D. Simon (1930), the text developed from his papers to NABIM in 1913, 1923, 1928.

38. Leetham: *Milling*, October 1928, 401; *The Miller*, November 1928, 668.

39. 'New era', *The Miller*, September 1929, 545; 'Remedy', *Milling*, August 1929, 236–37.

40. Confidentiality: *The Miller*, December 1929, 820. General description: G. H. Ball, 'The rationalization of the flour milling industry', April 1935, 387–88.

41. Purchase Finance Co Ltd, Certificate of incorporation, No 240631 of 27 June 1929; Annual return, naming directors, 10 October 1930.

42. Robertson to Spillers Ltd AGM, *Milling*, May 1932, 546; Nicholls, January 1932, 124.

43. Lord Peel, 'The Wheat Act': *Milling*, November 1932, 510–11.

44. Gampell, *The Miller*, January 1932, 22–3; March, 201, 206–11; April, 293.

45. ALFM AGMs, *Milling*, July 1931, 65–6; July 1932, 98–101. Constituent members: December 1932, 652–56.

46. Robertson: *The Miller*, June 1931, 412, 418.

47. AGM, *Milling*, May 1932, 548; June 1934, 619–24; November 1934, 519; June 1935, 722. *The Miller*, June 1936, 503–6.

48. In relation to the 1933 results, *Milling*, December 1933, 772.

49. Solent Mills: *The Miller*, June 18, 1934, 552–54; *Milling*, July 1934, 33–41.

50. *The Miller*, November 1933, 1043.

51. *Milling*, December 1932, 674. With ALFM, a new project was acquired at Silvertown, the Empire Mills: see Joseph Rank Ltd (1955).

52. Rank's statement in *The Miller*, and *Milling*, November 1933, 'The nation's bread', listing mills and capacities. Their Clarence Mills at Hull, Premier Mills at Silvertown, Atlantic Mills at Liverpool, and Ocean Mills at Liverpool still formed a strong basis.

53. Henry Simon Ltd, *Modern Flour Mills* (1937). Joseph Rank Ltd (1955), 64 referred to their Pacific Mills at Belfast, opened in 1934; see also *Milling*, March 1934.

54. Sun Mills: *Milling*, December 1934, 670–74.

55. E. D. Simon (1930), 10.

56. E. D. Simon's paper to NABIM, 'Watercooling of rolls', *The Miller*, June 1934, 547–50.

57. 'Steady national progress', *Milling*, December 1934, 770.

58. 'Leslie Smith': *Milling*, May 1923, 504.

59. *The Miller*, February 1934, 133; *Milling*, January 1935, 17; *Henry Simon Ltd Occasional Letter*, May 1934.

60. Dence and Hovis: *Milling*, June 1933, 603–4.

61. 'Flour imports', *Milling*, February 1934, 179; March, 329.
62. 'Sliced bread', *Milling*, July 1929, 65; *The Miller*, March 1930, 172.
63. 'Bread', with permission from *Punch*, *Milling*, October 1932, 402.
64. Humphries' new awareness, NJIC AGM, *Milling*, October 1934, 440.
65. Article for *American Miller*, also printed in *Milling*, June 1936, 710–11.

Notes to Chapter 16: The later twentieth century

1. Joseph Rank Ltd, *The master millers* (1955), 70–1.
2. Anthony Simon (1947), 39.
3. Le Corbusier, *Towards a new architecture* (1923, translated F. Etchells 1989), 31.
4. *Henry Simon Ltd Occasional Letter*, October 1953.
5. Thomas Robinson & Son Ltd, *The rebirth of the Solent Mills* (1950).
6. Joseph Rank Ltd (1955).
7. Conversation with C. P. Rishworth (1993 & 1996).
8. J. H. Scott, 'Flour mills of the future', *Milling*, July–August 1949.
9. Conversation with C. R. B. King (1999).
10. The Monopolies and Mergers Commission, *Flour and bread* (1977), 27.
11. D. W. E. Axford, N. Chamberlain, T. H. Collins & G. A. H. Elton, 'The Chorleywood Process', *Cereal Science Today* (1963) vol 8, No 8.
12. Conversations with C. W. Chitty and H. W. Andrews (1975 & 1976).
13. Conversations with John Mannering (1975 & 1976).
14. Conversation with Herbert Hooker (1975).
15. Conversations with Leslie Garnham (1975).
16. E. Marriage & Son Ltd, *The annals of one hundred years of flour milling, 1840–1940* (Colchester 1950) gave their early history.
17. The British Baking Industries Research Association was merged with the Research Association of British Flour Millers in 1967.
18. 'Bread for success?', *World Grain*, March 1999 stated the numbers of UK flour mills in 1950, 1960 and 1970 as 252, 202 and 118 respectively, citing NABIM as data source.
19. '150 years of Spillers, 1829–1979', *Milling Feed and Fertiliser*, December 1979, 26–8.
20. 'RHM, 1875–1975', last page.
21. W. Richardson, *The CWS in war and peace, 1938–1976* (1977), 315; CWS Business Information Unit; MMC (1977) para 177.
22. *Milling*, September 1977, 9.
23. MMC: *Flour and bread* (1977) chapter 1, paras 27–62.
24. MMC (1977) paras 87, 94.
25. MMC (1977) paras 164, 133, 190, 78.
26. Satake Corporation UK Division.
27. MMC, Tomkins plc and Kerry Group plc (1998) Cm 4031.
28. J. H. Scott, series of articles, *Milling*, July–August 1949; J. Speight, many articles, particularly in 1957, 1960, 1962, 1963.
29. *Milling*, October 1963, 422, 424.
30. A. Wilkinson, for E. Timms & Son Ltd, Goole, *The old five-sailer* (1996). The mill has been reported closed in April 2001.
31. B. C. McGee, 'The Peritec process and its application to Durum wheat milling', *Association of Operative Millers*, Calgary, Canada (1995); H. J. Schoch, 'Recent developments in flour milling' in W. Bushuk and V. F. Rasper, *Wheat production, properties and quality* (1994).
32. J. Watson, *The role of the computer in the flour milling industry*, NABIM gold medal paper (1984); B. C. McGee, 'Automation in flour milling', *Association of Operative*

Millers, Atlanta, Georgia (1982); Neil Walker, *Process control within the mill*, NABIM gold medal paper (1999).

33. *Milling*, November 1985, 16–18, 33.

34. Morton S. Sosland, 'Project Apollo', *World Grain*, May 1999, 9, including the Coronet Mill at Manchester, 8–14, 66, 69.

35. Gavin Owens, 'Roller mills: the flat facts', *Cereals International*, August 1997, in a series of articles.

36. NABIM 'The UK flour milling industry 1999'.

37. Conversations with A. D. Evers (2000); Branscan technical information.

38. Kent & Evers (1994), 66.

39. NABIM Flour milling industry correspondence course (versions from 1988 to 1999).

40. NABIM (1999).

41. Simon (1892), 22.

Bibliography

Abbreviations in the text and source notes:

NABIM National Asociation of British and Irish Millers
NJIC National Joint Industrial Council for the Flour-Milling Industry
Proc.I.C.E. Proceedings of the Institution of Civil Engineers
Proc.I.Mech.E. Proceedings of the Institution of Mechanical Engineers
JRASE Journal of the Royal Agricultural Society of England

Specialist Journals

The Miller from March 1875 to August 1950
Milling from November 1891, and successor titles, including *Cereals International* and
   Grain & Feed Milling Technology
The Millers' Gazette for the 1880s
American Miller 1873–1876; 1889–1891 (Chicago)

Official reports and publications

Board of Agriculture (1893) *Corn Prices 1892*
Board of Trade (1912) *Final report on the First Census of Production of the United Kingdom,
   1907*
—— (1931) *Final report on the Third Census of Production of the United Kingdom , 1924*
Home Office (1899) *Final report of the departmental committee appointed to inquire into
   and report upon certain miscellaneous dangerous trades*
—— (1912) *Annual report of the chief inspector of factories and workshops for the year 1896*
House of Lords (1895) *Appeal in the case Parkinson v. Simon, judgements delivered July
   1895.* (Previous stages reported in The Miller: March, April, July 1894; August 1895)
Ministry of Agriculture and Fisheries Departmental Committee on distribution and prices
   of agricultural produce (1923) *Interim report on cereals, flour and bread*
Monopolies and Mergers Commission:
—— (1977) *Flour and bread*
—— (1998) *Tomkins plc and Kerry Group plc*
NABIM Annual reports of the transactions of the National Association of British and
   Irish Millers (published extensively in *The Miller*; until 1886 the only record but from
   1892 also in *Milling*). The transactions were published annually and privately to
   members, apparently from 1886. References in this text cite the milling journals, as
   they are publicly available, and were concurrent with events.
—— (1887) 'Report of special committee of the National Association of British and
   Irish Millers appointed to investigate the present depression in the milling trade',
   Ninth annual report of the transactions, August 1887 and *The Miller*, July 1887
—— (1976 & 1979) The practice of flour milling
—— (1988 onwards & 1998 onwards) *Flour milling industry correspondence course*
NJIC (1926–1935) Technical education papers see Birch, Fisher, Green, Marston,
   E. D. Simon, Thompson, Williams
Patents for inventions, for which abridgements of specifications assist searches:
   class 58: Grain and seeds, treating, including flour and meal
   class 59: Grinding, crushing, pulverising
   class 117: Sifting and separating

Patents for inventions, sixteenth report of the Comptroller-General of Patents, Designs, and Trade Marks for the year 1898 (HMSO, 1899)
Reports of Royal Commissions:
    (1884) Technical instruction
    (1886) The depression of trade and industry
    (1893 & 1894) Labour
    (1894, 1896 & 1897) Agricultural depression
    (1902) The administration of the Port of London
    (1905) Supply of food and raw materials in time of war
    (1921) Wheat supplies
    (1925) Food prices

Milling process technology texts

Amos, P. A. (1912) Processes of flour manufacture
Birch, J. R. (1930) *The roller mill* (NJIC 6)
Dedrick, B. W. (1924 *Practical milling* (Chicago, Illinois)
Gibson, L. H. (1885) *Gradual reduction milling* (Minneapolis)
Halliwell, W. (1904) *The technics of flour milling*
Kick, F. (1888) *Flour manufacture. A treatise on milling science and practice* (Trans. H. H. P. Powles of 1878 German ed. and Kick's supplement of 1883)
Kozmin, P. A. (1917) *Flour milling* (Trans. M. Falkener & T. Fjelstrup from Russian)
Lockwood, J. F. (1945) *Flour milling*
Scott, J. H. (1936) *Flour milling processes*
—— (1972) *Development of grain milling machines* (Edinburgh)
Smith, L. (1936, 1937) *Flour milling technology* (Rochdale)
Voller, W. R. (1889, 1892 & 1897) *Modern flour milling* (Gloucester)

Other texts

Bennett, R. & Elton, J. (1900) *History of corn milling* 3
Beveridge, W. H. (1928) *British food control*
Bradfield, E. (1920) *Wheat and the flour mill* (Liverpool)
Brown, R. C. (1877) *The new process milling* (Elgin, Illinois)
Bühler (1961) *100 years of Bühler Brothers* (Uzwil, Switzerland)
Burnett, R. G. (1945) *Through the Mill*
Coles Finch, W. (1933/1976) *Watermills and windmills* (Sheerness)
Cooperative Wholesale Society Ltd (1914) *Annual for 1914*
—— (1930) *The people's year book*
Corn Trade News (1938) *George Broomhall's Corn Trade News 1888–1938* (Liverpool)
Davenport, N. (1979) *The United Kingdom Patent System* (Havant)
Jago, W. (1886) *The chemistry of wheat, flour and bread and bread and technology of breadmaking* (Brighton)
—— (1895) *A text-book on the science and art of bread-making*
Jago, W. & Jago, W. C. (1911) *The technology of bread-making*
Jones, B. (1894) *Cooperative production* (Oxford)
Kent, N. L. (1975) *Technology of cereals* (Oxford)
Kent, N. L. & Evers, A. D. (1994) *Technology of cereals* (Oxford)
Kent-Jones, D. W. (1939) *Modern cereal chemistry* (Liverpool)
Kent-Jones, D. W. & Amos, A. J. (1950) *Modern cereal chemistry* (Liverpool)
Kent-Jones, D. W. & Mitchell, E. F. (1962) *The practice and science of breadmaking* (Liverpool)
Kuhlmann, C. B. (1929) *The development of the flour-milling industry in the United States* (Boston, Massachusetts)
Leigh Pearson, E. (1925) *Organisation and management in the flour milling industry*
Macrosty, H. W. (1907) *The trust movement in British industry*

Northern Publishing Co Ltd (1921) *The roller mill and silo manual* (revision of a book by J. Donaldson) (Liverpool)

O'Hagan, H. O. (1929) *Leaves from my life*

Percival, J. (1934 & 1948) *Wheat in Great Britain*

Redfern, P. (1913) *The story of the Cooperative Wholesale Society Ltd 1863–1913* (Manchester)

—— (1938) *The new history of the CWS* (Manchester)

Rew, R H (1920) *Food Supplies in peace and war*

Richardson, W. (1977) *The CWS in War and Peace 1938–1976*

Simon, B. (1997) *In search of a grandfather. Henry Simon of Manchester 1835–1897*

Storck, J. & Teague, W. D. (1952) *Flour for man's bread* (University of Minnesota)

Thiel, G. (1955) *Milling phrases and definitions* (in German) (Braunschweig)

Basic papers and essays

Axford, D. W. E., Chamberlain, N., Collins, T. H. & Elton, G. A. H. (1963) 'The Chorleywood process', *Cereals Science* 8

Baker, W. P. (1872) 'On the Buchholz process of decorticating grain, and making semolina and flour by means of fluted metal rollers', *Proc.I.Mech.E.*

—— (1882) 'On the various systems of grinding wheat, and on the machines used in Corn-Mills', *Proc.I.Mech.E*

Ball, G. H. (1928) 'The history of the National Association', *Milling*, June

—— (1935) 'The rationalisation of the flour milling industry', *The Miller*, April

Bates, W. T. (1907 & 1908) 'Twenty five years of roller milling', *The Miller*, April 1907–May 1908

Edwards, H. V. (1948) 'Flour milling' in M. P. Fogarty ed. *Further studies in industrial organisation*

Fisher, E. A. (1935) *Flour quality: its nature and control* (NJIC 3)

Graham, R. (1966) 'A British industry in Brazil. Rio Flour Mills 1886–1920', *Business History* 8

Green, L. H. ed. (1928) *Some basic principles of flour-milling* (NJIC 2)

Hamill, J. M. (1911) 'Report to the Local Government Board: The bleaching of flour and the addition of so-called improvers to flour', *The Miller*, May

—— (1911) 'Report to the Local Government Board: The nutritive value of breads', *The Miller*, September

Humphries, A. E. (1905) 'The improvement of English wheat', *The Miller*, November–December

—— (1907) 'Modern developments in flour milling', *The Miller*, January

—— (1907) 'Causes of the quality of strength in wheat and flour', *The Miller*, September

—— (1909) 'Ideal British wheats', *The Miller*, August

—— (1912) 'The milling of wheat in the United Kingdom', *JRASE*

—— (1935) 'War-time control of breadstuffs', *The Miller*, April

Jenkins, R. (1887) 'Roller mills: a historical sketch', *The Miller* July 1887 and *The collected papers of Rhys Jenkins* (Cambridge 1936)

Lawes, J. B. & Gilbert, J. H. (1893) 'Home produce, imports, consumption and price of wheat, over forty harvest-years, 1852–53 to 1891–92', *JRASE*

Little, G. (1887, 1888) 'Modern Milling – its birth and development', *The Engineer*, July, August, November 1887; January, March 1888

Marston, H. (1931) *The development of the modern British roller mill* (NJIC 7)

McGee, B. C. (1982) 'Automation in flour milling', to *Association of Operative Millers*, Atlanta, Georgia

McGee, B. C. (1995) 'The Peritec process and its application to Durum wheat milling', to *Association of Operative Millers*, Calgary, Canada

Milling (1923) 'Review of the industry. Special issue, September

Milling (1928) 'Review of the industry, NABIM Jubilee, June

Owens, G. (1997) 'Roller mills: the flat facts', *Cereals International*
Russell, T. (1925) 'Expansion of markets at home and abroad', paper to NABIM Convention, *The Miller*, July
Scott, J. H. (1949) 'Flour mills of the future', *Milling*, July, August
Scott, J. H. (1962) 'Value of purifiers in flour milling', *Milling*, September
Speight, J. (1957) 'The milling industry. 1938–1970', *Milling*, November
Speight, J. (1962–63) 'Flour milling progress' and other speculative articles, *Milling*
Thompson, W. S. (1934) *A historical study of wheat conditioning* (NJIC 11)
Voller, W. R. (1923) 'Five decades of flour milling', *Milling*, September
Watson, J. (1984) 'The role of the computer in the flour milling industry', NABIM gold medal thesis
Williams, A. E. (1935) *Purification* (NJIC 12)

Simon publications

Simon, E. D. & A. (1947 & 1953) *The Simon Engineering Group*
Simon, E. D. (1913) 'Analysis of the power required to drive a flour mill', *The Miller*, July
—— (1923) 'The principles of wheat conditining', *The Miller*, June
—— (1926) *Power* (NJIC 1)
—— (1928) 'Flour milling research', *Milling*, June
—— (1930) *The physical science of flour milling* (Liverpool)
—— (1934) 'Water cooling of rolls', *The Miller*, June
Simon, H. (1879) 'Daverio system', *The Miller*, July
—— (1882) 'Modern flour-milling in England', *Proc.I.C.E.*
—— (1886) *On roller flour milling* (Manchester), also catalogue
—— (1887) 'Records of tests as to the power consumed by various machines used in roller mills', *The Miller*, July, and Transactions of NABIM, August
—— (1888–1898) Letters (unpublished)
—— (1889) 'On the latest development of roller flour milling', *Proc.I.Mech.E.*
—— (1890) *The patent Reform purifier* (Manchester)
—— (1892) *The present position of roller flour milling* (Manchester), also catalogue
—— (1898) *Modern flour mill machinery* (Manchester), also catalogue
(1892–1896) *Henry Simon's Circular*
(1897–1899) *Henry Simon's Occasional Letter*
(1899–1947) *Henry Simon Ltd Occasional Letter*
Henry Simon Ltd (1908, 1913, 1914 & 1930) *Catalogues*
Henry Simon Ltd (1923) *Granaries, elevators & grain handling plants*

Among many conversations, the following were recorded:

W. H. Andrews (1975); C. W. Chitty (1975 & 1976); P. Hancock (1975); H. Hooker (1975); J. Mannering (1975 & 1976)
D. W. Kent-Jones (1976)
C. P. Rishworth (1993 & 1996)
C. R. B. King (1999)

Milling companies' records

E. Marriage & Son Ltd. (1940) *The annals of one hundred years of flour milling, 1840–1940* (Colchester)
Joseph Rank Ltd (1955) *The story of the House of Rank 1875–1955*
Williamson, A. (1996) *The old five-sailor. A history of E. Timm & Son, Flour-millers, of Goole*

A substantial collection of miscellaneous non-technical records from milling businesses acquired by Joseph Rank Ltd has been preserved at Reading University. When FMBRA was absorbed into the Campden & Chorleywood Food Research Association in 1995, a now rare set of the journal *The Miller* was transferred to Reading University, along with a special collection of texts on milling technology. Some non-technical records from J. Reynolds & Co. Ltd (Voller's mill) are stored at Gloucester Record Office. In both cases there are access restrictions. Elsewhere, minute books and wheat puechase books have survived, but during the rapid diffusion of roller milling in the late nineteenth century most milling innovators were members of private firms or companies, leaving few records outside the milling journals. Off-prints of journal articles, describing developments in particular mills, were often the only highly informative, carefully preserved and available records.

For some companies, including Spillers, Vernons, Liverpool North Shore Co., Coxes Lock Co., and Marriages at Colchester and Felixstowe, the journal record is more extensive than for most others. Only in the case of the engineer Henry Simon has a collection of letters been available, all out-going correspondence. Henry Simon and Henry Simon Ltd have left a varied fund of information.

It is hoped that where further material becomes available concerning individual innovative millers this particular study may be helpful.

Index

Allied Bakeries Ltd 322
Allied Mills Ltd 5, 327, 330, 335 (Figure 125), 338
Allis, E. P. & Co. 32, 62, 69
Alphega method *see* roller mill
Alsop Flour Process Ltd 248
American flour, competition 55, 56, 227
 see also New Process milling
Amme, Giesecke & Konegen 261
Andrews, J. & S. 248
Appleby, Arthur 208
Appleby, Edgar 208, 219
Appleby, Joseph & Sons 208, 209 (Figure 75), 309 (Figure 109), 327
Carolina Mills at Bootle 208, 307
Appleton French & Scrafton Ltd 203
Appleton, R. H. 44. 67, 133, 201, 202 (Figure 69), 215
Archer Daniels Midland Co. 330
Armstrong, Samuel (NABIM president) 277, 278, 282, 314
 'Mr Armstrong's pig' 279
Ashby, F. 38
Ashby, Son & Allen at Croydon 88
Associated British Foods Ltd 6, 322
Associated London Flour Millers Ltd 281, 305, 307, 327
Austria-Hungary 11, 23, 37
automatic process control 106, 337
automatic working 106

Baker, Arthur (NABIM president) 204, 205, 220
Baker, Proctor 204
 as examiner 41, 151, 152
 papers 41, 51, 68, 148
Baker, William & Sons 41, 64, 204
Ball, G. H. (NABIM secretary) 271, 283 85
Barlow, Collins 38, 64
Barnard & Lea in Illinois 72
Bates, W. T. 125, 129 (Figure 49), 213, 218
 and Bread Reform League 122

commentaries 127, 261, 263
letters to journals 56, 58, 122
on Carter's bogey 107
on wheat mixing 59
plansifters *v.* centrifugals 258
Baumann, J. & Simon 188, 193
Baxendell & Sons 213, 231
Beerbohm, J. E. 19
Beveridge, W. 272, 276
Bevin, Ernest 275, 300
Biffen, R. H. 216
Boland's aleurometer 60
Bovill's patent 132, 211
Branscan instrumentation 338
bread 339 (Figure 126)
 brown or white 50–2, 119–23
 'Eat More Bread' campaign 285 (Figure 101)
 sliced 314
 Standard Bread 249, 250
 wrapped 294
 see also Chorleywood process
Bread Reform League 119–23
 Campbell Morfit process 119–21
Briddon & Fowler 255 (Figure 93), 256, 263
Britannia Flour & Bread Co. Ltd 89
Broomhall, G. J. S. 1, 206, 236, 291
 starts *Milling* 20, 206
Brown, Charles & Co. Ltd 282
Buchanan & Co. Ltd at Birkenhead 192, 211
Buchanan, W. at Liverpool 191
Buchanan's Flour Mills Ltd 192, 194, 238, 281, 327
Buchholz, G. 37, 39–42
 machinery 41
 patents 40
Buchholz, J. Λ. Λ. 19, 38, 44, 62, 63–7, 134
 & Ganz 39, 63, 65 (Figure 19)
 and NABIM 138
 on Hungarian milling 64
 system 38, 106

Budapest *or* Buda Pesth 4, 23, 27, 28
   (Figure 11), 35
   visit to mills 38
   see also Waltzmuhle
Bühler, Adolf 88, 196
   factory 160 (Figure 58), 161 (Figure 59)
   roller mill manufacture 160–61, 164 (Figure 61)
Bühler Brothers 196, 253–54, 297

C.W.S. & Cooperative Movement 5, 202, 240–44, 295, 303, 315, 319, 328
   at Dunston on Tyne 202, 203 (Figure 70), 241
   at London (Silvertown) 241, 242 (Figure 90), 320 (Figure 115)
   flour mills 243, 295
   Scottish C.W.S. 243
   Sun Mills at Manchester 242, 309, 311 (Figure 111)
Cabane purifier 29, 37
Cannon & Gaze Ltd 233
Cardiff & Channel Mills Ltd 281
Cardiff Milling Co. Ltd 203
Carr, Thomas at Bristol 68
Carr, W. T. (NABIM president) 276, 306
Carrs Flour Mills Ltd 248, 306, 313, 331, 332 (Figure 122)
Carr-Touflin disintegrator 68
Carter, J. Harrison 100–7, 100 (Figure 37), 203
   3-roller mill 101 (Figure 38)
   4-roller mill 100
   and Vienna exhibition 38
   advocates exhibitions 146
   achievements 104
   as consultant 41
   automatic working 89
   claims 89
   criticises Oexle 46
   letters to journals 46, 137
   papers 52, 125, 140
   patents 103
   system 100, 103, 104 (Figure 40)
   with Turners 102 (Figure 39), 100–7
Carves, Francois 86
Case Co. of Ohio 79, 112
Census of Population 14
Census of Production 14, 237, 239, 285
centrifugal 67, 86, 163, 259
Chatterton, J.H. 131, 133, 139 (Figure 50), 282

and NABIM 113, 141
   on records and data 57
   on technical education, 151
Childs, A. B. 45
Childs, A. B. & Co. 18, 37, 45–9, 77–9
   disc mills 77
   system 79
chilled iron rolls 24, 49, 83, 100, 103, 145
Chisholm, S. S. of Chicago 77
Chitty, Charles W. 1, 219, 251, 287 (Figure 102), 288 (Figure 103), 289, 298, 299, 323
Chitty, G. W. & Co. 323
Chorleywood bread process 322, 330
Christian, George H. 29
Cincinnati exhibition 34, 146
City & Guilds studies 143, 150, 156
   see also Voller
Clapham, J. H. 12
Clarke & Dunham 37
Clarke, Henry 19
Cleveland Flour Mills Ltd 203
company formations 220–21
continuous working 114, 115
Corcoran, B. 37, 123, 125, 127
   letters to journals 127
   papers 125, 128 (Figure 48)
Corcoran, Witt & Co. 46, 66
Cosgrove roller mill 42, 74
Country millers – the bitter cry 216–19
   categorisation 239
Coxes Lock Milling Co. 221, 235 (Figure 87), 321 (Figure 116), 327
Cranfield Bros Ltd at Ipswich 233, 311 (Figure 112), 328, 329 (Figure 120)
crease dirt 66, 112, 256

Dalgety Ltd 330, 331
Daverio, Gustav 64, 86
   roller mills 11, 32, 88
Davidson, John & Sons 43, 205
de la Barre, William 32
debranning 336
decontrol and reconstruction 274–81
Dell, W. R. & Co. 42, 72–3, 73 (Figure 22), 124
   plansifter 169, 258
Dence, A. (NABIM president) 314
disc mills 62, 67–9, 77, 79
Dornbusch, George 18, 214, 237
Downton, R. L. 31
Dunham, William 1, 18 (Figure 7), 20
   achievements 50

on technical education 150
starts *The Miller* 18–21

Elsdell & Soundy 67
endosperm 25
Escher Wyss & Co. 37, 42, 48
exhibitions, international *see* Cincinnati;
    Islington; Kilburn; Vienna
extraction rate 25

Fairbairn, William 19
Fairclough & Sons Ltd 327
Fairclough, John 38, 64, 138, 139
Fairclough, W. in Cornwall 127
First World War control 267–73
    see also decontrol
Fischer, Adolf 32, 66
Fisher, E.A. 247, 287, 297
Fison & Co. 41
flour, bleaching 248, 252, 298
    see also Flour Oxidising Co. Ltd; Alsop
    demand for white 50–2, 119–23
    first break 165
    imports 23, 38, 55–8, 215, 229
    improvers 249, 251, 252
    strength 246–47
    treatment, Departmental Committee
        298
    see also American flour
Flour Milling Employers' Federation 274,
        300, 304
Flour Mills Control Committee 269, 272,
        278
Flour Oxidising Co. Ltd 248
Food Controllers 268, 269, 274, 276, 277,
        278
Food Council 290, 292
Food, Ministry of 268, 277
Frost, F. A. & Sons at Chester 64, 89, 240
    (Figure 89), 280, 323 (Figure 117)
    at Ellesmere Port 240–41, 261, 280

Ganz Abraham 39
Ganz & Co. 26 (Figure 9), 32, 38, 39, 62,
    63
Garnham, H. L. 332
Gardner, William & Sons at Gloucester
    42, 74, 76 (Figure 24), 77
Germ Milling case 67, 130–36
    Germ Defence Association 133–34
    see also Henry Simon; J. & H.
        Robinson
Glen, A. & W. at Glasgow 69

Gloucester millers technical class 153
gluten 246
    composition of 247, 338
    gluten and strength 59, 246
    see also flour; wheat
gradual reduction 23, 24 (Figure 8), 25
Graham, Prof. Charles 60, 120, 121
gravity purifiers 25, 63, 88, 92 (Figure
    31), 165, 173
Gray, W. D. 28, 32, 34
    roller mill 32, 62, 69, 70 (Figure 20),
        71 (Figure 21)
Green, L. H. 274, 300
Greenwood, John & Sons Ltd in
    Lancashire 105, 126, 208, 315, 327

Hadley, S. C. (NABIM president) 16, 138
Haggenmacher plansifter 107, 166–69,
    167 (Figure 62)
Hall, A. D. 216
Hamill, J. M., reports 248, 249
Hardy, W. B. 247
Healing, S. & Sons 327
Heath Robinson 63, 336
Hepburn, William 21, 50, 138
Herdman, John & Sons Ltd 281
Heygates Ltd 331
Hibbard, T. W. (NABIM president) 215
    American tour 34, 141
    on soft wheats 130
Higginbottom, J. of Liverpool
    disc mill 79
    roller mill 80
    plansifter 169
    purifier 176
Hind & Lund 113, 169
Hooker, W. & Son 325
Hosegood Industries Ltd 315, 331
Hosken, Trevithick, Polkinhorn & Co.
    Ltd 205
Hovis Bread Flour Co. Ltd 232 (Figure
    86), 260, 314, 321
Hovis McDougall Ltd 327
Hudson, C. J. Ltd 325
Hughes, Bernard 44, 90
Humphries, A. E. (NABIM president)
    224, 247, 251, 268 (Figure 97),
    287, 298, 299, 301, 304, 314
    wartime executive 270, 272, 273, 275,
        286, 290, 291
Hungarian milling 23, 25–8, 40, 42–4
    flours 23
    millers 23

system 37, 43, 44
Huntly, Holcombe & Heine purifier 111
Hutchinson, Edward at Liverpool 94, 209, 238, 327
Huxley, G. & Simon 184, 187, 196, 253, 255, 257, 262

Ingleby, Joseph 185 (Figure 68)
  & Simon 182, 184, 187, 188, 193, 194, 195, 196, 262
Ingleby, J. A. & Sons at Tadcaster 38, 88
Institution of Civil Engineers (I.C.E.) 51, 62, 68, 148
Institution of Mechanical Engineers (I.Mech.E.) 12, 41, 89, 116
Islington exhibition 12, 141, 142 (Figure 51), 146–47

Jackson, John & Son Ltd 281
Jago, William 19, 60, 120, 143, 248, 249, 251, 289
Jenkins, Rhys 27
Journals, importance 1, 188
  see also Milling; The Miller

Kalnoky & Simon reports 38
Kelly's Directories 15, 239
Kent millers 323, 325
Kent-Jones, D. W. 60, 288, 289 (Figure 104), 298, 299
Kick, Friedrich 25, 37, 46, 132, 156, 157
  plansifter appraisal 168
Kidd, Samuel & Co. 214
Kilburn exhibition 145
King Flour Mills at Ellesmere Port 263
Kirbys Ltd 281

La Croix 29, 30
Lawes & Gilbert, reports and papers 52, 216, 217
Leetham, Henry & Sons 5, 44, 223 (Figure 82), 238, 303, 306, 326 (Figure 119)
Leetham, S. (NABIM president) 188, 222 (Figure 81), 223, 229, 248, 273, 284, 285, 293, 296, 303
Limited Companies registration 220–21
Little, Gilbert 41, 105
  articles 105, 106
Lockwood, J. F. see Henry Simon Ltd
London bread 122
Luther, G. 39, 66
  plansifter 168, 169, 258

Mallett, W. R. 218
  for country millers 218
  on port mills 236
Manchester Ship Canal 231
Mannering, W. & E. 325
Marriage Neave & Co. 213, 314
Marriage, Wilson 38, 130, 217
  at Colchester 154 (Figure 55), 155 (Figure 56), 324 (Figure 118)
  at Felixstowe 237 (Figure 88), 233
Marshall, William & Sons, Grimsby, Ltd 233, 306
Martin, Edward 21
McDougall Bros at Manchester 11, 88
McDougall Bros at Millwall 214
Mechwart, Andreas 39
Metford, F. K. S. (NABIM president) 296, 300, 301, 314
middlings 22, 25
Miller of Dee 239
Miller, George 125, 127
  paper to operatives 126
Millers' Mutual Association (MMA) 276, 303, 306, 315
Milling foundation 206
milling experts 38, 41, 100, 111, 112, 184, 256, 310, 313
milling process (break; dressing; grading; purification; reduction; scalping) 22–5, 24 (Figure 8)
mills, flour, numbers in UK 115, 116, 144, 330
  working hours 114, 115
millstones see Corcoran; G. T. Smith; rollers v. stones
Minneapolis 4, 31–5
Monopolies & Mergers Commission 328, 330, 339
Moss, Frederick 103, 115, 121, 133
Muir, Matthew & Sons 43
Muir, Thomas of Glasgow 16, 131
  patent 130–31
  see also Germ Milling Case
Mumford, Peter at Vauxhall 16, 64, 212 (Figure 80), 213, 216, 281
  and NABIM 139
Mumford, S. & P. at Deptford 213
Munden, Armfield & Co. 113

Nagel & Kaemp 67–9
  centrifugal 67
  system 44, 140
National Association of British & Irish

Millers (NABIM) 17, 137–56,
222, 339
affiliated associations 140
and journalists 144
and milling engineers 144
annual conferences started 143, 148
annual reports 283
conference at Buxton 224
conventions 148, 149, 283 (Figure 100)
Education Committee 286
foundation 137–40
incorporation 222
lectures (1884–90)148
members 17, 143–44
objectives 138, 144
presidents 276
special committee 1887 113, 114
technical education 150–56, 339
usefulness 222
visits to mills 149
see also Carter; Chatterton; Hadley;
H.Simon
National Joint Industrial Council (NJIC)
275, 298, 300, 312
Nelstrop, William & Co. Ltd 331, 333
(Figure 123), 336
New Cardiff Milling Co. Ltd 203, 233
New Process milling 28–31, 40, 72–3
Nicholls, W. E. (NABIM president) 226,
234, 236, 251, 252, 270 (Figure
98), 271, 286, 291, 293, 296, 305
& Spillers 233
for port millers 218
on numbers of mills 238, 263
North Shore Flour & Rice Co. Ltd 16,
43, 90, 114, 209, 210 (Figure 77),
211 (Figure 78), 231, 315
North-Eastern Millers Association 225
North-Eastern Milling Co. Ltd 201
Noye, J. T. of Buffalo 74

Odell roller mill 42, 77
Oexle, Oscar 27, 32, 39, 42, 111
articles 37, 45
O'Hagan, H. O. 264–65, 271, 272, 284,
291
Operative millers, London 125, 127, 275
visit to Burnley and Blackburn 127
overlapping 215–19, 225
see also Mallet

Pappenheim, Gustav 25, 157
Parkinson, T. & G. M. of Doncaster 176

v. Simon 178–81
Paur, Ignaz 25
Pekar, Emrich 39
test for whiteness 59
Perrigault, Joseph 29
Pillsbury mills 29, 30
Pillsbury, C. A., 30
Pillsbury, C. A. & Co. 34
plansifter 166–69, 259
v. centrifugals 258, 260
see also Haggenmacher; Higginbottom;
Kick; Speight; Stringer; Voller
Pledge, H. S. & Sons Ltd 325
pneumatic handling 321
porcelain rolls 46–9
Port Millers' Committee 238
Purchase Finance Co. Ltd 303
purifiers *see* gravity; sieve; Higginbottom;
Robinsons; Simon Reform;
G. T. Smith

Radford, J. R. & Simon 185, 191, 193,
194
Radford, W. J. & Sons 41, 211
Rank Hovis Ltd 330, 334 (Figure 124),
337
Rank, James V. (NABIM president) 302,
303
Rank, Joseph (NABIM president) 99,
206, 208 (Figure 74), 225, 228,
275, 286
Alexandra mill at Hull 206 (Figure 72)
Atlantic mill at Cardiff 229 (Figure
85), 231, 244
Clarence mills at Hull 190, 205, 207
(Figure 73), 244, 320
London mill 231
progress 3, 231, 244
Rank, Joseph Ltd 5, 206, 238, 281, 296,
302, 303, 307, 308, 310 (Figure
110), 315, 319, 320
at Liverpool 244
at Southampton 307
Ocean Mills, Birkenhead 245 (Figure
91)
Premier Mills 228 (Figure 84), 306
Ranks Hovis McDougall Ltd 327
Research Association 286–89, 297, 298,
323, 335
revolutionary change 1, 11–14, 90
Reynolds, J. & Co. 13 (Figure 5), 15
(Figure 6), 153 (Figure 54), 250,
327

Reynolds, P. R. (NABIM president) 290,
    293, 294, 301
Rieger, George 25
Rio de Janeiro Co. & Simon 188, 189,
    195, 213
Rishworth, C. P. 321
Rishworth, Ingleby & Lofthouse Ltd 281,
    320
Robinson, J. & H. at Deptford 16, 71,
    133, 212 (Figure 79), 213
    see also Germ Milling Case
Robinson, Oswald (NABIM president)
    267, 271
Robinson, Thomas & Sons Ltd 107–13,
    108 (Figure 43), 109 (Figure 44),
    112 (Figure 46), 202, 297, 309
    4-roller mill 110 (Figure 45)
    diagonal roller mill 253
    Koh-i-Noor purifier 177
    plansifter 259
    progress as milling engineers 107, 113,
        117, 242, 253, 258, 320, 334
    with Frederick Nell 111
Robinsons Milling Systems Ltd 330
roller mill plants: capacity in 1887 114
    largest in 1887 114
    numbers 114, 234
roller mill:
    3-roller mill 84 (Figure 26), 85 (Figure
        27), 101 (Figure 38), 159
    4-roller mill 95, 96, 100, 107, 108,
        110, 159–61, 162 (Figure 60), 164
        (Figure 61)
    8-roller mill 336
    Alphega system 255 (Figure 93), 256,
        263
    design 157–63
        basics of modern design 157
        patents 157
rollers v. stones controversy 123–30
rolls, lengths 88
    diagonal placement 253, 254 (Figure
        92)
    surface 255, 309, 336
    water cooling 310
    see also chilled iron, porcelain
Royal Agricultural Society of England
    (R.A.S.E.) shows 145
Royal Commissions:
    on Food Prices 290, 291, 292, 293
    on Food Supply 52, 53, 55, 230
    on Supply of Wheat & Flour 267, 276,
        278, 291

on Technical Instruction 152
Rush, J. W. 144
    paper 54
Russell, Thomas on advertising 294–95

Samuelson, Sir B. & Simon 187, 194, 256
Sanderson, H. J. 67–9
    paper to NABIM 140
Satake Corporation 330, 336, 338
Scott Lings on amalgamations 226
Scott, J. H. 333, 335–37
Seck, Heinrich 86
    & Simon 185, 193
    centrifugal 86 (Figure 28)
    system 44
Sellnick, F. 48
semolina 22, 25
Shackleton, E. & Sons at Carlow 88, 89
Shone, J. A. (NABIM president) 276,
    278
sieve purifiers 25, 63, 93, 94, 173
    see also Simon Reform
sieving and separating 163–69
Simon, E. D. 262, 288, 297, 309, 313
    papers 261, 302, 338
Simon, Bühler & Baumann 193, 194
Simon, Henry 3, 12 (Figure 4), 13, 83,
    183 (Figure 66), 196, 223
as leader 3, 13
    at Mount Street, Manchester 182, 184
        (Figure 67)
    'no finality' 174, 252–63, 340
    associates see Baumann; Buchanan;
        Bühler; Carves; Daverio; Seck
    machines:
        design problems 87, 158, 170, 253
        roller mills 157–63
        flow diagrams 91 (Figure 30), 165
        machine testing 130, 191
        Seck granulator 42, 87 (Figure 29),
            88
        2-roller mill 86, 160
        3-roller mill 84 (Figure 26), 85
            (Figure 27), 86, 159
        4-roller mill 86, 95 (Figure 34), 96
            (Figure 35), 159–60, 162 (Figure
            60)
        patents 174
    projects:
        Liverpool & Birkenhead mills 98,
            221
        numbers of plants 38
        record of work 99, 116, 118, 129

publicity and papers:
  advertising 89
  catalogues 43, 98
  Circulars 189
  counter to J. Muir
  letters to journals 44, 121, 126,
    130, 132
  Occasional Letters 190
  on Islington exhibition 147
  papers 12, 48, 49, 51, 62, 68, 89,
    116, 140, 148
  The Miller 188
Reform purifier 93 (Figure 32), 94
    (Figure 33), 171 (Figure 63),
    173–81
  channels 172 (Figure 64), 174, 175,
    176, 179 (Figure 65)
  contention with Parkinsons 176–81
  deflector
staff 182–197
  see also Huxley; Joseph Ingleby;
    J. R. Radford; Stringer
system 86–99, 91 (Figure 30), 98, 170
  see also Reform purifer
Simon, Henry Ltd 221, 233–34, 289, 334
  8-roller mill 254, 261
  diagonal 253, 254 (Figure 92)
  at Cheadle Heath 297, 302, 312
    (Figure 113), 313
  Lockwood, J. F. 22, 310, 312, 315, 339
  major projects 315
  MQ purifier 262 (Figure 96)
  plansifter 258 (Figure 94), 260 (Figure
    95)
  scalpers 257
  registered 195
Smith, George T. 30 (Figure 12), 72, 123
  millstones 30, 62, 124 (Figure 47),
    125
  purifier 29, 31, 33 (Figure 13), 72
  roller mill 74
Smith, L. on technical education 312
Smith, Samuel 34
Smiths Flour Mills (Northern Foods) 331
Soundy, S. M. 17, 67
Speight, John 333–36
  plansifter 333
Spiller & Co. Ltd 204
Spiller, Joel 204 (Figure 71), 331
Spillers & Bakers Ltd 5, 205, 233, 238,
    271, 279
Spillers Ltd 297, 302, 303, 304, 306
    (Figure 106), 307 (Figure 107),

308 (Figure 108), 313 (Figure
    114), 328
  Sir Malcolm Robertson, chairman 304,
    306
Spillers Milling & Associated Industries
    Ltd 279, 296
St Davids, Lord 269, 273
Stevens rolls 74, 75 (Figure 23)
strength 60, 247, 288, 302
  see also flour; wheat
Stringer, W.:
  machine testing 130
  plansifter appraisal 166–67
  sieve ideas 176
  and Simon 184, 188
Sulzberger, Jacob 27, 43

Tariff commission 228–29
Tattersall, A.R. 30
  on text books 154
Taylor, Seth 5, 17, 42, 144 (Figure 52)
  main mills 16, 92, 114, 115, 213, 280
    (Figure 90)
Technical education for milling 150–56,
    312, 339
  see also Chatterton; Dunham;
    Proctor Baker; Smith; Tattersall;
    Voller
The Miller, foundation 18–21
  importance 188
Throop, J. W. 32, 34, 62, 69–72, 211
  and Cincinnati exhibition 34
  and Vienna exhibition 38
Timm, E. & Son 336
Trade Organisation 264, 282, 283
traditional milling 11, 13 (Figure 5),
    14–18, 22, 23, 128
  see also Corcoran; G.T.Smith
Tucker, James Ltd at Cardiff 106 (Figure
    42), 107, 203
Turner, E. R. & F. 41, 100–7, 105 (Figure
    41), 231, 260, 308
  see also Carter

Ure, John at Glasgow 16, 64, 115, 281

Vernon, N. (NABIM president) 305
Vernon, W. A. (NABIM president) 252,
    271, 294, 295, 301, 320
Vernon, William (NABIM president) 95,
    208, 225
  at Fole 208, 210 (Figure 76)
  at Liverpool 208

Vernon, William & Sons 5, 97 (Figure
    36), 238, 279
  at Birkenhead 3, 192, 196, 221, 227,
    231, 261, 331 (Figure 121)
Vernons' Millennium flour 227
Vernons' Millennium Mill 227 (Figure
    83), 230, 279, 293 (Figure 105),
    320
Vienna exhibition 38, 145
Vienna party 1, 36 (Figure 14 & 15), 101
Voller, W. R. 145 (Figure 53)
  on City & Guilds
  on crease dirt 112
  on Islington exhibition 147
  on plansifter appraisal 167
  on roll arrangement 158 (Figure 57)
  on technical education 151, 153–56
  on text books 59
  on trade optimism 3, 12, 227
  on wheat mixing 59–60
Voss, T. 125, 126

Waltzmuhle, Pesther 13, 27 (Figure 10),
    37, 42
Washburn, Crosby & Co. 35
Washburn, C. C. 32
Washburn mills 29, 30, 31, 32
Watson, Todd & Co. Ltd 280
Weaver & Co. Ltd 205

Wegmann, Friedrich 45, 48 (Figure 18)
  roller mills 32, 38, 39, 45 (Figure 16),
    47 (Figure 17)
  system campaign 18, 45–9, 66
Weston, Garfield 322
wheat, acreage in UK 217, 278
  Canadian 54, 228, 230, 332
  English 11, 304, 314
  foreign 11
  Home Grown Wheat Committee 246,
    278
  Hungarian 23
  milling quality 4, 246
  soft see T. W. Hibbard
  strength 4, 59, 246
Wheat Act 304
Wheat Commission 304
wheat conditioning 288
wheat mixing 58–60
wheat supply 52–55, 59
  from America 52, 54, 55
Whitley report 274
Whitmore & Binyon 78 (Figure 25) 169,
    203, 208
Wilson, W. O. & J. at Liverpool 211, 217
Wood, James 43
Wood, T. B. 247

Zimmer, G. F. 103